Nietzsche
and the
Modern Crisis
of the
Humanities

Peter Levine

Nietzsche
and the
Modern Crisis
of the
Humanities

STATE UNIVERSITY OF NEW YORK PRESS

Production by Ruth Fisher
Marketing by Nancy Farrell

Published by
State University of New York Press, Albany

For information, address the State University of New York Press,
State University Plaza, Albany, NY 12246

Library of Congress Cataloging-in-Publication Data

Levine, Peter, 1967-
  Nietzsche and the modern crisis of the humanities/Peter Levine.
    p. cm.
  Includes bibliographical references and index.
  ISBN 0-7914-2327-1 (alk. paper).—ISBN 0-7914-2328-X (pbk.:
alk. paper)
  1. Nietzsche, Friedrich Wilhelm, 1844-1900—Contributions in
concept of the humanities. 2. Humanities. I. Title.
B3318.H87L48 1995
193—dc20   94-11021
                                                          CIP

10 9 8 7 6 5 4 3 2 1

For my mother and father:
scholars, teachers, humanists

CONTENTS

Contents

A Note On Sources

For ease of reference, I have wherever possible quoted from a widely available English translation of Nietzsche's works. These are identified in the text as follows:

Citation:	Refers to:
Arrowsmith	Arrowsmith, William: *Unmodern Observations* (New Haven: Yale University Press, 1990), comprising: *David Strauss: Writer and Confessor*, translated by Herbert Golder; *History in the Service and Disservice of Life*, translated by Gary Brown; *Schopenhauer as Educator*, translated by Arrowsmith; *Richard Wagner in Bayreuth*, translated by Brown; and *We Classicists*, translated by Arrowsmith. Used by permission of Yale University Press. (To avoid confusion, I have used the standard English titles of these works, viz., *Untimely Meditations*, *Use and Disadvantage of History for Life*, *We Philologists*.)
Faber	Faber, Marion, with Steven Lehmann (trans.): *Human, All-Too Human: A Book for Free Spirits* (Lincoln, Nebraska, 1984).
Kaufmann	*Beyond Good and Evil* by Friedrich Nietzsche, translated by Walter Kaufmann. Copyright © 1966 by Random House, Inc. *The Will to Power* by Friedrich Nietzsche, translated by Walter Kaufmann with R.J. Hollingdale. Copyright © 1967 by Walter Kaufmann. *The Gay Science* by Friedrich Nietzsche, translated by Walter Kaufmann. Copyright © 1974 by Random House, Inc. *The Birth of Tragedy* by Fredrich Nietzsche, translated by Walter Kaufmann. Copyright © 1967 by Random House, Inc. *On the Genealogy*

of *Morals* by Friedrich Nietzsche, translated by Walter Kaufmann with R.J. Hollingdale. Copyright © 1967 by Random House, Inc. Quotations from all of these works are reprinted by permission of Random House, Inc.

Gilman   Sander Gilman, Carole Blair, and David J. Parent, *Friedrich Nietzsche on Rhetoric and Language* (New York: Oxford University Press, 1989), Includes: "Description of Ancient Rhetoric" (1872-3); "History of Greek Eloquence" (1872-3); and "On Truth and Lying in an Ultramoral Sense" (1873). Used by permission of Oxford University Press.

In some cases, there is no reliable English translation. In those instances, I have generally cited the following German edition, which is the most widely available:

Schlechta, Karl (ed.): *Werke*, (Frankfurt: Karl Hanser Verlag, 1972). Cited as "Schlechta."

When the Schlechta edition does not contain a particular passage, I have used the following edition:

Colli, Giorgio, and Montinari, Mazzino (eds.): *Werke*, Berlin, 1967. This is often called the *Kritische Gesamtausgabe*. A part of the *Kritische Gesamtausgabe*, the *Nietzsche Briefwechsel* (correspondence), is cited separately.

I have had to use other German editions for a few remaining passages from Nietzsche's letters and unpublished fragments; these editions are cited in full in the footnotes.

Quotations from Ludwig Wittgenstein's *Philosophical Investigations*, third edition, translated by G.E.M. Anscombe, are reprinted with permission of Macmillan Publishing Company. Copyright © 1958 by Basil Blackwell & Mott, Ltd. Earlier edition copyright 1953 by Macmillan Publishing Company, Inc.

Introduction

This book offers an account of the modern humanities and a
defense of humanism against two prevalent schools of criticism.
On one hand, some critics argue that the humanities have become
essentially relativist and therefore morally useless; they complain
that scholars and educators have abandoned a commitment to
what Walter Lippman once called "the central, continuous and
perennial culture of the Western world."[1] But at the opposite end
of the spectrum, other critics attack the pretensions of scholars
who still claim to know truths about texts from the past; they call
for humanists to abandon one remaining aspect of Lippman's
"perennial" Western culture, its commitment to objectivity and
rationality. Each school has many partisans who disagree with
each other on important points. But I will concentrate on defending
the humanities against two particularly radical groups of critics:
Leo Strauss and his followers (including Allan Bloom); and the
deconstructionists, especially Jacques Derrida.

More than a century ago, Friedrich Nietzsche engaged in a
similar quarrel about the humanities, and endorsed *both* positions
that I have described here. In other words, Nietzsche feared that
cultural relativism was undermining the moral role of the humanities
and thus abetting the growth of nihilism; but he also hoped that
relativism would, if pushed to its logical extreme, destroy the
implicit ideals of objectivity and impartiality that still guided
Western scholars. Even relativism, scholars would discover, was
relative to a particular culture. A recognition of this paradox,

Nietzsche thought, would make room for a radical and creative new kind of scholarship and education that could serve as an antidote to modern nihilism. Both Strauss and Derrida have been directly and decisively influenced by this aspect of Nietzsche's thought. They have not merely adopted many of his general ideas, but have borrowed his specific doctrines and modes of exposition. In particular, they have inherited his understanding of what constitutes a culture—as have many other contemporary thinkers. But I believe that Nietzsche's understanding of culture was fundamentally mistaken. Therefore, I will offer a critical reading of Nietzsche's philosophy, in order to provide the groundwork for a defense of the modern humanities.

Nietzsche, Strauss, and Derrida—despite their profound differences—have all argued that the chief enemy of humanism is historicism. I am using "humanism" to mean the study of history, literature, and the arts, intended for moral purposes. Many defenders of humanism have claimed, like Walter Lippman, that one coherent set of moral values is contained in a universal canon of great literature, and that exposure to this tradition is an effective means of moral education. But "historicism" implies that people from different ages and places possess radically different values or ways of reasoning; so the ideas of any author may not be relevant to all cultures. Since humanism can be defended without recourse to the idea of a homogeneous and universal canon, historicism is not necessarily fatal to the humanities and their moral purposes. However, historicism does raise serious ethical and epistemological challenges, which Nietzsche explored. If all beliefs and values arise from specific cultural contexts, then the concepts of truth and virtue implicit in traditional humanism seem to require serious modification.

Most modern scholars in the humanities endorse historicism, and hold that scholarship should aim to understand human thought in all its diversity. But many scholars are also "humanists," for they still believe in the moral value of an education in literature, history, and the other humanities. Nietzsche—and those he has influenced—oppose this synthesis of humanism and historicism; but I will defend it. In what follows, I will attempt to demonstrate the moral value of the humanities, without ignoring the fact of profound cultural and historical diversity.

It may appear that, in concentrating on Nietzschean critics of humanism, I am ignoring those people who simply argue about the content of humanistic curricula, claiming either that existing canons are narrow and exclusive with regard to gender, race, and class, or that curricula have become too broad and indiscriminate. I hope that my account of the humanities can help provide a new framework within which to conduct such debates. (My account generally favors a more inclusive stance.) But arguments about the content of the humanities are healthy and useful parts of humanistic scholarship; they do not constitute an attack on humanism. For implicit in the claims of reformers and conservatives alike is the belief that some kind of curriculum would have useful moral effects, and that truth is a legitimate goal for scholars and teachers. In this book, my intention is to defend the humanities against the far more radical criticism implied by modern Nietzscheans. Allan Bloom, wrong about so much else, is right to claim that practically all contemporary thinkers who argue about the fundamental value and meaning of the humanities derive their problems and paradigms from Nietzsche.[2]

Nietzsche was educated at a famous grammar school in a highly traditional, humanistic manner; but he went on to receive a rigorous training in the methods of nineteenth-century classical scholarship, which presupposed that historicism was an accurate theory. This training caused him to despair about traditional methods of moral education, with their claims to "universal culture," and ultimately led him to turn against scholarship and rationality in general. When Nietzsche first considered the phenomenon of historical diversity that he encountered as a philologist, he concluded that people must be the products, results, or mere "fluctuations" of real entities that he called cultures or *Weltanschauungen*—world-views.[3] Each *Weltanschauung* encompassed a consistent, homogeneous and clearly delimited set of values. Later, Nietzsche abandoned the idea of a causal connection between cultures and individuals; this was too metaphysical for him. Besides, he gradually developed a subtler idea of culture, one that could accommodate evidence of diversity and change within each society. Nevertheless (he continued to think), everyone had to *believe* that he or she belonged to a homogeneous, consistent culture, and that people outside its borders were uncultured savages. This belief, false as it might be, provided the necessary grounds for concluding that one's own ideas and values were justified. Nietzsche often wrote that the belief in "truth" depended upon myth or error; and no myth was more important than a belief in one's own culture as consistent, unalterable, clearly delimited and unrivaled in every way. Thus Nietzsche clung to the notion that everything important about human life—our ideas of good and evil, truth and falsehood, madness and sanity—depended upon our participation in local, contingent *Weltanschauungen*. These might be myths, but so was everything that we believed. There could, therefore, be no objective difference between truth and lie.

Anyone who recognized that the world contained many discrete cultures had what Nietzsche called the "historical sense." People with a historical sense possessed their own arbitrary and contingent values: they favored openness, tolerance, objectivity, cultural relativism and intellectual honesty. However, these were unusual and inferior values, for they immediately turned against themselves. Historicists who thought about the matter rigorously enough would soon recognize that their own values were merely arbitrary and deserving of no allegiance. Belonging to a culture meant being closed to the claims of rival *Weltanschauungen*; it required ignorance and blind allegiance. But modern historicists had recognized the plurality of cultures and the diversity within each society; they had therefore lost allegiance to any values at all, even the values of historical objectivity and cultural relativism. Nietzsche feared that for the ordinary modern, whom he called the "Last Man," this loss of values would lead to a passively nihilistic inability to act at all, a merely vicarious, eclectic and voyeuristic study of past cultures. A similar concern has been eloquently stated by Leo Strauss and his followers, who regard contemporary America as the regime of the Last Man.

On the other hand (Nietzsche thought), a recognition of nihilism is a *liberating* event for those who have the strength to act creatively despite their knowledge that nothing is true or false, good or evil. Nietzsche called such people Overmen. Like Last Men, Overmen are beyond culture, but they are able to exploit this as an advantage. For example, Nietzsche felt that nihilism had liberated *him* from the strictures of conventional rationality and given him license to create a new, ahistorical philosophy that would not necessarily correspond to the findings of "scientific" philology. This philosophy represented his own *übermenschlich* affirmation, an actively nihilistic struggle against the passive nihilism of the Last Man. A similar effort to transcend truth and scholarship lies at the heart of Derrida's philosophy.

Thus I want to suggest that Nietzsche's thought followed a pattern that could be crudely summarized in five stages:

1. Historicism, or a recognition of diversity in values and ideas over time;

2. *Weltanschauung*-historicism, or the belief that an organic complex of ideas and values underlies each culture, deter-mining the course of human lives and thought;

3. Relativism, or the theory that ideas are only true or good *within* a specific *Weltanschauung*;

4. Nihilism, or the loss of all ideas of good and evil, truth and falsehood; thus proposition (3) is turned against itself— even relativism is merely relative;

5. Dionysian philosophy, or a creative journey beyond culture and rationality.

This pattern of thought is evident in the early history of Nietzsche's ideas, before he wrote any of his published books. By the time he finished *The Birth of Tragedy*, he had already arrived at the last stage. Because Nietzsche moved beyond stage (3) in his mature work, it would not be strictly true to call him a "relativist," although he was certainly willing to use relativist arguments against the dogmas of the past. It would also not be true to say that he retained a belief in the *Weltanschauung*, for all such metaphysical concepts soon fell prey to the critical stance represented by stage (4). The theory that each culture possessed its own *Weltanschauung*, Nietzsche thought, was itself just the arbitrary product of one culture's world-view. However, Nietzsche did depend on the concept of the *Weltanschauung* at an early stage in his development; without it, the later stages would not have followed. From the standpoint of Dionysian philosophy, the steps (1–3) that had led Nietzsche beyond reason, morals and culture now appeared hopelessly arbitrary, the merely contingent products of nineteenth-century European culture. Nevertheless, they were necessary stages on the road to the active nihilism that Nietzsche preached. Thus Nietzsche's thought led to a conclusion which made his own premises seem untrue; like Wittgenstein, he could have said:

> anyone who understands me eventually recognizes [my premises] as nonsensical, when he has used them— as steps—to climb beyond them. (He must, so to speak, throw away the ladder after he has climbed up it.)[4]

But, unlike Wittgenstein, Nietzsche was making a *historical* claim: he thought that the Western discovery of cultural relativism was undermining the belief in objective truth that had led to relativism in the first place. It was this pattern of thought that made Nietzsche a powerful and influential critic of the modern humanities.

When Nietzsche is described as an "anti-humanist," this often means something different from what I mean. Nietzsche believed that all values and beliefs inevitably depend upon metaphysical theories. For example, he asserted that every time we use the verb "to be,"

we are assuming "the error of Being [*Sein*]."⁵ If it is true that all
values depend upon metaphysics, then it would seem that the
basic metaphysical idea upon which humanists depend is the concept
of the human subject, self, ego or soul. But Nietzsche denied that
the subject, the "I" of Descartes and Kant, exists; he held the
"existentialist" view that human actions just happen, and we
invent a fictional self as their cause.⁶ This view is sometimes
described as "anti-humanism," since it denies the existence of a
metaphysical *human* subject.

Moreover, some philosophers have claimed that if one denies
the existence of the human self, then one must also renounce the
humanities as they have traditionally been understood. For example,
Heidegger argued:

> Every humanism is either grounded in a metaphysics or
> makes itself the ground of one. Every determination of the
> essence [*Wesen*] of men ... is metaphysical, whether it knows
> this or not. That is why, considering the way in which the
> essence of men is determined [generally, by the study of history],
> the peculiarity of all metaphysics lies in the fact that it is
> 'humanistic.' In the same way, every humanism remains
> metaphysical.⁷

Thus, according to Heidegger, we cannot study the works of
authors from the past (in a conventional way), nor draw moral
lessons from their writings, without being committed to the idea of
metaphysically independent, conscious, human beings. For him,
humanism—the study of the history of culture—is inevitably an
investigation into the metaphysical nature of Man, unless it simply
assumes some theory about this nature. Since Heidegger opposed
metaphysical interpretations of Being, he also opposed traditional
humanistic scholarship. Nietzsche, too, frequently assumed that
institutions and practices (such as humanistic scholarship)
presuppose or entail metaphysical theories; and since he rejected
the theories, he also attacked the institutions and practices.
However, I think—following the pragmatists, the later Wittgenstein,
and others—that it is a mistake to believe that ordinary language,
moral practices, political values, and the ability to understand
other people necessarily depend upon the truth of any metaphysical
theory, either implicitly or explicitly. These values and beliefs
either gain consensus because they work, or fail in competition
with other values and beliefs; but no metaphysical grounding for
them is usually necessary. Thus, regardless of whether Nietzsche

was right to attack the metaphysical subject, this has little to do
with questions about the moral relevance of the humanities. I will
make this argument in more detail below. But in any case,
Nietzsche's basic attack on the moral value of the humanities
emerged not from his attitude toward the self, but from his
extreme reaction to cultural relativism—and it is this influential
aspect of his thought that I will consider here.

From time to time in this book, I will refer to another classicist
who received his education just a few years after Nietzsche and
from many of the same teachers: this was Ulrich von Wilamowitz-
Möllendorff, who has often been called the greatest Hellenist of
the nineteenth century.[8] Wilamowitz published a hostile review
of Nietzsche's Birth of Tragedy, and thereby initiated a quarrel
over the humanities that foreshadowed modern debates. Until his
last years, Wilamowitz remained loyal to the historicist methodology
that he and Nietzsche had both learned as young men, but he saw
no conflict between historicism and rationality. His work epitomized
the philological attitude that Nietzsche criticized as inherently
nihilistic; but Wilamowitz conceived of his own project as morally
useful and scientifically valid. As Rector of the University of
Berlin during the Weimar Republic, and author of 70 books,
Wilamowitz was a standard-bearer for the humanities, which had
already taken on substantially their modern form.[9] I will use his
career and his criticisms of Nietzsche to help illustrate Nietzsche's
originality and radicalism, and the nature of his departure from
the mainstream of nineteenth-century scholarship.

In the second part of this book, having explained the reasons
behind Nietzsche's decision to turn against humanism and scholarship,
I will explore several of his experimental alternatives. Each of
these involved an effort to transcend the modern sense of history
in all of its manifestations, for Nietzsche believed that our
consciousness of history—of perpetual change and diversity—
would lead the West into nihilism by revealing the relativity of all
beliefs. Nietzsche's first effort to arrive at stage (5), and thus to
provide an alternative to relativism and nihilism, was articulated
in The Birth of Tragedy (1871). Here he declared music and
Dionysian impulses to be essentially nonhistorical, natural and
life-affirming. At the same time, he attacked rationalist scholarship
as the enemy of the nonhistorical, nonreflective way of life that he
advocated. Nietzsche was later to declare this first constructive
project "Romantic" and abandoned it; I will devote only one chapter to it.

One aspect of *The Birth of Tragedy* that remained alive in Nietzsche's later work was an apparently nostalgic desire to return to pre-historicist attitudes toward the classics and classicism. In this spirit, Nietzsche revived some doctrines long favored by the party of the "ancients" in the famous quarrel between the ancients and the moderns. (The "ancients" had argued for the superiority of classical civilization to everything modern.) For example, Nietzsche revived the "Eternal Return," a pre-Socratic doctrine that had been widely held by the "ancients"—this doctrine, I will argue, served as one of Nietzsche's ways out of historicism and the contingencies of culture. Furthermore, Nietzsche glorified those civilizations, especially Rome and seventeenth-century France, that most naively imitated the Greeks. According to Nietzsche, the various renaissances in the Western tradition had resulted from a naive but enviable belief in transcendent cultural standards: standards that were allegedly epitomized in classical civilization. Nietzsche also revived the eighteenth-century genre of the anti-scholarly satire, as practiced by such "ancients" as Swift and Pope, in order to undermine the authority of philologists as interpreters of the past. As an alternative to the critical and historical attitude of philology, Nietzsche advocated an unquestioning allegiance to ancient genius.

It may seem that Nietzsche was being inconsistent when he endorsed a pre-historicist belief in the universal superiority of ancient Greece, after he had accepted as valid the relativist assumptions of modern historicism. I think that an explanation lies in Nietzsche's strategy of teaching different doctrines to two distinct audiences. He hoped to preach a naive version of humanism to the "herd" as a way of avoiding cultural collapse, while keeping nihilism a secret for "Overmen" to share. Thus I will explore Nietzsche's doctrines of Eternal Return and Will to Power as the exoteric teachings of an apparent cultural reactionary; but these teachings also contained an implicit message of liberation for Nietzsche's *übermenschlich* readers, whom he wanted to help move beyond culture. Dissatisfied by the vicarious, eclectic, and passively nihilistic life of the modern cultural pluralist, Nietzsche tried to steer his ordinary readers backwards into a pre-historicist stage at which cultural norms were still regarded as natural and permanent; but at the same time, he tried to push his true disciples into a post-modern stage at which no values appeared objective at all. It is this aspect of Nietzsche's thought that Leo Strauss adopted. I will therefore argue that Strauss and his followers are essentially duplicitous writers, holding an exoteric, conservative doctrine for the herd, and an esoteric, postmodern position for their *übermenschlich*

readers. Thus Allan Bloom and other Straussians are not as closely
allied to conservative proponents of a coherent Western canon as
they may appear at first glance: as Nietzscheans, they do not actually
believe that such a canon could contain "the accumulated wisdom
of our civilization... the best that has been said, thought, written,
and otherwise expressed about the human condition."[10]

Thus the exoteric message in both Nietzsche and Strauss is a
call to return to a homogeneous Western canon, uncontaminated
by historicism. But Nietzsche's esoteric philosophy represents an
attempt to supersede the "historical sense" by leaving truth and
objectivity behind altogether. Like Derrida a century later,
Nietzsche used historical perspectivism to attack the privileged
position of morals, logic, metaphysics, and even grammar; but
above all, he used historicism to undermine itself. Practitioners of
this kind of critique would, Nietzsche hoped, turn into "free spirits"—
transcending tradition, dogma, and culture, they would move into
a space beyond history. Their path out of history would consist in
a rational critique of the very structures of rationality, culminating
in an intoxicating sense of freedom and forgetting that can only be
described in Nietzschean terms. In this book, I try to show that
Nietzsche's Dionysian state was attained by first endorsing the
idea of a *Weltanschauung* and cultural relativism; this position
then deconstructed itself, leaving Nietzsche with no philosophical
position at all, in the traditional sense, but with an attitude of
liberation and creativity. However, since I think that the data of
historical diversity can be explained better without recourse to the
notion of a *Weltanschauung* in the first place, I argue that
Nietzsche's Dionysian attitude resulted from a mistake.

In my final chapter, I propose a new paradigm as an alternative
to *Weltanschauung*-historicism. This is intended to make better
sense of the phenomenon of historical diversity, without leading to
irrationalist conclusions. I do not argue here against Nietzsche's
view that ideas are completely conditioned by their contexts. (Nor
do I endorse this view, however.) Instead, I argue against the
notion that cultures are—or must seem to their members to be—
isolated, delimited entities with clear boundaries. I suggest an
alternative paradigm which treats the cultural context surrounding
a work as a heterogeneous collection of ideas, experiences, influences
and prejudices. Thus, I argue, it is wrong to think of texts as
products or phenomena of separate, organic, homogeneous cultures,
each culture unintelligible to any other. Instead, "cultures" merely
represent useful categories within which to place people who share
some element of background that happens to be of interest; but
these categories can be defined in numerous ways. In fact, almost

any two people could be described as belonging to different cultures, if the cultures were defined appropriately. Thus, I argue, cultural boundaries have no objective existence and cannot fatally block communication or understanding. Every author betrays, in principle, a *unique* set of influences and prejudices; and the experience of understanding a text from far away or long ago is just a perspicuous example of the process of understanding that always takes place between two people.

Scholars in the humanities have pointed out profound differences in perspective that divide men from women, ancients from moderns, Westerners from Asians or Africans, bourgeois from proletarians, African-Americans from European-Americans. My paradigm in no way suggests that these claims are false. On the contrary, I believe that many of them are true—but true at one and the same time. Thus no single cultural category has a definitive role in determining human lives and thought; we result rather from the interplay of many cultural categories. It seems impossible to say definitively to what degree cultures condition us. But if it is true that each person is conditioned by multiple, overlapping cultures, then we are all potentially unique. Moreover, we must be able to understand people across cultural borders, because this is what we do even when we communicate with those who are most similar to us. Thus my paradigm does not so much refute the dilemmas of cultural conditioning and relativism, as defuse them.

In defense of the modern humanities, I argue that the practice of trying to understand ideas and texts from alien backgrounds is morally valuable in itself, regardless of any universal moral truths that may or may not inhere in such texts. I claim that a rigorous study of other people's viewpoints has inherent ethical preconditions and political ramifications. Therefore, the modern humanities are not morally nihilistic, even if they are relativist with regard to the ideas contained in the texts which they study.

The nihilist Last Man, according to Nietzsche, is a creature inferior to any member of a naive, closed society; he is also inferior to the post-modern, Dionysian Overman. Nietzsche's caricature (like Allan Bloom's) depends on the view that only members of a "culture" can find a grounding for their ethical and aesthetic preferences—so only members of a "culture" (and Overmen) can find the strength to act. Nietzsche did not regard the eclectic, historicist regime of the Last Man as a "culture" at all, and therefore he did not believe that Last Men were capable of creativity. But the alternative paradigm that I propose to explain cultural diversity dispenses with the very notion of a *Weltanschauung*, and thereby allows us to see the so-called Last Man in a new light: not as different in kind from anyone else, but as relatively free, broad-minded and humane. I argue that the humanities can still be defended as having great moral value—not because they inculcate a fixed set of universal moral truths—but because they make us more tolerant, open-minded and consequently fit for citizenship in the regime of the Last Man. Nietzsche recognized that a historicist form of humanistic education was the best means to engender the attitudes of the Last Man. Nietzsche therefore attacked historicism and modern humanistic education in virulent terms. But I will try to use my alternative paradigm to provide a new theoretical understanding of the modern humanities—and also to vindicate the life of the modern humanist, Nietzsche's Last Man.

Thus I hope to describe Nietzsche's effort to move "beyond culture," to transcend or overcome the definition of humans as cultural and historical creatures. This constitutes my interpretation of the Overman, Eternal Return, Dionysian philosophy and the Free Spirit in Nietzsche's thought. At the same time, I want to suggest that Nietzsche's derivation of cultural relativism and nihilism from the historical methodology of his day began with his endorsement of what Hayden White has called the "culturalist fallacy."[11] This belief in reified, homogeneous, isolated *Weltanschauungen* seems to me a prejudice of much modern philosophy, and one that should be discarded. Even the so-called "Western tradition" (viewed as a discrete, coherent, delimited entity) is a legacy of philosophical idealism that has created pseudo-problems for modern theorists of humanistic education. Thus I want to suggest that in order to defend the humanities against a Nietzschean critique, we too should move "beyond culture"—but only in order to make way for a richer and more convincing account of what education and scholarship mean.

Part One

The Path to Nihilism

Gradually it has become clear to me what every great philosophy has been so far: namely, the personal confession of its author and a kind of involuntary and unconscious memoir....

Beyond Good and Evil (Kaufmann), 6

Chapter 1

The Humanistic Tradition

I. Birth of a Philologist

At the age of 12, in his first year as a student at the pre-eminent German boarding school, Schulpforte, Friedrich Nietzsche attempted his first original philological proof. He had read in Livy about the Roman patriot Gaius Mucius Scaevola, who had thrust his hand into a fire to demonstrate his contempt for pain, thereby intimidating an enemy of the Roman Republic. In order to prove that this might actually have happened, Nietzsche held a handful of burning matches under the palm of his outstretched hand until he had burned himself badly; only the intervention of a prefect saved him from doing himself an even greater injury.[1]

This was the remarkable act of a remarkable child. A schoolmate recalled that "there was something extraordinary in his voice and tone, as there was in his choice of expressions, that made him quite different from other boys of the same age." One of Nietzsche's friends in primary school said that he "looked at you in a way that made the words stick in the back of your throat"; and another compared this future "antichrist" to the child Jesus, disputing with the elders in the temple. But although Nietzsche's actions were always, even in childhood, extraordinary and calculated to shock his bourgeois contemporaries, his daring defense of Livy was in many ways merely an example of the educational methods of Pforta taken to a pathological extreme.[2]

3

Nietzsche's interest in Livy was, in the narrow sense, "humanistic"—that is, he wanted to draw a moral lesson from a reading of classical literature, just as the humanists of the Renaissance had done. Perhaps he had developed this aspiration as a result of his early experiences at Pforta, for his humanist teachers assumed that literary classics epitomized universal values, and that the great works could serve as powerful sources of moral instruction for the young. At the same time, the moral lessons that the 12-year-old Nietzsche attempted to draw from Livy happened to conform to the militarist ethos of neighboring Prussia. Thus the education that Nietzsche received at Pforta could be characterized as humanism which had been deliberately placed at the service of pan-German nationalism. This kind of appropriation came naturally to Pforta's teachers, who believed that their own morals were epitomized throughout the canon of the classics of literature. They believed that both they and the ancient Romans belonged to a single world-culture to which the only alternative was barbarism. Finally, Nietzsche showed a precocious concern for finding out whether the story of Mucius Scaevola could actually be true; thus he showed an inclination, typical of German humanism in the nineteenth century, toward a positivist reading of the classical past. In 1824, Leopold von Ranke had formulated the slogan of historical positivism with his claim that historians could discover "what actually happened." But he did so, characteristically, in the hope that objective history would help to justify a specific modern political ethos and the aspirations of the incipient German state. Thus positivism furnished the *method* of much nineteenth-century humanism, and nationalism frequently provided its motivation.[3]

Nietzsche was to renounce the militarist, positivist, and (above all) the humanist presuppositions that underlay the curriculum at Pforta. At the beginning of this book, I defined "humanism" as the project of teaching virtue using a canon of exemplary literary and his-torical texts. This was a project that Nietzsche associated with a whole tradition of Western thought, beginning with Socrates, Euripides, and the Sophists, passing through the humanists of the Renaissance and the Enlightenment, and continuing in his own day in the educational system that prepared him to be a classicist. Nietzsche believed that humanism was essentially associated with several other tendencies in Western thought, so that the word could be used almost interchangeably with a whole set of abstract terms. First of all, humanists chose their exemplary texts and discussed them using critical, rational means. By "rational," I do not mean a commitment to any particular mode of reasoning, nor a belief in any specific truths. I just mean that people who are rational attempt to convince others of their views by offering *reasons* for them; and if other people do not accept their methods of reasoning, then they try to offer reasons for their methods. These are practices that Nietzsche associated with Socrates, who refused to take traditional values on faith but demanded that they be justified. Thus, for Nietzsche, humanism was a species of Socratic rationalism.

Secondly, humanism implied that virtue and wisdom were teachable; good character was not, therefore, a matter of birth, but belonged to anyone who had the opportunity and intellect to receive a humanistic education. Thus humanism was at least in theory a democratic project. Furthermore, humanism was in principle cosmopolitan; if the criteria of excellence were universal, then each work had to be assessed on its merits without regard to its national or ethnic origins. And finally, humanism seemed to Nietzsche to require a specific set of ethical values. For example, in order to live up to the ideals of humanism, scholars had to treat both the texts they read and the students they instructed with tolerance, empathy, candor, reasonableness, and (where appropriate) respect. Anything else would have interfered with the process of rational inquiry and thus betrayed the project of humanism.

Thus, in Nietzsche's thought, "humanism" became a far richer concept than the one with which I began this book. In the following pages, I will offer an account of humanism as I think Nietzsche understood it. Nietzsche's understanding of humanism has been shared by many other thinkers, both humanists and anti-humanists. Moreover, his account of the connections linking humanism, democracy, cosmopolitanism, rationality and empathy seems reasonable. In order to illustrate the presuppositions and consequences of humanism as Nietzsche understood it, I will offer a brief account of both the specific educational practices that were employed at Pforta, and the tradition of humanistic thought that lay behind these practices. Nietzsche never defined "humanism" explicitly, and he used it less frequently than some related concepts, particularly rationalism and democracy. But something like the following was, I think, what he meant by the term.

II. The Humanistic Tradition

Schulpforte was an ancient and highly respected school for boys, situated four miles from Nietzsche's home at Naumburg, within the high walls of a twelfth-century Cistercian abbey. As an educational community—in the words of the Rector, "a whole school-state"—it conformed to Voltaire's description of the court of Frederick the Great: "Sparta in the morning and Athens in the afternoon."[4] But, despite the apparent schizophrenia in Prussian mores that Voltaire had satirized so perceptively, the militarist and intellectual sides of German culture did not come together entirely accidentally. On the contrary, at Pforta, the search for knowledge about the past was conducted with discipline and self-sacrifice worthy of the battlefield, while the nationalist, militarist ideology of the period was bolstered with lessons taken from classical texts.[5]

The "Athenian" side of Pforta's educational atmosphere was a direct legacy of the humanistic project of the Italian Renaissance. The term "humanist" had originated as a fifteenth-century Italian slang-word meaning a professor of the *studia humanitatis*, i.e., grammar, rhetoric, poetry, history, and moral philosophy, all taught using Greek and Latin classics. Renaissance humanists believed that all classical authors had addressed the same moral issues from essentially the same perspective, and had drawn similar moral conclusions, which, they thought, had the virtue of being correct for all time. Their belief in an eternally constant "human nature" led them to mine history for examples of wise and virtuous action from the past, which they considered directly applicable to the present. John Dryden eloquently restated a humanist commonplace when he wrote of history that:

> It informs the understanding by the memory: It helps us to judge of what will happen, by shewing us the like revolutions of former times. For Mankind being the same in all ages, agitated by the same passions, and mov'd to action by the same interests, nothing can come to pass, but some President of the like nature has already been produc'd, so that having the causes before our eyes, we cannot easily be deceiv'd in the effects, if we have Judgment enough but to draw the parallel. ... All History is only the precepts of Moral Philosophy reduc'd into Examples. ...[6]

The genealogy of this idea can easily be traced from the age of Renaissance humanism down to the mid-nineteenth century, when a highly rigorous, historically based education in ancient literature became an almost universal ideal for the European ruling classes. It may seem strange to us today that the sons of Prussian Junkers should have been forced to study Greek for six hours each week throughout their secondary education, and Latin for ten or 11 hours, and that the classical languages should have been the major intellectual accomplishment that they were expected to acquire. The responsibility for this lies with the leading figures of the German Enlightenment, who, like their counterparts throughout Europe, had successfully reinforced and reinvigorated the humanists' commitment to teaching virtue by exposure to classical texts.[7] Leibniz, for example, had written that the goal of history, like that of poetry, is "to teach wisdom and virtue by example." For him, even the moral truths of revealed religion were historical facts (since they came to us in texts from antiquity); and only history could demonstrate the coincidence of reason and faith that was so central to his thought.[8] At Pforta in the 1860s, a tradition of fundamentalist Lutheranism still remained alive, if only in the person of the chaplain; but there was also a Leibnizian effort under way to teach the Hebrew and Greek Bibles as historical texts just like all the rest.[9] And along with this new willingness to subject the Bible to positivist criticism, biblical scholars still hoped, with humanist optimism, to draw moral lessons from Scripture, as they had from the other privileged texts of antiquity. "Moderns" like Leibniz had long argued for the expansion of the humanist canon to include non-classical texts, from the Bible to Machiavelli and Bacon. So, although Pforta remained for the most part a "Latin school" in which even Greek was treated as a somewhat exotic subject, both Nietzsche and Wilamowitz quickly learned (as Leibniz had) that humanist methods could be applied to a wide range of texts, many of them lying far outside the classical canon. They also learned the practical value of these methods; when Nietzsche's friend Paul Deussen was disappointed in love, Nietzsche tried to console him "with examples from history and literature."[10]

Above all, Pforta students were expected to develop a literary style by imitating those canonical authors whom the curriculum presented. At the age of 14, Nietzsche criticized the writing he had done before coming to Pforta, none of which "contains even a spark of poetry." Nietzsche recalled that in these first, failed efforts, "I had no models. I could hardly imagine how anyone could imitate a poet, and I molded [my poems] as my soul suggested them."[11] This was to change once Nietzsche began to study the classics seriously at school. In 1888, Nietzsche was still grateful for what he had learned about style at Pforta. In a section of *Twilight of the Idols* entitled "What I Owe to the Ancients," he recalled:

My sense of style, of the epigram as style, was awakened almost immediately when I encountered Sallust. I have never forgotten the astonishment of my honored teacher Corrsen when he had to give the highest grade to his worst

Latin scholar.... One will recognize in all my writings, even in my *Zarathustra*, a very serious ambition for *Roman* style, for the *'aere perennius'* in style.—It was no different when I first met Horace.[12]

In some respects, then, Nietzsche remained permanently devoted to the core principles of humanism as they had been articulated during the Italian Renaissance. Above all, he retained a typically humanist belief in the value of learning style through the imitation of the classics.

III. The Origins of Humanism

I hope to have shown that humanistic education meant something quite similar in Renaissance Florence and nineteenth-century Pforta. The precise values that humanists tried to impart through the study of classical texts might have changed between the fifteenth and the nineteenth centuries, but Pforta's humanists continued to believe that the classics epitomized universal values, both moral and aesthetic. They even used many of the same authors (mostly Latin orators and poets) who had already been treated as canonical during the Renaissance.

The history of humanism can also be traced back into antiquity, to its roots in the Sophist school, which, as Nietzsche saw, anticipated most of the important characteristics of Renaissance humanism. The Sophists had taught virtue and eloquence to the young by exposing them to a canon of classical literary models, but they had treated these models critically, valuing reason (*gnomē*) over myth, emotion, or mere chance.[13] Nietzsche associated these values not only with the Sophists, but especially with Socrates, whom he considered the founder of science and reason. In fact, Nietzsche considered Socrates to have been "the first and supreme *Sophist*, the mirror and epitome of all sophistical tendencies."[14] Socrates and the Sophists had taught people to assess customs and myths by applying rational criteria to them: i.e., by asking *why* any particular myth should guide people. More specifically, Socrates' method was "rational" in that he proposed and defended specific methods and rules of reasoning, which were supposed to be universally valid and which could be used to evaluate myths, customs and received norms. Thus "Even the most sublime ethical deeds, the stirrings of pity, self-sacrifice, heroism and ... *sophrosune*, were derived from the dialectic of knowledge by Socrates and his like-minded successors, down to the present, and accordingly designated as teachable."[15] This, in a nutshell, was the educational philosophy that modern humanists such as Leibniz had propounded. They taught wisdom and virtue from historical and literary texts, but they chose their examples using the light of critical reason (although they differed in their precise definitions of rationality).[16]

In the tradition-bound culture of Greece before Socrates (Nietzsche thought), the received values had been left unquestioned and it had been bad taste—at best—to seek reasons for them:

> With Socrates Greek taste turns in favor of dialectics: what really happened there? Above all an *aristocratic* taste was thereby conquered; with dialectics the rabble rises to the top. Before Socrates, one declined dialectics in good company: it was considered bad manners, it laid things bare. One warned the young to stay away from it.[17]

By testing the received values of Athenian society against rational criteria, Socrates implicitly adopted a vantage point *beyond* his culture. From there, he could see "behind the aristocrats of Athens," recognizing the groundlessness of their beliefs.[18] He began to pick and choose his values from a variety of cultures, using reason as his guide. Thus, with the arrival of Socrates and the Sophists:

> The *polis* loses its faith in the uniqueness of its culture, in its right to rule over every other *polis*—One exchanges cultures, i.e., "the gods"—one thereby loses faith in the sole prerogative of the *deus autochthonous* [the indigenous god]. Good and evil of differing origin are mingled: the boundary between good and evil is blurred.... [19]

In Nietzsche's view, such a process must ultimately end in nihilism. Despite what Socrates might have thought, there were no universally valid or compelling grounds on which to choose one ethical view over another; such choices were always culturally contingent. So, by allowing the claims of reason to trump the *"deus autochthonous,"* Socrates was leading the way to moral nihilism. Besides, Socrates' quest for foundations and reasons would ultimately have to be applied to his own method; people would ask whether rationality had grounds—in other words, whether there was any reason to choose reason.[20] No such ultimate foundation was available,

except via God; and God was dead, killed when Socratic rational-
ists discovered a plurality of religious beliefs and realized that all
gods must be the mere products of local values and preferences.[21]
Robbed of its (ultimately religious) foundations, Socratic rationalism
appeared to be nothing but a compound of arbitrary values—
a culture—and no more secure than any other. Anyone who
looked "*behind* Socrates" would see that the Socratic way of life
depended upon "divine naïveté and sureness"—in other words, on
a complete lack of doubt regarding its own core principles.[22] Any
culture, even the rational, objective culture of humanism, could
preserve its values only by failing to view them rationally and
objectively; that is why one had to warn the young to shun
Socrates. Nietzsche believed that Socrates had, in the end, recognized
the nihilistic consequences of his own method and had therefore
committed suicide.[23] Thus, in his diagnosis of Socrates—as
elsewhere—Nietzsche collapsed humanism, Sophism, and rationalism
(not to mention democracy and enlightenment) into a single category
and viewed them as part of a single project, the effort to view tradition
in a critical light. But he called the value of this project into question,
suggesting that it contained the seeds of nihilism.[24]

IV. Humanism and Philosophy

Nietzsche was being contentious or even paradoxical when he
claimed that Socrates was a Sophist, for the Socrates who appears
in Plato's works was a great *enemy* of the Sophists.[25] Socrates and
most of his Sophistic contemporaries probably had at least one
thing in common: their commitment to rationality over myth.
Thus Protagoras and several other Sophists were convicted, like
Socrates, on charges of impiety and corrupting the young, because
they had openly criticized Athenian myths and traditional laws on
rational grounds.[26] On the other hand, the Sophists' critical methods
differed from those of Socrates, resulting in a controversy that was
depicted in detail (but not necessarily fairly) by Plato. In my view,
such Sophists as Protagoras and Gorgias were more like the
humanists of the Renaissance and Nietzsche's Pforta than was
Socrates. What distinguished them from Socrates was their attitude
toward metaphysics: Socrates argued that values had to be
grounded in general, abstract, *a priori* truths about the cosmos,
whereas the Sophists believed that morality could be derived
directly from the concrete particulars of history and literature.
    For example, Protagoras refused to concede the relevance of

metaphysics to his educational methods. In Plato's *Protagoras*, Socrates repeatedly seeks to engage Protagoras in metaphysical discourse (wanting to discuss, for example, the abstract nature of virtue), but Protagoras keeps trying to change the subject to literary criticism. Protagoras' book entitled the *Antilogiae* apparently contained pragmatic attacks on speculative religion, and on many other *a priori* disciplines.[27] Instead of deriving moral truth from dialectic, he promised, like Leibniz, to "teach wisdom and virtue by example."[28] In the dialogue that bears his name, Protagoras describes his pedagogy as follows:

> the works of the best poets are set before [children] to read on the classroom benches, and the children are compelled to learn these works thoroughly; and in them are displayed many warnings, many detailed narratives and praises and eulogies of good men of ancient times, so that the boy may desire to imitate them competitively and may stretch himself to become like them.[29]

As I have suggested, Protagoras' educational methods were still very much alive at Pforta in the nineteenth century. Even the list of "good poets" remained remarkably constant, at least from the Roman period on.[30] It was because of the Renaissance humanists' opposition to metaphysics that they had replaced the scholastic curriculum of the middle ages with one based upon history and literature, i.e., concrete particulars; and this remained the dominant educational philosophy at Pforta in Nietzsche's time: philosophy was not taught there at all, and even religion was given a historical grounding.

However, Socrates (as depicted by Plato) raised the following objection to this form of pedagogy: Sophists, he argued, possessed no independent means to decide which actions were virtuous and which immoral. Evil men had frequently chosen to imitate liars and scoundrels whom they found described in poetry and history; therefore, Socrates thought it prudent to expel the poets from the Republic altogether. If any stories were to be told to the young, they would have to be tales fashioned by philosophers, who always kept one eye on The Good.[31] A similar objection to the humanist method was made 2,000 years later by followers of Réné Descartes, who believed that "clear and distinct" moral ideas were not obtainable in literature and history, but only by means of rational introspection or divine revelation. And Kant wrote:

One cannot damage morality more than by seeking to borrow it from examples. For each example that is set before me must itself be judged first by principles of morality, whether it is worthy to be a primary example, *i.e.*, to serve as a model, but it no way can it dependably provide the conception of morality.[32]

Similarly, Nietzsche believed that it was impossible to make discriminations between good and evil—such as those which the Sophists and humanists made—without having at least a covert commitment to an absolute standard of the True and Good. Descartes, Kant, and probably Plato thought that such a standard was available by way of philosophy or religion; Nietzsche thought that no such standard existed, and therefore he abandoned both humanism and philosophy. Thus Nietzsche called Socrates a Sophist because he believed that the Sophists (and their humanist descendants) ultimately relied upon abstract standards of truth and value like the ones that Socrates had sought. They were just philosophers in disguise.

Some scholars believe that the Sophists tried to avoid establishing an *a priori* grounding for morals by finding morality inherent "in the objective historical structure of [their] nation's spiritual life."[33] In other words, instead of asking abstract questions about ethics, they advocated imitating the virtuous acts that were depicted in their culture's literary heritage. However, as Nietzsche knew well, this approach would run into profound difficulties as soon as people realized that the world contained *numerous* cultures with conflicting notions of virtue; then, lacking an absolute and nonempirical standard of morality, every thoughtful person would have to become a relativist. The Sophists of antiquity were almost certainly not cultural relativists (although they have been consistently caricatured as such): they probably believed that the myths and historical narratives of Greece were superior to all others.[34] Nevertheless, critics of Sophism and humanism worried from the beginning that these schools (since they failed to articulate abstract, universal truths) offered no firm bulwark against relativism; and this fear only grew worse in the modern period, when Europeans began to practice comparative studies of diverse cultures and discovered what Jürgen Habermas calls "a rationally irresoluble pluralism of competing value systems and beliefs."[35] This discovery was to lie at the heart of Nietzsche's questioning of traditional values:

Just because our moral philosophers knew the facts of morality only very approximately in arbitrary extracts or in accidental epitomes—for example, as the morality of their environment, their class, their church, the spirit of their time, their climate and part of the world—just because they were poorly informed and not even very curious about different peoples, times, and past ages—they never laid eyes on the real problems of morality; for these emerge only when we compare *many* moralities.[36]

According to Nietzsche, humanists (like philosophers) rely on "accidental epitomes" to tell them the "facts of morality"; but they take these arbitrary collections of custom and art to be universal. For Nietzsche, any preference for one moral example over another (unless it is the preference of an Overman) must result from an underlying *Weltanschauung*; and these are plural and contingent. Nietzsche consistently asserts that we must either accept the implicit metaphysical preconceptions of our culture, or else, like Socrates, we can attempt to derive absolutely valid metaphysical doctrines to guide us. The first option is closed-minded and naive; the second is futile. However, contrary to Nietzsche, I think that there is another alternative: we can develop ethical standards through a universal discussion that is aimed at consensus.

This, I believe, was the humanists' approach. For example, Isocrates argued that truth could emerge from a collective, rational discussion of law and literature, provided that all free men could participate and that the participants were trained in the critical, rational methods of the Sophists. And Protagoras believed that all men possessed a sense of justice and reverence that enabled them to arrive at moral truth through discussion.[37] In a daylong argument with Pericles, Protagoras apparently claimed that what is right *just is* what is universally believed by human beings.[38] These were central tenets of humanism. But Nietzsche thought that humanists had failed to recognize the existence of fundamental differences in perspective that would make communication—let alone consensus—impossible. Literature could not successfully instruct the young in ethics, because the standards that it contained would vary from culture to culture, and none could ever be universally valid.

V. Humanism and Liberalism

In later chapters, I will argue that Nietzsche was wrong in his mature critique of humanism. But for now it will be useful to examine a little more closely the consequences of traditional humanism, in order to see what was at stake in Nietzsche's critique. In Nietzsche's view, the Sophists founded humanism by trying to turn the body of Greek literature, history and law into an objective entity to be studied and, if necessary, criticized. In the process, they contributed greatly to Greek notions of individuality, personal responsibility, and progress. To borrow categories invented by Karl Popper (which are, however, already implicit in Nietzsche's *Untimely Meditations*), the Sophists participated in the move from a Closed Society to an Open Society that occurred in Greece during the classical period.[39] Closed Societies, in Popper's view, are marked by a "magical or irrational attitude towards the customs of social life, and [a] corresponding rigidity of these customs." Members of a Closed Society are unable to differentiate "between the customary or conventional regularities of social life and the regularities found in 'nature'...."[40] It would be a mistake to treat Popper's dichotomy of wholly open and wholly closed societies as anything more than a pair of ideal types. I will say more about this in Chapter IX, when I re-examine the closed/open distinction in the light of a paradigm that makes the very notion of a totally Closed Society appear implausible. But it does seem clear that societies become *relatively* more or less open in different periods, and that humanism plays a generally rationalizing and liberating role in any culture where it is allowed to operate. The enemies of humanism are the first to admit as much; for example, Heidegger's *Letter on Humanism* of 1947 is a sustained critique of the critical interpretive methods that the Sophists began, which, he says, imply a definition of humans as essentially rational. But such a definition, in Heidegger's view, alienates us from authentic "Being," and overvalues progress, ethics, and science.[41] Along similar lines, Nietzsche praised the pre-Socratics for having avoided the disease of objectivity that bedevils any society in which humanism is dominant.[42] He argued that Euripides, that alleged mouthpiece for Sophism and Socratic rationalism, had taught the Greeks for the first time to treat their myths objectively and critically:

> Euripides brought the spectator onto the stage in order to make him truly competent to pass judgment.... [F]rom him the people learned how to observe, debate, and draw conclusions

according to the rules of art and with the cleverest sophistries....
If the entire populace now philosophized, managed land and
goods, and conducted lawsuits with unheard-of circumspection,
he deserved the credit, for this was the result of the wisdom
he had inculcated in the people.[43]

But Nietzsche also found much to criticize in this new democratic
spirit. His attitude towards the Closed Societies of the ancient
world was not the pure nostalgia that many of his Romantic
contemporaries felt, for he did not believe in the "indigenous gods"
that had given these societies their coherence and direction. But
Nietzsche also had serious reservations about modern, "open,"
democratic societies, which, he thought, teetered on the edge of
nihilism. In 1860, his future colleague and friend at Basel, Jacob
Burckhardt, described the humanistic culture of the Italian
Renaissance as an Open Society, in contrast to the Closed Society
that had preceded it:

In the Middle Ages both sides of human consciousness—that
which was turned within as that which was turned without—
lay dreaming or half awake beneath a common veil.... Man
was conscious of himself only as a member of a race, people,
party, family, or corporation—only through some general category. In Italy this veil first melted into air; an objective
treatment and consideration of the State and of all the things
of this world became possible. The subjective side at the same
time asserted itself with corresponding emphasis; man
became a spiritual individual, and recognized himself as
such.[44]

Burckhardt described the Greeks in much the same way as he had
described the Renaissance humanists: "The Greeks had a
panoramic eye and an objective mind, and accordingly wrote the
history of their own people and of other peoples as well. They were
the first to observe something with detachment...."[45] Thus
Burckhardt traced a tradition of enlightenment, beginning with
the Greeks, passing through the Renaissance, and moving on into
modernity. This tradition, for Burckhardt, was identical with the
phenomenon of humanism. But Burckhardt spoke for many
Germans of the mid-nineteenth century when he described the
critical attitude of humanism in largely negative terms. For
Burckhardt, as for the adult Nietzsche, the alienation of objective

and subjective worlds—in Max Weber's phrase "the specific and peculiar rationalism of Western culture"—had split the authentic Greek person in two, and had led to the disintegration of the holistic, all-encompassing community of the preclassical polis.[46] Thus, when Nietzsche worked out his early criticism of humanism in *The Birth of Tragedy*, he naturally turned to Greece before the Sophists as an example of a time when there had been no division of subjectivity and objectivity, in part because there had (allegedly) been no human subjects in the modern sense. But Nietzsche began to feel more and more strongly that the naive age of archaic Greece had become utterly unrecoverable, given the power and ubiquity of Socratic rationalism; and that nostalgia was an impediment to cultural rejuvenation.[47]

Thus Nietzsche certainly went far beyond a mere nostalgia for pre-Socratic, pre-rational culture—after all, he was a confirmed anti-Romantic. But there was one defining characteristic of pre-Socratic culture that Nietzsche found attractive throughout his life, and that he attempted to revive in his mature philosophy. This was the pre-Socratics' absolute antipathy to everything historical, to any sense that things could change fundamentally or that profane events could matter. Without a belief in the possibility of change, an Open Society is impossible. But, as Mircea Eliade has written in his *Myth of the Eternal Return* (the title is deliberately Nietzschean): "interest in the 'irreversible' and the 'new' in history is a recent discovery in the life of humanity." In pre-Socratic times, one "tolerates 'history' with difficulty and attempts periodically to abolish it."[48] Thus all the events which do occur in pre-Socratic culture are taken to be either repetitions of timeless archetypes, or else punishable infractions of the law. Individual decisions and opinions are of little importance. Nietzsche described Greek tragedy before Euripides as a ritual act in which the gods were actually present and archetypal myths repeated themselves on stage with the participation of a univocal audience. Until the "demise of tragedy," Nietzsche writes,

> the Greeks had felt involuntarily impelled to relate all their experiences immediately to their myths, indeed to understand them only in this relation. Thus even the immediate present had to appear to them right away *sub species aeterni* and in a certain sense as timeless.[49]

Euripides' "sin" was to treat the same myths as quasi-historical events, whose meaning was open to interpretation by a critical audience, responsible for its own role in making history. Thus Euripides, as a father of humanism and the Open Society, helped to introduce the Greeks to history—but Nietzsche considered this a mixed blessing. Along similar lines, Nietzsche expressed a lifelong interest in the ancient myth of the Eternal Return of the Same, which (writes Eliade), "as interpreted by Greek speculation, has the meaning of a supreme attempt towards the 'staticization' of becoming, toward annulling the irreversibility of time."[50] One fundamental aspect of Nietzsche's philosophy was his revival of this myth. Finally, he often expressed his admiration for those philosophers who seemed to stand aloof from time and history, showing contempt for historical events and disdain for the collective labors of scholarship that humanists advocated. Thus, for example, in his book on *Philosophy in the Tragic Age of the Greeks*, Nietzsche described the opposite of "a republic of scholars," namely, "the republic of geniuses: each giant calls to his brother across the desolate intervals of the ages, and, undisturbed by the wanton noises of the dwarfs who carry on beneath them, they continue their high spirit-talk."[51]

As Nietzsche would be eager to admit, this "republic" of geniuses differs in some basic ways from an open society. For example, Popper argues that, insofar as a society is open, social change is possible and "we recognize rational personal responsibility."[52] And Habermas concludes that in a society where particular norms are criticizable, the corresponding values must arise, not out of "an interpreted lifeworld immune from critique," but out of "the interpretive accomplishments of the participants themselves, that is, by means of risky (because rationally motivated) agreement...."[53] Since the ability to participate in the formation of a rationally motivated agreement belongs, according to humanists, to all rational creatures, the move to an Open Society has strong egalitarian consequences. Sincere humanists, like Isocrates, abandon notions of racial or class superiority, and argue that all people can and should participate in the Open Society.[54] The Sophists were widely censured for charging money to teach rhetoric. But G. B. Kerferd argues that this disapproval cannot have resulted from the mere fact that they treated ideas and books as commodities, for poets and physicians who sold their products faced no similar condemnation. Rather, the Sophists attracted criticism for selling their ideas and skills to *anyone* who could pay for them; thus they made a potent kind of political expertise—rhetoric—available to a wide array of people without regard for hereditary status or nationality. In fact, some Sophists may not have been quite as egalitarian as their collective reputation suggested; but their elitist critics were well aware that the skills they taught were potentially subversive and democratic.[55] As Bernard Knox writes in a discussion of the Sophists:

> that group of studies we call the humanities came into being as an education for democracy, a training in free citizenship; all through its long history it has been the advocate of free thought and speech; it has flourished most brilliantly wherever those freedoms were respected and faced repression and banishment wherever they were not. And this is the strongest argument for the humanities today.[56]

The individualism, liberalism, egalitarianism and cosmopolitanism that are often associated with humanism stem not so much from the specific moral lessons that humanists draw from literary texts (for these lessons differ greatly), as from the methods that they use. Nietzsche recognized this; describing the Sophists, he wrote that theirs was an

> essentially *republican* art: one must be accustomed to tolerating the most unusual opinions and points of view and even taking a certain pleasure in their counterplay; one must be just as willing to listen as to speak; and as a listener one must be able more or less to appreciate the art being applied.[57]

Humanists, as Nietzsche saw, generally believe that truth will emerge from a rational discussion which allows all participants to express themselves freely. For this reason, they often resist tyranny and censorship as irrational, and they are frequently democrats. According to Nietzsche, any form of objectivity and rationality has democratic implications: *"la science* belongs to democracy, that is clear as day."[58]

Needless to say, most humanists from the past seem to us to be seriously lacking in respect for the rights of large groups of human beings. Thus, for example, Seneca and Jefferson, both humanists par excellence, also owned large numbers of slaves; and few humanists before the modern age was willing to include women among those considered worthy of being educated. Nevertheless, it can be argued that humanism tends to undermine and oppose any effort to exclude rational human beings from education and public discourse. Humanists who do exclude groups of people from their definition of rational beings do so because of received opinions about the alleged inferiority of these groups—opinions that they have as yet failed to test by rational means. When they do attempt in good faith to provide educational and political opportunities to such once-excluded groups, they invariably discover that members of these groups are competent to participate politically and socially as equals.[59] Thus, while humanism has by no means prevented the evils of racism, sexism, and class prejudice, it has tended, through-out history, to serve progressive, egalitarian, and increasingly inclusive political causes. Or, to describe the same phenomenon in Nietzsche's terms, humanism has been an anti-aristocratic, level-ling force—an instrument "of the *ressentiment* of the rabble"—which has served the interests of "shopkeepers, Christians, cows, women, Englishmen, and other democrats."[60]

VI. The Ethics of Humanism

In addition to its democratic, rationalistic, and cosmopolitan implications, humanism seemed from the beginning to engender some specific modes of personal behavior. Thus by the late-Roman period, the two meanings of "humane"—on the one hand, learned; on the other, philanthropic—had already become confused, so that, according to Aulus Gellius, "humanism" had come to mean, in common language, "*philanthropia*,' signifying a kind of friendly spirit and good feeling towards all men without distinction...." Gellius therefore found it necessary to remind his readers that "humanism" really meant only "education and training in the liberal arts." Men who were *maxime humanissimi* would, for example, be acquainted with the works of Praxiteles from the books they had read. Gellius adds that the word "humane" does not mean, as "the common people" think, "good natured, amiable, and kindly, although without knowledge of letters, [but it means] a man of 'some cultivation and education'...."[61] In a similar way, the humanists of the Renaissance were often described in ethical terms—as revealing an "emphasis on man and his dignity"—when all they essentially shared was a common educational method.[62]

Gellius implies that *any* connection between the word "humane," as it is commonly used, and the technical term "humanities," is merely coincidental. But scholarly methods have strongly ethical consequences, and this perhaps accounts for the perennial confusion of "humanists" with "humane" people. The humanizing effect of the humanities was already a cliché when Ovid wrote, "to study the liberal arts faithfully makes behavior (*mores*) gentle and permits people not to act savagely."[63] But the fact that this sentiment is ancient and a mainstay of platitudinous commencement addresses does not make the essential insight any less valid; the humanities really do engender or require certain standards of ethical behavior. For example, because humanists' goal is to interpret texts and ideas created by other people, they must show both empathy and detachment in their work. Without some degree of empathy, interpreters are likely to miss the full meaning and value of texts from alien periods; but without detachment, they can lose their ability to criticize these texts. Similarly, humanists frequently find that to hold opinions dogmatically would clash with their generally critical attitude towards authority, textual or otherwise; they are therefore forced to adopt a relatively modest and cooperative attitude. Even the technical apparatus of humanist scholarship—footnotes, bibliographies, and the like—signifies that humanists place themselves within a tradition and a community, that they attempt to justify their conclusions rationally, and that they expect their work to be criticized by scholars of the future.

Moreover, the success of their whole enterprise depends upon a certain amount of candor; for unless scholars make their sources and methods clear, others cannot readily build upon their work. Although scholars in the humanities, like any large group of people, are susceptible to snobbery, pedantry, deceit, and narrow-mindedness, their goals cannot be achieved unless they are open-minded, empathetic, candid and cooperative. The fact that scholars frequently fail to live up to these ethical standards means that the progress of humanistic disciplines is constantly being retarded. However, humanism at least depends upon ethical conduct for its very success, which distinguishes it from war, business, and even the fine arts. Moreover, the specific interpretive skills that humanists use are particularly important in a democratic society, where reaching consensus depends upon mutual understanding; and this, in turn, requires such "humane" values as openness, candor, empathy and detachment.[64]

For these reasons, it often proves difficult for true humanists to justify excluding any individual or group from the process of collective discussion and cultural interpretation, because to do so might interfere with the search for truth. In this regard, Wilamowitz provides an interesting case study. Despite his rabid anti-Semitism, for many years he readily acknowledged the contributions of Jewish scholars and even worked with them collaboratively.[65] For, as Nietzsche remarked, "nothing is more democratic than logic; it is no respecter of persons and makes no distinction between crooked and straight noses."[66] However, during the Weimar period, Wilamowitz became an activist for the right-wing

Fatherland Party, which had a proto-fascist program and advocated dictatorship.[67] But at the same time, Wilamowitz renounced his lifelong commitment to scholarly values, writing a "biography" of Plato that has been called a "historical novel" and a "cryptoautobiography, Wilamowitz' *Zarathustra*."[68] All his life, Wilamowitz had seen Nietzsche and Nietzscheans (notably the circle of the poet Stefan George) as the enemies of dispassionate scholarship who used the past to promote their own philosophical and political views.[69] In his last years, having lost his son in the First World War, having seen Prussian civilization succumb to "self-destruction [and] self-castration," and having committed himself to the cause of the "German sword, which alone can bring salvation to a diseased world," Wilamowitz was ready to make his peace with the Nietzscheans.[70] The official publication date of his biography of Plato was Nietzsche's 75th birthday.[71] Thus Wilamowitz' intellectual biography shows that humanism cannot by itself hold back the tides of history and personal embitterment. However, Wilamowitz could not remain simultaneously a humanistic scholar and a proto-fascist; as he knew, the two attitudes were incompatible, for humanism requires an attitude of openness, cosmopolitanism and rationality. Therefore, once he came to oppose these values, he had to abandon humanism as well. Although it would be inaccurate to call Wilamowitz' last work "Nietzschean" (for it lacked Nietzsche's irony, subtlety and political aloofness), Wilamowitz at least came to share Nietzsche's rejection of scholarly values.

VII. Humanism Under Threat

Thus it seems clear that humanism is what turned the Prussian "Sparta" of Pforta into an "Athens"—at least some of the time.[72] But Pforta's Spartan character was nevertheless highly evident: for example in the disciplined organization of the boys' lives—they even swam in military formation.[73] Wilamowitz recalls some "liberal opposition to Bismarck at school" that influenced him temporarily, but this did not stop him from delivering a Latin elegy in honor of the Iron Chancellor at the school festival in 1867.[74] Like most students and teachers, he says: "I was black and white to the core."[75] Moreover, his "unconditional devotion to the fatherland, and the belief in its greatness, its honour, and its claim to a corresponding position in the world" went hand in hand with two other typical characteristics of nineteenth-century Prussian nationalism: contempt for the Slavs, and bitter anti-Semitism.[76]

Nietzsche, for his part, was unusually ambivalent about Bismarck's Prussia, as he was unusual in almost every other way. However, he found support for an even more radical German nationalism than Bismarck's as he began to read ancient Nordic sagas and Romantic poetry. Nonclassical texts still lay outside of the organized curriculum at Pforta, but the school's literary historian, Koberstein, nevertheless found time to introduce Nietzsche to the sagas of the Ostrogothic King Ermanarich, about whom Nietzsche wrote poetry and music.[77] In a typically Romantic fashion, Koberstein was trying to broaden the scope of Nietzsche's humanistic education to include texts from cultures that were alien to the classical tradition, but supportive of claims to German greatness. The values that these texts taught were far different from the lessons that could be picked up from Cicero or Isocrates. Nevertheless, Nietzsche acted like a good scholar and "rummaged around a great deal in pigskin-bound volumes and chronicles" until he had written a sixty-page essay on Ermanarich.[78] And the purpose of this essay was inspirational: "That twilight of the gods," he wrote, "as the sun goes black, the earth sinks into the sea, and whirlpools of fire uproot the all-nourishing cosmic tree, flames licking the heavens— it is the greatest idea human genius ever produced, unsurpassed in the literature of any period, infinitely bold and formidable, but melting into magical harmonies."[79] In the same spirit, Nietzsche read Novalis, and wrote heavily Romantic poetry; he admired Shakespeare and Byron, calling the latter's characters *übermen-schlich*; and he picked out the then almost unknown Romantic author Hölderlin as his favorite poet. He wrote that whenever Hölderlin says "cutting truths" against the Germans, "not only are they well grounded all too often," but they are also "compatible with the greatest patriotism, which Hölderlin genuinely had in the highest degree. What he hated in the Germans was mere special-ization, philistinism."[80] Nietzsche's final work at Pforta, his Latin dissertation, was a study of the Archaic poet Theognis of Megara. "I plan to complete the work with proper philological thorough-ness," he wrote, "and as scientifically as I can."[81] But once again, Nietzsche's purpose was ethical and political; he was interested in the conflation of "good" with "aristocratic" that he found in Theognis.[82]

Thus Nietzsche was still very much a humanist when he left Pforta. The extent of his revolt against the school consisted in a rather sober reinterpretation of one classical text and some extra–curricular work on a few nonclassical books. Both Nietzsche and Wilamowitz left Pforta vowing to dedicate themselves to truly rigorous, positivistic scholarship in the service of humanistic learning and education. As yet, neither felt any misgivings about the value of his chosen profession. On leaving Pforta, Nietzsche wrote that he wanted "a science that could be pursued with cool reflectiveness, logical coldness, equable effort, and would not yield results that seize hold of the heart."[83] Wilamowitz, at his graduation, deplored his own "unstable and passionate ways, even in my learning, which had in it something of the Polymath...." Like Nietzsche, he vowed to correct his natural leanings with serious scientific discipline.[84]

However, even within the conservative walls of this Renaissance-style "Latin school," hints of radical new ideas had already been felt, ideas which would soon throw the whole program of humanistic education into doubt. I think that Jaap Mansfield goes too far when he claims that Pforta's curriculum was already dominated by the historicist and Romantic tendencies that could then be found in German universities.[85] This is explicitly denied in Wilamowitz' *Recollections*. Nevertheless, some Pforta teachers—notably Koberstein—already possessed the radical historicist insight that each past culture was a unified whole, internally consistent, but alien to the present. This idea had not yet taken its full toll on the curriculum at Pforta, where no aspects of Greek culture except poetry were seriously taught, and Greek literature was still presented as containing universally valid models for direct stylistic and moral imitation. But the insights of historicism were to have negative ramifications for humanism, since humanists had always claimed that the actions and ideas of the past were directly applicable to the present. Moreover, historicism in its most radical form brought into question the authority of the humanist scholar as an objective reader of texts—for weren't his views merely the product of their time, alien and inapplicable to the distant past? At the same time, historicism raised difficult questions about the possibility of knowing anything about a cultural artifact from a distant period, since each artifact could only be understood in its context, and its context, in turn, was made up of many artifacts all requiring interpretation. Finally, the idea that cultures were so radically different that some (like those described in Nordic sagas) might even lack Western notions of rationality, individualism, and cosmopolitanism raised the possibility that the best culture might not, in fact, be a humanistic one. But if such thoughts were passing through the minds of many German intellectuals in the mid-nineteenth century, they had not as yet achieved a victory within the gates of Pforta, over which still hung the motto: "*ecce porta coeli*"—behold the gate of heaven.[86] As Nietzsche's biographer writes:

Time stood still in this cloistered realm, the German reality of 1858 did not penetrate its thick battlements; the youth who grew up here—a select company—came of age in the world of Hellas and Rome and in the world of Goethe and Schiller.[87]

Chapter 2

The Historical Method

I. Historicism

At the University of Bonn, Nietzsche and Wilamowitz each made a fairly quick decision to pursue a professional career in classics.[1] Thus the transition between Pforta and Bonn was, in a way, fairly smooth. But the pedagogy and curriculum in German universities in the mid-nineteenth century was infused with a radically different spirit from that rather archaic humanism which had predominated at Pforta. The guiding ideology at Bonn was historicism. So prevalent was historicism in German higher education at this time that Isaiah Berlin has called it "an almost official national philosophy of history."[2] The term "historicism" has been defined in numerous, sometimes contradictory ways. Nietzsche rarely uses the word, which had not yet gained any currency in his day; but he uses "the historical sense" (*das historische Sinn* or *Bewußtsein*) to denote a sensitivity to historical context and cultural difference.[3] This is roughly what Berlin means by "historicism": it implies a general picture of humans as embedded in a web of cultural practices, which differ profoundly from epoch to epoch and place to place. Such a picture can support numerous more specific theories and attitudes. For example, some historicists merely hold that cultural contexts should be considered when we study literature and art; while others treat all ideas and events as the mere side effects or "reflex functions" of cultural or historical movements.[4]

Thus the general picture which Nietzsche called the "historical sense" is so vague that most people today probably hold it: Nietzsche calls it our modern "sixth sense."[5] But although it is vague, it is not without content: certain beliefs can be identified that necessarily follow from it, and that would be absent without it.[6] Nietzsche thought that the "historical sense," like humanism, had broad cultural, ethical, epistemological and political consequences. For one thing, historicism makes possible the notion of "cultures" as important entities to be understood and, if possible, compared. Before historicism, "culture" had been largely used in the singular, as a description of those (presumably universal) attributes that every civilized person possessed. But historicism raises the possibility that there are many cultures; that cultures should be treated as actually existing entities; and that cultures can belong in causal chains, affecting the lives of people, and being affected by historical events.

Moreover, historicism imposes methodological requirements on scholars, for it entails that a knowledge of cultural context is at least relevant (if not essential) if we are to understand texts and ideas from the past. The process of understanding thus becomes more difficult than it appeared before historicism, when it was widely believed that identical values were contained in all worthwhile books. This new-found difficulty in interpretation can lead to the conclusion that intercultural communication is not possible at all: a view with profound political ramifications. Or it can simply imply that we must attempt to shed our own cultural prejudices when we read texts from the past: a view with a different kind of ethical and political consequences. Furthermore, to the degree that someone is a historicist, he or she believes that social practices belong to history; that is, that they are not decreed by something outside history, whether nature, God, or pure reason. Thus historicism implies that at least some aspects of "human nature" (if the phrase can be used at all) in fact vary from culture to culture and may be open to deliberate change. The modern notion of a social or cultural revolution—above all in Marxism—is therefore predicated on historicism. Thanks to historicism, it becomes conceivable that instead of *homo sapiens* as we have known him, we might one day see *homo sovieticus*, or some other radically new kind of human being.[7] Nietzsche's example of "the revolutionary of society"[8] was Wagner, who

> observes qualities in modern men that do not belong to the
> human being's immutable character and skeletal frame, but

are mutable, indeed transient, and [sees] that precisely *because of these qualities* art must be without a home among them and he himself must be the messenger and forerunner of another age.[9]

Finally, historicism at least raises the possibility that any ideas about universal values to which we might commit ourselves—whether ethical, logical, or metaphysical—are not truly objective, but are mere objectifications of our own culture's values.

Clearly, one can be more or less historicist, depending on how much one includes in the list of those aspects of human nature, logic, morality, and experience that belong to the flux and variety of history. Herodotus already showed a certain degree of historicism, at least relative to earlier Greek thinking; and therefore historicism was not a completely new discovery in the eighteenth century, as Newtonian physics had been. But the eighteenth century did mark a profound change in attitudes toward history, sufficient to qualify "historicism" as a movement. Although it might be hyperbolical to call this movement "the greatest spiritual revolution of the Western world,"[10] I will try to demonstrate in the following pages that it was reasonable, at least, for Nietzsche to consider historicism an important, new, and problematic aspect of modern culture.

As a philology student, Nietzsche was first exposed to historicism as a methodological outlook. In Nietzsche's day, *Philologie* meant a search for contextual material through interdisciplinary historical research, conducted as a preliminary to the appreciation of literature. Thus philology was essentially imbued with a "historical sense." Echoing what he had learned at the University of Bonn, Wilamowitz wrote:

> the task of scholarship is to bring that dead world [of Greece and Rome] to life by the power of science—to recreate the poet's song, the thought of the philosopher and lawgiver, the sanctity of the temple and the feelings of believers and unbelievers, the bustling life of market and port, the physical appearance of land and sea, mankind at work and play.[11]

Wilamowitz held that "to grasp all historically produced phenomena in terms of the assumptions of the time in which they developed..., this is at least in principle [the] scientific and generally accepted method... ."[12] And Nietzsche frequently wrote as if he, too, tried to understand the thought of the ancients within its context. Consider, for example, the following passage from *The Gay Science*:

> The illumination and the color of all things have changed. We no longer understand altogether how the ancients experienced what was most familiar and frequent—for example, the day and waking. Since the ancients believed in dreams, waking appeared in a different light. The same goes for the whole of life, which was illuminated by death and its significance; for us 'death' means something quite different.[13]

Nietzsche proceeds to point out several other fundamental differences between ancient life and modernity (e.g., ideas of truth, passion, joy and philosophy), and then concludes the section by commenting, "We have given things a new color: we go on painting them continually." This is the essential insight of nineteenth-century historicism, summarized in a sentence. Balzac uses a similar metaphor when he writes that "periods rub off on the men who pass through them... the historical coloring [is] imprinted upon their physiognomies, their talk, their ideas, their clothes."[14]

Nietzsche's early exposure to the methodology of historicism is evident in the curriculum he followed at Bonn; in his choice of reading; in his professional relationships and apprenticeships; and, finally, in his theoretical reflections on history and culture which he published in 1873-1876 as his *Untimely Meditations*. At Bonn, Nietzsche was exposed to whole new disciplines, such as the history of art, which had entered the university curriculum as a consequence of the rise of historicism.[15] He encountered auxiliary historical sciences—numismatics, archaeology, linguistics—which had become respectable in higher education only because, to historicists, they seemed valuable for the light that they could shed on literature.[16] He began a close apprenticeship with Ritschl, who was engaged in contextualizing and historicizing the doctrines of the early Christian church.[17] And around Christmas, 1864, Nietzsche read the latest edition of David Strauss' *Life of Jesus*, a historicist treatment of Jesus' biography which attempted to undermine the universal truth of Christian doctrine by explaining Jesus' teaching as a mere consequence of his culture and time. Nietzsche's friend Paul Deussen was willing to give up Christianity as a result of reading Strauss, but Nietzsche hesitated: "There is a serious consequence—if you give up Christ, you will have to give up God too."[18] Needless to say, Nietzsche soon gave up

both, and for largely historicist reasons, which he inherited from
Strauss and Hase (he had read Hase's *Life of Jesus* in 1860).
Defending his turn to atheism, Nietzsche told his sister Elisabeth
in 1865 that he considered all religious beliefs to be historically
conditioned and culturally relative:

> [If] we had believed from our childhood that all salvation for
> the soul depended, not on Jesus, but on another, for example
> Mahomet, would we not certainly have felt the same blessed-
> ness? Surely only faith sanctifies, not the objective reality
> that is behind it... . True enough, faith never fails us; it
> furnishes the believer with anything he desires from it, but
> without ever offering any support for grounding it in objective
> reality.
>   It is here that the roads which humans follow divide. Do
> you want a peaceful soul and happiness?—then believe.
> Would you rather serve truth?—then seek it.[19]

At this stage in his education, Nietzsche was ready to relativize
every past religious system of values and beliefs, but he still maintained
that the scientific search for truth, as practiced by philologists,
was universally valid. Thus, as a young university student, he
was an earnest devotee of David Strauss' "New Faith": the critical
application of modern historical methods to all received opinion, a
process that Strauss considered to be as spiritually rewarding as
traditional religion (the "Old Faith"), which was now discredited
by science. Thus Nietzsche demonstrated a tendency, typical of
much historicism, to place himself outside the realm of history as
an utterly unbiased onlooker, as if he were free of the conditioning
forces that had made all past ideas historically relative. Some
years later, Dilthey would try "to justify the knowledge of what
was historically conditioned as the achievement of objective science,
despite the fact of the knower's being conditioned himself."[20] But
Nietzsche revealed, as yet, none of the conscious realization of the
dilemmas of historicism that made Dilthey a fruitful thinker.[21]
Instead, Nietzsche's "first attitude to the study of philology was
conventional, or naively historical."[22] The naive theory of an unbiased
historical onlooker was not to survive for long in Nietzsche's
thought. Nevertheless, it raises an important question: Can historicism be justified as having some relation to truth, or is it—like
all the theories it dismisses as culturally determined—merely a
historical phenomenon that can be fully explained as the result of

historical forces; for example, as a "reflex function" of the German reaction to the French Revolution?[23] In short, does historicism fall into a vicious circle, or is it a coherent picture? And beyond that, was there any compelling reason for Nietzsche to accept historicism, even if we admit that it is coherent?[24]

II. The Empirical Foundations of Historicism

It is my contention that Nietzsche became a historicist because this was the outlook that he was taught at Bonn. Moreover, I believe that there were good empirical reasons for Nietzsche and his teachers to adopt historicism: its value as a picture had been demonstrated over the course of a century's historical research. At the end of the eighteenth century, practical advances in the methodology of classical scholarship were brought to bear on traditional questions of aesthetics and cultural criticism. For example, new philological insights were introduced by both sides in the old quarrel between the "ancients" and the "moderns"—i.e., between those humanists who defended classical models in the arts and sciences as absolute and universal, and those who advocated the introduction of some modern standards. This was a typically prehistoricist argument, because the goal of each side was to posit one set of absolute aesthetic and intellectual models for imitation.[25] However, the contribution of the most advanced classical scholars of the day to this quarrel tended to historicize both ancient and modern perspectives, thereby changing the terms of the argument altogether. For example, the "modern" Richard Bentley—himself no historicist— attempted to undermine the value of the Epistles of Phalaris as models for contemporary letter-writers by showing that they were forgeries. To do so, he applied his encyclopedic knowledge of early Greek culture, implicitly claiming that the Epistles, had they been genuine, would have necessarily reflected the institutions and mores of their specific time and region.[26] Similarly, Bentley and Vico both made Homer seem increasingly alien to modernity by applying advanced philological methods to the interpretation of the epics, thereby contextualizing them. And Winckelmann, attempting to argue the "ancient" side in the quarrel with the "moderns" by demonstrating the eternal value of Greek art, actually began the process of relativizing aesthetic standards by inaugurating a scientific history of art in its development. Wilamowitz said of Winckelmann that he "provides an imperishable example" of the insight that "aesthetic evaluation is possible only from the perspective of the time in which the artwork was situated, out of the spirit of the people which brought it forth."[27]

New advances in classical scholarship tended to demonstrate the alien nature of ancient culture, and this coincided with new discoveries of alien cultures around the world. It became an eighteenth-century commonplace to compare the indigenous societies of America with Homeric culture. Bentley, whose knowledge of Greek civilization allowed him to recognize the alien nature of Homer's time, attacked Pope's translation of the *Iliad* for its historical naïveté. In Nietzsche's time, the debate over the alien quality of Homeric poetry and society still raged—Nietzsche claimed that the "Greeks are much more ancient that anyone thinks"[28]—but the terms of the argument had shifted far in the historicist direction. No one in a German university in the 1860s would have accepted Pope's courtly appropriation of the *Iliad*. Nietzsche cited this increasing accuracy in the translator's art as a sign that his age had become essentially historicist:

> *Translations*—the degree of historical sense of any age may be inferred from the manner in which this age makes translations and tries to absorb former ages and books. In the age of Corneille and even of the Revolution, the French took possession of Roman antiquity in a way for which we would no longer have courage enough—thanks to our more highly developed historical sense.[29]

The tragedians of the French Baroque had appropriated Greek drama without much awareness of the gulf that lay between their culture and that of ancient Athens. On the other hand, Homer gained popularity among the German Romantics precisely because historicism had revealed his alien nature, his alleged naïveté.[30] For much the same reason, German Romantic historians gained a new appreciation of the Gothic style, which architects like Schinkel in Prussia and Nash in England began to copy. Meanwhile, novelists like Sir Walter Scott invented the genuinely historical novel, complete with local color and sensitivity to period, as an alternative to the literary works of Voltaire and his contemporaries, which had been placed only superficially in a historical period. Scott was a major influence on Ranke and the whole "antiquarian" school of German historical scholarship.[31] Scott's historicism is starkly different from the prehistoricist attitude of the "ancient" Racine, who wrote in his Preface to *Iphigénie*:

I recognized with pleasure—by the effect produced on our theater by all that I imitated from Homer and Euripides—that good sense and reason are the same through all the ages. The taste of Paris is found to conform to that of Athens; my audience was moved by the same things which once upon a time set the wisest people of Greece to weeping....[32]

Two hundred years later—as if to announce his distance from Racine—the self-consciously historicist Balzac wrote at the beginning of his *Père Goriot* (a historical novel set *precisely* in 1819):

Will [this] story be understood outside Paris? It is doubtful. The peculiarities of the scene, abundant in local color and personal notations, can be appreciated only between the hills of Montmartre and the heights of Montrouge....[33]

The early historicists thought that they were engaged in a process of objectifying—with ever increasing thoroughness and empirical rigor—the world that they described. Burckhardt identified the origins of this process in the Italian Renaissance, which was itself a rebirth of an objectifying attitude towards the world prevalent in antiquity. Renaissance artists had placed themselves at a single, imaginary point in front of the objects that they painted. They then depicted these objects in linear perspective, i.e., as they would be seen from one point in space. This represented a radical break from the nonperspectival art of the middle ages, and it has often been compared to a similar "Copernican turn" evident in other areas of culture.[34] Later, with the historicism of the late eighteenth century, the point of view from which objects and events were depicted was relativized not only spatially, but also historically. The art of the Renaissance had shown a remarkable lack of historical consciousness. For example, in his "Fête champêtre" of 1508, Giorgione had depicted men in Renaissance costumes sitting together with naked women on a lawn. This image, although not easily identifiable, seemed vaguely mythological and other-worldly, and therefore not morally suspect. Sixteenth-century viewers did not read the costumes and trappings in Giorgione's picture as specifically contemporary, although they now appear unmistakably as products of sixteenth-century Venice. But when Edouard Manet set his nude women and clothed men in a contemporary setting ("Le déjeuner sur l'herbe," 1863), he created a great scandal. To nineteenth-century viewers, his picture was easily identifiable as a scene from the present, not from any remote past. Manet's art was fundamentally concerned with the portrayal of people in their precise social roles and contexts; and in "Le déjeuner sur l'herbe," the roles he portrayed were considered scandalous.[35]

The Renaissance artist had already occupied a specific vantage-point in space, but his position within the history of culture was left unspecified. Biblical scenes, for example, were depicted as if they took place in the present. But by 1808, the German Romantic Franz Pforr was already painting highly accurate historical depictions of scenes from Medieval history; and in these paintings, Pforr had to be imagined as a kind of eyewitness, present at the historical moment. Thus by the period when Nietzsche and Manet were active, the eye of the painter, the novelist, the translator and the historian had been firmly relativized in time as well as in space. And just as the Renaissance invention of linear perspective resulted from a scientific, objectifying attitude towards nature, so the historicists' discovery of historical perspective originated with their rigorous, philological study of the distant past. Historicism was a radical new form of perspective, in which the contingent viewpoint of the artist was specifically acknowledged in a new, more fundamental way. Painters now pretended to be present at a specific historical moment, aware of the costumes and customs of the day. Even when they ignored this awareness and depicted scenes from the past in anachronistic settings, they did so consciously and deliberately.[36]

Thus historicism emerged out of the empirical research of the eighteenth century, and not out of the great historicist philosophies of history, none of which the young Nietzsche or his colleagues in philology knew particularly well anyway. Wilamowitz would not have agreed with this verdict. In his *History of Classical Scholarship*, he argued that "the birth of a real [i.e., historicist] science of antiquity was completely unconnected with [the discoveries of] esoteric scholarship... . The decisive factor was the awakening of a new spirit in Germany, which had an equally powerful effect on poetry and philosophy."[37] But the awakening of a "new spirit" sounds suspiciously mystical; it explains little, and in any case, it depends upon the historicist presupposition that each age possesses its own discrete "*Geist.*" Like Wilamowitz, George Iggers argues that it was not the advent of new philological methods, which "were developed by an earlier generation of historians, philologists, classicists, and Bible-Scholars," that had led to the rise of historicism. The new "critical method," he writes, "became the common property of honest historical scholars everywhere." But what "distinguished the writings of the historians in the main tradition of German historiography was rather their basic theoretical convictions in regard to the nature of history and the character of political power."[38]

Iggers' view may apply to those metaphysical versions of historicism that invoke a concept of the *Weltanschauung*, but it does not explain the rise of a generally individualizing and historically conscious attitude towards the social world. Yet this attitude almost always underlay the metaphysical speculation of philosophers of history: consider, for example, the preliminary philological labors of Vico, Marx and Nietzsche.[39]

Looking at a nineteenth-century artistic depiction of a scene from the past, it is difficult to avoid reaching the conclusion that the historical sense shown by the artist conveys more realism than would have been demonstrated by any painter of an earlier century, who would almost certainly have depicted the same scene in a setting drawn from his own time. The same can be said of nineteenth-century histories, translations, novels, poetry, and other media of historical representation. Of course, one could argue that the modern recognition of cultural diversity is just a prejudice of our age—but one would thereby be admitting the historicist thesis that each age views the world in its own way. Even the existence of historicism as a "standing ingredient of modern thought"—the effects of which "an alert mind can trace... in almost every important judgment on human structures"[40]—counts in favor of the historicist idea; for we appear to live in a historicized age, in contrast to all others. Thus Nietzsche noted that "we live in the age of comparison, we can verify as has never been verified before: we are in every way the self-consciousness of history." And this new vantage point of historicism was enough to guarantee our difference from all preceding epochs, our "pre-eminence." "We enjoy differently, we suffer differently: our instinctive activity is to compare an unheard-of number of things."[41] Nietzsche held that historicism was now identical with rationality, so that to abandon historicism would require a deliberate and irrational (but possibly desirable) act of forgetting what we had learned. And certainly, it seems true that the empirical discoveries of historicism have at least put traditional philosophy on the defensive, so that philosophers must now avoid speaking naively of "human nature" or "objective truth," unless these can be shown to be truly universal and not merely local cultural norms writ large. Even opponents of historicism must admit that it has created a new range of theoretical problems, and has caused philosophy to cede much of its authority (rightly or wrongly) to the empirical historical disciplines, especially linguistics and the social sciences. Because of his commitment to the historicist picture, Nietzsche held that "historical philosophy is from now on necessary...."[42] At one point in his *Untimely Meditations*, Nietzsche seems to want to step outside historicism in order to discuss it in an objective way; but he quickly concludes that this is impossible, for historicism and rationality are now thoroughly interdependent. "Our high estimation for history may be merely a Western prejudice," he concludes, "but let us at least progress within such prejudices, and not stand still!"[43] Whether we like it or not, there is no rational alternative to historicism for modern thinkers.

III. Varieties of Historicism

Nevertheless, historicism is a general picture that can serve as the basis of numerous more specific theories. Some such theories are relativist, but this is not a necessary consequence of historicism. I believe that Nietzsche's commitment to radically historicist and relativist ideas stemmed from his training as an empirical philologist, and the validity of his later ideas therefore stands or falls depending on the rigor of his deduction of these ideas from scholarly practice. Even if we accept that Nietzsche's historicist and relativist theories are consistent, we are entitled to ask why he (or anyone else) should adopt them. The best answer that Nietzsche could give, I think, was that historicism had been borne out by the methods and findings of modern scholarship. A thousand empirical discoveries had made a recognition of cultural diversity unavoidable for modern Europeans. However, the more specific theories that Nietzsche derived from his historicist picture were not, I believe, grounded in the facts or ultimately satisfactory.[44]

Historicist theories (i.e., theories supported by a historicist picture) can be categorized according to three criteria. First, historicists have diverged in holding that different kinds of human phenomena are products of the cultural environment, rather than essential and universal. For example, some theorists exempt the laws of logic from the historical diversity that they think applies in the realm of ethics. The tendency in Nietzsche's mature thought is to reject distinctions between facts and values, rationality and morality, and to suggest that the whole of human psychology (including even the "laws" of logic) is equally contingent. Nietzsche argues that science and rationality always rest upon subjective choices and preferences; so no fact/value distinction can be maintained. But this still leaves two questions unanswered. First, how widely shared are the contingencies of psychology: are they shared by the entire species, by whole cultures, or by no two people? And second, how "open"—i.e., commensurable, comparable, or translatable—

are the perspectives of diverse cultures, species or individuals? The union of these two questions yields a taxonomic chart of possible forms of perspectivism (only some of which are strictly historical):

PERSPECTIVES ARE SHARED BY:	PERSPECTIVES ARE:	
	ISOLATED	IN DIALOGUE
INDIVIDUALS	Subjectivism	Nominalist Historicism
CULTURES	*Weltanschauung* Historicism	Dialogic Historicism
THE SPECIES	Psychologism	Transcendent Perspectivism

"Subjectivism" would mean that each person is trapped within the bounds of his or her own, purely private experience. This is not necessarily a historicist position, since differences among people could be caused by physical rather than cultural factors; but it is a form of perspectivism. "Nominalist historicism"—which I will ultimately endorse—would hold that human perspectives are in principle unique, since each person occupies a subtly individual historical position; but this view would also imply that perspectives can be shared or mutually understood. "*Weltanschauung*-historicism," on the other hand, would imagine entire cultures much as "subjectivism" imagines individuals. Cultures would be unique and isolated, and all members of a culture would share fundamental values or ideas. Some characteristics, in other words, which nonhistoricists credit to "human nature" would be identified as functions of culture, each culture producing a different kind of human being. On this theory, individual thoughts and ideas would be relative to an underlying cultural structure, and would carry a different meaning (or none at all) outside of their original context.

"Dialogic historicism," too, would view cultures as internally homogeneous, but this theory would hold that members of one culture can potentially understand or even learn from members of another. "Psychologism" would imply that all humans share a contingent perspective on the world—probably as a result of biological factors— but that we have no access to other perspectives. And "transcendent perspectivism" would mean that humans share a common, contingent perspective; but that we can also understand another perspective, such (for example) as that of God.

Nietzsche endorsed at least three of these forms of perspectivism, but without distinguishing among them clearly or recognizing that each form requires its own justification and entails a unique set of consequences. He certainly endorsed psychologism.[45] As I will argue more fully below, he also clearly endorsed *Weltanschauung*-historicism, and this served as the basis for his discovery of nihilism and his deconstruction of the antithesis between truth and lie.[46] Finally, he makes isolated comments that seem to imply an adherence to either nominalist historicism or dialogic historicism, but these do not amount to a significant strand in his philosophy.[47]

In passing, it should be noted that certain forms of historicism are simply varieties of relativism, while others do not entail relativist conclusions. All "closed" forms of perspectivism lead to relativism. If it is impossible in principle for me to understand other perspectives—yet I believe that these perspectives exist—than I have no means of judging whether mine is right or wrong, better or worse than someone else's. The only exceptions to the rule that "closed" forms of perspectivism are relativistic might be religious varieties of psychologism, which hold that humans have no access to the perspective of God, but that the divine perspective is, by definition, true. But such positions are, admittedly, irrational. "Open" forms of perspectivism, on the other hand, are compatible with relativism, but do not entail it. It is conceivable that I could understand another person's perspective, but have no way of judging its truth or value relative to mine. But some theories about the nature of communication among diverse perspectives suggest that truth *can* emerge from such dialogue—or even that it must, for "truth" has no higher definition than a consensus achieved through intercultural dialogue. I will argue in Chapter IX for a nonrelativist theory of communication that is built on nominalist historicism.

There are only two versions of perspectivism from the chart above that Nietzsche fairly certainly did *not* endorse. The first I have simply called "subjectivism," meaning the doctrine that "each person is the measure of all things," and that no true mutual understanding is possible. To suggest that each person's perspective is unique and utterly incongruent with everyone else's is equivalent to solipsism, and Nietzsche was not prepared to go so far. Such "individual relativism," writes Husserl, "is such a bare-faced and (one might say) 'cheeky' skepticism that it has certainly not been held in modern times."[48] Apart from any other problems with this doctrine, it is unclear how I can know that other people have different perspectives from mine, if I am aware that everything I know is the mere product of my own psychology. The other version of perspectivism that Nietzsche did not hold was transcendent perspectivism: the notion that human beings as a species share a contingent perspective on the world, but that we also have access to other species' ways of thinking. This view could perhaps be attributed to some Christians, who believe that human rationality and perception are limited, but that we have access to God's knowledge through revelation. However, it certainly was not Nietzsche's position. If we could communicate with a gnat, he writes in his essay "On Truth and Lying," we would learn that it considers its worldview to be as objective as ours. But, Nietzsche adds, we *cannot* see "now like a bird, now like a worm, now like a plant," so differences among species' perspectives are ineffable.[49]

Psychologism is the form of perspectivism that is most widely recognized in Nietzsche's work, but it will not concern me directly in this book. Psychologism holds that rationality, perception, and all values are in no sense universal or objective, but are products of human physiology. However, psychologism also holds that we have no means of understanding any perspectives other than that of homo sapiens. "Between ourselves: since no one would maintain that there is any necessity for men to exist, reason, as well as Euclidean space, is a mere idiosyncrasy of a certain species of animal, and one among many—"[50] Nietzsche ridicules the "naiveté" with which traditional philosophers take our species' idiosyncrasies as a measure of "'truth in itself.'"[51] However, psychologism is a theory that admits of no empirical refutation or confirmation, and it therefore seems vacuous to me. It is, writes Husserl, "in all its forms... a relativism."[52] In Nietzsche's version (which Husserl would label "anthropologism" or "special relativism"), it appears to be a form of *historical* relativism, for Nietzsche remarks frequently that the structures of logic and epistemology arose at a specific time—"the most arrogant and untruthful moment in 'world history'"[53]— with the emergence of homo sapiens. However, Nietzsche could not have derived psychologism from historical data, as he did his other forms of historicism. Nietzsche encountered psychologism when he read Schopenhauer and F. A. Lange (on whom I will say more below); and similar ideas could also be found in the works of J. S. Mill, Bain, Sigwart, Erdmann, Lipps, and other nineteenth-century philosophers.[54] Psychologism was a very popular theory in Nietzsche's day, and an equally popular target of critique at the turn of the century. Whether it is a tenable view is beyond the scope of this book, but it should be clear that even if it were true it could have little impact on educational or cultural issues, since the deepest structures of epistemology, perception, and logic would be

fixed by biology and immutable. Psychologism may appear to be
an important axiom in works like Nietzsche's essay on "Truth and
Lying in an Extra-moral Sense," where he attacks the notion of an
objective description of the world. In fact, pyschologism is a *conclusion*
of this essay, as I will show below. What makes Nietzsche believe
in the first place that "word and thing do not necessarily coincide"[55]
is his recognition of the diversity of ways of thinking that humans
in different cultures reveal. "The various languages, juxtaposed, show
that words are never concerned with truth, never with adequate
expression; otherwise there would not be so many languages."[56]
In other words, cultural diversity is the empirical basis for
Nietzsche's attack on objective "truth"; and pyschologism merely
follows from this premise.[57]

It is possible that at times Nietzsche had a kind of dialogic
historicism in mind. Dialogic historicism would characterize individuals
as essentially placed within a culture or age, but would leave open
the possibility that one age can understand—or even subsume—
another through a process of communication. Hegel is a great
example of a dialogic historicist; Gadamer is an important contemporary
case.[58] At times, Nietzsche (like Hegel and Gadamer) seems to
advocate a program of research into the mores and beliefs of alien
cultures. In fact, Nietzsche says, true "humaneness" would mean
"being a person whose horizon encompasses thousands of years...
being the heir of all nobility of past spirit."[59] It would mean comprehending
the vast diversity of human perspectives on their own terms:
a project which is by no means ruled out by dialogic historicism.
But dialogic historicism, for all its promises of universal understanding
and "humaneness," brings its own problems into play. For one
thing, if difficulties in communication increase only in degree as
we move across cultural barriers (as some dialogic historicists
claim), then it is unclear why we should invoke the notion of barriers
and horizons at all. But if there is something *qualitatively* different
about intercultural communication (as opposed to interpersonal
communication), then this difference requires explanation, and it
will be necessary to contrive a complicated theory about the definition
and boundaries of a "culture." A nominalist theory therefore
seems much simpler and more promising.

Although Nietzsche's thinking is in many ways highly nominalist—
for he rejects almost every universal as a fiction—the notion of the
cultural *Weltanschauung* retains an important place in Nietzsche's
thought. *Weltanschauung*-historicism holds that all humans are
trapped within the horizon of a culture, unable to understand anything beyond. Its impact on educational and hermeneutic issues is
particularly severe. It makes the goal of understanding alien per-

spectives appear foolish, since it implies that we will always utterly misread texts from distant cultures and times: their meaning will be inaccessible, indeterminate, or at best, useless to us in our very different *Weltanschauung*. Our interpretation of any author will itself be a "text" immanent within our own culture, and will have no transcultural validity. Thus Nietzsche noted that "the act of evaluation" could only appear potentially objective to a philosopher like Kant, "who belongs *before* the great historical movement."[60] In the age of *Weltanschauung*-historicism, all interpretation is seen as subjective. It was because of his early espousal of *Weltanschauung*-historicism that Nietzsche sometimes argued against trying to imitate the Greeks at all; they were an utterly alien civilization.[61]

As a *Weltanschauung* historicist, Nietzsche argued that communication requires a shared outlook on the world, so only members of a single culture or "herd" are able to understand each other. He hinted that communities originally arose as people deliberately abandoned differences in perspective in order to communicate and cooperate: "All unity is only as organization and co-operation—just as a human community is a unity... ."[62] Thus Nietzsche imagined that in its "natural" state, mankind was composed of individuals with diverse perspectives, but *Weltanschauungen* were created in order to create agreement and thereby to end the primitive war of all against all. Human beings prior to the establishment of cultures had no language, no ability to distinguish (however arbitrarily) between truth and falsehood, and were therefore hardly human at all. Members of a culture gained their belief in truth and morality as a result of their unswerving allegiance to a coherent set of values which seemed necessary to them because the only alternative was madness. As early as 1872, Nietzsche conceived the philologist's task as an effort to "comprehend *the internal coherence and necessity of every true culture.*"[63] But the philologist could see that there were many true cultures and that their criteria of truth and goodness were always merely local and incommensurable with those of other civilizations. Zarathustra (who knows the good and evil of all nations) says:

> Never did one neighbor understand another: his soul always wondered at his neighbor's madness and evil.
> A table of values hangs over every people. Behold, it is the table of their overcomings; behold, it is the voice of their will to power.[64]

Nietzsche appropriated the Enlightenment figure of a social contract as the foundation for society, but in his version, the contract governed everything that separates humans from beasts, including rationality itself. Logic and grammar differed from culture to culture and always originated as a result of arbitrary decisions. Nietzsche writes of the primeval contract:

> this peaceful agreement apparently leads to the first step towards man's acquisition of his mysterious desire for truth. For what 'truth' will be from now on is fixed; a uniformly valid and binding terminology for things is invented and the legislation of languages also enacts the first laws of truth. For now, for the first time, the distinction between truth and lying arises.[65]

However, the first *Weltanschauung* did not arise out of an achievement of true communication or consensus among individuals; it arose when many individuals decided to renounce their own perspectives entirely in order to adopt one arbitrary perspective. This perspective established the arbitrary limits and rules of discourse that made thought possible. Nietzsche writes: "man's greatest labor so far has been to reach agreement about very many things and to submit to a *law of agreement*—regardless of whether these things are true or false."[66] Thus, "consciousness does not really belong to man's individual existence but rather to his social or herd nature... . We simply lack any organ for 'truth', for knowledge... ."[67] Human "herd nature" manifests itself in a plurality of forms, governed by a diversity of arbitrary "agreements." Each form, each culture, is an organic whole, unified by the common perspective of all its members: "our values, our yeas and nays, our ifs and buts, grow out of us with the necessity with which a tree bears fruit—related and each with an affinity to each, and evidence of *one* will, *one* health, *one* soil, *one* sun."[68] There can be no communication among separate *Weltanschauungen*, for there are no arbitrary rules available to guide inter-cultural communication. Cultures are defined as groups of people sharing a common adherence to a set of rules which allow them to communicate; so, by definition, people belonging to different cultures cannot understand each other. Nietzsche thought that if two cultures came to adopt a common perspective, this only meant that one had overcome the other, so that there was now just one culture. For Nietzsche, as a *Weltanschauung*-historicist, rationality was totally contingent and communication meant conformity, renunciation of individuality— in short, noncommunication.

Discernible in Nietzsche's *Weltanschauung*-historicism is a holistic theory of truth and meaning; this is fundamental to his thought. If we take truth to inhere in individual ideas, words, or propositions, then it makes no sense to argue that alien cultures cannot be understood. Only if meaning inheres in a *Weltanschauung*, is it possible to imagine great difficulties in understanding the beliefs and values of another culture. Otherwise, value "x" in culture "a" can simply be translated into the equivalent terms used by culture "b." Some difficulties might arise, for example if we tried to translate words like *virtù*, *Schadenfreude*, or *polis*; but even these words could be replaced with longer phrases in our own language, or simply appropriated as new English words. But Nietzsche, like many nineteenth-century historicists, thought that truth was a function of the "whole." Words, ideas, and propositions were only comprehensible in terms of other words and ideas. What made ideas appear "true" or "false" to members of a culture was the ungrounded commitment which these people felt toward a whole, internally consistent vocabulary and world-view, which was based on implicit valuations and assumptions, all of them arbitrary. As soon as people recognized that world-views were plural and culturally relative, they lost faith in the universal validity of their own *Weltanschauung*, and so, Nietzsche thought, slipped down the slope towards nihilism, recognizing that all truth was contingent.[69]

It is reasonable enough to believe that truth inheres in something larger than individual propositions. For example, if we want to understand what a word means, we often have to look it up in a dictionary, which is only comprehensible if we know the meaning of many other words. If we are taught what a word means by someone who points at an object to define it, we still have to know in advance what "pointing" means. For something like this reason, Hegel held that "the true is the whole"; it is a function of the entire *Geist* of an age.[70] Similarly, Wittgenstein located meaning only in utterances that belong to preunderstood language-games and shared "forms of life." The empirical discoveries of historicism lend support to some kind of holistic theory of meaning, since such a theory can account for radical differences of thought between people far distant in space or time: they belong to different "wholes." However, it seems to me that it was a mistake on Nietzsche's part to imply that the meaning that is accessible to an individual is a function of one particular whole: his or her "culture." My access to meaning is not a function of my being an English-speaker, *or* an American, *or* a modern, *or* a Westerner, *or* someone who has read Nietzsche; rather, all of these forms of context have some kind of bearing on how I think. Wittgenstein, therefore, allows that language–games are multiple, overlapping and constantly evolving. Thus the Wittgensteinian individual belongs to a variety of cultures and subcultures (to use non-Wittgensteinian terms), some of which he or she has had a role in creating. Indeed, every Wittgensteinian individual is in principle unique; all forms of life are shared by groups of people, but each person can participate in a unique *set* of such shared forms of life. In what follows, I will say more about the difference between Nietzsche and Wittgenstein on this question, and I will try to claim Wittgenstein for a nominalist form of historicism: a theory that takes each human being as in principle unique.

Chapter 3

Nietzsche's Concept of "Culture"

I. *Weltanschauung*–Historicism

Much of the debate about the soundness of historicism seems to have been limited to the belief in *Weltanschauungen*, which Nietzsche certainly endorsed early in his career and which he helped to make popular. This view rests upon the observation that all individuals who belong to a single age or culture share a common and contingent shape of consciousness, conceptual scheme,[1] epistemic foundation, "'form of life,' 'life-world,' 'practice,' 'linguistically mediated interaction,' 'language game,' 'convention,' 'cultural background,' 'tradition,' 'effective history,' or what have you....."[2] It is a view that has political implications, as Nietzsche recognized.

For example, many of the prominent historicists of Nietzsche's day championed this doctrine because it allowed them to imbue their own German culture with an unchallengeable legitimacy. Historicism had made all allegedly universal standards of value appear culturally relative (Ranke's school called this "*Antinormativität*"); therefore, each individual culture and nation could no longer be held accountable to any standards that were alien to it. The nation-state could thus be seen as entirely self-justifying and sovereign; Ranke called Prussia "an idea of God."[3] Meinecke argued similarly. For him, the authenticity and naturalness of a culture's actions and values were the only criteria appropriate for judging it.

Morality, he wrote:

> has not only a universal but also an individual side to it and
> the seeming immorality of the state's egoism for power can be
> morally justified from this perspective. For nothing can be
> immoral which comes from the innermost, individual character
> of a being.[4]

(Note the idealist assumptions that allowed Meinecke to describe
the state as a "being" with its own "character.") Thus Meinecke
and his predecessors used *Weltanschauung*-historicism to defend
the actions of an aggressive, expansionist nation state. But precisely
the same logic is frequently invoked today in the struggle *against*
ethnocentrism and cultural imperialism. Modern relativists often
deny "that the norms governing other cultures' beliefs and practices
[can ever be] invalid," because such a claim might lead to
"'programmes of action detrimental to the well-being of other
peoples.'"[5] Put more forcefully, the modern *Weltanschauung*-
historicist "wants us to stop using 'philosophical B-52's' ... to read
our truth, logic and rationality onto" another society."[6]

Nietzsche was later to call the historicist nationalism of
Ranke and his school "antiquarian history." This, he said,

> is the healthiest, most generally beneficial sort of unreason—
> a fact known to everyone who ... has studied the plight of a
> people that has lost its loyalty to the past and succumbed to a
> restless cosmopolitan craving for the new and always newer.
> The opposite feeling, the satisfaction of a tree in its own roots,
> its happiness in knowing that it is not a wholly arbitrary and
> chance growth, but the inheritor, the blossom, and the fruit
> of a past, and that its existence is thereby excused and even
> justified—this feeling is what I now prefer to call the real
> historical sense.[7]

On the other hand, Nietzsche doubted the historical accuracy of
much antiquarian history, which was by definition "unreason."
Moreover, as an enemy of the popular cultural norms of his day,
he recognized the apologetic and even self-congratulatory purposes
of much officially sanctioned, academic historical research in the
school of Ranke. "Historians," he wrote, "are diligently engaged in
demonstrating the proposition that every age has its own legitimacy,
its own conditions—in order to prepare [a] defense for the future
tribunal which our age must face."[8] Throughout his mature work,
Nietzsche argues consistently that cultures must think of themselves

as homogeneous and organic if they are to be healthy. Thus he defines culture as a "unity of artistic style in all the vital manifestations of a people.... A people to whom we attribute a culture must be a vital unity in every aspect of reality."[9] However, from the beginning Nietzsche was worried about the tendency shown by historicist moderns who wanted to *create* a homogeneous *Weltanschauung*, even though the sophistication of their "historical sense" told them that their societies were actually full of diversity. A clear danger was that this desire for organic homogeneity would turn to violence against those who differed from the norm. The "mendacious racial self-admiration and racial indecency that parades in Germany today," Nietzsche wrote, is "a sign of a German way of thinking that is doubly false and obscene among the people of the 'historical sense.'"[10] Nationalism, he thought, requires "cunning, lying, and power to maintain its reputation."[11] Of course, all antiquarian historians were not racists—nor was "antiquarianism" by any means limited to Germany—but Nietzsche detected an implicit racism in the antiquarian endeavor.

Thus, partisans of *Weltanschauung* historicism have defended the doctrine because of its political implications; and conversely, historicism's enemies have charged it with leading to pernicious political effects. Some authors have claimed, in particular, that historicism is incompatible with liberalism, because liberalism depends upon such alleged absolutes as the "rights of man," which historicism deems culturally relative.[12] And Carlo Antoni considers it a "tragic error" on the part of historicism to "negate the existence of universal human values."[13] But none of this debate gets at the question of the soundness of historicism as a methodology.

The problem, moreover, is that authors like Iggers, Antoni and Meinecke deal with historicism only in one of the versions outlined above: namely, the theory that there are a certain number of discrete, hermetic cultures in the world, which are more or less unintelligible to each other and based on radically different "tables of values." In order for these cultures to survive and function, their basic values must be consistent, homogeneous and uncritically endorsed by members of the culture. Such a notion of culture leads to a form of historicism that treats human beings as ontologically dependent on *Weltanschauungen*, Hegelian "shapes of consciousness," or other abstract intersubjective entities. This kind of theorizing did have a prominent place in Nietzsche's mature thought. Moreover, he encountered reified notions of culture early in his university career, for Ritschl and his colleagues defended classical philology precisely because they wanted to understand—and perhaps even to revive—"hellenism" as an abstract entity. Jaap Mansfield provides a useful account of that school of German philology, well-known to Nietzsche, which treated "the Greeks" as an ideal concept, an abstract, organic unity.[14] For example, Nietzsche's teacher at Pforta, Koberstein, had produced one of "the more important creative, nonacademic views of Antiquity, and of 'the Greeks.'" Ritschl, on the other hand, was a critical, objectivistic scholar whose work tended to break down stereotyped notions about hellenic culture—but he had known Schlegel in his youth and "did not totally reject the grand romantic impulse." Mansfield also mentions F. G. Welcker (1784–1868), "whose nonrationalist *Griechische Götterlehre*, published near the end of his long life, was read by Wilamowitz when a student at Bonn"; August Boeckh (1785–1865); and K. O. Müller (1797–1840) as partisans of the holistic conception of Greek civilization. These three authors were favorites of Wagner; and Nietzsche read them assiduously during his Wagnerian phase.[15] So Nietzsche was well acquainted with frankly creative depictions of "the Greeks," which served to buttress his *Weltanschauung*-historicism. But the critical methodologies of historicist scholarship that Nietzsche learned from Jahn, Ritschl, and his other teachers should not have committed him to anything beyond the nominalist version of historicism outlined above: i.e., the theory that all texts belong to some kind of local context and must be so interpreted.[16]

Nevertheless, like so many of his contemporaries, Nietzsche could not resist positing abstract, idealized, a prioristic notions of ancient culture. For example, in his essay on "Homer and Classical Philology" (1869), he turns the "Homeric Question" into a general question about the philosophy of history: "is an idea formed by a person, or a person formed by an idea?" He tentatively concludes the latter—that individuals are the products of the underlying concept (*Begriff*) of their culture; "the individual means nothing, except as a fluctuation of the folk-soul...." More specifically, he introduces the idea of a distinctively Greek folk-soul, and claims that this "found expression in representative personalities, concentrated its essence in particular poetic characters." Thus all events and characters from Greek history should be interpreted as representative of a communal psyche. Nietzsche credited modern philology with having, for the first time, recognized "the great mass-instincts, the unconscious national forces as the real support and dynamic of so-called universal history."[17] Only the genius could be credited with any independence from the contingencies of culture; this was his "untimeliness." But the genius' achievement was non-rational, mystical, and thus impossible to understand. Anything rational was the mere automatic product of a culture's

"Begriff"—its notion of truth and falsehood, sanity and madness. Nietzsche thought that "Nature always produces two opposite phenomena: first the dull, slumbering masses, proliferating by instinct; and then, at a far higher remove, the great solitary contemplatives, equipped for the production of immortal works."[18] Here lay the seed of Nietzsche's vision of the Overman, who lay *beyond* culture. But when it came to an analysis of a specific historical problem, Nietzsche thought that the best philology could do was to detect the modest aberrations in works of literature that revealed them to be the products of an "untimely" genius, rather than the purely automatic creations of a "folksoul." In the case of Homer, no such aberrations could be discovered, if only because the Homeric poems were our sole source for the mores of the time. In general, the thoughts and beliefs of people—with the possible exception of geniuses—were the pure products of their cultural background, their *Weltanschauung*. Summing up his theoretical position on the study of culture, Nietzsche announced a "brief formula of a confession of faith." He wrote: "each and every philological activity should be surrounded and fenced in by a philosophical *Weltanschauung*, in which everything single and isolated is discarded and evaporates, while only the whole and unified remains."[19]

In his first lectures as professor of classical philology at Basel, Nietzsche continued to argue that the true scholar "concerns himself with pure essential things," guided not by scattered empirical data but by a philosophical conception. In order to understand the Greeks, the scholar would have to abandon modern preconceptions (especially the overvaluation of science) and adopt the *Weltanschauung* of classical antiquity, which had been revived by Schopenhauer; thus Schopenhauerian pessimism provided the key to the holistic world-view of the Greeks. Instead of seeking to understand individual phenomena from classical antiquity in modern, rational terms, the philosophically informed philologist should behold an ideal "picture of the time of Aeschylus, the great harmony of being: essential devoutness, deep world-contemplation, a bold philosophical standpoint, warriors, politicians, and everyone whole and harmonious."[20]

II. Historicism and Relativism

Nietzsche at various times described people as trapped within the horizons of their individual psychology, their professional culture, their national tradition (or "folksoul"), their epoch, their language, their place in a broadly defined group such as "Christianity" or "Europe", and their very species.[21] Most of these forms of context could be used by the philologist or the historical novelist to reveal ways in which people's thought is shaped and limited. But historical research shows that individuals belong to many overlapping contexts, so that they both share perspectives with their neighbors and yet remain in some sense unique. This is something that the young Nietzsche did not fully recognize. Discussing Nietzsche's essay on *The Use and Disadvantage of History for Life*, Gadamer asks:

> Are there such things as closed horizons, in [Nietzsche's] sense?... Or is this a romantic reflection, a kind of Robinson Crusoe dream of the historical enlightenment, the fiction of an unattainable island, as artificial as Crusoe himself for the alleged phenomenon of the *solus ipse*? Just as the individual is never simply an individual, because he is always involved with others, so too the closed horizon that is supposed to enclose a culture is an abstraction.[22]

In the case of classical philology, it is easy to see the temptation to explain individual writings in terms of "the Greek spirit," or some similar holistic abstraction. There is little more specific information to go on, especially in the case of the pre-Socratics, who especially interested Nietzsche. But a lack of empirical evidence does not justify the use of a priori concepts and the imposition of reified notions of culture—Robinson Crusoe islands. For some philosophers, however, these notions prove attractive because they seem to justify relativist theories. Thus both Hegel and Nietzsche saw the individual ideas and values of any epoch as all reflective of a single, contingent perspective which they, the philosophers of the nineteenth century, had in some sense revealed and overcome.[23] This view of history as a series of contingent perspectives was an important ingredient in Nietzsche's attack on truth, objectivity and traditional metaphysics.[24] In his essay "On Music and Words" (1871), Nietzsche argued against objectivity by claiming that each language was the contingent creation of a culture: "In the multiplicity of languages the fact at once manifests itself, that word and thing do not necessarily coincide...."[25] For Nietzsche, the diverse perspectives of human cultures and languages were, to use Donald Davidson's phrase, "conceptual schemes," or:

> points of view from which individuals, cultures, or periods survey the passing scene. There may be no translating from

one scheme to another, in which case the beliefs, desires, hopes, and bits of knowledge that characterize one person have no true counterparts for the subscriber to another scheme.[26]

Nietzsche argued that languages were decisive in conditioning thought, each language in its own way:

The strange family resemblance of all Indian, Greek, and German philosophizing is explained easily enough. Where there is an affinity of languages, it cannot fail, owing to the common philosophy of grammar—I mean, owing to the unconscious domination and guidance by similar grammatical functions .... It is highly probable that philosophers within the domain of the Ural-Altaic languages... look otherwise 'into the world'.... [The] spell of certain grammatical functions is ultimately also the spell of *physiological* valuations and racial conditions.[27]

Thus for Nietzsche, a recognition of the variety of contingent, incongruent perspectives on the world entailed that none could be objective. Objectivity was the dream of traditional philosophers, who lacked, above all, an "historical sense."[28]

Any historicist will admit that what seems true to him or her did not necessarily seem true to the pre-Socratic Greeks. This much is entailed by the findings of philology. But we still need to ask what is it whose truth-value seems to vary. If it is mere beliefs and propositions, taken individually, then no relativist thesis follows, for, as Hollis and Lukes argue:

[if] s and s' have the same meaning, whatever conditions make s true would [always] make s' true. So it is no surprise that relativists tend to favor holistic conceptions of truth and meaning, which make the primary semantic unit something more complex than the sentence.[29]

If a broad and holistic conception of truth is adopted, then the historicist may be forced to accept relativist conclusions. For, presented with any differences between the thought of two groups, the relativist will explain these in terms of different and incommensurable methods of reasoning. As Nietzsche put it, "the sum of all these [ways of seeing] is in every case totally *incongruent.*"³⁰ But a holistic conception of truth which ascribes meaning to "cultures" does not have to be held by historicists, since the historical data only present us unequivocally with marked differences in individual beliefs about the world. In making the leap to reified theories of culture, and associated concepts of truth and meaning, philosophers have sometimes moved beyond the conclusions that are required by the empirical data. The methods of historicist philology do call for authors from the past to be understood in terms of their environment—the questions that they were asked, the methods that were available to them, the thoughts that were deemed unthinkable. But no collapse of this environment into a single reified *Weltanschauung*, binding many authors within exactly one closed horizon, is called for by the findings of philology.

For Nietzsche, the most compelling example of a culture whose methods of reasoning were allegedly entirely alien to those of modernity was the culture of Greece before Socrates. Nietzsche's descriptions of Dionysian frenzy and collective consciousness seem to presume that the Greeks of the "tragic age" would have denied the relevance of modern rationality to their beliefs; and Nietzsche said as much explicitly (see Chapter IV). If Nietzsche thought that the gulf between Greek culture and our own represented empirical evidence in favor of *Weltanschauung*-historicism and relativism, then he has been joined by numerous modern ethnologists and philosophers of culture, who argue that "On the level of empirical investigation ... there is more evidence to be cited for relativism than against it."³¹ Their radical species of relativism depends on the view that forms of reasoning differ from culture to culture and are incommensurable or untranslatable. To quote Peter Winch, they hold that "The criteria of logic are not a direct gift from God but arise out of and are only intelligible in the context of ways of living and modes of social life."³² Thus no argument can be conducted between two holders of separate conceptual schemes, for the reasons adduced to support each person's position will be unintelligible or suspect to the other. In Nietzsche's phrase: "the question which of the two world-perceptions is more right is a completely senseless one, since it could be decided only by the criterion of the *right perception*, i.e., by a standard *which does not exist.*"³³

But in order to hold this view, the relativist must provide some kind of evidence to support the idea that there are separate and incommensurable conceptual schemes operating in different cultures. This is frequently assumed a priori. For example, Barnes and Bloor derive their argument for relativism from a situation in which two utterly discrete "tribes," T1 and T2, are observed by an anthropologist.[34] It is precisely this assumption of unrelated schemes of consciousness that underlay Nietzsche's relativism. But it is difficult to see how we can know that another scheme is alien to ours unless we can understand it in principle and can articulate its differences from our scheme in terms that are comprehensible to us. It is certainly hard to see how we can know that there are *several* alien cultures beyond the limits of our own horizon, unless we can understand them well enough to recognize their differences. Thus Davidson remarks that modern relativists are always giving accounts of alien conceptual schemes that make these schemes perfectly comprehensible (if not convincing) to us. For example:

> Whorf, wanting to demonstrate that Hopi incorporates a metaphysics so alien to us that Hopi and English cannot, as he puts it, 'be calibrated', uses English to convey the contents of sample Hopi sentences. Kuhn is brilliant at saying what things were like before the revolution using—what else?—our post-revolutionary idiom. Quine gives us a feel for the 'preindividuative phase in the evolution of our conceptual scheme', while Bergson tells us where we can go to get a view of a mountain undistorted by one or another provincial perspective.[35]

The same could be said of Nietzsche's accounts of pre-Socratic life in *The Birth of Tragedy* and elsewhere: he makes that life appear not only comprehensible, but even appealing. If understanding of the sort that Nietzsche seems to claim in *The Birth of Tragedy* is possible, then relativism is ruled out, for "the possibility of translation entails the falsehood of relativism."[36] And translation is a fact of life: "we know [from experience] that unequivocal translation evolves between any two communities in contact."[37] But some antirelativists claim that, if translation "is to be possible, there must be, in Strawson's phrase, 'a massive central core of human thinking which has no history.'"[38] Martin Hollis posits this core of eternal truths a priori as a transcendental requirement for communication and translation, broadly conceived. But vacuous conclusions tend to result from the effort to identify these cultural universals through empirical research. Thus, for example, Clyde Kluckhohn argues:

> Zuñi culture prizes restraint, [but] Kwakiuti culture encourages exhibitionism on the part of the individual. These are contrasting values, but in adhering to them the

Zuñi and Kwakiuti show their allegiance to a universal value; the prizing of the distinctive norms of one's culture.[39]

This is the kind of meaningless result that often arises from a *consensus gentium* approach. The underlying problem is that no theory about the universal features of human epistemology can rebut a relativist critique, for any such theory can be dismissed as the mere product of the theorist's cultural background. Thus it is not surprising that Hollis makes "no serious attempt to describe the common core, or mark its boundaries."[40] Yet to *deny* the existence of such a core seems equally unjustified; for it is not an empirically falsifiable entity. Rather, it seems more promising to suggest, with Davidson, that the very idea that people think through the prisms of contingent and distinctly separate conceptual schemes is bankrupt. For, given "the underlying methodology of interpretation, we could not be in a position to judge that others had concepts or beliefs radically different from our own." Thus, he concludes, "we have found no intelligible basis on which it can be said that schemes are different."[41]

Nietzsche claimed that the structures of modern rationality were inapplicable to an understanding of pre-Socratic Greek life. Thus, for example, the "consistency we praise in a scholar is pedantry when applied to the Greeks"[42]—for the Greeks (allegedly) had only contempt for consistency. A similar point has been made recently about the so-called witchcraft rituals of the Azande, described by the anthropologist Evans-Pritchard. Evans-Pritchard discovered that Zande laws for deciding who was a witch had an incoherent result when systematically applied: everyone could be called a witch. But the Azande refused to "press their ways of thinking about witches to a point at which they would be involved in [such] contradictions." Peter Winch uses this anecdote to draw a Nietzschean conclusion against the Western anthropologist who wants to speak of "the superior rationality of European over Zande thought, in so far as the latter involves a contradiction which it makes no attempt to remove and does not even recognize ...." Against this view, Winch argues "that it is the European, obsessed with pressing Zande thought where it would not naturally go—to a contradiction—who is guilty of misunderstanding, not the Azande. The European is in fact committing a category mistake."[43]

But it is possible to understand the Zande resistance to Evans-Pritchard's discovery in purely rational terms. They recognized the social disintegration and powerlessness that would ensue if they were forced to face a contradiction that was made apparent only through a collision with another culture; and they made a calculated rational decision to abjure rationality in the realm of witchcraft, although they had always used it in other realms. The same thing has happened numerous times within Western culture as religious views, among others, have come under rational scrutiny. Examining the doctrine of the Trinity— or superstitions about black cats—no one would conclude that the West has an essentially irrational *Weltanschauung*. Nor would an anthropologist, watching an Azande going about his or her daily chores in a "rational" fashion, conclude that the Azande have a rationalist world-view. But for some reason, evidence of irrationality in one sphere of Zande life is taken to prove that their perspective or epistemology is fundamentally alien to ours. Instead of comparing "Zande culture" with "occidental rationalism," we surely should compare specific practices, beliefs, and people. Some Azande are probably more rational than others, just as some aspects of Zande life are irrational and some rational, measured by any standard. When we look at that vast array of people and institutions which we call the "West," it seems unlikely that one perspective or worldview can underlie everything, from the actions of medieval mystics to those of corporate raiders. But some philosophers seem eager to read exotic cultures as essentially homogeneous and alien to "our civilization"—however that is defined.

The Zande way of life before Evans-Pritchard arrived was in many ways enviable. The anthropologist Robin Horton has chosen to live in an African society resistant to "Western rationality" because of a *"discovery of things lost at home ...*, an intensely poetic quality in everyday life and thought, and a vivid enjoyment of the passing moment ...."[44] Discussing Horton's choice, Habermas asks: "Shouldn't we, beyond all romanticizing of superseded stages of development, beyond exotic stimulation from the contents of alien cultures, recall the losses required by our own path to the modern world?"[45] The challenge, then, is to examine in an objective way the uses and disadvantages of rationality, by comparing rational with apparently irrational institutions and practices. This is a quintessentially Nietzschean project; it is apparent already in the title of his essay "On the Use and Disadvantage of History for Life." And he opens *Beyond Good and Evil* with the following question: "Suppose we want truth: *why not rather* untruth? and uncertainty? even ignorance."[46] But Nietzsche's attempt to step outside the "culture" of Socratic rationalism did not excuse him from interpreting alien customs in a rational way, nor did it justify his depiction of exotic cultures as homogeneous and "essentially" irrational. To examine alien customs rationally is not, as Stephen Lukes has suggested, a matter of "charitably" assuming that they are themselves rational. On the contrary, in order to discover that they are *not* rational by our standards, the social scientist must, as Habermas writes, "proceed from the presumptive rationality of [each] questionable assumption in order, if necessary, to assure himself step by step of its irrationality." Only "hermeneutic *severity*"— or the measuring of alien statements against "criticizable validity claims"—can lead to understanding at all.[47]

Jürgen Habermas is one philosopher who agrees with Nietzsche that "Forms of life are totalities which always emerge in the plural."[48] But, like Davidson, he abandons the idea of discrete and unrelated forms of life: "their coexistence may cause friction, but this *difference* does not automatically result in their *incompatibility*." For Habermas, as for Gadamer, all languages "are in principle intertranslatable" and this "guarantees their transcendental unity." Otherwise, we would be unable to say anything meaningful about alien languages, learn to speak them, or even recognize them as languages. Although each language works in a different way, nevertheless "the same unity of speech [asserts] itself everywhere ...." Thus, the "dialectical confrontation of what is one's own with what is foreign" can in principle lead to mutual understanding. In fact, when two cultures understand each other, this is only a radical example of the process of mutual interpretation and "fusion of horizons" that always takes place in communication. "Translation is only the extreme variant of an achievement upon which every normal conversation must depend." Needless to say, the "brokenness of intersubjectivity" that occurs between different cultures can be greater than that existing between people of the same background. Nevertheless, "in such cases where understanding proves difficult owing to great cultural, temporal, or social distance it is still possible for us to state in principle what additional information we require in order to fully understand ...."[49]

To summarize the conclusions of this section, it seems that the holistic notion of "culture" that most relativists implicitly endorse is incoherent. Nietzsche would no doubt reject the whole contemporary discussion of relativism as question-begging. It assumes the universal validity of certain facts and practices— including, for example, the validity of anthropological data and of logical arguments—that Nietzsche would call culturally contingent. Nietzsche, like Davidson and Habermas, ultimately concludes that *Weltanschauung*-historicism is inadequate. But Davidson and Habermas reject the theory as a premise, whereas Nietzsche begins by endorsing the notion of the *Weltanschauung*; he then points out that such a concept makes all universalizing theories and all objectivity impossible. Thus it seems to me that Nietzsche is as guilty of begging questions as the modern analytic philosophers are. He too begins by assuming the validity of the data to which he had been exposed as a philologist: in fact, he assumes the validity of a rather contentious, idealist *interpretation* of these data. A much more reasonable approach, it seems to me, would abandon *Weltanschauung*-historicism as a *premise*, and search for an alternative paradigm to explain cultural diversity.

III. Nietzsche's Mature Theory of the *Weltanschauung*

I have tried to show that, as a young man, Nietzsche believed in an uncompromising version of *Weltanschauung* historicism. People, he thought, were the mere "fluctuations" of the "concept" (*Begriff*) of their culture; and each culture had a distinct *Begriff*.[50] This view was much too metaphysical for the mature Nietzsche. Besides, it ignored the diversity within cultures that he was sometimes willing to recognize; and it implied an objective understanding of past cultures, which, as a mature philosopher, he did not think possible. Thus, for example, in *The Birth of Tragedy*, Nietzsche worked out a "concept" of the Greeks in terms of a grand synthesis of Dionysian and Apollonian impulses. However, as I will argue in Chapter V, he did not mean this interpretation to be a hypothesis that would actually describe the historical data; it was something more like a deliberate myth. Nevertheless, Nietzsche continued to rely on the epistemological conclusions that he had derived from his early commitment to *Weltanschauung* historicism; and he continued to write, now and then, as if he still believed in it.[51]

Thus in some places Nietzsche seemed to use the idea of *Weltanschauungen* as an objective fact from which to derive a critique of truth; while in other places he admitted that *Weltanschauungen* were myths, simplifications, subjective impositions on the past. But this apparent inconsistency was far from a careless error. From the perspective of the modern scholar, *Weltanschauungen were* myths which could no longer be sustained. But from the perspective of people living within what Nietzsche called "the completed original folk cultures,"[52] their own local *Begriff* appeared real enough. In fact, their *Weltanschauung* was of the highest importance to them, constituting the very structure of their rationality and their only criterion for distinguishing between civilization and barbarity, sense and nonsense. For a culture to recognize internal diversity or the contingency of its own norms meant death. Thus Nietzsche noted:

It is a form of faith, of instinct, that a kind [*Art*] of men fails to perceive its limitation, its relativity in comparison to others. At least, it seems to be the end for a kind of men (a people, a race) when it becomes tolerant, grants equal rights and no longer thinks that it wants to be master —.[53]

"It is a general law," Nietzsche wrote, "that no living thing can become healthy, strong, and productive except within a horizon."[54] In reality, Greeks of various ages and regions might have spoken different dialects, held different ideas to be axiomatic, and reasoned using different methods. Such differences no doubt even distinguished one Greek from his neighbor within a single *polis*. Meanwhile, some Greeks might have shared a great deal with their non-Greek contemporaries. Nevertheless (Nietzsche thought), up to a point the Greeks had *believed* that there was a homogeneous and eternal Greek way of life; that a clear horizon enclosed their nation and fenced off the barbarians.

There were centuries in which the Greeks found themselves in a similar danger to ours, namely of being destroyed by the inundation of the past and the foreign, by "history." [But they] gradually learned to *organize the chaos* .... Thus they retook possession of themselves and did not long remain the over-loaded heirs and epigones of the whole Orient; they became themselves, and through difficult struggles with themselves, ... became the happiest enrichers and enlargers of their inherited treasure and the first-born and pattern of all subsequent cultured peoples.[55]

Nietzsche's *Ecce Homo* is subtitled "How One Becomes What One Is." Nietzsche holds that existence precedes essence, that people *are* only the sum of what they *do* in the world (see Chapter VI). Similarly, the Greeks became what they were, not by realizing an inherent potential or essence, but by deliberately forming a *Weltanschauung* which they began to treat as if it were their essence. Nietzsche is consistent in treating all forms of identity— personal as well as cultural—as myths; but he also believes that such myths are indispensable.

Scholars ultimately destroyed what had been an objectively powerful illusion: the *Weltanschauung* called "Hellas." Nevertheless, imitators of classical civilization from the Middle Ages to nineteenth-century Pforta had drawn strength from their vision of ancient civilization as a homogeneous *Weltanschauung*. These beliefs, "false" as they might have been, served as the structures within which people thought; and without such structures, there could be no difference between "true" and "false" at all. According to Nietzsche's holistic theory of truth, individual ideas and propositions could have no meaning unless they belonged within a culture whose values were left unquestioned. Nietzsche described

> the obligation which each society, in order to exist, imposes: to be truthful, i.e, to use the customary metaphors, or in moral terms, the obligation to lie according to an established convention, to lie collectively in a style that is mandatory for everyone. Now, of course, man forgets that this is his situation; so he lies in the designated manner unconsciously and according to centuries-old habits—and precisely *by this unconsciousness*, by this forgetting, he arrives at his sense of truth.[56]

To recognize the plurality of cultures meant to lose faith in the norms of one's own *Weltanschauung*. "There is a degree of ... historical awareness which injures and finally destroys a living thing, whether a man, a people or a culture."[57]

According to Nietzsche, it was possible to resist the slide towards nihilism by declaring allegiance to one particular culture, past or present, on the grounds that this was the best and most harmonious form of life. Many Romantics treated the Greeks in this way: they recognized the multiplicity of cultures, but fended off nihilism by declaring Hellenism to be somehow ideal. This move required a belief in the harmony and internal consistency of Greek culture, even though there was already plenty of evidence that the Greeks had been eclectic, diverse and subject to rapid change. If meaning was relative to culture, then ancient Greece could only serve as a transcendent source of meaning if it had been a genuine culture: i.e., dedicated to some consistent and all-embracing values, such as "sweetness and light." Thus to understand the Greeks in a stereotyped and idealized way, following Goethe and Wagner, paradoxically meant to understand them in the only way that could preserve the illusion of truth, objectivity and meaning. "Meaning"—always dependent on a leap of faith—could be preserved by a commitment, not to modern values, but to the values of the ancient Greeks. Thus Nietzsche wrote that there "could be a kind of historical writing that had not a drop of common empirical truth in it and yet could claim in the highest degree the title 'objective'."[58]

The alternative was to apply the devices of modern scholarship in order to destroy the notion of "Greek civilization" or "Hellas" as a useful abstraction. But the modern discovery that *Weltanschauungen* were myths and simplifications was itself the product of a contingent perspective—that of the "historical sense." The "historical sense" could claim no objectivity, since it was based, like everything else, on arbitrary rules and conventions. Nietzsche's *Untimely Meditations* were full of examples intended to demonstrate the historical contingency of the "historical sense." This was also a primary theme of his *Genealogy of Morals*, written some years later. Modern historicism had its own table of arbitrary values, the positivist canon of objectivity, impartiality, and so on. However, Nietzsche generally refused to call historicism a "culture" or a *Weltanschauung*; cultures were defined by an unquestioned faith in their own values, but historicism denied the objectivity of *any* values (including, ultimately, its own), and turned instead to a nihilistic, voyeuristic study of superseded ways of life.

In his lectures on "The Future of Our Educational Institutions," Nietzsche advocated a blind adherence to the arbitrary norms of some culture—*any* culture—as preferable to the nihilism of historicized modernity:

> The historical style has become so familiar in our time that even the living body of language is sacrificed to its anatomical study: but this is precisely where culture [*Bildung*] begins— one must understand how to treat the living as living; and it is here too that the mission of the master of culture begins: in suppressing the "historical interest" that tries to impose itself where one must above all act correctly, but one must know nothing ... *Bildung* begins with obedience, subordination, discipline, and subjection.[59]

Thus Nietzsche was aware that a belief in a homogeneous *Weltanschauung*—whether that of one's own culture, or that of a past age—required irrational commitment and "subordination." Nietzsche's revised theory of the *Weltanschauung* was an effort to account for the diversity within cultures which the "historical sense" had revealed, but which the "folk cultures" had (for good reason) succeeded in suppressing. Although people might believe that their countrymen were all playing by the same rules and speaking the same language, in fact each person's perspective might be subtly unique. Following historical scholarship to its logical conclusion, Nietzsche was therefore led to abandon the notion of the *Weltanschauung* as a causal force, an actually existing entity of which individuals were mere "fluctuations." Nietzsche's more sophisticated version of historicism replaced talk of a "folk-soul" with metaphorical language about contracts, games and rules. For example, logical reasoning was analogous to a game of chance: "Within this game of concepts ..., 'truth' means: to use each die as it is designated, count its spots accurately, forming the correct labels, and never violating the caste system and sequence of rank classifications."[60] It was possible, on Nietzsche's more sophisticated theory of culture, that people might succeed in playing a game together, and yet have subtly different ideas about the rules. This was the case, for example, when classical Greeks considered themselves part of the same culture as their Homeric predecessors, or when teachers at Pforta naively tried to make the classics part of modern civilization. Historical research might succeed in breaking up such a game, by revealing that the parties were playing at cross purposes. But once the game was broken up, the parties lost all access to truth, sense and reason. Nietzsche still maintained, therefore, that consciousness was a function of social or "herd" nature.[61] Each "herd" might be a myth, a subjective construct— but consciousness was dependent on just such myths. "We have need of lies ... in order to live."[62] Or again, "without myth every culture loses the healthy natural power of its creativity: only a horizon defined by myths completes and unifies a whole cultural movement."[63] Thus the notion of a *Weltanschauung* slipped back into Nietzsche's thinking, not as something true, but as a mythical sine qua non for "truth."

Sophisticated as this theory was, it failed to avoid any of the traditional problems of *Weltanschauung*-historicism. People's commitment to their own culture had to be absolute if they were to think at all, but this made understanding any other *Weltanschauung* impossible; for what lay beyond the bounds of one's own "game of truth" (as one subjectively understood these bounds) appeared meaningless. It was therefore unclear how we could know that there were other *Weltanschauungen* in the world. Modern scholars *were* aware of cultural plurality, but they therefore lacked any *Weltanschauung* of their own, at least in the sense that "folk-cultures" had possessed *Weltanschauungen*. And without an unquestioned commitment to received norms of thought, they could not be "aware" of anything, even the existence of other cultures. Nietzsche thought that these paradoxes provided the grounds for a deconstruction of historicism and rationality, and a journey beyond good and evil, truth and lie. But Nietzsche could have the paradoxes altogether, if he had only been willing to create a coherent nominalist theory of culture, rather than reimporting an idealist notion and then declaring it incomprehensible.

IV. Wittgenstein Contra Nietzsche

Nietzsche's analogy of games and languages finds an echo in the later Wittgenstein; but Wittgenstein's use of language-games reveals the weaknesses in Nietzsche's metaphor.[64] Like Nietzsche, Wittgenstein holds that much of what we take to be metaphysics is actually a phenomenon of language. "What looks as if it *had* to exist, is part of the language. It is a paradigm in our language-game; something with which comparison is made."[65] And like Nietzsche, Wittgenstein thinks that there are multiple language-games, none of which have ultimate foundations: "the language game ... is not based on grounds [*ist nicht begründet*]."[66] Moreover, it is crucial to Wittgenstein's account that neither natural languages nor their constituent language-games can be defined precisely, for they do not have precise boundaries. Instead, "Our language can be seen as an ancient city: a maze of little streets and squares, of old and new houses, and of houses with additions from various periods; and this surrounded by a multitude of new boroughs with straight regular streets and uniform houses."[67] The multiplicity of language-games "is not something fixed, given once and for all; but new types of language, new language-games, as we may say, come into existence, and others become obsolete and get forgotten."[68] Nietzsche too believed that the *Weltanschauung* of Greece, for example, had evolved and grown; that it had vague borders. As a philologist, he was an expert on the subtle evolution of the Greek language and its Indo-European roots. In *The Genealogy of Morals*, Nietzsche uses the case of "punishment" to describe how a word and an institution which appears static to its users actually changes constantly. He reminds us that:

> whatever exists, having somehow come into being, is again and again reinterpreted to new ends, taken over, transformed, and redirected by some power superior to it; all events in the organic world are a subduing, a *becoming master*, and all subduing and becoming master involves a fresh interpretation, an adaptation through which any previous "meaning" and "purpose" are necessarily obscured or even obliterated ... [Thus] the entire history of a "thing," an organ, a custom, can

in this way be a continuous sign-chain of ever new interpretations and adaptations ....[69]

Wittgenstein uses a similar metaphor: he says that we add senses to a concept "as in spinning thread we twist fibre on fibre. And the strength of the thread does not reside in the fact that some one fibre runs through its whole length, but in the overlapping of many fibres."[70] But according to Nietzsche, in order for anyone to use a word or an institution, he must *believe* that it has only one meaning and purpose: he must be blind to its history. This is becoming more difficult in the age of historicism. Of the word "punishment," he writes:

> the history of its employment for the most various purposes, finally crystallizes into a kind of unity that is hard to disentangle, hard to analyze and, as must be emphasized especially, totally *indefinable*. (Today it is impossible to say for certain *why* people are really punished: all concepts in which an entire process is semiotically concentrated elude definition; only that which has no history is definable.) At an earlier stage, on the contrary, this synthesis of "meanings" can still be disentangled, as well as changed ...[71]

Thus Nietzsche holds that an ignorance about the vague borders of our language-games is necessary if we are to play them at all. Unless we think that the rules of the game are fixed, permanent and clear, we will not know how to play. This faith is dispelled by the "historical sense"—but the result is nihilism, or an inability to make choices and act. "When the uncontrolled historical sense prevails and reveals all its implications, it uproots the future by destroying illusions and depriving existing things of the only atmosphere in which they can live."[72] Hence, in the enviable world of the Greek polis, "There could be no *history*, no *development* in culture; everything had to be fixed for all time."[73] Historicism robs us of any confidence in the meaning of the words we use; ultimately it even reveals that any objective knowledge about the *history* of our words is impossible.

Wittgenstein, in contrast, sees no practical difficulty with vague boundaries and a consciousness of change and contingency. He builds this into his metaphor of ordinary play. Whereas Nietzsche imagined the ordinary player of the game of "truth" as a slavish follower of preordained rules, Wittgenstein prefers to imagine people amusing themselves in a field by playing with a ball so as to start various existing games, but playing many without finishing them and in between throwing the ball aimlessly into the air, chasing one another with the ball and bombarding one another for a joke and so on.[74]

In many cases, Wittgenstein thinks, it is impossible to identify the rule by which someone plays a game, for "he does not know it himself."[75] "And is there not a case where we play and—make up the rules as we go along? And there is even one where we alter them—as we go along."[76] Thus a crucial disagreement between Wittgenstein and Nietzsche can be stated as follows: for Nietzsche, "truth" is an illusion whose arbitrary character we cannot know if we are to remain "rational." For Wittgenstein, the ordinary practice of thinking and acting requires making up rules, experimenting with arbitrary signs and conventions, and entering into free, deliberate agreements with others, which allow communication to take place. But our recognition that the conventions we use are arbitrary human creations does not lead us to despair about their usefulness. A language, says Wittgenstein repeatedly, is an "instrument"; and a good instrument is one that works.

Wittgenstein, unlike Nietzsche, holds that there need not be rules underlying every aspect of a game—even implicit or unconscious rules. Wittgenstein's interlocutor in the *Philosophical Investigations* says: "But then the use of the word is unregulated, the 'game' we play with it is unregulated." Wittgenstein replies: "It is not everywhere circumscribed by rules; but no more are there any rules for how high one throws the ball in tennis, or how hard; yet tennis is a game for all that and has rules too."[77] For Wittgenstein, as for Nietzsche, language depends upon conventions; but Nietzsche imagines the underlying conventions of a game as rigid, uncompromising and all-encompassing.

Since Wittgenstein thinks that we have to create new language-games all the time in order to navigate our way around our own native languages, he sees no particular problem in learning a second language. In fact, he recognizes no clear boundaries among natural languages at all, for the same game may exist in several language at once, or may come into being as a means of translating *among* natural languages. Thus it would be impossible to isolate a *Weltanschauung*, to declare it a reified whole. Instead, "we see a complicated network of similarities overlapping and criss-crossing; sometimes overall similarities, sometimes similarities of detail."[78] A game of pointing at things and naming them, played by two people who shared no common vocabulary, would allow them to communicate and would serve as the nucleus of their mastery of each other's more sophisticated language-games. Ultimately, the possibility of learning multiple languages allows Wittgenstein to speak of human language in the singular: not as an ordered, understandable unity, shared by all people, but as a complex web of *differences* that includes us all. Wittgenstein needs to make no claims about uniformity in human behavior across historical distance in order to explain communication; but he does suggest that our differences are potentially reconcilable. Thus the "we" of which Wittgenstein writes is humanity as a whole; it is anyone with whom we can develop a language game. Since Wittgenstein can speak of human reason and human language, he is not a cultural relativist. Thus although Wittgenstein and Nietzsche share remarkably similar metaphors—and much besides—Wittgenstein's theory of language enables him to avoid relativism, and thereby to diffuse the paradoxes and deconstructive turns that Nietzsche used as a springboard to irrationalism.[79]

Chapter 4

Farewell to Reason[1]

I. Nietzsche on Contemporary Historiography

By 1874, when he wrote his meditation on *The Use and Disadvantage of History for Life*, Nietzsche had been exposed to several prominent forms of modern historical methodology. At Pforta, he had seen what he called "monumental history" at work. This was inconsistent with a "historical sense," since it pretended to discover universal models of virtuous action in the annals of the past. Nietzsche argued that "we simply cannot distinguish" between monumental history and "a mythical fiction." Accepting the historicist insights of his teachers at Bonn, Nietzsche warned that, if an "exemplary [*monumentalische*] study of the past *prevails* over the other modes of consideration—I mean antiquarian and critical history—then the past itself is *damaged*."[2] In other words, monumental history was essentially unrealistic as compared to the new historicist forms of philological methodology that Nietzsche had encountered at Bonn; it lived by making false analogies between actually incomparable epochs and events.

In his seminars at Bonn and in his reading of David Strauss, Nietzsche encountered, as an alternative to Pforta's naive humanism, the "New Faith" of critical history, which attempted to emancipate modern humanity from received opinion by contextualizing and relativizing all past dogmas. Nietzsche was later to express reservations about this attitude, but there is no evidence that he had

67

split with Albrecht Ritschl over the value of critical history as early as his departure from Bonn in 1865. On the contrary, he left Bonn partly in order to follow Ritschl to Leipzig as his devoted protégé.[3] So if Nietzsche had any historical ideology in 1865, it may have been something very much like the "New Faith" of Ritschl and Strauss. This ideology would have conflicted somewhat, as Nietzsche later recognized, with two other forms of historical consciousness that he encountered as a university student. First, as Nietzsche must have known, the dominant philosophical view of history at the time was that of Hegel, who (like Vico and Marx) had attempted to uncover the universal mechanisms driving world history. Nietzsche shows no sign of having had a close acquaintance with Hegel as a student, but upon his discovery of Schopenhauer in 1865, he quickly came to the conclusion that the Hegelian view of history was merely a form of Christian optimistic eschatology. For Nietzsche, to posit a single mechanism and a single optimistic telos for all history was to ignore the historicist discovery of individuation, and this was untenable. The effect of Hegel's philosophy had been to delay the recognition that God was a purely subjective creation, by using historicist insights as the foundation of an essentially unhistorical system: "Hegel in particular was [atheism's] delayer par excellence, with his grandiose attempt to persuade us of the divinity of existence, appealing as a last resort to our sixth sense, 'the historical sense.'"[4] Nietzsche found it particularly ridiculous that for Hegel, "the climax and terminal point of [the] world-process coincide with his own Berlin existence."[5] Hegel's world-historical narrative was—to a comical degree—the product of his own historical vantage point.

II. Romantic Historiography

By 1874, Nietzsche had identified one more contemporary form of historical consciousness to compete with the monumental, critical and Hegelian schools. This was the "antiquarian" ideology of Ranke and his followers, which Nietzsche must have encountered as a strong presence throughout the University of Bonn. Instead of seeking universal human models for emulation, as did the "monumental" historians, antiquarians sought to portray an entire culture in a positive light (thus antiquarians were "*Weltanschauung*-historicists"). The most significant version of antiquarian history for the classical philologist was the effort to portray Greek civilization as exemplary, but also as closely linked to modern Germany. Despite his commitment to Ritschl's critical methods, Nietzsche was interested in such Romantic Hellenism. In his *Untimely Meditations*, he was to suggest a deliberate synthesis of critical and reverential attitudes toward the past. Thus Nietzsche was willing to admit that antiquarian history had value, and he even called enthusiastically for modern Germans—as their "supreme reward"—to seek "models in that primitive and archaic Greek world of the great, the natural, and the human."[6]

Classical scholarship and efforts at radical cultural renewal had been closely linked ever since the age of the early Romantics in Germany. Wilamowitz was to write that these "men of [the] second renaissance," had "discovered the immortal Greek genius, to which they felt themselves akin, and eagerly drank in its life—the enhancing gospel of freedom and beauty."[7] German intellectuals in the early 1800s felt themselves alienated from the new regime of materialism, rationalism and capitalism, which had triumphed during the French Revolution. They labored to create a distinctively German alternative to the mainstream European culture represented by their French conquerors. In their view, modern European culture had begun with the appropriation of Roman civilization during the Renaissance, and had then rapidly degenerated into the baseness and triviality of bourgeois democracy. Their goal was to revive the civilization of the ancient Greeks, which they considered "a superior alternative to the contemporary world and the situation of Germany in it."[8] They had begun to turn the humanist project of reviving individual acts of virtue into a historicist project of reviving whole cultures.

The Greeks were especially attractive to the Germans because Hellenic culture had allegedly valued devotion to city above self-interest, beauty over profit, and grand religious insight over the gathering of piecemeal information. Moreover, the very distance of ancient Greece from contemporary European civilization and its Romano-Christian roots was appealing; classical Greek culture was the first that Europeans recognized as truly alien, and yet worthy of respect. But at the same time that the Greeks were held to be alien to the mainstream of modern European culture, they were also thought to share many racial and linguistic traits with the modern Germans. Thus one might realistically hope to recreate classical Athens in nineteenth-century Prussia. Wilamowitz writes in his *Recollections* that the

> final task of philologic-historical science is by the force of the
> scientifically trained fancy to revivify past life, feeling,
> thought, and belief in order that all the animating force there
> is in that past may continue to influence the present and the

future. Only Eros leads to the vision of truth and eternal life.[9]

This curious notion—that a passionate desire for the past can lead to a better future and a vision of the Universal—is quintessentially Romantic. And so it would not be an exaggeration to say, as Wilamowitz does, that the entire scholarly enterprise of Classical philology, in which he participated, was founded on a Romantic desire to "bring that dead [Greek] world back to life by the power of science"—in order to rescue the soul of modern humanity.[10]

The Romantics' desire to appropriate Greek culture for Prussian modernity came into conflict, from the beginning, with the central doctrine of *Weltanschauung*-historicists: that each culture was essentially unique. Certainly, there were Romantics who were *Weltanschauung*-historicists; indeed, the Romantic nostalgia for Hellenic civilization resulted precisely from a historicist realization that ancient Greek culture was very different from modern bourgeois society. Nevertheless, many early Romantics sensed a conflict between their desire to recreate the ancient world, and their belief in the individuality of each epoch. It took a sleight of hand on the part of scholars like K.O. Müller to posit a racial, or at least a linguistic, connection between the Greeks and the Germans as a way of legitimizing a modern appropriation of ancient culture; and this thesis was unsatisfactory to many Romantics. Thus, for example, Winckelmann had concluded his history of Greek art by describing himself in relation to Hellenic culture "as a lover standing on the sea shore [who] watches her beloved sailing away from her; she has no hope of ever seeing him again, yet her weeping eyes follow him into the distance, and think they can see his likeness mirrored in the sails as the ship draws further away."[11] And Nietzsche too, by the time he wrote his *Untimely Meditations*, had come to the pessimistic conclusion that his contemporaries were cut off forever from classical culture. "This would be a *thesis*," he wrote, "to describe Greek culture as irrecoverable..."[12]

This realization was slow in coming, however, and it is safe to say that when Nietzsche left Bonn in 1865, he still clung to some of the optimistic spirit of cultural reform that had driven the Germans to make historicist classical scholarship a major part of the university curriculum: like most of his colleagues, he still considered a renaissance of Greek culture to be both possible and worthwhile.[13] He even thought that the Greeks might provide an exception to the rule that all values are culturally contingent and morally equivalent. "Greek art," he wrote a few years later, "is the only one that overcame national requirements: here we come for the first time to Humanity: that is, not the average human being, but the highest manhood."[14] Thus Nietzsche left Bonn for Leipzig with a pair of conflicting ideologies driving his work: on the one hand, critical, positivistic scholarship; on the other, an antiquarian nostalgia for the ancient Greeks. Within ten years, he had rejected both of these ideologies, just as he had already left the naive humanism of Pforta behind him. But when Nietzsche left Bonn for Leipzig in October 1865, he still clung to the dominant mid-nineteenth-century ideology of historicism, albeit in a hybrid and somewhat contradictory form. The critical methods he was taught as a philology student had proved themselves to be effective and fruitful, and they committed him to a notion of historical difference. At the same time, the Romanticism that fueled his interest in the Greeks committed him (perhaps less reasonably) to the theory of hermetic, organic cultures. Nietzsche certainly did not as yet have any original contributions to make to the theory of culture, but a lifetime of contemplating the consequences of historicism had already begun.

III. Doubts About Philology

Between October 1865 and December 1868, Nietzsche studied classical philology at Leipzig under Ritschl. Early in 1866, Ritschl was already calling Nietzsche's work the most rigorous and professional that he had ever seen from so young a student.[15] Nietzsche, however, was beginning to tire of rigorous philology, and he found occasional solace from textual criticism in typically Romantic pursuits: "my Schopenhauer, the music of Schumann, and solitary walks."[16] At Leipzig, Nietzsche may have felt the first stirrings of a revolt against the ideology of historicist scholarship, or he may simply have suffered from occasional bouts of frustration and boredom. In any case, Nietzsche's dissatisfaction did not prevent him from producing a remarkable quantity of rigorous new philological research during his years at Leipzig. A lengthy article on the sources of Diogenes Laertius, which appeared serially in the *Rheinisches Museum*; a paper on Simonides' *Danae* and a study of Theognis, also published in the *Museum*; a formal lecture on the sources of Suidas; an essay in draft on the Democritean *spuria* intended for a festschrift for Ritschl; a paper on the satire of Varro and Menippus; and an index to 24 years of the *Rheinisches Museum*—Nietzsche produced all of this in three years, during which time he also wrote music and became thoroughly acquainted with Schopenhauer.[17]

His work on Democritus reveals a strong admiration for this iconoclastic rationalist who "devoted his life wholly to an attempt at penetrating all things with his [scientific] method. So he was the first to work his way systematically through everything knowable."[18] Nietzsche was here showing a preference for what he considered the scientific, almost positivistic method of Democritus over the metaphysical speculation of Plato and Aristotle. Nietzsche's own dedication in putting together a large index to a series of dry journal articles shows a similar commitment to the values of collective, scientific scholarship. On the other hand, by 1868 Nietzsche was already telling his friend Paul Deussen that he considered "philology the misbegotten son of the goddess philosophy, born an idiot or a cretin."[19] Nevertheless, when a former student of Ritschl's, Adolf Kiessling (a professor of classical philology) asked about Nietzsche's qualifications to succeed him at in his Chair at Basel, Ritschl predicted that Nietzsche would soon stand in the front rank of German philology. "Whatever he wants to do, he will be able to do," Ritschl told Kiessling;[20] and as a result, Nietzsche was quickly made Professor Extraordinarius of Classical Philology at the University of Basel. At 24, Nietzsche's career was off to a very fast start.

But by this time, Nietzsche was feeling a general alienation from the profession he had just entered, which he continually described as "philistine." Moreover, by now Nietzsche was almost certainly beginning to feel doubts about the theoretical underpinnings of historicism, and hence of his chosen discipline. In May or June of 1867, he had written some experimental aphorisms about history and historicism, in which he argued that the vantage point of the modern historian—like that of the people he studied—was culturally conditioned. "The historian is looking through a medium constituted by his preconceptions, those of his period and those of his sources. There is no hope of penetrating to the *Ding an sich.*"[21] To some degree, this was merely an empiricist attack on philosophical idealism. But it also pointed forward toward Nietzsche's thorough critique of rational, empirical scholarship. Nietzsche was beginning to believe that the rational outlook of the modern world was just another, arbitrary shape of consciousness, which could claim no absolute vantage-point from which to judge past periods. The Cartesian subject had been relativized and contextualized, the supposed Archimedean vantage point of rationalism shown to be historically conditioned. In the same way, the work of the historicist scholar might have to be declared historically relative. This was the basis of Nietzsche's transcendence of *Weltanschauung*-historicism. By the time he wrote *The Gay Science*, he was almost equally dismissive of ahistorical humanism *and* historical relativism; both views were merely contingent, the product of limited *Weltanschauungen* whose prejudices Nietzsche was prepared to identify precisely. For example, he thought, the "historians of morality (mostly Englishmen)," begin from the "mistaken premise" of

> some consensus of the nations, at least of tame nations, concerning certain principles of morals, and then they infer from this that these principles must be unconditionally binding also for you and me; or, conversely, they see the *truth* that among different nations moral valuations are *necessarily* different and then infer from this that *no* morality is at all binding. Both procedures are equally childish.[22]

Thus for Nietzsche it was "true" that morals differ from culture to culture, but precisely for this reason it was impossible to make any totalizing claims at all, even the claim that "no morality is at all binding." Indeed, it was ultimately impossible even to affirm the "truth" that there exists a plurality of cultures. "There are *no eternal facts*: therefore there is no absolute truth."[23] The "historical sense" made Nietzsche's ability to doubt received opinion much more potent than the ahistorical skepticism of someone like Descartes. Nietzsche could doubt that even skepticism had objective validity; he could reject the very structures of rationality which allow us to recognize truth and falsehood, opinion and fact. "We moderns are all opponents of Descartes and struggle against his dogmatic, frivolous doubt. One must doubt better than Descartes."[24] In 1866, Nietzsche had read F.A. Lange's *History of Materialism*, which not only attacked Kantian idealism, but also declared all forms of "truth" to be mere products of convention. Nietzsche called Lange's book "unequivocally the most important work of philosophy to have appeared in dozens of years"[25] And in developing Lange's thought, Nietzsche moved toward a radically deconstructive project. Karsten Harries writes:

> Was it not Nietzsche's great insight that there can be no escape from the prison-house of perspective? If following such suggestions we bring Kant's transcendental subject down to earth and replace his supposedly timeless categorical scheme with concrete historical language, we are also forced to deny the difference between objective and subjective appearance, between truth and illusion. With this collapse language

loses its measure and becomes free play. Carried to such extremes the Copernican comparative lets the Copernican theme deconstruct itself.[26]

This was to be a highly influential aspect of Nietzsche's thought. Indeed, Gadamer claims that there "is one thing common to all contemporary criticism of historical objectivism or positivism, namely the insight that the so-called subject of knowledge has the same mode of being as the object, so that object and subject belong to the same historical movement."[27] Such observations would only appear explicitly in Nietzsche's work in 1873, with the appearance of his essay "On Truth and Lying in the Ultramoral Sense." But there were hints of it already in his early aphorisms on history, and in his inaugural lecture at Basel, where he tried to walk a fine line between an absolute allegiance to rigorous scholarship, and a radical project of undermining his own discipline. Like Lange, he called for philological science to incorporate some of the creative spirit of art as a way of avoiding the pitfalls of a false objectivity and the naive positing of a vantage point outside history. But he stopped well short of declaring philology to be self-refuting. "Life is worth living, says art, the most ravishing temptress; life is worth knowing for what it is, says science." In Nietzsche's view, the two approaches should meet in the work of the classical scholar.[28]

IV. Wagner on Historicism

Nietzsche's ambivalence about his new position as a scientific philologist may have stemmed partly from his emerging critique of the historicist world-view; but a more direct cause was probably his simple dissatisfaction with the dry, unimaginative style of his colleagues and teachers. Nietzsche was casting around for an alternative to both historicism and academic philology. Appropriately enough, he celebrated the news of his appointment at Basel by resolving to hear Richard Wagner's operatic attack on traditional classicism, *Die Meistersinger von Nürnberg*, in Dresden. Shortly before, in November 1868, Nietzsche had met Wagner personally, and within a year, the two men would be friends. For Nietzsche, Wagner represented an exciting bohemian alternative to the life of a philologist at a provincial university. Wagner was a Schopenhauerian and a critic of contemporary optimistic philosophies of history. He had powerful theoretical ideas about culture—especially classical culture and its relation to modern civilization; and he seemed to Nietzsche to have avoided the intellectual weaknesses of Romanticism without lapsing into dry-as-dust positivism.

Wagner was a critic of historicism who blamed it for the demise of art; and his influence helped to reinforce Nietzsche's new feeling that historicist philology and art were somehow enemies.[29] Within a few months, Nietzsche had become a devoted Wagnerian.

Nietzsche quickly became familiar, not only with all of Wagner's music, but also with many of his theoretical works. By 1868, Wagner had already written voluminously about music, culture and history. *Die Meistersinger*, above all, served as an allegorical summary of his position on humanism and historicism, and it proved extremely attractive to Nietzsche.[30] The opera's hero and stand-in for Wagner is Hans Sachs, who was a real figure from sixteenth-century Nuremberg and a champion of Renaissance humanism. Humanistic German culture had sought to revive classical civilization as an all-encompassing alternative to the Middle Ages. Nuremberg had a special advantage in this, for in 1346 the large Jewish population of the city had been either massacred or driven away, so that their ghetto could be turned into a Renaissance market-place and a showpiece for the new humanism. In particular, the citizens of Nuremberg had constructed a huge *schöner Brunnen* (Beautiful Fountain), adorned with statues of the great thinkers of antiquity and embellished with symbols of the Holy Roman Empire, whose political capital was then at Nuremberg and whose propaganda suggested that the German Emperor was the true heir to the Caesars. To a confessed anti-Semite like Wagner, it may have seemed particularly appropriate that the new Nuremberg arose from the ashes of a Jewish ghetto, which had symbolized the presence of foreign ideas and foreign blood on German soil.[31] In a similar way, Wagner's music-dramas were intended to serve as a unified and holistic German alternative to the foreign, cosmopolitan, materialistic—in a word, Jewish—decadence that Wagner saw around him in nineteenth-century Germany. The Renaissance had turned to Rome for a cultural model, and had appropriated classical civilization for the German "Holy Roman Empire." Now Wagner intended to find alternative models for Germany in medieval epics and in ancient Greek tragedy—but the motivation for this new renaissance was essentially the same. Thus Wagner made Hans Sachs, that real-life propagandist for the Holy Roman Empire and Roman culture, pontificate against the Empire and in favor of a new, authentically German art. Sachs calls for "The Holy Roman Empire" to be replaced by "Holy German art."[32] Wagner seems to have meant that if Hans Sachs could speak to nineteenth-century Germans from the grave, he would declare the Romanizing Renaissance in which he had participated dead, and call for a new one.

The early modern Renaissance seemed to sophisticated Germans of the nineteenth century to have been a rather naive appropriation of ancient culture. Nietzsche thought that the humanist appropriation of Greek civilization depended upon a "*gross superficiality* in the idea of the ancient world—little more than regard for its formal skills and knowledge."[33] In the realm of music, for example, Monteverdi's invention of opera had arisen almost accidentally as part of a poorly informed effort to revive Greek tragedy. In opera as in architecture, poetry and philosophy, the ancients had been appropriated in a facile way by moderns who misunderstood their own fundamental distance from antiquity. The result had been a series of naive period-styles, from Augustan Rome to rococo Bavaria, each of which had appropriated ancient vocabulary in order to produce new cultural norms which took on a false authority by their alleged similarity to antiquity, but which were in fact quite parochial. Taken together, this series of period-styles is what Wagner calls either the "Roman Empire" or "French civilization," by which he means especially the French neoclassicism that had been adopted by the minor potentates of Germany as part of a "foolish restoration of a sham Greek mode of art."[34] Nietzsche, adopting a slightly different stance, celebrated this series of renaissances for their artistic creativity, but he admitted that their achievements were only possible because they had been ignorant of the classical past. For example:

> ... the French took possession of Roman antiquity in a way for which we would no longer have courage enough... .
> And Roman antiquity itself, how forcibly and at the same time naively it took hold of everything good and lofty of Greek antiquity! How they translated things into the Roman present! ... As poets, they had no sympathy for the antiquarian inquisitiveness that precedes the historical sense... . They did not know the delights of the 'historical sense'; what was past and alien was an embarrassment to them, and being Romans, they saw it as an incentive for a Roman conquest.[35]

Thus the very strength of humanist classicism was also its weakness: ignorant or dismissive of the gulf between past and present, it could not survive the discoveries of modern philology. In Wagner's view, the bottom had fallen out of French naive classicism when German Romanticism finally overthrew the last, most decadent Renaissance period-style, the rococo. The Romantics, with their more sophisticated understanding of the alien nature of Greek culture, began a new renaissance: they began a conscious appropriation of Greek civilization as something alien to Romanized modernity, yet akin in a profound way to the German spirit. "Hail Winckelmann and Lessing," writes Wagner, "ye who, beyond the centuries of native German majesty, found the German's Ur-kinsman in the divine Hellenes, and laid bare the pure ideal of human beauty to the powder-bleared eyes of French-civilized mankind!"[36]

And yet, despite his celebration of Goethe, Lessing and Beethoven, Wagner was not particularly satisfied with the Romanticism of his own day. Romanticism had begun in an eager attempt to appropriate the spiritual profundity of Greek civilization for modernity. The modern world had lost its gods and idols, so Romanticism could only return sentimentally, as Schiller said, to the naive art and religion of the past. Thus there was always an air of vicariousness and eclecticism inherent in Romanticism; and this became increasingly obvious as architects like Schinkel turned to Gothic, Eastern and classical models all at once; as Wagner's hero, Carl Maria von Weber, appropriated the magic of German folktales and Greek legends for his operas; and as poets like Byron and Hugo turned to the Orient, to Greece and to the Middle Ages for fuel for their poetry. In Wagner's view, the nadir of sentimental Romanticism came with the re-emergence of Jewish art in the European mainstream, for he viewed the Jew as the quintessential alienated outsider, the vicarious onlooker who, "with wondrous inexpressiveness," hurls "together the diverse forms and styles of every age and every master."[37] Wagner applied his own description of the educated Jew, standing "alien and apathetic" in the "midst of a society he does not understand," to the entire culture of Germany in the age of the Jewish artists: Heine, Mendelssohn and Meyerbeer.[38] Wagner attacked Mendelssohn in particular for appropriating the naive and authentic German spirituality of Bach for his own "washiness and whimsicality."[39] The ghetto had come back and recaptured the heart and soul of German culture—symbolized by Nuremberg's "Beautiful Fountain," for cosmopolitanism and eclecticism. "Judaism," wrote Wagner, "is the evil conscience of our modern civilization."[40]

V. Nietzsche Begins to Criticize Historicism

Similar thoughts concerning the vicarious condition of modern culture—although without Wagner's anti-Semitic prejudice—were to become staples of Nietzsche's writing.[41] Nietzsche feared that people in modernity had lost any essential qualities, any authenticity, so dependent were they on eclectic imitation:

> The hybrid European ... simply needs a costume: he requires history as a storage room for costumes. To be sure, he soon notices that not one fits him very well; so he keeps changing... . [A]gain and again a new piece of prehistory or a foreign country is tried on, put on, taken off, and above all *studied*: we are the first age that has truly studied "costumes"—I mean those of morality, articles of faith, tastes in the arts, and religions... .[42]

Beneath the costumes that moderns borrowed and discarded, lay— nothing. "The phenomenon of modern man has become nothing but illusion," Nietzsche wrote.[43] The word "nihilism" had not yet appeared in Nietzsche's work as a way to describe human nature that had become "nothing" beyond appearance, but the concept was already present, and he was already blaming the modern "historical sense" for its ascendancy. By understanding the past, he thought, the modern historian "might be able to elevate himself to a *supra-historical* vantage point," from which all norms appeared merely local and contingent. But historians in this position "would no longer feel tempted to go on living or taking part in history, because they would have recognized that the one condition for all events is the blindness and injustice in the soul of a man of action."[44] In order to act, a human being had to be unaware that the values guiding his or her actions were mere products of a local culture. "We must therefore regard the capacity for a certain degree of unhistorical awareness as [an] important and primordial capacity, since it provides the only foundation upon which any just, healthy, great, or truly human enterprise can develop."[45]

In 1885, Nietzsche was still worrying about the "nihilistic consequences of historiography and of the '*practical* historians,' i.e., the romantics."[46] Of the objective scholar, he wrote, "one [has] accorded him far too high honors and overlooked his most essential characteristics: he is an instrument, something of a slave though certainly not the most sublime type of slave, but in himself nothing— *presque rien!*"[47] In 1887 he wrote of pessimism and decline as "a sort of cosmopolitan fingering, as '*tout comprendre*' and historicism [*Historismus*]."[48] And he specifically called "modern historiography ... *nihilistic*." It was responsible, he said, for the "gloomy, gray, cold fog" through which these "historical nihilists" wander.[49]

A scholar who claimed to be open to everything was in fact closed to every distant culture, for he could not take any of their claims to absolute truth, goodness and beauty seriously. "Let us finally own it to ourselves," Nietzsche wrote, "what we men of the 'historical sense' find most difficult to grasp, to feel, to taste, to love once more ... is precisely the perfection and maturity of every culture and art, ... the moment when their sea is smooth and they have found halcyon self-sufficiency... ."[50] To the historicist scholar, every text was the same, and no text's claim to universal truth and perfection made any sense. Thus, said Nietzsche, scholars are eunuchs, and to "a eunuch any woman is as good as another, merely a woman. Woman-in-Herself, the ever-unapproachable."[51] The implication was that philologists lacked the spiritual equipment necessary to enter an alien text. All his life, Nietzsche ranted against the scholars' "rotting armchairs, [their] cowardly contemplativeness, [their] lascivious historical eunuchism, [and their] justice-tartuffery of impotence."[52] Nietzsche preferred even the ignorance of an animal, which is "totally unhistorical and living within a horizon no larger than a mere point, yet with a certain happiness, living at least without satiety or hypocrisy."[53] He concluded: "The unhistorical resembles an enveloping atmosphere; within its confines alone is life engendered, only to disappear with the annihilation of this atmosphere."[54]

Lamentations about the lack of authenticity in modern culture were common in nineteenth-century Germany, and the usual medicine prescribed was a return to the naive, the natural. Nietzsche was sometimes quite powerfully taken by this kind of rhetoric himself. In 1866 he described an experience to his friend von Gersdorff in the following terms:

Yesterday a heavy storm gathered in the sky; I hastened towards a neighboring hill... , I climbed it; at the summit I found a hut and a man, who, watched by his children, was cutting the throats of two lambs. The storm broke in all its power, discharging thunder and hail, and I felt inexpressibly well, full of strength and *élan*, and I realized with a wonderful clearness that to understand Nature one must, as I had just done, go to her to be saved, far from all worries and all our heavy constraints... . How happy they are, how strong they are, those pure wills which the mind has not troubled![55]

In Wagner's *Die Meistersinger*, back-to-nature Romanticism is represented by the untutored Walther, whose passionate *Meisterlied* triumphs over the music of his day, which is incapable of anything beyond "the presentment, stringing together, and entanglement of the most elegant, the smoothest and most polished figures ... but never where those figures were meant to take the shape of deep or stalwart feelings of the human heart."[56] Nevertheless, Walther is not the opera's hero—the educated scholar-poet Hans Sachs is. And in advocating something more sophisticated than vulgar Romanticism, Wagner was a major influence on Nietzsche, who soon abandoned the kind of melodramatic worship of nature that is evident in the letter quoted above. Wagner preached explicitly against a return to naive art and nature. "No," he wrote, "we do not wish to return to Greekdom; for what the Greeks knew not, and knowing not, came by their downfall, that know we."[57] The downfall of the Greeks came as a result of their parochialism, their indifference or ignorance regarding other cultures. A similar end ultimately befell the Germanic bards whose Nibelung myths Wagner appropriated. Wagner was certainly ready to use naive Greek and German art wherever he could, but he did so in a self-conscious way that recognized his sources for what they were: naive and parochial. Thus, Wagner claimed, he ran no danger of falling into cosmopolitanism, for he deliberately refashioned the parochial styles that he had appropriated into original creations of his own. Thus his way out of nihilism was the deliberate creation of new values, which he could achieve free of any historical conditioning because he was a genius. Nietzsche was eager to point out that, unlike ordinary people, Wagner could not be explained as "completely and solely the product of [the] present"; he is "unannounced."[58] Nietzsche never renounced the idea that geniuses (or "Overmen") are autonomous from history, even after he had renounced Wagner. In 1885 he wrote, "Against the doctrine of the influence of the milieu and external causes: ... A genius is not explained in terms of such conditions of his origin."[59] And Wagner had a powerful ally in his effort to transcend history through genius: music, a force that he considered trans-temporal and ahistorical. With music at his side, he hoped to "soar to the free manhood of art, with the star rays of the world soul." We moderns all desire, he said, "to grow to fair strong men, to whom the world belongs as an eternal, inexhaustible source of the highest delights of art".[60] Nietzsche later criticized Wagner's Romantic deification of music, but his description of the Wagnerian project was no doubt accurate:

With the extraordinary rise in the value of music that appeared to follow from Schopenhauerian philosophy, the value of the *musician himself* all at once went up in an unheard-of manner, too: from now on he became an oracle, a priest, indeed more than a priest, a kind of mouthpiece of the "in itself" of things, a telephone from the beyond—henceforth he uttered not only music, this ventriloquist of God—he uttered metaphysics....[61]

Thus the young Nietzsche borrowed at least three notions from Wagner: a diagnosis of historicism as nihilistic; a celebration of the free creativity of genius; and a theory that music lay beyond the realm of history. To these ideas he added his own deconstructive insight: that even historicism was a culturally relative phenomenon that could claim no objective perspective on the world. All of these ideas came together in his 1871 essay "On Music and Words." He begins this essay by applying the logic of radical historicism to undermine the alleged objectivity of language:

> In the multiplicity of languages the fact at once manifests itself, that word and thing do not necessarily coincide with one another completely, but that the word is a symbol. But what does the word symbolize? Most certainly only [subjective] conceptions ...; for how should a word-symbol correspond to that innermost nature of which we and the world are images? Only as conceptions we know that kernel, only in its metaphorical expression are we familiar with it; beyond that point there is nowhere a direct bridge that could lead us to it....[62]

Nietzsche's condemnation of the view that language describes the world is thorough: "even Schopenhauer's 'Will'," he writes, "is nothing else than the most general phenomenal form of Something otherwise absolutely indecipherable."[63] Philosophical discourse, like any discourse, is purely metaphorical, as Nietzsche claimed in his exegesis of Thales' statement, "All is water."[64] The noble philosophies of Thales and Schopenhauer (and of everyone in between) were merely allegorical and culturally contingent. But Nietzsche tried to escape, as Wagner had, from this relativist dilemma by positing a universal "tonal subsoil," common to all humans and "comprehensible beyond the difference of language."[65] In other words, Nietzsche was arguing that music—alone—is ahistorical and universal, for "the origin of music lies beyond all individuation...."[66] In prehistoric times, the first means of communication, the language of gestures, developed out of the "tonal subsoil" of music; and with this "begins the diversity of languages, whose multiplicity we are permitted to consider—to use a simile—as a strophic text to that primal melody of the pleasure-and-unpleasure language" of music.[67] Nietzsche was positing an ontological hierarchy, with music lying at the most basic level, the Schopenhauerian Will at an intermediate stage, and culture and language lying at the superficial fringes. This was also a hierarchy of value, with music seen as the most precious part of existence. Thus it had been an act of heroism— not unlike the Platonic philosopher's return to the cave—for Wagner to submit "to the language of culture, and all the laws of its expression, although he was the first to feel the profound inadequacy of this expression."[68]

VI. Nietzsche Against Scholarly Values

Nietzsche's commitment to Wagner allowed him to see himself as standing outside the culture of Socratic rationalism. Indeed, Nietzsche was beginning to see himself as beyond *all* culture, occupying an extra-moral perspective from which he could attack philology and historical scholarship. In an *Untimely Meditation* entitled *David Strauss, the Confessor and the Writer*, Nietzsche denounced Strauss for preaching a "New Faith" of scholarship that was inimical to life and to all creative human instincts. Nietzsche neglected to mention that he too had been a devotee of Strauss' *neuer Glaube*, and this may have accounted for his ad hominem and vitriolic tone.[69] Nietzsche claimed that Strauss expected modern human beings to find spiritual fulfillment in the pure effort to free themselves rationally from received opinion, and thus to become fully autonomous creatures. This, said Strauss, was the essence of humanity. But Nietzsche, armed with a historicist belief in the multiplicity of cultures, doubted that there *was* any single essence of humanity. Nietzsche argued that Strauss' imperative to "Live like a man" meant nothing, except perhaps that one should not live like "an ape or a seal." "Unfortunately," he wrote, "this injunction is totally inane and therefore utterly useless, since the concept of man encompasses such a multiplicity of types—from the Patagonian savage to Master Strauss."[70] Later, Nietzsche was to attack the "demand for 'humanization'" through scholarship as a deliberate fraud, "a tartuffery, behind which a quite definite type of man seeks to attain domination... ."[71] This was Nietzsche's critique of humanism in a nutshell.

Nietzsche had no objection to Strauss' call for a rational critique of received opinion. Although Nietzsche was not committed to

Strauss' Darwinism, he would (he said) have admired a rigorous effort to reveal the evolutionary—and therefore contingent—roots of "human kindness, love, compassion, and self-denial."[72] Nietzsche later praised "the unconquerably strong and tough virility of the great German philologists and critical historians (viewed properly, all of them were also artists of destruction and dissolution)... ."[73] But he criticized Strauss for failing to face the full subversive implications of his rationalist project. Above all, Strauss had failed to apply his critical method to the foundations of his own profession, classical scholarship. In other words, he had failed to ask whether there were reasons for rationality. Thus Strauss remained trapped within a culture—that of Socratic rationalism— even though he claimed to be critically detached from *all* cultural norms. From his vantage point beyond rationalism, Nietzsche expressed reservations about any culture that was dominated by knowledge—and especially historical knowledge—as opposed to myth and art:

> Culture is, above all, a unity of artistic style manifest in all the vital activities of a people. Vast knowledge and learning are neither the essential means to, nor even a sign of, culture; in fact, these generally accord much better with the opposite of culture, barbarism—the absence of style, or the chaotic confusion of all styles.[74]

The latter, of course, was what Nietzsche saw in contemporary German culture. "The modern German," he wrote, "amasses the shapes, colors, artifacts, and curiosities of all times and places, creating a motley carnival of culture, which scholars definitively regard as 'modern culture.'"[75] This "is not in fact a real culture," Nietzsche thought; it is "knowledge about culture."[76] Thus Strauss lacked the advantages of a traditional *Weltanschauung* (artistic style, for example), but he remained committed to scholarly values that were just as contingent. Nietzsche, on the other hand, had transcended *all* values and entered an extra-moral sphere.

Historical scholarship might have its own canon of values, including relativism, openness, and detachment; but the effect of these was to produce a "total lack of feeling for culture."[77] We "men of the 'historical sense,'" Nietzsche wrote, "also have our virtues, that cannot be denied: we are unpretentious, selfless, modest, courageous, full of self-overcoming, full of devotion, very grateful, very patient, very accommodating; but for all that we are not perhaps paragons of good taste."[78] These words applied perfectly to David

Strauss, as Nietzsche saw him. Nietzsche held that cultural relativism necessarily led to vicariousness and eclecticism, and that Strauss' "New Faith" was no spiritual match for art or naive faith. Discussing the relation between *Wissenschaft* and ascetic ideals in the *Genealogy of Morals*, Nietzsche wrote:

> Today there are plenty of modest and worthy laborers among scholars, too, who are happy in their little nooks; and because they are happy there, they sometimes demand rather immodestly that one ought to be content with things today, generally— especially in the domain of *Wissenschaft*, where so much that is useful remains to be done. I am not denying that; the last thing I want to do is to destroy the pleasure that these honest workers take in their craft; for I approve of their work. But that one works rigorously in the sciences and that there are contented workers certainly does not prove that *Wissenschaft* as a whole possesses a goal, a will, an ideal, or the passion of a great faith. The opposite is the case ...—*Wissenschaft* today is a hiding place for every kind of discontent, disbelief, gnawing worm, *despectio sui*, bad conscience—it is the unrest of the lack of ideals, the suffering from the lack of any great love, the discontent in the face of involuntary contentment.[79]

"Bad conscience" was a term that Nietzsche often used to describe scholars, who (insofar as they are "honest workers") feel a responsibility to take into account all relevant information and the views of all other scholars; to present evidence about the sources of their ideas; and to be forever uncertain about their views. Thus scholarship is conducive to a certain kind of morality—but precisely the kind which Nietzsche was to denounce. "The scholar is the herd animal in the realm of knowledge," he wrote. He "inquires because he is ordered to and because others have done so before him."[80] If someone should claim that a rigorous understanding of past cultures has improved people, Nietzsche wrote, then he would not argue—"only I should have to add what 'improved' signifies to me—the same thing as 'tamed,' 'weakened,' 'discouraged,' 'made refined,' 'made effete,' 'emasculated' (thus almost the same thing as *harmed*)."[81]

Nietzsche argued that, if the study of classical civilization according to traditional principles had a morally uplifting effect, then classical scholars should be admirable people. But he found instead that "our culture can only build on an utterly castrated and mendacious study of the classical world." And to "see ineffective this curriculum is," he wrote, "we need only glance at our classicists."[82] He compared them to the Greeks whom they studied by means of the following table:[83]

The Greeks	*The Classicists*
Pay homage to beauty	Are windbags and triflers
Develop the body	Are repulsive
Speak well	Stutter
Are religious transfigurers of ordinary things	Are filthy pedants
Are listeners and observers	Are hairsplitters and screech-owls
Are prone to symbolism	Are incapable of symbolism
Possess freedom as men	Are passionate slaves of the state
Have a pure outlook on the world	Are twisted Christians
Are intellectual pessimists	Are philistines

VII. The Philology of the Future

Thus Nietzsche's condemnation of his own profession was thorough. In his *Untimely Meditations,* he spelled out some of the characteristics of a "higher concept" of philology that he hoped would arise to sweep away the contemporary academic establishment. Most importantly, he argued that the philology of the future should match the Greeks' irrationalism, love of symbols, and propensity to simplify the world according to aesthetic principles with a similar *methodological* attitude. In other words, the methodology of the philologist should be unscientific, creative, aestheticizing and simplifying. The scholar of the future would not only study ancient culture dispassionately and objectively, but would follow the lead of Wagner, who

> has mastered the arts, the religions, and the various folk histories; yet he is the opposite of a polyhistor whose mind merely compiles and organizes; for he sculpts and breathes life into the material he has brought together, he simplifies the world.[84]

Modern, scholarly values such as consistency, objectivity and accuracy were inapplicable to the study of ancient culture. Objectivity was no virtue, for the "classicist castrated by objectivity, who ... dabbles in pure scholarship, is obviously a sorry spectacle."[85] Nor was it appropriate to use modern critical methods when looking at ancient art. Thus, for example, "Bentley summoned Horace before a tribunal which Horace would certainly have repudiated."[86]

Too much knowledge, too much *Wissenschaft*, would only serve to make the ancient world useless to us. Rational scholarship tended to break down stereotypes and holistic abstractions about distant cultures; it produced only piecemeal information in its effort to understand the past. But Nietzsche had a different objective. "Not to unloose the Gordian knot of Greek culture ..., leaving its ends to flutter in every direction; but rather to bind it again after it has been loosed—that is the present task." [87] "My method," Nietzsche wrote, "is to lose interest in single facts as soon as the wider horizon is visible... ."[88]   Later, he described the creative "will to mere appearance, to simplification, to masks, to cloaks, in short, to the surface," as the opposite of the attitude of science, "that sublime inclination of the seeker after knowledge who insists on profundity, multiplicity, and thoroughness, with a *will* which is a kind of cruelty of the intellectual conscience and taste."[89] Thus Nietzsche was willing to call the critical impulse of historians "sublime," if cruel. But *he* aimed instead at creative simplification. In 1870, Nietzsche had been pleased to tell Erwin Rohde that he was now approaching "a global vision of Greek antiquity, step by step, not without hesitation or surprises."[90] He was still thoroughly committed to the value of such holistic abstractions; and he was willing to invent them if they could not be sustained rationally. After all, his version of *Weltanschauung*-historicism depended on just such abstractions. And at about this time, the abstract categories of Dionysian and Apollonian art were developing in his mind.[91]

The history of classical philology in nineteenth-century Germany has been said to follow a tripartite scheme. First came the Romantic discovery of the Greeks as an ideal and striking contrast to the alienation of modernity. This was the achievement of the age of Schiller, Winckelmann and Hölderlin. But Romantic hellenism created an interest in every aspect of Greek civilization; and this interest could only be satisfied by a vast philological enterprise which gradually undermined any notion of "the Greeks" as an intelligible whole. Grand Romantic notions about Greek culture were replaced by learned monographs on esoteric subjects.[92] Following behind the "scholar poets," Nietzsche wrote, "plod the pure philologists," with their "nauseating erudition; lazy, passive indifference, nervous submission... ."[93] It was this situation that Nietzsche sought to address by deliberately creating new myths about the unity and perfection of Greek civilization, myths that would fall like a "cloak" over the incoherent mass of historical data unearthed by philology. But it is important to recognize that it was on these *frankly* irrational foundations that Nietzsche's *Weltanschauung*-historicist critique of truth rested. For his critique of truth depended, as I have said, on a notion of cultures as reified wholes; and his strongest example of such a culture, hellenism, could only be sustained by a deliberate effort to forget the historical facts.[94]

In suggesting that scholarship had created a spiritual problem for modern culture that could be solved only through the deliberate creation of all-encompassing myths, Nietzsche was following Lange and an entire school that Lange described in his *History of Materialism*—including Henrich Czolbe and Friedrich Ueberweg, both of whom Nietzsche read directly. These thinkers were all respectful of science and scholarship, which they credited with destroying Christianity and philosophical idealism, but to a greater or lesser degree they were also skeptical about the "facts of internal and external experience,"[95] and they believed that "truth" was a matter of convention. George Stack paraphrases Lange's proto-Nietzschean view of truth as follows: "Science does not discover 'Truth.' It is conventionalistic through and through, infiltrated by anthropomorphic notions, personifications, picturable entities and is built upon hypothetical foundations."[96] Lange and his allies argued that unadulterated *Wissenschaft* had a debilitating effect on modern culture and that it was an inadequate replacement for religion. Even granted that science could produce piecemeal truths about details of nature or history (which Lange doubted), it was certainly incapable of creating what Lange called *"ein großes Ideal."*[97] Lange argued that since truth was a matter of convention, it was the duty of philosophers to create uplifting myths that would serve as the accepted conventions of the future. These myths would have healthier effects than the modern devotion to science and materialism—although Lange sought myths that could not be *contradicted* by science. According to Stack, "Lange suggests that the need for a holistic *Welt-Bild* probably cannot be satisfied by science. Therefore, *Dichtung* must be joined to *Wissenschaft* in order to construct a view of the totality of actuality."[98] Similarly, even David Strauss had at one point called for a new form of pagan religion to supplement positivist science (although Nietzsche ignored this side of Strauss' teaching);[99] and Ueberweg demanded a *"neue religiöse Kraft"* and "a reunification of 'knowing, feeling and willing' that would be reflected in an ideal that would synthesize the theoretical, the ethical and the aesthetic."[100]

The heroes of Lange's *Geschichte des Materialismus* were all philosophers in the sense that Nietzsche meant when he *contrasted* philosophy and reason: philosophy's "feet are propelled by an alien, illogical power—the power of phantasy."[101] The tragic philosophers who lived before Socrates had known that "One must accept even illusion—therein lies the tragedy."[102] They had preferred grand metaphorical utterances (like Thales' "All is water") to empirical facts and the chimaera of scientific reason. Nietzsche's praise of the pre-Socratics as antirationalists paved the way for his early exercises in deliberate mythmaking and illusion: for example, his retelling of Greek history in terms of the Dionysian and Apollonian impulses. Like Lange's *"großes Ideal"*—or indeed like the doctrine of the Eternal Return—Nietzsche's aestheticized version of Greek history was probably intended to have enough empirical support to enable it to coexist with the findings of modern science. But at bottom it was an effort to transcend scholarship in the name of myth.[103]

Rational scholarship, Nietzsche thought, would destroy the Greeks as something useful to us. Greek civilization had been based upon a belief in "spirits, religious ritual, and the magical order of Nature," now undermined by science.[104] Nietzsche admitted that there "are numerous *vestigial* stages [of religious consciousness] surviving today, but these are already on the point of *collapsing*."[105] The modern rationalized world which was emerging from this collapse was superior to the Greek spirit in many ways. It was even morally superior—and here Nietzsche agreed with David Strauss:

> In natural and human history, we've surpassed the Greeks in *illuminating* the world; and our information is much greater, our judgment more moderate and accurate. Thanks moreover to the Enlightenment, a gentler humanity now prevails, which has *weakened* mankind—but this weakness, transformed into morality, looks very good and does us proud.... . [F]anaticism of opinion has become much milder.[106]

From the perspective of Socratic rationalism, the religious foundations of Greek civilization were now untenable. All such foundations, both "mythical and sociopolitical, have changed; our pretended culture has no stability because it's built on shaky, indeed already crumbling, conditions and beliefs.—So if we fully understand Greek culture, we see that it's gone for good."[107] Not only would scholarship reveal an unbridgeable gap between present and past; it would also show that there had been no such thing as "Greek culture" or "Hellas." Ancient Greek civilization comprised a vast diversity of perspectives held by speakers of a common (but evolving) language in many countries and situations during more than a millennium of intricate history. But this realization, although rationally supportable, would only weaken us by depriving us of "Greece" as a model for emulation. What was required, then, was not an accurate, objective—but castrating—depiction of Greek civilization in all its complexity and diversity, but rather a mythical, idealized vision of Greek life as a homogeneous, organic whole. The Greeks of the classical period had "become who they were" by inventing a concept of their own essential character which they held up as an ideal. That concept could now serve as a model for European civilization. But a revival of "Hellas" could not be achieved rationally or scientifically, for *Wissenschaft* would only make Greek culture appear plural and divided. It would have to be done creatively, aesthetically, with a simplifying vision and a heavy dose of symbolism: in other words, just the way Goethe and Wagner (to use Nietzsche's examples) had appropriated the past for their own creative purposes. These men were not Romantics, for they were neither naive about Greek culture nor did they hope sentimentally for its return. Instead they were "great men," creative geniuses, mythmakers, and the production of more people like them was Nietzsche's educational goal. "My hopes lie here," he wrote: "the training of significant men."[108]

VIII. Nietzsche's Critique of "Truth"

Thus Nietzsche hoped to see rationalist classical scholarship surpassed or even destroyed. The bitterness of his invective is difficult to convey, and it may have had partly personal motivations. But at the root of Nietzsche's attack on his profession was a philosophical position, articulated in his essay "On Truth and Lying in an Extra-Moral Sense." Here he argued that rationality was completely contingent and that any claims to objective truth were deeply mistaken. The most famous and influential claim in Nietzsche's essay was the following:

> What then is truth? A mobile army of metaphors, metonymies, anthropomorphisms: in short, a sum of human relations which were poetically and rhetorically heightened, transferred, and adorned, and after long use seem solid, canonical, and bind-ing to a nation. Truths are illusions about which it has been forgotten that they *are* illusions... .[109]

Complexes of metaphor seem true because they have become fixed for "a nation." Thus I think that Hollis and Lukes are right to point out that Nietzsche's "mobile army is a gang of local militias, each keeping order in its own province."[110] His insight that language is inadequate to express truth depends upon a recognition of radical cultural diversity and a commitment to the notion that each culture sees the world through a separate "conceptual scheme."

Nietzsche seemed to have unveiled a powerful and universally applicable argument against the distinction between truth and falsehood. He was careful to avoid using any arguments that could be considered attempts to make objective truth-claims. For example, he used the fiction of a prehistoric "social contract" to justify his argument that rationality was merely subjective— knowing that this would be taken as a metaphor and not a scientific hypothesis. Nevertheless, Nietzsche's early writings were littered with apparent truth-claims: about the Greeks, about modern Germany, about the diversity of cultures. Indeed, his argument against rationality seems to depend upon the allegedly objective fact that there are many incommensurable languages and world-views. It is one thing to claim in as many words that "truth" is meaningless; it is another thing to carry on with one's philosophical project, or even to defend this relativist position—without making any truth-claims. Thus Habermas argues that "the relativist is in the peculiar (and self-contradictory) position of arguing that his doctrine is somehow above the relativity of judgments he asserts exists in all other domains."[111]

But Nietzsche was not inconsistent in denying the truth-value of claims about the world, and then making such claims. First of all, Nietzsche can be construed as arguing that the truth-value of any statement is unknowable. This argument is not self-defeating; all we can conclude from it is that its own truth-value is permanently uncertain. Thus no one need believe it, but no one can declare it self-contradictory either. But more significantly, Nietzsche's philosophy after his transcendence of historicism constituted a statement made from *beyond* history, beyond culture, beyond truth and lie. Criteria like "consistency" were no longer applicable to his work in the normal way. Derrida says that in Nietzsche's writings, "opposition or contradiction no longer constitutes a law dictating prohibitions to thought. And that without dialectic."[112] Since all laws governing thought are cultural impositions, Nietzsche's thought is not so governed.

In his mature work (which began at the latest with *Human, All-Too-Human*),[113] Nietzsche directly faces the problem that the culturally contingent structures of grammar force us to make truth-claims, even when we say, for example, that all language "is" only metaphor which lacks an accurate relation to an objective world. Our language forces us to make implicit claims about allegedly objective things-in-themselves. For example, nothing "has a more naive power of persuasion than the error of being [*Sein*] ... it has every word, every sentence for it, whenever we speak!"[114] Nietzsche even feared "that we are not getting rid of God because we still believe in grammar... ."[115] Nietzsche no doubt realized that all of his claims appeared to be about truth, whereas "in fact" they were thoroughly metaphorical. As Derrida has written:

> We have no language—no syntax and no lexicon—which is foreign to ... history; we can pronounce not a single destructive proposition which has not already had to slip into the form, the logic, and the postulations of precisely what it seeks to contest.[116]

I think Nietzsche was aware of this problem. But he could not very well footnote every sentence of his *Werke* with the caveat: "this is solely a metaphor, created by a man who is beyond truth and lie." Instead, as both Nehamas and Derrida have argued, he constantly drew attention in his mature work to the fact that his claims were being uttered in the inadequate medium of language and within arbitrary grammatical structures, by making deliberate use of diverse styles, inconsistent arguments, and hyperbole— all of which served to remind the reader that the propositions he presented were not "true" in any objective sense, but were *his* creations and *his* utterances. Derrida claims that, for Nietzsche, "all statements, before and after, left and right, are at once possible (Nietzsche said it all, more or less) and necessarily contradictory (he said the most mutually incompatible things, and he said that he said them)."[117] And Nehamas adds: "Nietzsche uses his changing genres and styles in order to make his presence as an author literally unforgettable and in order to prevent his readers from overlooking the fact that his views necessarily originate with him."[118] Instead of announcing "the truth," Nietzsche announces what is true *for him*; and even this much is plural and often self-contradictory. For example, he writes that he will "state a few truths about 'women as such'—assuming that it is now known from the outset how very much these are after all only—*my* truths."[119] So, writes Nehamas, by "the strange artifice of calling his views true, Nietzsche underscores their deeply personal and idiosyncratic nature, the fact that they are his own interpretations."[120] Nietzsche even provides a clue to his method in a section of *Ecce Homo* where he explains "Why I Write Such Excellent Books." Here he calls attention to the diversity of his styles and the crucial importance of this diversity to the content of his philosophy: "I am capable," he says, "of many kinds of style—in short, of the most varied art of style that any man has ever had at his disposal."[121] It is this means of expression that makes Nietzsche's irrationalism so "excellent," so superior to most of its successors.

But in my view, there was one set of propositions which Nietzsche did *at one point* hold to be universally valid, and these were propositions concerning the relativity of conceptual schemes and the consequent inadequacy of language to represent truth. He came to these conclusions very early in his life—surely before he had begun to use exaggerated style as a *deliberate* means to undermine the apparent truth-value of his own language. Thus his early works on historicism should not be read as deliberately or self-consciously nonobjective; describing historicism and its self-destructive turn, Nietzsche believed that he was saying something true. Later, of course, he could re-read his own early comments about relativism as themselves thoroughly metaphorical; he could view them from an extra-cultural perspective. But this kind of perspectivist insight had to begin somewhere; there had to be some motivation for a young philologist who believed very strongly in truth to turn against his discipline. Nietzsche's hyperbolic and eccentric use of style goes back to his childhood, long before he could have conceived of a perspectivist philosophy. Therefore, it seems likely to me that *after* he had come to the conclusion that truth and lies were identical, he gradually discovered that his own diverse literary styles could be used deliberately to help him avoid making truth-claims in the "naive" way that most people do. In a note written in 1887, Nietzsche remarked:

> *On the genesis of the nihilist.*—It is only late that one musters the courage for what one really knows. That I have hitherto been a thorough-going nihilist, I have admitted to myself only recently: the energy and radicalism with which I advanced as a nihilist deceived me about this basic fact.[122]

Nihilism meant many things to Nietzsche—among them the death of God—but above all it meant the view that there was "nothing" except metaphor, the play of language, perspective and the vantage points of the historically situated viewer. But all of this depended upon the insight that every truth-claim is entirely immanent in a particular culture and language—and Nietzsche's reasons for adopting this position were weaker than he thought. He derived his nihilism from the notion that humans must be irrationally and totally committed to a holistic *Weltanschauung* that they call their culture, if they are to think at all. Moreover, Nietzsche's position depended on the view that such *Weltanschauungen* are plural and mutually incommensurable. Only once Nietzsche had adopted perspectivism and moved on, carried by "his energy and radicalism," did he construct his consistent attitude towards metaphor and style ("consistent" insofar as he unceasingly flouted such conventional values as consistency). But consistent as it might be, his mature perspectivism lacked the *raison d'être* that he had originally thought it to have; it derived from a faulty paradigm for culture.

So far, I have only criticized Nietzsche's original means of entry into what later became a consistent position. But consistency is not the only criterion for assessing a philosophical view; we also want to know whether what appeared to be the case to Nietzsche should seem to be the case to us. It is certainly true that the mature Nietzsche did not want to preach his version of perspectivism, or offer reasons for accepting it. "This—is now *my* way," says Zarathustra: "Where is yours?" And he adds, "*The* way—does not exist."[123] The mature Nietzsche believes in many things, but he does not believe in giving reasons for them. "'Why?' said Zarathustra, 'You ask why? I am not one of those who can be asked about their Why.'"[124] But a philosophical position is of little interest to us unless it makes a claim on our belief. Speaking of "The Higher Men," Zarathustra remarks, "I am a law only for my own, I am not a law for all."[125] Yet those who agree with Zarathustra are defined as "higher," so Nietzsche does seem to make at least a rhetorical effort to entice us to agree with him. Nietzsche even calls Zarathustra a "seducer."[126] One way for us to accept Nietzsche's philosophical insights would be to use the same point of entry into his mature thought that he had taken. In 1867 he wrote, "I try to stimulate in the reader the same sequence of thoughts that suggested themselves to me so spontaneously and so forcefully."[127] Yet the path that he took into nihilism—his analysis of *Weltanschauung*-historicism and its contradictions—was not as convincing as he thought it was.

But apart from any turning of historicism against itself, Nietzsche rejected "truth" partly because he could imagine no absolute, nonlinguistic standard by which to judge truth versus falsity. Habermas admits that any attack on the absolute "standard of right perception" is well-taken, for the "absolutist cannot call upon another First Principle to secure the status of the doctrine of First Principles."[128] However, Nietzsche's stance revealed a naive view of what constitutes rationality—his view was that a statement *had* to be grounded absolutely in order for it to be considered rational.

The alternative would be to judge the rationality of a statement not by assessing its immediate relation to truth, but by analyzing the way in which it is offered. Habermas states the problem thus:

> if the validity of arguments can be neither undermined in an empiricist manner nor grounded in an absolutist manner, then we are faced with precisely those questions to which the logic of argumentation is supposed to provide the answers: How can problematic validity claims be supported by good reasons? How can reasons be criticized in turn? What makes some arguments, and thus some reasons, which are related to validity claims in a certain way, stronger or weaker than other arguments?[129]

Habermas adopts an evolutionary approach to objective knowledge, arguing that progress can gradually be achieved in our efforts to describe the world, although absolute standards of truth may not be attainable. Nietzsche argued that hopes for absolute truth were bound to be disappointing. There was no transparent thing-in-itself against which to compare our beliefs; and the history of thought revealed a series of arbitrary ideas, each of which could be traced in large part to the contingencies of the age. However, the goal of absolute truth is Nietzsche's own straw man, and is not actually held by many traditional humanists, who believe rather in a continuous, collective search for truth. Indeed, in 1888, Nietzsche admitted that "the old philologist says, speaking out of the whole philological experience: there is no One Redeeming [alleinseligmachende] interpretation... ."[130] Claims made by humanists are held to be criticizable—not by comparison to some concept of the thing-in-itself, or the text-in-itself—but by an analysis of the methods with which these claims are offered. And certain kinds of method can be justified as more pragmatically effective than others: they contribute to a dialogue in which perspectives are shared and broadened. Thus, it is possible to uncover in the continuous and collective work of humanists over the centuries some of the "presumably universal bases of rational experience and judgment, as well as of action and linguistic communication."[131] For example, according to Toulmin, Rieke, and Janik, one universal criterion of rationality might be "openness":

> Anyone participating in argument shows his rationality or lack of it by the manner in which he handles and responds to the offering of reasons for or against claims. If he is 'open' to argument, he will either acknowledge the force of those rea-

sons or seek to reply to them, and either way he will deal
with them in a 'rational' manner.[132]

In his early theoretical works, Nietzsche was attempting to
free himself from the demands of a rational attitude—for example,
the presentation of empirical evidence to back up claims, the use of
footnotes, the mention of opposing points of view—because, he felt,
such an attitude would destroy the Greeks, would give him a permanent
"bad conscience," and would be inimical to life. Wilamowitz was to
say about Nietzsche's *Birth of Tragedy*:

> the main indictment against the book lies in its tone and
> inclination [*Ton und Tendenz*].... . For Herr Nietzsche does
> not proceed as a scientific researcher: by intuition he gathers
> wisdom which he presents partly in the style of the pulpit,
> partly quite *raisonnement*, and partly in a journalistic man-
> ner appropriate only in daily newspapers.[133]

According to Wilamowitz, Nietzsche lacked above all a rational
attitude, and this was more damning than any specific mistakes
that Nietzsche might have made. But Nietzsche defended his
renunciation of rationality in the sphere of classical scholarship by
suggesting that rationality was self-destroying anyway: it had produced
Weltanschauung-historicism, which in turn revealed the contingency
of all forms of reasoning. However, Nietzsche did not allow for the
possibility that his empirical understanding of the world as containing
multiple discrete cultures—so necessary as a foundation for his
deconstructive project—might be false or unintelligible, or might
later have to be amended in the light of new evidence. This attitude
of allowing for criticism is a crucial ingredient of rationality.
Therefore, it seems that Nietzsche was not, in fact, allowing rationality
to deconstruct itself; rather, he was allowing his own dogmatic
truth-claims to destroy their own foundations—and so much the
better for *Wissenschaft*.[134]

Part Two
Dionysus Versus The Crucified

Have I been understood?—*Dionysus versus the Crucified.* —

Ecce Homo, 'Why I am a Destiny,' 9

Chapter 5

The Birth of Tragedy

I. Nietzsche Leaves the University

During the five years after he met Wagner, Nietzsche continued to teach classics at the University of Basel, as well as at the local Pädagogium. Therefore, he was apparently still a classical philologist. However, during this time he produced a substantial piece of work on Greek civilization, *The Birth of Tragedy*, in which he demonstrated by example a radically new form of philology. In May of 1872, Wilamowitz published a scathing critique of Nietzsche's *Birth of Tragedy*; here he attempted to defend traditional philological methods by subjecting Nietzsche's claims to rational counter-arguments. In 1872, Nietzsche wrote to his friend Erwin Rohde: "It seems that the establishment has pronounced a sentence of death over me. But do they have the power to kill me?—this I doubt."[1] Still, by 1876, Nietzsche had lost interest in teaching philology, and on February 7 of that year, he taught his last class at Basel. Six years later, he wrote in *Thus Spake Zarathustra*:

> As I lay sleeping, a sheep ate at the ivy-wreath on my head,—it ate, saying: 'Zarathustra is no longer a scholar.'
> It said this, and went away clumsily and proudly.
> A child told me.

I like to lie here where the children play, beside the ruined wall, under thistles and red poppies.

A scholar am I still to the children, and also to the thistles and red poppies. Innocent are they, even in their evil.

But to the sheep [plural] I am no longer a scholar: thus my fate wills—blessings upon it!

For this is the truth: I have departed from the house of the scholars, and the door I have slammed behind me ....

Thus spake Zarathustra.[2]

The sheep are Nietzsche's colleagues; the proud and clumsy one is Wilamowitz. The slamming of the door was the publication of Nietzsche's attacks on traditional classical education. But was Nietzsche right to abandon humanistic scholarship for the thistles and the red poppies beyond?

II. Dionysus and Apollo

For several months after its publication in 1872, *The Birth of Tragedy* received no serious attention. Then in May 1872, Wilamowitz released his hostile pamphlet, and the famous quarrel began. In the book, Nietzsche outlined a comprehensive version of Greek history, relying heavily on his categories of the Dionysian and the Apollonian, which, he said, "in new births ever following and augmenting one another, controlled the Hellenic genius ...."[3] Greek civilization, Nietzsche claimed, emerged out of a Dionysian (i.e., natural and anarchic) state, with the imposition of Apollonian ordering principles, law and moderation. The Dionysian sphere was extra- or precultural; it corresponded to the precontractual state of nature that Nietzsche had imagined in his essay on "Truth and Lying," a state in which each person's perspective was unique, and no rules existed to limit thought or action. Nietzsche was still heavily under the influence of Schopenhauer, so he described the Dionysian sphere in terms of willing, suffering and Heraclitean flux. The Apollonian sphere, on the other hand, corresponded to the arbitrary rules that constituted a culture. The first civilized Greeks, the Apollonians of Homer's day, had distinguished their culture from both a pre-Apollonian age—the mythical period of the Titans—and an extra-Apollonian sphere—that of the barbarians. Following Schiller, Nietzsche calls Homeric Greece a culture of "naïve splendor."[4] But whereas Schiller defined naive art as a completely unself-conscious form of expression, rooted in an unquestioning belief in gods and myth, Nietzsche held that the achievement of naive Homeric culture was deliberate and significant. The Homeric, Apollonian artist, Nietzsche argued, had "triumphed over an abysmal and terrifying view of the world ... through recourse to the most forceful and pleasurable illusions."⁵ Homer and his contemporaries had escaped from the horrors of a state of nature, with its "titanic powers,"⁶ through the creation of *art*, and specifically through the deliberate aestheticization of their most horrible Dionysian memories, which took the form, in their poetry, of tragic myths and heroes: above all, Prometheus, Oedipus and Orestes. The beautiful poetry of Homeric Greece was an attempt to make suffering—which is "primal and eternal, the sole ground of the world"⁷—palatable; thus Homeric myths were related to the torments of a Dionysian state "as the rapturous vision of the tortured martyr to his suffering."⁸

Thus culture was initially created by means of an apparently deliberate illusion. In that case, why call it "naive" at all? Schiller had contrasted naive art with sentimental attempts to return to a mythical world view no longer held sincerely. Thus, unlike naive culture, a sentimental *Weltanschauung* was historically conscious, in Schiller's view, since it contrasted modernity against a distant, innocent past.⁹ Nietzsche suggested that Homeric artists had produced their illusions deliberately and consciously, with a full awareness of the Dionysian chaos that lay behind them: the "tragic myth is to be understood only as a symbolization of Dionysian wisdom through Apollinian [sic] artifices."¹⁰ Nevertheless, Nietzsche maintained that the pre-Socratic Greeks lacked the *historical* self-consciousness that is born when a society examines its own cultural institutions in the light of some extracultural standard—either a priori truths, or the myths and mores of other civilizations. Thus the Greeks *were* naive, but only insofar as they lacked the modern historical sense. They felt "impelled to relate all their experiences immediately to their myths .... Thus even the immediate present had to appear to them *sub species aeterni* and in a certain sense as timeless."¹¹ Homeric society epitomized what Nietzsche later called "master morality"; and in any master morality, the "noble type of man experiences *itself* as determining values; it judges, 'what is harmful to me is harmful in itself'; it knows itself to be that which first accords honor to things; it is *value-creating*."¹² By arguing that the Greeks were deliberate artists and creative lawgivers, Nietzsche could deny that he was engaged in a sentimental adulation of an innocent past; he could claim that he had begun a radically new kind of project. But the Greeks he advocated imitating were defined above all by their lack of the "historical sense"; they universalized their own perspective without compunction, not recognizing that any legitimate alternatives could possibly exist. Thus Nietzsche's project in the *Birth of Tragedy* still resembled to some degree the Romantics' efforts to return to a naive past—as Nietzsche himself was later to admit.

III. Dionysus and the Crucified

Since the Dionysian impulse is extracultural and universal, it negates cultural differences and produces similar effects throughout history. Thus Nietzsche compares the "singing dancers" of St. John and St. Vitus in the German Middle Ages with the "Bacchic Choruses of the Greeks, with their prehistory in Asia Minor, as far back as Babylon and the orgiastic Sacaea."[13] As one begins to approach the Dionysian sphere, Nietzsche writes, "all the rigid, hostile barriers that necessity, caprice, or 'impudent convention' have fixed between man and man are broken." The "veil of *maya* [is] torn aside and [is] now merely fluttering in tatters before the mysterious primordial unity."[14] In the state of nature, without the arbitrary conventions that allow people to make logical or moral distinctions, there is no *principium individuationis*, and all is One: a single flux of willing and suffering.

Nietzsche was to conclude his last book, *Ecce Homo*, with the enigmatic question: "Have I been understood? Dionysus versus the Crucified."[15] Any effort to decode this phrase is likely to be reductive and unsatisfying, but it is worth noting that Dionysus, for Nietzsche, was the apostle of extrahistorical forces—of nature— whereas the crucified Son of Man represented God's incarnation as a historical individual. Nietzsche, as the disciple of Dionysus, as the Antichrist, was above all interested in overcoming the historicity of modern life: the historical fixation of the West which had arisen, in part, because of the Judeo-Christian emphasis on narrative and history. Nietzsche was anti-Christian for many reasons, but above all because he rejected the world-narrative that centered on the crucifiction, a historical event. The Christian "historical sense"— apparent still in Hegel—made history central to life and treated it optimistically; it viewed events as meaningful only insofar as they contributed to the grand narrative of redemption. Nietzsche could not have been further opposed to this development, for he opposed the "historical sense" in any form, and loathed the additional trimmings of Christian historicism: optimism, eschatology and totalizing, metaphysical descriptions of the world. Christianity was a great historical religion, but its emphasis on history had led

ultimately to the discovery of the contingency of all beliefs. Thus
God had died not at Calvary, but in the archives and journals of
the modern historical scholar.[16] Dionysus was Nietzsche's figure
for the revolt against history in both its Christian and post-
Christian forms. But Nietzsche was a "believer" in historicism as
well as its enemy, and he derived from it the tragic fact of nihilism,
which he felt profoundly. Thus Nietzsche was also a victim of history—
he was the Crucified. In short, he was Dionysus *versus* the
Crucified, Nietzsche *contra* Nietzsche.[17]

To make matters even more complicated, it is important to
remember that Dionysus was, in a way, the Crucified: he was the
one Greek god who had been sacrificed and risen from the dead.
Meanwhile, Nietzsche sometimes describes Jesus in terms that
make him sound explicitly "beyond culture" and Dionysian;
Nietzsche even calls him a "free spirit."[18] Despite St. Paul's appropriation of Jesus as a teacher of life after death, the real Son of
Man was actually more or less interchangeable with Dionysus:

> such a symbolist *par excellence* stands outside all religion, all
> cult concepts, all history, all natural science, all experience of the
> world, all knowledge, all politics, all psychology, all books, all
> art—his "knowledge" is *pure foolishness* about the fact that
> such things exist. *Culture* is not known to him even by
> hearsay, it is not necessary for him to fight it—he does not
> deny it.[19]

So, as parablist and savior, Jesus does not even struggle
against culture; he is utterly beyond it. His attitude towards the
standards of his own civilization, embodied in Jewish Law, is one
of indifference; Nietzsche imagines him saying "What are morals
to us sons of God!"[20] Nor does Jesus endorse Christianity as a permanent new culture of his own creation. "What does Jesus *deny*?"
asks Nietzsche: "Everything that is today called Christian."[21]
Jesus was, Nietzsche thought, so far beyond culture as to make "no
distinction between foreigner and native, between Jew and non-Jew....
At no one is he angry, he disdains no one."[22] On the other hand,
Jesus can also be read as a sacrificial lamb on the altar of history,
subservient to his Father's will and bound to the preordained
course of world history. Interpreted thus, Jesus is far removed
from a Dionysian, intoxicated ignorance of culture, an existence
Beyond Good and Evil. It is this historical *interpretation* of Jesus'
role that makes him into the Crucified, and Nietzsche into an anti-
Christian [*Antichrist*]. But since fact "is precisely what there is

not, only interpretations,"[23] Nietzsche's Dionysian Jesus is no more
or less real than the "historical" Jesus of St. Paul and Hegel.
Thus the struggle between culture and extracultural forces goes on
within Dionysus and Jesus, just as it goes on between them and
within their disciple, Nietzsche.[24]

IV. The Greek Synthesis

Nietzsche was later to adopt the persona of Dionysus and to drop
Apollo from his mythical cosmology; but in *The Birth of Tragedy*,
he described and propounded a synthesis of Dionysian and Apollonian
impulses. The wave of Dionysian frenzy that overwhelmed post-
Homeric Greece, he wrote, would have led to nothing but "that horrible
mixture of sensuality and cruelty which has always seemed to me to be
the real 'witches brew.'"[25] But Dionysus was cheated of a complete
victory over civilization, as "the figure of Apollo, rising full of pride,
held out the Gorgon's head to this grotesquely uncouth Dionysian
power...."[26] The result was Doric culture: a stern, militarist spirit dedicated
to waging an unceasing war against Dionysian barbarism.[27]

At this point in his retelling of Greek history, Nietzsche
claims that a second synthesis of the Dionysian and Apollonian
arose to rival Homer's creation of beautiful images out of suffering
and strife. This was folk song—so important to the early German
Romantics—which, according to Nietzsche, originated in its literary
form with the poet Archilochus. Homer's art, as an art of illusion,
was essentially Apollonian; but Archilochus was Dionysian.
He created a first-person protagonist who was a "passionately
inflamed, loving, and hating man...."[28] But the real Archilochus
was the detached artist who created this Dionysian character as
his own illusion. In other words, he acted as an Apollonian image-
creator with a Dionysian spirit.

In elaborating on this view of lyric poetry, Nietzsche felt "impelled
to [state] the metaphysical assumption" that beneath everything
there is an *Ur-Eine*—"the truly existent primal unity"—which is
itself an artistic creator of images, so that even the Dionysian
world of nature or empirical reality—the realm of "perpetual
becoming in space, time, and causality"—is only an illusion.[29]
Thus Archilochus was a Dionysian creator of images, but himself
only an image created by the "primal unity" whose existence
Nietzsche postulated. In the light of what I said in the last chapter
about Nietzsche's attitude towards "truth," it seems likely that his
"metaphysical impulse" was actually a desire to create an illusion
of his own, a noble *"großes Ideal"* which, as Lange had hoped,

would "unhinge reality."[30] Positing the existence of a primal world-
artist allowed Nietzsche to claim, famously, that "it is only as an
aesthetic phenomenon that existence and the world are eternally
justified...." [31] But Nietzsche himself had created this image of the
primordial image-creator, the *Ur-Eine*, and had thereby revealed
his own project to be the production of a transfiguring "aesthetic
phenomenon" that would justify the world "eternally"—that is,
beyond all the contingencies of culture and historical change.

Using arrows to denote a process of artistic creation, Nietzsche's
"metaphysical" interpretation of the Apollonian art of Homer could
be diagrammed as follows:

Ur-Eine ➤ human beings and their world ➤ art

Thus the *Ur-Eine* "creates" the empirical world, including the poet,
Homer, who then creates art and culture. But the *Ur-Eine* itself is
an artistic creation of Nietzsche's, a product not of his will to
truth, but of his "will to mere appearance, to simplification, to
masks, to cloaks...."[32] In dreaming up this supremely metaphysical
entity, Nietzsche was "propelled by an alien, illogical power—
the power of phantasy."[33] Thus the above diagram could be redrawn
as follows:

Nietzsche ➤ *Ur-Eine* ➤ human beings ➤ art[34]

Archilochus and his folk songs heralded a change in this
"metaphysical" scheme. Describing Archilochus, Nietzsche
returned to the themes of his essay on music and words. Music, he
wrote, "symbolizes a sphere which is beyond and prior to all phenomena."[35]
Thus, as in Schopenhauer's system, music and the thing-in-itself
(Nietzsche's *Ur-Eine*) are all but identical. But in the poetry of
Archilochus, the primal unity of music spins out images and
metaphors that symbolize and imitate the basic, unindividuated
"stuff" of harmony. Since Archilochus had identified himself with
the *Ur-Eine* as a creator of Dionysian images, he had become identical
to music. But while Archilochus was uniting himself with music,
he was also creating a literary character which was his image.
Lyric poets like Archilochus therefore simultaneously fulfilled the
roles of *Ur-Eine* and image, creative will and representation, and
thus bypassed one stage in the above diagram. We now have a picture
something like this:

Nietzsche ➤ poets/musicians ➤ literary characters

But the whole of Nietzsche's work is merely a presentation of *his* visions and creations. Nietzsche "creates" a vision of Archilochus, for example, without any substantial reference to so-called historical facts. Thus Nietzsche already wanted his philosophy to be read as self-expression, rather than transcendent truth. Out of the void of nihilism, he made the existential choice to create something beautiful. He is both a poet/musician and his own literary character. In the last analysis, the "metaphysics" of *The Birth of Tragedy* can therefore be reduced to a single word: "Nietzsche."

Nietzsche's description of Greek lyric sets the stage for the emergence of tragedy, which he says, also grew out of music, and specifically out of the singing chorus, which was "the symbol of a whole excited Dionysian throng"[36]—the audience. The chorus was "a vision of the Dionysian mass of spectators,"[37] just as the stage and its setting was a vision of the chorus. By identifying with the chorus, the individual member of the audience "sees himself as satyr, and as a satyr, he sees the god...."[38] The god, in turn, is Dionysus, but it is Dionysus seen in the form of an Apollonian image created by the chorus, and so, vicariously, by the audience. "That he [Dionysus] appears at all with such epic precision and clarity is the work of the dream-interpreter, Apollo, who through this symbolic appearance interprets to the chorus its Dionysian state."[39] Nietzsche claims that in early Greek tragedy, "the only stage hero was Dionysus himself,"[40] and that even later on, all the protagonists were veiled versions of the god. However, as protagonists appearing on the stage, they were, like Homeric heroes, Apollonian. Thus a synthesis of the Apollonian and the Dionysian took place in tragedy whenever the audience identified itself with the chorus. This synthesis was further aided by the fact that the audience as a whole, arrayed in a "terraced structure of concentric arcs,"[41] and busily creating Apollonian images on the stage, itself served as an image for each individual audience member to contemplate as if he were outside of culture observing it as a Dionysian chorist. The characters on the stage, meanwhile, were Apollonian images, but represented Dionysus in the form of both good and evil characters: i.e., in his "dual nature of a cruel, barbarized demon [Dionysian] and a mild, gentle ruler [Apollonian]."[42]

All this is too complicated to diagram, but suffice it to say that Nietzsche had tried to describe an enviable synthesis of nature and culture, individuation and wholeness, reality and illusion, author and audience, which he thought took place in Greek tragedy.

This was based in part on an overtly metaphysical scheme. But Nietzsche surely cannot have meant to offer his metaphysics in the same spirit that most philosophers after Socrates had: i.e., as a hypothesis about the objective world, arrived at by means of observation and dialectic. Rather, Nietzsche's metaphysics was overtly metaphorical. This was to be expected, since he believed that all truth-claims were metaphors; but it did not imply that he took his scheme lightly. "For a genuine poet," he wrote, "metaphor is not a rhetorical figure but a vicarious image that he actually beholds in place of a concept."[43] Thus Nietzsche, the would-be artist and image-creator, was holding up a beautiful and intricately detailed metaphysical scheme for the reader to behold. Perhaps this scheme reflected a deeper musical force that lay beneath it and that could be identified with its creator, Nietzsche, just as Archilochus the poet had been identified with the spirit of music. But even if such a relation existed, it was necessarily a relation of imperfect imitation or symbolism; and it would therefore be impossible to describe the *Ur-Eine* below, at least in words. Thus, rather than analyze the historical phenomena which were being described or symbolized by his prose, Nietzsche wanted us to revel in the symbolism and metaphor per se, to take pleasure in the illusory world that he had created. In this way, the prophesies of Schiller and Lange could be fulfilled; scholarship would be superseded by art.[44]

Thus Nietzsche's extraordinary text set forth an account of the origins of tragedy—although not one which was meant to be taken as positivist history. Immediately thereafter, he also set forth an account of the *death* of tragedy. More specifically, he claimed that tragedy died as a result of the rise of humanism, especially as this new anti-Hellenic movement was embodied in the persons of Euripides and Socrates. I have said that Sophism can be described as a Greek antecedent of Renaissance humanism; and Nietzsche describes Euripides as the quintessential Sophist, from whom "the people have learned how to observe, debate, and draw conclusions according to the rules of art and with the cleverest sophistries."[45] Euripides was also a democrat, according to Nietzsche, with typically humanist ambitions to educate the masses for citizenship. Nietzsche claims that Euripides, although a democrat, undoubtedly felt himself "superior to the people in general."[46] But Euripides only differed from the people in one way: "he did not comprehend tragedy and therefore did not esteem it."[47] Instead, he held the plots and morals of traditional myths up to the critical eye of reason; and furthermore, he "brought the spectator onto the stage in order to make him [also] truly competent to pass judgment."[48] Euripides' plays dealt with wild, irrational subjects, but he always held these subjects up to the cool light of reason, and, like Brecht, attempted to break down the audience's irrational identification with the protagonists by means of deliberate improbabilities of plot, such as the *deus ex machina*. Euripides also produced a Brechtian alienation effect by giving away the whole plot in the prologue—a device that he invented. With his keen eye for psychology, Nietzsche detected a hint of superiority in the spirit of humanists who, like Euripides, criticize popular beliefs and natural impulses, and attempt to educate the people to think as they do. Euripides, furthermore, was guilty of fighting a lifelong battle against Dionysus and of replacing Apollonian illusion with "cool, paradoxical thoughts."[49] In his struggles against both Apollo and Dionysus, Euripides was personally unsuccessful and ended his life in suicide; but the baton of rationality and humanism was picked up by the one humanist of truly god-like powers, Socrates, for whom Euripides had only been a mouthpiece all along.

Nietzsche accepts Aristophanes' portrait of Socrates "as the first and supreme Sophist, as the mirror and epitome of all sophistical tendencies."[50] Despite the arguments of the Platonic Socrates against the notion that virtue is teachable, Nietzsche holds that "Socratic philosophy is absolutely practical.... *It is for all and popular: for it holds virtue to be teachable.*"[51] Thus Nietzsche considered Socrates to be the originator of the process of rational moral education that Nietzsche had himself encountered at Pforta. But Socrates' criteria for good and evil were not to be found in the traditions and past achievements of his culture; rather they were (allegedly) universal and objective:

> What, then, is the significance of the reaction of Socrates, who recommended dialectics as the road to virtue and made mock when morality did not know how to justify itself logically?—As if this were not part of its virtue—without unconsciousness it is no good —
> ... *In praxi*, this means that moral judgments are torn from their conditionality, in which they have grown and alone possess any meaning, from their Greek and Greek-political ground and soil, to be denaturalized under the pretense of sublimation.[52]

Thus, Nietzsche thought that Socrates' search for ahistorical moral criteria was misguided. Socrates was also the founder of the urge to reform reality by comparing it to intellectual ideals: like all humanists, Nietzsche wrote, he "conceives it to be his duty to correct existence...."[53] Nietzsche found this goal equally foolish. Moreover, Nietzsche claimed that the real ideal of modern civilization was not Socrates or Socratism but the Death of Socrates: that is, rationality having completed its task after fully understanding and shaping the world. But Nietzsche treats this ideal ironically, since, he says, "we see clearly how after Socrates, the mystagogue of science, one philosophical school succeeds the other, wave upon wave," each one claiming to explain the world, and each one failing in the eyes of the succeeding age.[54] As in his *Untimely Meditations*, Nietzsche was here standing outside of the history of science and contemplating it with irony. His claim that "logic... finally bites its own tail"[55] summarizes his arguments in the essay *On Truth and Lying* about the relativity of modern rationality—arguments that were allegedly derived by rational means. Thus, says Nietzsche, Socrates showed "divine naïveté"[56] in creating a New Faith of science which stood on weak foundations; science was inevitably speeding towards its own shipwreck;[57] and Lessing could be considered "the most honest theoretical man," since he alone "dared to announce that he cared more for the search after truth than for truth itself—and thus revealed the fundamental secret of science."[58]

Nietzsche revered Socrates as a figure comparable to two gods, Apollo and Dionysus. His "driving-wheel of logical Socratism" had even been powerful enough to send these gods into retreat.[59] But in 1886, Nietzsche was ready to claim explicitly what he had hinted at in *The Birth of Tragedy*: Socrates himself had been aware of the provisional and limited nature of knowledge; he had been aware that even science was a "subtle last resort against truth."[60] Indeed, this knowledge was the crowning glory of Socrates' genius. Socrates' *daimon* had always spoken up to dissuade him from making the kind of (Nietzschean) argument which is intended to undercut the very foundations of rationality. But in his last days, Socrates had a dream-vision which told him to practice music and write a prelude to Apollo. This led Nietzsche to conclude that even Socrates knew that "there is a realm from which the logician is exiled," and that art is "a necessary correlative of, and supplement for science."[61] Later, Nietzsche was to hypothesize that Socrates had secretly *wanted* to die because he had realized that the spirit of pure dialectic, which he embodied, was inadequate and dangerous.[62] Thus what culture needed, according to Nietzsche, was a new synthesis of art and science, a solace for the logician who has watched science bite its own tail, the whole ensemble created by an "artistic Socrates."[63]

Wagner had called for a deliberate, aesthetically motivated appropriation of all the art and culture of the past that is known to us through historical science. Nietzsche too had advocated the transformation of history into art. Now, in *The Birth of Tragedy*, the rational philologist Nietzsche—a child of Socrates—was creatively reinterpreting the findings of his profession in order to make the past serve the future in a beautiful and constructive way. Who then was this "artistic Socrates"? It was Hans Sachs, cited in Section I of *The Birth of Tragedy* as a creative interpreter of dreams. It was Wagner, who had sought to "soar to the free manhood of art" by means of "conscious musical doings."[64] But above all, it was Nietzsche, as the creator of an artistic work of philology, *The Birth of Tragedy*.

V. Nietzsche's Repudiation of *The Birth of Tragedy*

Wagner had attempted to avoid the perils of Romanticism, but today his appropriation of primitive Germanic culture appears typically Romantic, based as it was on a sentimental aestheticization of a naive culture. In the same way, by 1886, Nietzsche was ready to denounce his own first book as Romantic through and through. Despite his disclaimers about the barbarity of the Greeks, he had idealized them and made them a direct inspiration for the present. The Greeks, he had written, "as charioteers, hold in their hands the reins of our own and every other culture, but ... almost always chariot and horses are of inferior quality and not up to the glory of their drivers...."[65] Thus Nietzsche had lacked "the strength ... to shatter and disintegrate the past"; he had failed to live up to his own call to bring "the past before a tribunal, interrogating it carefully, and in the end condemning it."[66] In *The Birth of Tragedy*, moreover, he had expressed a typically Romantic "hatred against 'the Now,' against 'reality' and 'modern ideas'," which may have sprung, in part, from his own youthful, Werther-like alienation and *ressentiment*.[67] Instead of acting as a superhistorical "free spirit," he had embroiled himself in a criticism of his age. In *The Gay Science*, Nietzsche wrote that the

> human being of such a beyond [i.e., the super-historical individual] who wants to behold the supreme measures of value of his time must first of all "overcome" this time in himself—this is the test of his strength—and consequently

not only his time but his prior aversion and contradiction *against* this time, his suffering from this time, his un-timelyiness, his *romanticism*.[68]

This Nietzsche had manifestly failed to do. Moreover, with a typically Romantic optimism about the revolutionary capacities of art, he had "appended hopes where there was no ground for hope, where everything pointed all too plainly to an end."[69] In particular, he had been optimistic about German culture and German music, which he now denounced as romantic, un-Greek, intoxicating, and "a first-rate poison for the nerves."[70] His own style and substance in the *Birth of Tragedy*, he now claimed, had been a mirroring—not of the timeless *Ur-Eine*—but of decadent Romantic German music. The main ingredients of Nietzsche's mature philosophy—genealogy, the Eternal Return, the *Übermensch, amor fati*—would all serve as more satisfactory, "existential," post-Romantic alternatives to the arguments of *The Birth of Tragedy*, as I will argue in the following chapters.

VI. Wilamowitz Contra Nietzsche

Notwithstanding his later criticisms, *The Birth of Tragedy* did give a powerful, substantial form to Nietzsche's early theoretical attacks on humanism. But Nietzsche's professional colleagues were quick to respond to his attack—in particular Wilamowitz, whose pamphlet entitled *Zukunftsphilologie!* charged Nietzsche with deliberately obscuring historical facts in order to make Greek civilization conform to Wagnerian ideals. Even if this had been true, it would not have been as serious a blow against Nietzsche as Wilamowitz thought, for Nietzsche had already argued that there was value in the project of intentionally misinterpreting the past to suit modern needs. Still, Wilamowitz hoped to defend rational scholarship by showing that the findings of classical philology could be used to disprove altogether Nietzsche's themes in *The Birth of Tragedy*. His polemic ended with a charge of "ignorance and lack of the love of truth."[71]

It would not be useful to assess Wilamowitz' claims against Nietzsche by referring to the findings of modern classical scholarship as if these were objective and absolute. Nevertheless, despite Nietzsche's lack of concern for rationalist methods and the opinion of his colleagues, his intuitive reading of the Greeks did later find much support among conventional philologists. F.M. Cornford was just one British classicist who claimed that *The Birth of Tragedy* was a "work of profound imaginative insight, which left the scholarship of a generation toiling in the rear."[72] Cornford was referring to Nietzsche's recognition of the importance of mystery cults, Bacchic festivals, and other aspects of the irrational in Greek culture. The "primitive" and irrational side of Greek civilization became an important new subject of scholarly study in the early part of this century; and the new generation of classicists hailed Nietzsche as their inspiration. But this new school worked by applying rationalist methods to the analysis of irrational historical phenomena, and they therefore had more in common with Socrates and Euripides than with Nietzsche, since the latter had wanted to match the objective irrationalism of the Greeks with a similar methodological attitude. Besides, a similar new interest in the prehistory of human culture and psychology was apparent in the works of numerous other thinkers around the turn of the century: Frazer, Freud and Jung being only three examples. So the new interest in the irrational had other sources besides Nietzsche.

Nietzsche seems to most modern scholars to have been right in viewing Homer as an early and primitive poet, whereas Wilamowitz claimed that Homer belonged to the Archaic period at the earliest. But Nietzsche achieved this insight not because of a radical new methodology of his own; rather, he was, in this case, simply more successful than Wilamowitz in applying the historical sense that they both shared. After all, Vico had reached the same conclusion more than a century earlier; and the best evidence came with the empirical discoveries of the comparative ethnologist, Milman Parry. Conversely, Wilamowitz was successful in refuting some of Nietzsche's claims by using the same historicist methods—at least if we accept modern scholarship as the standard of judgment.[73]

But Nietzsche was right to claim that if we treat the findings of modern scholarship as absolutely valid, this will only lead to skepticism about the value of rationality, since contemporary arguments will soon appear to be (in part, at least) the subjective products of their time. In his essay on philology, Nietzsche had claimed that "The ancient world has in fact always been understood in terms of the present...."[74] Thus we would be making a mistake if we judged *The Birth of Tragedy* false because modern scholars disagreed with it on some points. However, there is an alternative criterion that we could apply in order to judge the rationality of Nietzsche's works—a criterion that applies only if we imagine the history of classical scholarship, not merely to be a sequence of discrete new prejudices, but rather to consist in the gradual amassing of diverse perspectives, the synthesis of divergent views attained by rational means. If we could show that scholarship had achieved pragmatic advances in the understanding of Greek culture, attained through a rational discussion among philologists of succeeding generations, then we could argue that to produce a deliberately irrational work of scholarship means to cut oneself off from the continuous, collective effort to attain the truth. We could then judge the rationality of a given work by its "performative attitude." We would ask: To what degree does the author seek to further a rational dialogue?

Wilamowitz' diagnosis of *The Birth of Tragedy* along these lines was unequivocal:

> ... Herr Nietzsche is also a professor of classical philology; he handles a series of very important issues of Greek literary history.... This is what I will illuminate, and it will be clear that the imaginary geniality and insolence in the presentation of his assertions stands in a direct relation to his lack of wisdom and disregard for truth.... His expedient is to revile the historical-critical method, to insult any aesthetic insight which dissents from his own, and to lay aside the generation in which philology in Germany, especially through Gottfried Hermann and Karl Lachmann, was raised to an inimitable height, calling [their work] 'a complete misunderstanding of classical scholarship'....[75]

Wilamowitz argued that the "generally accepted historical-critical method," perfected by Lachmann and Hermann, should lead us to judge each epoch by its own standards; but Nietzsche was being deliberately unhistorical in applying Schopenhauerian "dogmas" to the understanding of Greek aesthetics. He was thus insulting "any aesthetic insight which dissents from his own...."[76] Wilamowitz was willing to admit that his criticisms meant nothing if Nietzsche were trying to write a myth, rather than history; but he concluded his pamphlet with a piece of advice:

> Let Herr Nietzsche keep his word. Let him take up his thyrsos. Let him journey from India to Greece. But let him descend from the lecture platform from which he should be teaching *Wissenschaft*. Let him gather panthers and tigers at his knees but not the philological youth of Germany, who should, with ascetic, self-denying work, seek everywhere truth alone,

in order, through willing submission, to be freed of prejudice....[77]

Nietzsche was perfectly willing to accede to Wilamowitz' request, since his contempt for the "philological youth of Germany" was already on record; his critique of the ascetic attitude was forthcoming; and he was about to resign from his Chair of Philology. On the other hand, Wilamowitz no doubt exaggerated his own influence when he wrote late in life that Nietzsche "did what I called on him to do, gave up his teaching office and science, and became the prophet of a non-religious religion and an unphilosophical philosophy. His dæmon justified him in that: he had the genius and strength for it."[78] Nietzsche's renunciation of humanistic scholarship was far too deeply embedded in his philosophical attitude to have anything to do with Wilamowitz' advice.

Moreover, if we apply Wilamowitz' standards of rationality to his own pamphlet, it falls short. He relied too heavily on the *ad hominem* argument that Nietzsche was unqualified to judge Greek culture, given his youth and lack of scholarly credentials. Wilamowitz set forth no strong arguments against Nietzsche's reading of Greek culture, while he himself made grand and unsubstantiated claims about the Greeks. For example, in contrast to Nietzsche's picture of Homer as pessimistic and Wagnerian, Wilamowitz described a "joyful, exuberant" Homeric world, which "dreamed the dream of life most beautifully."[79] Wilamowitz sensed, correctly, that Nietzsche's performative attitude—his *Ton und Tendenz*—was irrational; but he failed to act any more rationally himself. In exasperation, he called Nietzsche a disgrace to their common mother, Pforta.[80]

Wilamowitz was soon to apologize for his irrational and hyperbolic tone, and in later years he may have thought that he had failed to respond to Nietzsche in a convincing manner.[81] However, Nietzsche's work *can* be criticized effectively by measuring it against the standard of a "rational performative attitude." Consider an example of an argument from the *Birth of Tragedy*. In Section XIII, in order to justify the claim that Socrates and Euripides were intellectual allies, Nietzsche cites the rumor that Socrates helped Euripides to write his plays. The conventional philologist would state openly that this rumor comes from a notoriously problematical source, Diogenes Laertius' *Lives and Views of Eminent Philosophers* [1.4.ii]. Nietzsche happened to be an expert on this text and its sources, about which he had written a lengthy essay.[82] Much of his professional work had been devoted to the techniques of source-criticism.[83] He should therefore have explained where Diogenes could have found proof for such a subtle and distant rumor about two men living hundreds of years before his time.[84] If a conventional philologist wanted to use the rumor to back up his general thesis about Socrates and Euripides, he or she would first provide a detailed account of the arguments for and against accepting Diogenes' testimony. But Nietzsche takes Diogenes seriously solely because the rumor fits his argument. Thus Nietzsche acts like those nonrationalist Bible scholars who accept whatever variant text of the New Testament fits their theology. Moreover, on the grounds that rational scholarship is weakening and inimical to life, Nietzsche altogether neglects to say where he gets his rumors: he doesn't even mention Diogenes in *The Birth of Tragedy*. Thus he shows a lack of concern for helping readers to make critical and productive decisions about the accuracy of his account, just as he shows a lack of interest in the existing professional literature on the origins of tragedy. True enough, the insights of Nietzsche's *Birth of Tragedy* were later incorporated into the rational dialogue about Greek culture by classical scholars who were willing to provide evidence to back up at least some of Nietzsche's claims. But Nietzsche made this difficult by disguising his sources, and therefore—as he must have realized—the average reader was likely to be misled by some of his claims.

Of course, if we argue that Nietzsche "misled" his ordinary readers, we are thereby assuming that professional philologists know something valuable, that philology has a point. Nietzsche denied this in his theoretical essays. Wilamowitz's mature response was to show that the "horizons" of different cultures— and particularly, the perspectives of different ages as they reread the Greek classics—can be melded together to produce a view that is ever richer, ever broader, and ever more rational. In Nietzsche's view, "Every historical school has tried its hand with classical civilization...."[85] The implication is that each of these schools has been completely conditioned by cultural forces operating in its own time, and completely unconnected to the perspectives of any other school or period. Nietzsche's denial of the possibility that horizons can be fused and perspectives shared among discrete *Weltanschauungen* led him to doubt that scholarship could achieve any advances in objectivity. Instead, he called the story of classical scholarship an altogether "miserable history."[86] Thus it was only with the publication of his *History of Classical Scholarship* as a mature professor that Wilamowitz really answered Nietzsche. In this book, he laid out a progressive history of his discipline in which he showed how the insights of each age had been incorporated into the modern view of the Greeks. Thus the modern view could be considered richer and less narrowly subjective than any previous reading of Hellenic culture.

Wilamowitz himself believed in the existence of recognizable *Weltanschauungen*, especially that of "Hellenism." He even explained developments in classical scholarship as the result of changes in the "spirit" of the age. But Wilamowitz in no way suggested that the beliefs of any generation were inaccessible to the next; on the contrary, he constantly described great classicists from the past as thinkers from whom we could learn directly. In other words, he was a "dialogic historicist," in the tradition of Hegel. Late in life, he wrote: "Only knowledge of a language that possesses another mode of conceiving the world can lead to the appropriate knowledge of one's own language."[87] Wilamowitz was right to recognize the possibility of understanding across great cultural distance, but wrong to espouse the idealist doctrine of *Weltanschauungen*. It seems to me that a more promising response to Nietzsche's skepticism about scholarship could be made by jettisoning altogether the idea of cultures as reified entities having independent existence. Nevertheless, Wilamowitz' defense of classical scholarship by means of a history of his own discipline at least had the merit of showing that perspectives can be "open," i.e., subject to communication and comparison with alien viewpoints. Projects like Wilamowitz' *History of Classical Scholarship* were popular in the late nineteenth century among scholars who wanted to defend historicism from charges that it was self-contradictory or self-defeating.[88]

The view that the history of classical scholarship is a collective, progressive—although frequently interrupted—process of fusing perspectives serves as a refutation of Nietzsche's attack on humanism in several ways. First, it undermines Nietzsche's claim that an iron cage of subjectivity inevitably and completely binds all allegedly rational students of the past. Secondly, it makes the process of humanistic scholarship appear empowering rather than weakening, and life-enhancing rather than life-denying. For to escape from the narrow bounds of our cultural or individual background by fusing horizons with scholars and thinkers from the past means to free ourselves, at least in part, from the limitations of a single perspective; and thereby we approach the kind of freedom that Nietzsche could only imagine to be a trait of geniuses. Finally, this view makes us all the more wary of those who, like Nietzsche, seek to disrupt the collective process of rational dialogue by "slamming the door" of the "house of scholars."

Chapter 6

The New 'Ancient'

I. Nietzsche in the Quarrel Between
the Ancients and Moderns

In the preceding chapter, I stated that Nietzsche repudiated *The Birth of Tragedy* because its idealization of the Greeks was Romantic. His mature philosophy represented a more sophisticated effort to escape from modern historicity and nihilism. Yet Nietzsche's relation to antiquity remained an important aspect of his work, and understanding it can help to throw light upon some central doctrines of his mature philosophy: Eternal Return, Will to Power, and the Overman. In turn, an interpretation of these doctrines and their relationship to historicism will help to explain some central techniques and precepts in the work of the modern Nietzscheans, Leo Strauss and Jacques Derrida.

Nietzsche was, as I have said, a believer in historicism. One of its consequences was a solution to that most ancient of humanist controversies, the quarrel between the "ancients," who advocated imitating classical models in all areas of culture, and the "moderns," who argued for the possibility of progress. By suggesting that the achievements of each age could only be judged according to the values of the time itself, historicism had put to rest the question of the superiority of classical civilization to all succeeding epochs. Ancient culture was neither superior nor inferior to modernity;

it was incomparable. This discovery of value-relativism in history can be seen as a logical consequence of the historical fixation of the "ancients" and "moderns." Johan Huizinga writes:

> Engrossed in antiquity as a result of an admiration for it and a desire to imitate it, people became more and more aware of its *historical* character: seeking for what could unite, they found what divided. Via antiquity and from antiquity man learned to think historically, and once he had learned to do so he had to give up historical ideals of life with a general significance... . Hence it is history itself that has banished historical ideals of life as tenuous shadows.[1]

But Nietzsche viewed historicism as a mixed blessing: he thought it damaging to any healthy culture. And as an opponent of the idea of objective "truth," Nietzsche no longer thought that a harmful doctrine needed to be sustained, no matter how "scientific" or rational it might appear. Thus Nietzsche was ready to reopen the quarrel between the "ancients" and "moderns," despite his earlier adherence to *Weltanschauung*-historicism; and he was even prepared to take up the cause of the "ancients," those most credulous, unscientific and antihistorical of humanists.

Nietzsche's *ancienneté* is evident at once in his antischolarly diatribes, which should be understood as a revival of the witty polemics that the "ancients" of the seventeenth and eighteenth centuries had launched against professional philologists, whose potential to undermine an idealized view of the classics they already feared. When Nietzsche calls classical scholars "windbags and triflers," "repulsive," and "filthy pedants," he is raising the ghosts of Swift and Pope.[2] Swift had satirized the philologists of his day, above all Richard Bentley, by means of an allegory in which "a malignant deity called Criticism," as well as the gods of Dullness, Positiveness, and Pedantry, come to the aid of the "moderns" in their battle to unseat the classical authors from the slopes of Parnassus. Momus, the patron goddess of the "moderns," delivers a speech which recalls Nietzsche's caricature of "Socratic men" from Euripides to Wilamowitz:

> "Tis I," said she, "who give wisdom to infants and idiots; by me children grow wiser than their parents; by me beaux become politicians, and school-boys judges of philosophy; by me sophisters debate and conclude upon the depths of knowledge;

and coffee-house wits, instinct by me, can correct an author's style, and display his minutest errors, without understanding a syllable of his matter or his language."[3]

Nietzsche's *Untimely Meditations*—especially "We Philologists"— are very close in genre and style to the polemics of the eighteenth-century "ancients." His personal library contained a set of Swift's works, and it seems certain that they influenced him.[4] Like the "ancients" of the preceding centuries, Nietzsche had no use for scholarship that was not useful, or erudition that did not unveil a unified and attractive vision of the past. And like them, he preached the view that the Greeks were superior to all subsequent civilizations. Moreover, he constantly expressed his admiration for those cultures that were most naive and enthusiastic in their efforts to revive the classical world. His cultural ideal was seventeenth-century France, but Augustan Rome and Renaissance Florence also won his consistent praise. He credited the French of the age of Corneille with taking possession of Roman antiquity "in a way for which we no longer have courage enough," just as the Romans had boldly appropriated Hellenic civilization.[5] Similarly, he praised the Baroque French for resurrecting the "Stoic Roman ideal" [*die stoisch-großen Römertums*]: they had thereby continued "the task of the Renaissance in the worthiest fashion," giving us, through imitation of the ancients, "the best books and the best human beings."[6] In the words of Peter Heller, Nietzsche himself "generally inclined toward an *imitatio* of Voltaire and a mythical self-identification with Voltaire"—but the Voltaire he imitated was, in turn, a self-conscious imitator of Roman virtue and style.[7] Nietzsche never gave up seeking to revive the *Romanitas* of Sallust and Horace in his literary style.[8]

II. Zarathustra

Thus I want to suggest that Nietzsche was a new "ancient," engaged in a self-conscious borrowing of others' naive appropriation of the classical past. This was one of his ways of overcoming the modern "historical sense," and it was evident in his choice of cultural models and literary genres. It also throws light on the figure of Zarathustra, his chosen mouthpiece. Nietzsche's academic specialty had been ancient histories of philosophy, especially those by Diogenes Laertius and Suidas. Both of these authors had considered Zarathustra to be a founder of philosophy and a font of perennial wisdom.[9] Diogenes claims that Zarathustra was the first philosopher of all, a Persian mage who lived 5,000 years before the sack of Troy.[10] As Nietzsche must have discovered when he wrote his dissertation on Diogenes, the vast majority of previous commentators—coming down at least as far as Leibniz—*agreed* with Diogenes in treating Zarathustra as a prime source of the *philosophia perennis*, the core truths that God had initially revealed to man.[11] In the Middle Ages, Zarathustra had been identified with Noah's son, Ham;[12] from Antiquity down to the nineteenth-century, the "Chaldaic Oracles" were attributed to him;[13] Aristotle had considered him an intellectual ancestor;[14] and Proclus said that his Oracles were so wise that they, along with the *Timaeus* alone, could be allowed to fall into the hands of laymen.[15] In 1582, an English commentator found "verie many plaine speeches of the sonne of God" in Zarathustra's works;[16] Leibniz thought Zarathustra a likely author of the *I Ching*;[17] and Newton was so taken by the idea that Zarathustra had anticipated his physics that he liked to be called *"mon cher Zoroastre."*[18] For premodern humanists of a certain radically antihistorical school, attributing positions to Zarathustra meant giving them the stamp of authority, for he had come before the history of philosophy proper, *in illo tempore*, when God's truths were still unsullied. Pietro Critino puts the following, quintessentially "ancient" speech in the mouth of Pico della Mirandola:

> In every age there have been a few predominant thinkers, supreme both in judgment and knowledge, such as Moses, Pythagoras, Hermes, Zoroaster [alias Zarathustra], and Solon, who all agreeing together, believed these things [sc. Christian neoplatonism], but also powerfully proclaimed them... undoubtedly the whole of ancient philosophy, being like-minded, asserts one and the same thing.[19]

Nietzsche, the *Weltanschauung*-historicist, could not have believed that ancient philosophy was objectively or universally true. Nor could he have considered Moses and Solon "like-minded," since they surely belonged to different cultures. However, his willingness to appropriate prehistoricist rhetoric as part of his revolt against historicism is apparent when he describes the pre-Socratic philosophers as a "republic of geniuses: each giant calls to his brother across the desolate intervals of the ages."[20] But by Nietzsche's period, much was known about philosophy before Socrates, and in particular about the real Zarathustra. His authentic works, the *Zend-Avesta*, were now known in the West, and many details from *Thus Spake*

Zarathustra conform to what appears in any modern encyclopedia of myth. Thus modern scholarship should have made it impossible for a scholar of Nietzsche's erudition to appropriate the rhetoric and methodology of an "ancient" like Pico della Mirandola.[21]

What then was Nietzsche doing, despite all his scholarly knowledge, putting his own doctrines of the death of God and the *Übermensch* in the mouth of an ancient Persian prophet? The simple answer would be to say that he was parodying the "ancients'" search for perennial wisdom, much like Mozart, who had put freemasonry in the mouth of "Sarastro" (alias Zarathustra) in *The Magic Flute*.[22] But, like Mozart, Nietzsche was at least half serious. First of all, Nietzsche's appropriation of the idea of a *philosophia perennis* was one of his many ways of showing that he didn't mean to be objective or scientific, for he certainly did not believe in a perennial wisdom. But beyond that, Nietzsche was serious about the view that a new existential philosophy, based on atheism, *amor fati*, and the Eternal Return, had to be created as an antidote to the nihilism of historicist modernity. And what better way to begin a new antihistorical philosophy than by appropriating the methods of the naive "ancients" whom historicism had defeated?

Zarathustra was Nietzsche's mouthpiece, situated deliberately outside or beyond history: a Persian prophet speaking as if he were being appropriated by a Renaissance believer in the perennial philosophy, at the same time using the language of the New Testament to preach atheism and alluding frequently to modern German issues. In *Ecce Homo*, Nietzsche remarks, "Zarathustra was the first to consider the fight of good and evil the very wheel in the machinery of things: the transposition of morality into the metaphysical realm, as a force, cause, and end in itself, is *his* work." Indeed, this achievement constitutes the "tremendous historical uniqueness of that Persian." So far, Nietzsche has simply described the historical Zoroaster, who was a founder of Persian dualistic theology. But he continues, "Zarathustra created this most calamitous error, morality; consequently, he must also be the first to recognize it." So Nietzsche's Zarathustra has an existence spanning the centuries, from the prehistoric age of myth, to the posthistoric age of the *Übermensch*. He has "more experience in this matter, for a longer time, than any other thinker," for he has watched from afar the entire course of history, which is merely "the refutation by experiment of the principle of the so-called 'moral world-order'... ."[23] Zarathustra knows the character of all history better than anyone, for he is not trapped within the confines of any limited part of history, any contingent culture. He observes history from offstage, having no contingent beliefs or values himself.

"Zarathustra has seen many lands and many peoples: so he has discovered the good and evil of many peoples."[24] But Zarathustra, uniquely, is *beyond* good and evil. In creating this character, Nietzsche had broken all the rules of modern perspectivism, for Zarathustra has no historical or cultural location. Nietzsche's reaction against historical realism foreshadows Kafka, Beckett, Eliot and Camus, whose fictions are often set in deliberately undefined settings and periods. But Nietzsche's literary antihistoricism also looks back to the eighteenth century and before, when all literary authors were (at least relatively) insensitive to historical change and difference. This insensitivity allowed them to appropriate the stories of the past for their own uses, without being paralyzed by relativism.[25] The "ancients" had been particularly anxious to defend the notion that classical myths were of timeless value and direct relevance to the present. So in creating Zarathustra, Nietzsche revealed himself to be a new "ancient," appropriating the appropriative methods of his predecessors, but in a deliberate and radical way.

III. The Eternal Return

In order to understand better Nietzsche's role as an "ancient" and his mature attitude towards history and historicism, it is worth taking a closer look at Zarathustra's "fundamental conception," the "Eternal Return of the Same."[26] This has been convincingly described as the categorical imperative of Nietzsche's existentialism. Nietzsche holds the existentialist view that "There is no 'being' behind doing, effecting, becoming; 'the doer' is merely a fiction added to the deed—the deed is everything... ."[27] In order to show that you accept the sum total of your past deeds as authentically your own—as equal to your essence—you must will that your own life should be repeated infinitely. Only an *Übermensch* will have the strength of character to make this wish; and only he will therefore be capable of facing up to fate and his own identity. Anyone who wishes that he had acted differently in the past is in fact wishing his own annihilation, for his acts *are* his essence. The "Eternal Return" is therefore a test of *amor fati*, "the highest formula of affirmation,"[28] and, incidentally, a way to will the transcendence of history by willing one's own endless recurrence. The Eternal Return is commonly taken as an antidote to nihilism, to the modern "paralyzing sense of general disintegration and incompleteness";[29] and this is true in part because it is a willful denial of history. A sense of history, of the irrevocability of profane events, a feeling that one is "powerless against what has been done,"[30] and a belief in *"eternal novelty"*[31]—this, according to Nietzsche, is the source of every melancholy and "gnashing of teeth."[32] The Eternal Return is "the will's revulsion against time and its 'it was.'"[33] The *Übermensch* looks back on the irrevocable events of his own life and resists alienating them as his "history"; instead, he proclaims them to be his eternal, ahistorical essence. He translates every "it was" into a "thus I willed it,"[34] thereby overcoming history— if history is defined as an objectified series of irrevocable events.[35]

The function of the Eternal Return as a categorical imperative and a salutary myth is easy to see, at least if we accept Nietzsche's existential preconceptions. By willing his activities to go on forever, the Overman grants them the same kind of eternal validity that religious rituals used to enjoy when people still believed in God and objective morality. The Overman creates his own values, refuses to preach them to anyone else, but wills their eternal recurrence. In other words, he has the strength to treat his values *as if* they were God-given and universal, knowing full well that they are not. The Overman recognizes that Being is just a phenomenon of grammar—that there are no permanent facts—but he nevertheless treats his own values as permanent, for "To impose upon becoming the character of being—that is the supreme will to power."[36] He loses himself wholly in the enjoyment of his own acts, just as the Greeks had lost themselves in the timeless ritual of their tragedy. Nietzsche says that he has erected the Eternal Return "In place of 'metaphysics' and religion... as a means of breeding and selection."[37] Thus it is not so much a theory, as a way of identifying overmen and defeating nihilism. But Nietzsche also called it "the most *scientific* of all possible hypotheses."[38] Still a loyal follower of Lange, Nietzsche wanted a myth that was compatible with science—for he wanted it to be effective, and he knew that "Rational thought is interpretation according to a scheme that we cannot throw off."[39] Accordingly, much has been made of Nietzsche's notes to the effect, for example, that the "law of the conservation of energy demands eternal recurrence."[40] But any attempt to ground the eternal return in physics seems likely to fail, and it does not sound like a particularly Nietzschean project. After all, he had written that "physics, too, is only an interpretation and exegesis of the world... and not a world-explanation."[41] And Nietzsche even remarks that "one must guard against" thinking of Eternal Return on the model of "stars, or the ebb and flow, day and night, seasons... ."[42] Whatever it is, the Eternal Return is not centrally a hypothesis about the structure of nature or the universe.[43] Once again, it seems to me that viewing Nietzsche as an "ancient" can help to shed a stronger light on his apparently obscure methods, and in particular, his effort to unite myth with *Wissenschaft*.

The "Eternal Return" was, after all, an ancient doctrine, frequently recurring itself throughout pre-Socratic philosophy and the humanistic tradition. So when Nietzsche called it a *wissenschaftlich* theory, perhaps he meant a concept of *Wissenschaft* much like that which believers in the perennial philosophy had held: that is, *Wissenschaft* as scholarship, and above all as the search for truth from ancient sources. Even Newton had considered it an important proof of his discoveries that they had been anticipated by ancient philosophers: this made his physics more scientific, more *wissenschaftlich*. Nietzsche borrowed the idea of Eternal Return from pre-Socratic thinkers, and also from "ancients" who had believed the doctrine because it came on such good (i.e., ancient) authority.[44] Nietzsche recalled that he had thought of the doctrine when he was "6,000 feet beyond people and time"[45]—i.e., when he was beyond or outside of history, just as Zarathustra was situated outside of history. He remarked, "Immortal is the moment when I begat Return."[46] And he praised his own *Zarathustra* in terms which echoed the "ancients'" adulation of their favorite books of perennial wisdom, composed *in illo tempore*, such as the supposed Oracles of the mage Zarathustra:

> This book, with a voice bridging centuries, is not only the highest book there is...—the whole fact of man lies *beneath* it at a tremendous distance—it is also the deepest, born out of the innermost wealth of truth, an inexhaustible well, to which no pail descends without coming up again filled with gold and goodness.[47]

The "cosmological" formulation of the Eternal Return is given by Nietzsche's Zarathustra as follows: "Everything goes, everything comes back; eternally rolls the wheel of being. Everything dies, everything blossoms again; eternally runs the year of being."[48] A strikingly similar formulation can be found in the works of the pre-Socratic "republic of creative minds": Anaximander, Empedocles, Heraclitus and Pythagoras. At least one modern scholar suggests that this pre-Socratic cosmology of eternal return actually did arise from "Irano-Babylonian origin," i.e., from the culture that brought forth Zarathustra.[49] Mircea Eliade has tried to make explicit the roots of Nietzsche's ahistorical philosophy by identifying the myth of the Eternal Return in societies that reveal a "revolt against concrete, historical time, [a] nostalgia for a periodical return to the mythical time of the beginning of things, to the

'Great Time.'"[50]   Eliade finds in several modern authors, notably Joyce, Eliot and Nietzsche, philosophies that "tend to reconfer value upon the myth of cyclical periodicity, even the myth of the eternal return." He writes:

> These orientations disregard not only historicism but history as such. We believe we are justified in seeing in them, rather than a resistance to history, a revolt against historical *time*, an attempt to restore this historical time, freighted as it is with human experience, to a place in the time that is cosmic, cyclical, and infinite.[51]

Thus Eliade reads Nietzsche as a philosopher engaged in a revolt against history, and willing to turn sentimentally back to prehistorical cultures.[52] And certainly, Nietzsche does write against the modern "historical sense" in all of its formulations, saying that he prefers even the ignorance of an animal, which, "absolutely 'unhistorical,'" lives at least without ennui.[53] "Indeed," he writes, "if I had to choose, I might even opt for some unhistorical, antihistorical person (such as Dühring...)."[54] These are strong words from Nietzsche, who despised Dühring almost as much as Marx and Engels did. So at least on a literal level, Nietzsche seemed to be opposed to history in all of its forms and eager to revive the ahistorical cosmologies of the pre-Socratics. Moreover, he was willing to utilize the ahistorical *methods* of the "ancients" as a means to support his new philosophy. Nietzsche's attack on the distinction between truth and lie perhaps justified his use of a myth in the place of what we would normally call "scholarship." But such deliberate mythmaking, used to glorify and revive a past culture, would seem to be only a species of Romanticism, and therefore no advance over *The Birth of Tragedy*, or even over Wagner's *Parsifal*. Since Nietzsche was an avowed anti-Romantic, he could be charged (at least) with hypocrisy, if this was all that he meant by the Eternal Return.[55]

IV. Esoteric Nihilism

But Nietzsche's presentation of the Eternal Return is more complicated, to say the least. Zarathustra relates a straightforwardly cosmological version of it to his animals, but it is unclear whether we are to take this seriously. The animals reply enthusiastically that Zarathustra is the one who "must first teach this doctrine."[56]

The absurdity of their response at least reveals that Nietzsche is somewhat detached from their wholehearted acceptance of Eternal Return—so perhaps we should not accept it as straightforwardly as they do. Nehamas points out that, after Zarathustra's animals have spoken, he "remains totally silent and does not once acknowledge the idea his animals attribute to him."[57] But despite his reluctance to acknowledge his vision of recurrence or to correct his animals' absurd use of it, Zarathustra again proclaims it, this time to a dwarf who is annoying him. Now his proclamation of Eternal Return serves a clear purpose: it frightens off the dwarf. Thus Nietzsche is doubly distant from his "doctrine" of the Eternal Return, which is presented as a "truth" only by the fanciful figure of Zarathustra, who may have ulterior motives in preaching it to dwarves and little animals. In passages where Nietzsche writes of recurrence in his own voice,[58] he presents it merely as a thought-experiment, useful for defending *amor fati* and his related view that a human being *is* only the sum of his deeds. On the basis of this evidence, it is possible to imagine that Nietzsche wanted to use the Eternal Return in two ways: as a thought-experiment for his *übermenschlich* disciples; and as a myth, a "golden lie," to teach to naifs like his animals, who would accept it wholeheartedly and thus avoid (or be frightened away from) nihilism. Perhaps this latter group would provide the audience for books that Nietzsche only dreamt of writing, with titles like "The Eternal Recurrence: A Book of Prophecy."[59] But the clever reader of *Zarathustra* (subtitled "A Book for Everyone and No One") would notice the irony in Nietzsche's presentation of the Eternal Return, and accept it only as a convenient myth. This realization would be made easier for those disciples who read all of Nietzsche's published works, and read them carefully, with attention to irony. This kind of reader would be offered no escape from the abyss of nihilism; but, *übermenschlich*, he would remain unfazed by the sight of the abyss, and would preach the new religion of Eternal Return to the weaklings who needed it.[60]

Nietzsche comes close to admitting that his project is duplicitous in notes which (appropriately enough) may never have been intended for publication. Nietzsche's collapse into madness robbed him of any control over his fragmentary manuscripts, and allowed some of his comments about his own esotericism to be made public. For example, already in 1884, he wrote:

> Our presuppositions: no God: no purpose: no finite force. Let us guard against thinking out and prescribing the mode of thought necessary to lesser men![61]

And in 1886 or 1887, he wrote:

> No 'moral education' of the human race: but an enforced schooling in errors is needed, because 'truth' disgusts and makes one sick of life—unless man is already irrevocably launched upon his path and has taken his honest insight upon himself with tragic pride.[62]

This latter stance was of course that of the *Übermensch*, who could recognize that "Everything is false! Everything is permitted!"[63]— and yet, like Nietzsche, remain disciplined, committed to classical or neoclassical ideals of style, devoted to "honest insight," and capable of presenting noble lies to his inferior fellows, who might otherwise be destroyed by his knowledge.

This reading of Nietzsche as presenting both an exoteric myth for the herd, and an esoteric doctrine for those able to bear nihilism, is further supported by his comments about what he expects from his readers. Like the humanist teachers of an ancient esoteric philosophy, Nietzsche says that he "deserves" a reader "who reads me as the good old philologists read their Horace": that is, with minute care and attention to possible double or triple meanings.[64] After all, the *philosophia perennis* had always been considered an esoteric doctrine, associated with mystery cults, the private teachings of ancient philosophical schools, coded double meanings in Virgil and the Torah, the secret wisdom that God had imparted to Moses, and the arcane knowledge possessed by such closed societies (real and imagined) as the Rosicrucians, Templars, Masons and Cabalists.

In *Ecce Homo*, Nietzsche writes, "When I imagine a perfect reader, he always turns into a monster of courage and curiosity; moreover, supple, cunning, cautious; a born adventurer and discoverer." And he adds:

> In the end, I could not say better to whom alone I am speaking at bottom than Zarathustra said it: to whom alone will he relate his riddle?
> "To you, the bold searchers, researchers, and whoever embarks with cunning sails on terrible seas—to you, drunk with riddles, glad of the twilight, whose soul flutes lure astray to every whirlpool... ."[65]

The "terrible seas" that Nietzsche means are the seas of nihilism, arrived at by modern humanity after voyaging through historicism and relativism. But Nietzsche's readers will only understand his nihilist teaching if they are among those capable of solving his riddle. Moreover, they will have to be sufficiently courageous and liberated from herd morality not to be frightened away by Nietzsche's deliberate self-demonization, his self-presentation as the Antichrist, as "dynamite," as the one who philosophizes with a hammer. There "attaches to my name a quantity of doom that is beyond telling," Nietzsche told his sister in 1888.[66] And Nietzsche remarks, "It is important that as few people as possible should think about morality... ."[67] Since his death, Nietzsche's demonic mask has effectively prevented many people from thinking along the lines that interested him, for to think like Nietzsche means to think like the Antichrist (or, as some would now say, like a Nazi).

If someone complained that Nietzsche should, in the name of honesty, reveal the "truth" of nihilism to all of his readers, regardless of the cost to them, he would respond as he did in his Preface to *The Dawn*: "But, after all: why must we say so loudly and with such enthusiasm what we are, what we want, and what we do not want?... . Let us say it as if among ourselves, so privately that all the world fails to hear it, and fails to hear *us*!" Nietzsche then explains how he will keep what he is (a nihilist) secret from all but the most cunning few:

Above all, let us say it *slowly*... One does not become a philologist in vain—perhaps one is a philologist still, that is, a teacher of slow reading. [Philology] teaches how to read *well*, that means slowly, profoundly, respectfully, carefully, with inner thoughts, with the mental doors ajar, with delicate fingers and eyes... my patient friends, this book desires only perfect readers and philologists: *learn* to read me well![68]

Similar comments appear throughout Nietzsche's works, so he is at least candid enough to remind his readers constantly that he is not being entirely frank with them. As early as *The Wanderer and His Shadow* (1880), Nietzsche publicly airs his concerns about the potentially destructive impact of his esoteric philosophy on the herd:

Stylistic caution. A: But if *everyone* knew this, the *majority* would be harmed. You yourself call these meanings dangerous for those susceptible to danger, and yet you express them openly?
B: I write so that neither the mob, nor the *populi*, nor the Parties of any kind wish to read me. Therefore these mean-

ings will never become public. A: But in that case, how do you write? B: Neither usefully nor pleasantly—for those I mentioned.[69]

In 1885, Nietzsche wrote (in a note that may not have been intended for public consumption):

> *Good Europeans* that we are—what distinguishes us from the men of fatherlands? First, we are atheists and immoralists, but for the present we support the religions and moralities of the herd instinct: for these prepare a type of man that must one day fall into our hands, that must *desire* our hands.
>
> Beyond good and evil—but we demand that herd morality should be held sacred unconditionally.[70]

There is also a note from 1886–1887 where Nietzsche actually uses the words "esoteric" and "exoteric" in a way that seems indubitably to refer to his own philosophy. The cryptic note reads as follows:

> *Exoteric-Esoteric*
>
> 1. all is will against will.
>
> 2. there is no will at all.
>
> 1. causalism
>
> 2. there is no such thing as cause and effect.[71]

The statements labelled (1) correspond to the exoteric arguments in *Beyond Good and Evil*, which Nietzsche was writing at about the same time.[72] Here Nietzsche suggests as an "experiment" that we consider "nothing else to be 'given' as real except our world of desires and passions... ." He then remarks that "the conscience of *method*" demands that we push this thought-experiment "to its utmost limit (to the point of nonsense, if I may say so)," and thereby reduce all causality to the "causality of the will." Read carelessly, this passage appears to be an argument for a cosmology of Will to Power: it concludes with the statement: "The world viewed from inside, the world defined and determined according to its 'intelligible character'—it would be 'will to power' and nothing else."[73] But the careful reader will notice that this is merely a hypothesis, which Nietzsche says we must make if we are to push the Schopenhauerian methodological principle of homogeneity to its nonsensical conclusion. In fact, he believes that the world lacks any "intelligible character." In case there were any doubt that the cosmology of Will to Power is therefore merely an exoteric doctrine, like the Eternal Return, we have Nietzsche's private note stating quite clearly his esoteric views: "there is no will at all... there is no such thing as cause and effect." In *Beyond Good and Evil* itself, Nietzsche pleads that he be read very slowly and with an eye to duplicity. This plea itself is couched in cryptic language: "It is hard to be understood," he remarks, "when one thinks and lives *gangasrotagati* [slowly like the Ganges] among men who think and live differently—namely, *kurmagati* [like a tortoise], or at best 'the way frogs walk,' *mandukagati* (I obviously do everything to be 'hard to understand' myself)... ."[74] Nietzsche distinguishes between the literalist approach of the exoteric— who "comes from the outside and sees, estimates, measures and judges," trying to understand the world in metaphysical or ethical terms—from the esoteric who "looks *down from above*," from a space beyond truth and objectivity.[75] The careful reader will heed such warnings. The careful reader will also note that the Will to Power is deliberately self-defeating as a cosmological doctrine, for it reduces even the Will to Knowledge, which allegedly *produced* this cosmology, to a mere Will to Power—specifically, Nietzsche's *übermenschlich* will to produce an exoteric doctrine, to say "yes" despite his knowledge of the abyss.

Chapter 7

The Free Spirit

I. Nietzsche's "Intentions"

In the last chapter, I suggested that Nietzsche deliberately created works that hid an esoteric doctrine of nihilism. He presented Eternal Return and Will to Power as substitutes for traditional metaphysical and religious doctrines, but without believing them himself. Here, I will try to give a fuller account of how one might live according to Nietzsche's esoteric, nihilist message. But claiming that Nietzsche had a "message" immediately raises the controversial question of his intentions. Certainly, Nietzsche never stated his message explicitly, even in his private notes, because any prosaic description of nihilism—still expressed in the metaphysical form of grammar—would be inadequate, immediately destroying itself. It is impossible to express the thought that "nothing is true" in so many words, without stating a mere paradox. Stanley Rosen remarks that for Nietzsche, "The esoteric truth is then that there is no truth and no theory.... But this means that the distinction between the esoteric and the exoteric collapses."[1] Nevertheless, it seems to me that Nietzsche pointed deliberately and clearly in a direction beyond sense, grammar and culture. His exoteric teachings (Will to Power, Eternal Return, etc.) were carefully designed to undermine themselves in order to point in the direction of "nothing."

It could be argued that Nietzsche would reject any reading of his texts that imposed upon them such a determinate intention,

131

however epistemologically radical. But Nietzsche's rejection of the
distinction between truth and lie did not commit him to reject the
difference between intelligent and unintelligent interpretations of
texts—especially of his own texts. In 1888 he wrote of St. Paul
and other "misinterpreters" of Jesus:

> None of these holy epileptics and seers of visions possessed a
> thousandth part of that integrity of self-criticism with which
> a philologist today reads a text or proves the truth of an his-
> torical event.—Compared with us, they are moral cretins—[2]

Nietzsche had, of course, denounced philologists for their overvaluation
of truth in interpretation, and admired some "moral cretins" of the
past who had appropriated the ancients for their own purposes.
For him, truth was not the highest value, and a useful misinterpretation of a text could be preferable to a harmful but accurate
interpretation. However, that did not mean that there was no difference
between an accurate reading and a misinterpretation. Furthermore,
Nietzsche asked that his own books be read using careful, philological
methods. If his disciples did not read his arguments against truth
as determinate—indeed, as valid—then his deconstructive project
would be stillborn.[3] "Hear me!" he wrote in *Ecce Homo*: "For I am such
and such a person. Above all, do not mistake me for someone else."[4]

In France in the early 1960s, a school of "postmodern" philosophers
(heavily influenced by Heidegger) began reading Nietzsche as a
critic of "truth."[5] They made little of Nietzsche's explicit discussion
of his own esotericism, nor did they describe him as presenting a
"noble lie" for the herd. Instead, they avoided, as far as they could,
ascribing *any* intentions to Nietzsche, but suggested that his texts
had a highly unusual quality of constantly subverting themselves
in order to gesture in a direction beyond sense. Thus they adopted
what they took to be Nietzsche's view: that authorial intentions
can never be objectively known. "Whoever thought he had understood
something of me, had made up something out of me after his own
image...."[6] But the postmodernist reading can be restated as an
account of Nietzsche's *deliberate,* deconstructive project.
As Robert Pippin writes, Nietzsche's philosophy "is, in more fashionable
language, a solution [to the crisis of modernity] that deconstructs
itself, but what is responsible for the deconstruction is not textuality
itself but Nietzsche."[7]

Thus several questions arise. First, do Nietzsche's texts subvert themselves? In the last chapter, I offered evidence in favor of
this idea. Not only are such doctrines as Will to Power and

Eternal Return self-refuting, but (as the postmodernists have pointed out) Nietzsche also adopts a variety of contradictory poses and masks. Second, did Nietzsche *mean* his texts to subvert themselves? His comments about his own writing suggest that he did, but his philosophical position seems to rule out the possibility of our ever understanding an author's motives. Indeed, the very existence of an author is made problematical in Nietzsche's philosophy, for "'the doer' is merely a fiction added to the deed."[8] Any account of a statement that ascribes it to a subject, and describes this subject's motives, is pure fiction, the product of the reader's perspective. The "reader," too, is a fiction, but one that we cannot avoid so long as "we" speak in the "lies" of grammar, appending the pronoun "I" to "our" thoughts. These quotation marks begin to multiply to such an extent that Derrida writes of "an epochal regime of *guillemets*."[9] Thus a Nietzschean reader of Nietzsche is forced to back away from any reading that confidently ascribes motives and strategies to the author on the basis of textual evidence. Paradoxically, the postmodernist reading therefore seems faithful to Nietzsche's philosophical position—or, as it is almost impossible to avoid saying, to his intentions. On the other hand, those of us who are not committed to using Nietzschean methods to read Nietzsche are not forced to dance around the issue of intention, and can simply restate the postmodernist interpretation as a hypothesis about Nietzsche's intentions.

To some degree, this may be a merely formal question, a choice between using "Nietzsche" or "Nietzsche's texts" as the subject of sentences that describe a series of utterances associated with Nietzsche. (At one point, Derrida even uses "the Nietzsches" as a subject, in order to imply the multiplicity of Nietzsche's voices and the fiction involved in imposing a singular identity on them.)[10] But there may also be a substantial issue separating postmodernist and humanist discourse. Throughout this essay, I have been making hypothetical claims about Nietzsche's beliefs, motives, strategies, intellectual development, and so on. Derrida would not approve. What "ridiculous naiveté," he writes, "what sly, obscure, and shady business are behind declarations of the type: Friedrich Nietzsche said this or that, he thought this or that about this or that subject...."[11] Unlike naive and shady humanist interpreters of texts, Derrida does "not teach truth as such; I do not transform myself into a diaphanous mouthpiece of eternal pedagogy."[12] Derrida seems to me to be setting up a straw man here, for his humanist rivals do not consider themselves diaphanous mouthpieces either; they seek to make criticizable hypotheses and back them up with as much evidence as they can muster, in the expectation that their work will some day be surpassed. But Derrida believes that liberating himself from the alleged pretensions of traditional hermeneutics also liberates him from the scholarly "bad conscience" that Nietzsche had criticized:

> I would like to spare you the tedium, the waste of time, and the subservience that always accompany the classic pedagogical procedures of forging links, referring back to prior premises or arguments, justifying one's own trajectory, method, system, and more or less successful transitions, reestablishing continuity, and so on. These are some of the imperatives of classical pedagogy with which, to be sure, one can never break once and for all. Yet, if you were to submit to them rigorously, they would soon reduce you to silence, tautology, and tiresome repetition.[13]

Thus the Last Man is as much a target for Derrida as he was for Nietzsche. Derrida seeks to escape from the burdens of a collective and cumulative scholarly enterprise, in order, perhaps, to become one of Nietzsche's "solitaries." "You solitaries of today," says Zarathustra, "you who have seceded from society, you shall one day be a people: from you, who have chosen yourselves, shall a chosen people spring—and from it, the Overman."[14] In contrast to the "tedium" and herd-like docility of humanistic scholarship, Derrida provides a reading of Nietzsche in *Spurs* which is an avowed testament of self-expression, the utterance of a (proto-) Overman. He claims explicitly that his interpretation is not meant to be in any way objective. Like Nietzsche, he too uses eccentric styles to call attention to his own subjectivity and contingency as an author. Derrida reveals his attitude towards the "truth" of his own interpretation when he writes that Nietzsche's text "is cryptic and parodic (now I tell you that it is, from beginning to end, and I can tell you this because it doesn't help you at all, and I can lie in acknowledging it because one can only dissimulate in telling the truth, in saying that one is telling the truth)...." Nietzsche's text is "indefinitely open, cryptic and parodic, that is to say closed, open and closed simultaneously or in turn"—and so is Derrida's.[15] Nevertheless, in explaining Nietzsche's often contradictory statements as a strategy to avoid dogmatism, Derrida refers to specific passages in Nietzsche's books and offers them as reasons for us to believe that these works are interesting and subversive, rather than merely confused and contradictory. Intentionally or not, Derrida conjures up a picture of Nietzsche as an intentional agent, and a profoundly creative and subtle one at that. Derrida's reading appears plausible, but it could perhaps be criticized on the basis of evidence that he does not cite, or from a different perspective. In short, Derrida's reading of Nietzsche is interesting, but only insofar as it constitutes a rational hypothesis about a philosopher's intentions: that is, a hypothesis supported by reasons and evidence, and open to criticism by others.

II. Nietzsche as Woman

In the following sections, I will present a view of Nietzsche's esoteric teachings which draws heavily on postmodernist interpretations—although the postmodernists would deny that they have objectively understood Nietzsche. Derrida's reading, for example, stresses the diverse styles in Nietzche's texts, which serve to undermine the texts' status as objective truth-claims. "The heterogeneity of the text shows it well. Nietzsche never allowed himself the illusion—in fact, he *analyzed* the illusion—that he understood the effects called [for example] woman, truth, castration, or the *ontological* effects of presence or absence."[16] Thus when one reads that Nietzsche's statements about women are only *"my* truths," this "implies without doubt that these are not *truths*, because they are multiple, variegated, contradictory."[17] It is in discussing women that Nietzsche makes an explicit point of his own avoidance of truth-claims, because women represent a model for Nietzsche of people who transcend the distinction between truth and lie. Nietzsche's women appear in conventionally moral terms to be contemptible because they do not care for truth. But, viewed from his own "extramoral" perspective, Nietzsche's account of "the Eternal Feminine" is a hymn of praise and a self-description, hidden amid diversionary comments about women as cooks, and so on. After all, he tells us that the "perfect woman is a higher type of human than the perfect man, and something much more rare."[18] The following words about women apply to Nietzsche's own apparent efforts to discover the "truth" about himself:

> Unless a woman seeks a new adornment for herself [sc. by seeking to "know" herself]—I do think adorning herself is part of the Eternal-Feminine?—she surely wants to inspire fear of herself—perhaps she seeks mastery. But she does not *want* truth: what is truth to woman? From the beginning, nothing has been more alien, repugnant, and hostile to women than truth—her great art is the lie, her highest concern is mere appearance and beauty.[19]

Nietzsche remarks that "Whatever is profound loves masks...."[20] Nietzsche wears many masks, and constantly draws attention to their illusory character. But women are consistently described in his works as the real experts in the art of mask-wearing. "There are women," he says, "who have no inner life wherever one looks for it, being nothing but masks. [And] just these women are able to stimulate man's desire most intensely: he searches for their souls—and searches on and on."[21] Thus women have the advantage over men that they recognize, as Nietzsche does, that they have no souls, no essences; moreover, they have the Nietzschean advantage that they are beyond truth and lie, in a realm where all choices are made groundlessly and freely, because no choice is better than any other:

> *Inspiration in the judgments of women.* Those sudden decisions about pro and con which women tend to make... have been enwreathed by loving men in a glow, as if all women had inspirations of wisdom.... However, if one considers that something positive can be said for any person or cause, and likewise something against it... then it is almost difficult to go astray by such sudden decisions; indeed, one could say that the nature of things is arranged in such a way that women always win the argument.[22]

For Nietzsche the male/female distinction has no more objective validity than any other dichotomy, so it is not "false" for him to imply that he is a "woman."[23] Indeed, he implies it very forcefully. "There are realities," he writes, "that one may never admit to oneself: after all, one is a woman, one has a woman's *pudeurs*...."[24] Like women (as he describes them), Nietzsche enjoys adorning himself, making himself attractive, and yet hiding his private thoughts under an exoteric veil of modesty. But this does not amount to a reproachable act of dishonesty or guile, for it is done naively:

> Given the tremendous subtlety of woman's instinct, [her] modesty remains by no means conscious hypocrisy: she divines that it is precisely an actual naive modesty that most seduces a man and impels him to overestimate her. Therefore woman is naive—from the subtlety of her instinct, which advises her of the utility of her innocence.... Wherever dissembling produces a stronger effect when it is unconscious, it *becomes* unconscious.[25]

Similarly, Nietzsche describes the Greeks as "superficial—*out of profundity!*"[26] This apparently paradoxical move of *deliberately* becoming naive is central to Nietzsche's philosophy. It emerges when he calls for humanity to "produce wise, innocent (consciously innocent) men";[27] or when Zarathustra prophesies the final transformation of the spirit from the lion—who "creates freedom" through his nihilistic skepticism—to the child, who is "innocence and forgetting."[28] The same phenomenon is evident in the Greeks' deliberate creation of naive art; in "Woman's" deliberate self-creation as a creature of mere appearances; in Nietzsche's deliberate return to the naïveté of the "ancients"; and even in the unfathomable, ultimately meaningless, but endlessly alluring quality of "life" herself. Life deserves this feminine pronoun, for she "is covered by a veil interwoven with gold, a veil of beautiful possibilities, sparkling with promise, resistance, bashfulness, mockery, pity and seduction. Yes, life is a woman."[29]

The deliberate naïveté shown by women, the Greeks, Nietzsche, and life itself is apparently paradoxical or hypocritical— but only as long as one retains a Socratic distinction between truth and lie, reality and appearance. Once this distinction has been undermined, the paradox disappears; and it may even be the most "truthful" way of life to live deceitfully. Nietzsche can be called deceitful only insofar as he modestly shields his "true essence" beneath masks—but that essence never existed in the first place. It is, writes Eric Blondel, only the "idealist philosopher who invents or reinstates a hidden reality, who turns naïveté into a hypocritical eroticism—i.e., who conceals only in order to suggest and exhibit."[30] But Nietzsche suspects that "all philosophers, insofar as they were dogmatists, have been very inexpert about women." Their "gruesome seriousness" and "clumsy obtrusiveness" have failed to part the veil of life's dissimulation—because there is nothing more to life than this veil.[31] Nietzsche, on the other hand, conceals only to reveal the message of nihilism, the message that there is "nothing" concealed beneath the dissimulation which he draws our attention to *as* dissimulation. "The will to appearance, illusion, deception, to becoming and change is deeper, more 'metaphysical,' than the will to truth, to reality, to being."[32] Writing metaphorically and poetically—as one must in dealing with women—Nietzsche ascribes a womanlike guile to nature and truth. Nietzsche's feminization of nature is itself a "feminine" (i.e., duplicitous) move. He covers his implicit message of nihilism in a veil of attractive metaphor that will misdirect the average "male" reader into a search for Nietzsche's doctrines, while he seduces his subtler audience into joining him in a game of deception that lies beyond truth and lie.[33]

III. The Politics of Nihilism

Thus, read from a certain perspective, Nietzsche appears a prophet and proponent of nihilism. But for him, a great question mark hung over the whole issue. Nihilism was *"ambiguous,"* he wrote; it could be a "sign of increased power of the spirit"—that is, *"active* nihilism"—or it could mean "decline and recession of the power of the spirit," which Nietzsche called *"passive* nihilism."[34] Thus he describes his own doctrine of the Eternal Return as "the most extreme form of nihilism";[35] but in this case he means an *active*, affirmative kind of nihilism—the creation of new values in the face of the abyss. The effects of the passive variety of nihilism, on the other hand, are evident in the case of the "most contemptible man," the "Last Man," who is paralyzed by his recognition of the contingency of all beliefs. In politics, the Last Man's values include a benign indifference to all ideology, an equal tolerance for all opinions, and therefore no capacity to take any political program seriously. Under these circumstances, "Who still wants to rule? Who obey? Both are too much of a burden." The result: "No herdsman and *one* herd!" Nietzsche would prefer to see many herds in bitter conflict, rather than one composed of passive nihilists. In the age of the Last Man, when every value is equally tolerated and none given allegiance, "Everyone wants the same thing, everyone is the same: whoever thinks otherwise goes voluntarily into the madhouse."[36] The age of the Last Man is one of Nietzsche's nightmares for the future of a nihilist society. The Last Man is the opposite of a "bridge to the overman"; he prevents the affirmation of new values by forgetting how to string the arrow of human longing. He declares himself happy living in a purely vicarious and passive culture where no one seeks to overcome himself, or sees any reason to do so. The Last Man has achieved "the imperative of herd timidity: 'we want that some day there should be *nothing any more to be afraid of*!'"[37]

The paralysis of nihilism can be well illustrated in the realm of aesthetics. Traditionally, in what Nietzsche calls "the completed original folk cultures,"[38] formal canons of style exist to regulate creative expression. Examples would include the vocabulary of the classical orders in architecture, or metrical rules in poetry. These are not merely arbitrary, for they serve to produce works of art that meet cultural expectations, and some forms prove more effective at this than others. Corinthian columns in white marble are useful as a way to communicate impressions of gravity and solemnity, for instance, particularly to viewers accustomed to buildings that use this vocabulary. But once it is recognized that "all artistic styles

[are] bound in place and time"[39]—and that the cultural expectations which these styles serve are contingent—then the rules and grammars of traditional art no longer have any legitimacy, and to use them may appear vicarious and insincere. Nietzsche defines the "modern spirit's lack of discipline" in politics as "tolerance," or "the incapacity for Yes and No," and analogously in aesthetics as "'freedom' versus rules (romanticism)."[40] For the Overman, freedom is a boon. But for ordinary human beings, absolute freedom spells disaster when they try to set pen to paper. Life itself requires "estimating, preferring, being unjust, being limited...."[41] For most people, "preferring" one style or value over another means deferring to the preferences built into a culture—in other words, being "limited." The historical sense of the modern individual leaves him or her without criteria of choice and preference, and hence in the paralytic state of the Last Man. Therefore, Nietzsche wrote, the condition of being

> unhistorical, antihistorical through and through—is the womb not only of an unjust act, but of every just act as well. No artist would ever paint a picture, no general would win a victory, no people would gain its freedom without first having longed for and struggled toward that end in such an unhistorical condition.[42]

This was written before Nietzsche conceived of the Overman, who has the strength to act *despite* his knowledge of historical contingency. One example of an effort at *übermenschlich* aesthetics is the architecture of the Bauhaus. In his manifesto for high modernism, Walter Gropius announced, "We have had enough and to spare of the arbitrary reproduction of historical styles."[43] Instead of vicariously imitating the naive styles of the past, the "modern building should derive its architectural significance solely from the vigour and consequence of its own organic proportions. It must be true to itself...."[44] Gropius supplemented this Nietzschean call to authenticity with a claim that he had moved *beyond* the culturally bound styles of the past, "A breach has been made with the past," he wrote, "the morphology of dead styles has been destroyed; and we are returning to honesty of thought and feeling."[45] Gropius saw historical contingency as the essential challenge that modernism faced. The architects of the early nineteenth century had already recognized this problem, and had responded with an aesthetic of eclectic historicism; Gropius therefore saw himself as a descendent of the great Prussian eclectic, Schinkel.[46] But Gropius' *übermenschlich* architecture was intended to solve the problem of contingency once and for all, by moving beyond the realm of style and culture. "The object of the *Bauhaus* was not to propagate any 'style,' system, dogma, formula, or vogue, but simply to exert a revitalizing influence on design."[47] However, the architecture of the Bauhaus, seen from the perspective of a half-century later, bears the unmistakable stamp of its time; it is just another period style (and perhaps not a very successful one). Gropius foresaw this and lamented it. "A 'Bauhaus style'," he wrote, "would have been a confession of failure and a return to that very stagnation and devitalizing inertia which I had called it into being to combat."[48]

Thus Gropius' hopes for a final end to culture were not fulfilled. In the age of postmodern architecture, the eclecticism and vicariousness of the Last Man is back in style, and the Bauhaus has become yet another source of material to be appropriated. However, Nietzsche might say that Gropius at least had the strength to create something new, to found a style and to put his stamp on an age. Nietzsche thought that the "phenomenon 'artist' is still the most transparent [manifestation of] the basic instincts of power, nature, etc."[49] Thus Gropius' achievement in creating a new style is paradigmatic of the way all ideas and institutions are founded, and even of the way nature, viewed as Will to Power, operates. In any case, creating a new—if ephemeral—style may have been all that Nietzsche expected from the Overman. It is probably a mistake to read the *übermensch* as the founder of a final era beyond good and evil. What makes Zarathustra choke and retch is his recognition that the Last Man will always return, revealing the contingency of any Overman's creations.[50] It is in this sense that the Last Man is—in a constantly repeating sequence of historical development—always "last." Therefore, in order for Zarathustra and Nietzsche to affirm the Overman, they must also affirm the regime of the Last Man, whose nihilism breeds *übermenschlich* acts of revolt, but who always reappropriates the creations of Overmen for a culture of comparison. Indeed, the Overman "can maintain and develop himself most easily in a democratic society...."[51] The genuinely *übermenschlich* art of the Bauhaus was therefore not a permanent departure from the culture of historicism, but a mere moment in this culture. Nevertheless, for Nietzsche, just such moments and individual acts of genius justify an entire age. In a similar way, Nietzsche recognized that his own affirmations—the Eternal Return, the Will to Power, the Overman—were doomed to appropriation by the weak. He probably did not believe that his philosophy would gain anything like a universal or permanent following; that it would ever be seen widely as "true." Nevertheless, it had the *übermenschlich* value of a creative revolt, an authentic affirmation of self. And this was enough to justify it politically: "Mankind must labor unceasingly to produce great individuals. This and nothing else is its function."[52]

Apart from the regime of the Last Man, the other nightmare that plagued Nietzsche was the "long plenitude and sequence of breakdown, destruction, ruin, and cataclysm that is now impending" as a result of the Death of God.[53] The Death of God resulted when Christianity's chief virtue, truthfulness, was at last turned against religion. The search for historical truth resulted in skepticism about the transcendent claims of religion, and "eventually turned against morality, discovered its teleology, its partial perspective...."[54] Luther was an archetypical Christian who, impelled by the love of truth, "surrendered the holy books to everyone—until they finally came into the hands of the philologists, who are the destroyers of every faith that rests on books."[55] At times, it appears that for Nietzsche the death of God was a supremely liberating event, and one to be celebrated. On the other hand, he also speaks of an "approaching gloom"[56] which will overwhelm Europe as morality gradually perishes: "this is the great spectacle in a hundred acts reserved for the next two centuries in Europe—the most terrible, most questionable, and perhaps also the most hopeful of all spectacles.—"[57] So although Nietzsche harbors hopes for an eventual transvaluation of all values, he does not by any means consider this a foregone conclusion, nor does he look forward to the gloom and cataclysm that will result between the death of the old values and the birth of the new. "Nihilism represents a pathological transitional stage," he writes; and he wonders "whether the productive forces are not yet strong enough, or whether decadence still hesitates and has not yet invented its remedies."[58]

Nihilism contained at least one more danger. Nietzsche was well acquainted with "antiquarian historians" who believed in *Weltanschauung*-historicism, but who deplored the failure of pluralist modernity to live up to the ideal of a *Weltanschauung*. Like Nietzsche, these Romantics thought that modern society was nihilistic—but Nietzsche disapproved of their reactionary proposals for reform. Nietzsche thought that it was dangerous to apply ideas about organic, homogeneous cultures to the pluralist states of the nineteenth century. He too detested pluralism and admired the homogeneity of the Greek polis; but he did not want to step backward culturally, like his Romantic contemporaries. A consistent enemy of the "Men of the Fatherlands" (among them, his brother-in-law), Nietzsche worried that *Weltanschauung*-historicists would try to *make* their societies homogeneous through violent suppression of differences.[59]

The deep problem for Nietzsche was that he possessed no criterion for preferring *übermenschlich* authenticity to the banality of the last man's happiness, or disciplined self-overcoming to militarism, cataclysm and political cruelty. His own loathing for German nationalism is clear, for example, but he can give no *reasons* for this attitude. Zarathustra, after all, is not one of those who has a "Why?" Even if we accept Nietzsche's dictum that cruelty is a sign of weakness, he cannot give us any reason to prefer strength. In 1888, he wrote:

> It is my good fortune that after whole millennia of error and confusion I have rediscovered the way that leads to a Yes and a No.
> I teach the No to all that makes weak—that exhausts.
> I teach the Yes to all that strengthens, that stores up strength, that justifies the feeling of strength.[60]

But this judgment is neither neutral and uncontroversial, nor grounded in any transcendent "truth." At times, Nietzsche uses "life" as if it were a transcendent value, on the basis of which strength can be preferred to weakness, creativity to cruelty. But this sounds suspiciously metaphysical and therefore unlikely to be Nietzsche's real, esoteric position. In fact, he comments that "Judgments, value judgments about life, for or against, can in the end never be true...."[61] So Nietzsche is unable to provide a grounding for his political preferences even by complaining that a given form of decadence harms "life." Nietzsche recognized the decadence of the Last Man in his own society, and he also predicted the arrival of a weak species of nihilist who would take advantage of the Death of God to spread cruelty and cataclysm. But he had no firm ground on which to criticize these awful developments.

IV. The Overman

However, insofar as Nietzsche sought to teach or exemplify anything, his message to potential Overmen seems to have been an attitude of authenticity and liberation from the contingencies of culture. Since the dominant culture of modernity is composed of Socratic rationalism and historicism, liberation from it means freedom from objectivity and seriousness; it means a call to "play" and "dance" and "laugh," to be a "free spirit," to practice a "gay science."[62]

The Overman must live beyond culture, but he must show no resentment or resistance against cultural norms, for this would reveal his continued embroilment in the web of history:

> *"The Wanderer Speaks"*—If one would like to see our European morality for once as it looks from a distance ..., then one has to proceed like a wanderer who wants to know how high the towers in a town are: he *leaves* the town. "Thoughts about moral prejudices," if they are not meant to be prejudices about prejudices, presuppose a position *outside* morality, some point beyond good and evil to which one has to rise, climb, or fly.[63]

Nietzsche is perfectly willing to admit that the desire to move beyond culture may itself be a contingent value, "a minor madness," "a peculiar and unreasonable 'you must'—for we seekers for knowledge also have our idiosyncrasies of 'unfree will'—[but] the question is whether one really *can* get up there." The answer is a qualified yes; but in order to do so, one has to be *"very light."*[64] In a section of *Zarathustra* entitled "The Wanderer," the "Hour" tells Zarathustra: "You ... have wanted to see the reason [*Grund*] for things and their background: so you must climb above yourself— up, beyond, until you have even your *stars* under you."[65] Zarathustra responds by taking up the challenge fully, even daring to hope that he can gain a vantage point from which to see the illusion of himself as a grammatical subject: "Yes! To look down upon myself and even upon my stars: that alone I would call my *summit*, that has remained for me as my *final* summit!"[66] When all footholds disappear for Zarathustra in the rarified atmosphere beyond culture, objectivity, selfhood, grammar and truth, he learns to use his own head and heart as means of ascent, climbing "upon" them—that is, above and beyond them. "Lift up your hearts, my brothers," cries Zarathustra to the Higher Men: "high, higher! And don't forget your legs! Lift up your legs, too, you fine dancers: and better still, stand on your heads!"[67]

One of the most important metaphysical fictions that the Overman seeks to transcend is the category of "man" itself. However "man" (or "human") is defined within a given culture, it is (according to Nietzsche) a construct created by people from their contingent perspectives in order to serve their wills to power. Thus the Overman is not only above and beyond grammar, reason and morals; he is over-man. Zarathustra is always saying: "Man is something that should be overcome."[68] Of course, one cannot think without falling back on the construct "man" or "person" as long as one uses verbs and pronouns. Even my statement, a few sentences back, that "people" create arbitrary definitions of "man," is, from the Overman's perspective, a fiction. That is why Zarathustra holds out the transcendence of man as a perpetual goal, but not one which he has attained in any satisfactory sense.[69]

The world that the Wanderer would find if he could ascend beyond culture is one that Nietzsche had tried to describe metaphorically, in *The Birth of Tragedy*, as the sphere of Dionysus. It is a world that defies literal description, because within it, the subject (a socially constructed fiction) no longer has any objective distance from reality, and can no longer make distinctions or observations. That is why Nietzsche says in *The Birth of Tragedy* that once the cultural veil of *maya* is lifted, what is revealed is a "mysterious primordial unity."[70] In his later work, Nietzsche is more likely to say that the soul that moves beyond culture enters an abyss, "plunges joyously into chance, ... dives into becoming."[71] This abyss can only be described negatively, as the absence of being and the subject. Any positive description presented in grammatical form would be inadequate, because grammar itself presupposes the category of being. Nietzsche's philosophy therefore has something in common with the mystical Negative Theology of Pseudo-Dionysius the Areopagite or Meister Eckhart—except that the world Nietzsche's Overman beholds is our own mundane world, merely viewed from an extrahistorical perspective. Nietzsche thought that Heraclitus had grasped something of the spirit of this perspective when he conjured up a vision in which "qualities struggle with one another, in accordance with inviolable laws and measures that are immanent in the battle."[72] Heraclitus' genius was, Nietzsche thought, to recognize that "things, in whose definiteness and endurance narrow human and animal minds believe, have no real existence."[73] In a note written in 1885, Nietzsche asks, "Do you know what 'the world' is to me?" The quotation marks around "world" already give away the fact that Nietzsche will not be able to provide an objective description of the world as it is; and he makes this even more clear in the next sentence: "Shall I show it to you in my mirror?"[74] The image of a world reflected in a mirror allows Nietzsche to suggest, first, that his cosmology is immanent in the cosmos, the product of physical processes like everything else; second, that he will only show us the world from *his* perspective; and third, that his image requires interpretation by the reader and even by him, the author, for he holds his vision at arm's length. This said, the world that

Nietzsche shows us in his mirror is Heraclitean, a product of subtracting being and the subject from our concept of nature. It is a

> monster of energy ... enclosed by 'nothingness' as by a boundary; not something blurry or wasted ... but set in a definite space as a definite force ... as force throughout, as a play of forces and waves of forces ... a sea of forces flowing and rushing together, eternally changing ... a becoming that knows no satiety, no disgust, no weariness ...

"This world," says Nietzsche, "is the will to power—and nothing besides!"[75] A world of will to power, of mere quanta of energy, is what is left (as Nietzsche thought Heraclitus had discovered) when we cut through the veil of *maya* imposed by language and discover a universe without being. But this image, too, is only the product of a will to power—Nietzsche's will to power. And since it annihilates the notion of the human subject, it is a vision that is impossible to contemplate: "To think away the subject—that is to want to represent to oneself a world without a subject: this is a contradiction: to represent without representation!"[76] Nevertheless, to behold this vision is Zarathustra's "final summit." Nietzsche speculates that "it might be a basic characteristic of existence that those who would know it completely would perish, in which case the strength of a spirit should be measured according to how much of the 'truth' one could still barely endure—or to put it more clearly, to what degree one would *require* it to be thinned down, shrouded, sweetened, blunted, falsified."[77]

Thus Zarathustra is beyond culture because he is able to say No to all that culture constructs, including grammar, being and his own existence: these are all forms of "falsification." Yet this does not leave him, Hamlet-like, in a state of paralysis; from some mysterious source, he gains the strength to say Yes:

> The psychological problem in the type of Zarathustra is how he that says No and *does* No to an unheard-of degree, to everything to which one has so far said Yes, can nevertheless be the opposite of the No-saying spirit; how the spirit who bears the heaviest fate ... can nevertheless be the lightest and most transcendent—Zarathustra is a dancer—how he that has the hardest, most terrible insight into reality, that has thought the "most abysmal idea," nevertheless does not consider it an objection to existence, not even to

its eternal recurrence—but rather one reason more for
being himself the eternal Yes to all things.[78]

Tracy B. Strong has demonstrated convincingly that
Zarathustra's attitude is formed from a synthesis of Jesus and
Socrates.[79] Both men were in some sense "beyond culture," rejecting
the explicit laws of their community. Socrates responded to the
uncritical affirmation of local customs that was shown by Greek
culture with a dialectical method that said No to everything.
Jesus, on the other hand, grew up within a society that functioned
by rejecting all *non*-local practices; his response was an unqualified
Yes to the whole world, Jew and gentile. "While every noble
morality develops from a triumphant affirmation of itself, slave
morality from the outset says No to what is 'outside,' what is 'different,'
what is 'not itself'; and *this* No is its creative deed."[80] Socrates was
a nay-sayer born within a master morality; Jesus, a triumphant
yes-sayer born among slaves. But Socrates lacked the strength to
affirm the nihilistic world that his dialectic revealed; whereas
Jesus lacked any recognition of nihilism to accompany his joyous
affirmation. Zarathustra takes Socrates' No and adds Jesus' Yes,
thereby exemplifying the Overman.

Thus the Overman is characterized by his liberation from all
arbitrary bonds of culture. He has used his recognition of the multiplicity
of *Weltanschauungen* as a kind of ladder up to the heights at
which rationality no longer appears binding. From these heights,
even the notion of multiple cultures no longer seems true; so the
Overman has, so to speak, pulled his ladder up after him. But the
Last Man, too, is defined as a person who feels no conventions to
be binding. A similar freedom is the defining mark of the Free
Spirit, also, and even of the Good European. For the purposes of a
diagnosis of modern culture, Nietzsche describes these characters
separately, just as human virtues and vices might be treated as
discrete characters in an allegory. But it seems to me that the
same person could be described at once as admirably free from
social conventions, *and* as deprived of all sense of meaning or purpose.
Thus Walter Gropius was a Last Man insofar as he considered no
style of architecture to be inherently beautiful; but he was an
Overman simultaneously, insofar as he nevertheless chose to build
buildings. I use Gropius as an example of an Overman because he
thought, at least, that he had cultivated his *übermenschlich* qualities
to an outstanding degree. He was, so to speak, deeper along the
axis of "Overman" than along that of "Last Man." But if we wanted
to gain a truly three-dimensional picture of Walter Gropius—or of

anyone else—we would have to see him from *many* perspectives. This is something that Nietzsche calls for explicitly: "Problem: to see things as they are! Means: to be able to see them from a hundred eyes, from many persons."[81] And it is a project that Nietzsche carries out to a remarkable degree. Constantly changing his perspective, he disparages modernity for its nihilism, and then praises it for its creativity in the next breath. This is a classic example of Nietzsche's effort to avoid objectivity by wearing a series of masks. The sum total of his work is a three-dimensional picture of modernity, analogous to a photograph taken from many angles at once. "The wisest man," Nietzsche wrote in 1884, "would be the one richest in contradictions, who has, as it were, antennae for all types of men—as well as his great moments of *grand harmony* ..."[82]

Nietzsche tells us that the essence of a thing (for example, "punishment") is its history, its genealogy. A genealogy (in normal usage) is a tool for describing a set of people in terms of their relations to one individual. Thus many family trees can be drawn of the same set of people: for example, the Tudors could be described as Henry VII's progeny or as Elizabeth's ancestors. So it comes as no surprise that the modern human being, the citizen of a "culture of comparison," belongs at once to several family trees. Describing the origins of the modern nihilist, Nietzsche therefore provides several genealogical stories: this is equivalent to saying that he describes the present from several perspectives. Thus the modern nihilist (for example, Walter Gropius) could be placed, first of all, in a story about the loss of value in Western art. This story would constitute a kind of family tree of the Last Man. It might begin with medieval religious painting, which was not representational or perspectival, but attempted to capture the essence of the sacred by means of a talismanic or iconic stand-in.[83] This art was supplanted by Renaissance painting, which depicted religious events as they would appear to a human viewer. As part of the story of the rise of the Last Man, e.g., Walter Gropius, this development could be described as a profound loss of meaning and value, even as the first stage in the death of God. But as part of the family tree of the Overman, e.g., Walter Gropius, the same event would take on the character of an act of liberation.

Renaissance painting still depicted the inherited moral norms of a culture without the more radical perspectivism that results from a "historical sense." But another generation of Walter Gropius' ancestors arose when historicist nineteenth-century artists began to depict the ideals of numerous cultures in an eclectic, vicarious—Nietzsche would say "nihilist"—fashion. Nineteenth-century art became the object of Nietzsche's ridicule because of its vicariousness, its lack

of substance; but it was also the art of the Good European and the
Free Spirit, who had been liberated from the arbitrary closed societies
of the Men of the Fatherlands. Finally, yet another "generation"
arose to supplant historicism in the era of high modernism, when
Braque and Picasso, among others, began to treat even the
perspectival space of Old Master paintings as something arbitrary
and invented; they experimented with alternative forms of spatial
perspective. This development paralleled Nietzsche's turning of
science against itself, and it resulted in a further loss of meaning—
but also in a further dose of freedom. Thus the "seeds" of nihilism
were present in the Last Man's "family" all along:

> why is the arrival of nihilism *necessary*? Because our previous
> values themselves draw it in their wake; because nihilism is
> the logical result of thinking through our greatest values and
> ideals to the end—because we must experience nihilism first,
> to be able to uncover precisely what the worth of these values
> was...."[84]

But it would be just as much in the spirit of Nietzsche to say that
the arrival of the *Overman*, rather than the nihilist, was a necessary
and logical result of thinking through our values. In a few paragraphs
of *Twilight of the Idols*, Nietzsche tells the "History of an Error"
(metaphysics) from Plato's concept of Forms to the "zenith of
mankind"—Nietzsche's philosophy—at which point: "INCIPIT
ZARATHUSTRA." This is just a positive way of retelling the story
which, in its pessimistic version, ends with nihilism and the Last
Man.[85]

Part Three

A Vindication of the Last Man

Chapter 8

Nietzsche Today

I. The Modern Quarrel in the Humanities

In recent years, the humanities have become the focus of a heated debate. Some of the controversy has involved the *content* of curricula: critics have charged that the experience of large groups of people—women, the working class, or nonwhites—is systematically ignored. I will have something more to say about this kind of criticism (which I generally endorse) in the next chapter. But, as I argued in the Introduction, critics of the content of the modern humanities are not critics of humanism per se. They believe, in general, that it is possible to understand texts and ideas from the past, and that doing so has moral and political value. These were two beliefs which Nietzsche criticized; and several contemporary parties in the quarrel over the humanities share Nietzsche's more fundamental skepticism.

On one side (which it seems fair to call the "right"), are those who believe that the modern humanities—having accepted the insights of historicism and committed themselves to studying a potentially endless diversity of cultures—have lost their moral function. These Right Nietzscheans believe that a culture must be unhistorical and closed if it is to survive and retain its capacity to differentiate between good and evil. They therefore advocate a return to an allegedly universal and univocal canon of Western

151

classics, much like that which Nietzsche encountered at Pforta. On the other side are those who argue openly that no objective meaning or values can be discovered in works of literature. These critics, equally Nietzschean, argue that the methods of the humanities must be replaced with something new: the attitude of a Free Spirit who is somehow beyond culture. In the following pages, I will offer an account of the contemporary Right and Left Nietzscheans, as represented, respectively, by Leo Strauss and Jacques Derrida.[1] Each author's reading of Nietzsche is fruitful, and each project demonstrates what it might mean to be his disciple. Strauss and his followers are helpful in showing how Nietzsche's esotericism can be kept alive, and how the regime of the Last Man might be resisted in a Nietzschean spirit. Derrida, on the other hand, openly preaches Nietzsche's esoteric views, and applies them in interesting ways to the study of culture. In the last chapter, I made use of Left Nietzschean interpretations to illustrate Nietzsche's "womanly" mask, and his position outside metaphysics. But I will suggest here that both Left and Right Nietzschean positions depend upon a notion of "culture" that is much like Nietzsche's, and that this dependence constitutes their Achilles' heel.

II. A "Right" Nietzschean: Leo Strauss and his Followers

In *Ecce Homo*, Nietzsche heaps contempt upon those who misinterpret him, and remarks that if some people don't understand him, this is "perfectly in order." But he adds that part of his audience does understand him, for "... I have even real geniuses among my readers."[2] This sounds slightly optimistic, given the total number of readers Nietzsche had in 1888; but his wish may have come true more recently. (After all, Nietzsche speaks of himself as one of those "posthumous people" who are only truly born after their death.)[3] There is a school of philosophers who, I believe, have entered into a kind of secret discipleship of Nietzsche. This school is composed of followers of Leo Strauss, who have exercised a powerful influence on humanistic education in the United States and to a lesser extent in Germany and Italy.[4] Straussians hold professorships at many major universities in North America. One orthodox Straussian text, Allan Bloom's *Closing of the American Mind*, became a bestseller, as did a book by one of his students, Francis Fukuyama.[5] Strauss has been called the "guru of American conservatism";[6] during the Reagan and Bush administrations, his influence extended to the State Department's policy planning staff, the Department of Education and the Office of the Vice President.

My thesis that Strauss was an esoteric Nietzschean is contentious; at first glance, Strauss appears to be a passionate *critic* of historicism and nihilism and a believer in natural law. However, there is substantial evidence that he was a secret Nietzschean. The most important indication is his method of interpreting the writers of the past: he says, for example, that they always state their sincere views only at the precise center of their books, and put their own ideas in the mouths of other authors. As a general hermeneutic method, this seems eccentric at best. But Strauss asks us to apply his method to his own works,[7] in which case nihilism emerges like the solution to a puzzle. In addition, Strauss began life as an overt historicist who later attacked this doctrine, but only because of its alleged immoral effects; he never provides an argument against it. Furthermore, although he claims to be a natural law theorist, merely transmitting the doctrines that all great Western thinkers have always held, he never states the content of these doctrines, and the most he says about natural law is that it is always "changeable."[8] Finally, Strauss alludes systematically to Nietzsche without acknowledging his debt in a straightforward way; and in particular, he borrows Nietzsche's methods of writing esoterically.[9]

Like Nietzsche, Strauss began as a historicist, believing that "truth is a function of time (historical epoch) or that every philosophy belongs to a definite time and place (country)."[10] From historicism he moved to nihilism, or the rejection of all truth, including even the "truths" of history; and he continued to hold nihilism as a secret position. But like Nietzsche, he also began to preach an exoteric antihistorical doctrine, which has been widely read and admired. Leo Strauss therefore serves as a quintessential example of a certain kind of *übermensch*.

The closest Strauss comes to revealing the true nature of his ideas is in a 1961 essay entitled "Relativism." Here he denounces liberals and positivists for claiming to accept relativism, while inconsistently treating tolerance and objectivity, respectively, as absolute standards. Nietzsche—in contrast to these well-meaning but intellectually dishonest versions of "the last man"—is *"the* philosopher of relativism: the first thinker who faced the problem of relativism in its full extent and pointed to the way in which relativism can be overcome."[11] Immediately Strauss adds, "Relativism came to Nietzsche's attention in the form of historicism... ."[12] And the aspect of historicism that concerns Strauss is the belief in *Weltanschauungen*:

i.e., the theory that science (for example) "may depend... on the spirit of the age."[13] Strauss' own *Weltanschauung*-historicism is evident, for example, in his belief that "the human species consists by nature of tribes or nations, *ethne;*"[14] or in his claim that "there can only be closed societies... ."[15] He argues that for Nietzsche, history "teaches a truth that is deadly."[16] This "truth" is that the norms of each culture are thoroughly arbitrary; but people must nevertheless believe in the transcendent value of these norms, "which limit their horizon and thus enable them to have character and style."[17] Historical research reveals the contingency of all values, and thereby paralyzes us. The Romantic response—"that one fabricates a myth"—is "patently impossible for men of intellectual probity."[18] The "true solution" is not Romanticism but Nietzschean philosophy, which reveals, first of all, that historical research is as contingent as everything else: "Objective history suffices for destroying the delusion of the objective validity of any principles of thought and action; [but] it does not suffice for opening up a genuine understanding of history... ."[19] Any such understanding is a chimera; and with the very distinction between truth and lie removed, space is opened up for a "new project—the revaluation of all values... . It is in this way that Nietzsche may be said to have transformed the deadly truth of relativism into the most life-giving truth ..."[20]

Strauss, a lifelong admirer of Heidegger, agrees with him that Nietzsche may have faltered in the end and produced merely a new, dogmatic version of metaphysics with his doctrine of the Will to Power. (This seems untrue to me, since the Will to Power was merely Nietzsche's *exoteric* doctrine.) But Strauss describes Heidegger's "existentialism" as an "attempt to free Nietzsche's alleged overcoming of relativism from the consequences of [Nietzsche's] relapse into metaphysics or of his recourse to nature."[21] Thus, according to Strauss, Heideggerian philosophy is simply a more consistent version of Nietzscheanism. Heidegger was a nihilist: in other words, he was a relativist with "angst."[22] Strauss summarizes Heidegger's position as a Nietzschean discovery of nihilism, reached through a recognition of relativism, and arriving at last at the following point:

> The fundamental phenomenon, the only phenomenon that is not hypothetical, is the abyss of freedom: the fact that man is compelled to choose groundlessly; the fundamental experience, i.e., an experience more fundamental than every science, is the experience of the objective groundlessness of all principles of thought and action, the experience of nothingness.[23]

Thus even historical scholarship rests, ultimately, on a groundless choice to pursue a certain kind of arbitrary procedure. "Rationalism itself rests on nonrational, unevident assumptions; in spite of its seemingly overwhelming power, rationalism is hollow."[24] Strauss' article ends almost as soon as he has invoked Heidegger's name, and before he has given any exposition of Heidegger's positive doctrines. "I can allude here only to one point," he writes, "to Heidegger's teaching regarding historical truth." About even this he says practically nothing, except that, for Heidegger, "true understanding of a thinker is understanding him creatively, i.e., understanding him differently from the way he understood himself."[25] This is the key to Strauss' own philosophy, which consists almost entirely of creative (mis)readings of thinkers from the past. Thus Strauss owes much to Heidegger, whose ideas are "of the greatest importance to man as man."[26] Heidegger, he claims, "surpasses in speculative intelligence all his contemporaries and is at the same time intellectually the counterpart to what Hitler was politically [i.e., a nihilist]"[27] Strauss is a nihilist too, esoterically; his only insight is a knowledge of the Nietzschean\Heideggerian abyss. But he wants to turn back from this spectre of groundlessness, *übermenschlich*, to produce a comforting illusion for the herd. Yet in order that this myth should not to be a mere Romantic fabrication, it must *at the same time* reveal the secret of nihilism to those clever enough to follow Strauss' hints. Strauss' vehicle for preaching this double-edged message is the deliberate misinterpretation of past philosophers, whom (just like Heidegger) he "understands creatively."

A typical Straussian text begins with an apparent denunciation of historicism. For example, in *Natural Right and History*, he contrasts the "self-evident truths" of the liberal Enlightenment, which constituted a version of natural right, against the modern "historical sense," which has led us "eventually to unqualified relativism." According to historicists, he says, "all societies have their ideals, cannibal societies no less than civilized ones."[28] This kind of moral *reductio* is meant to prevent the conventionally moral herd from endorsing historicism. Richard Schacht summarizes Strauss' rhetorical strategy as follows: "These developments [sc. historicism and relativism] lead to Nietzsche. It would be too horrible if Nietzsche were right. Therefore Nietzsche must be wrong."[29] According to Strauss, historicism "asserted that all human thought and action are essentially dependent on historical situations, the sequence of which proves to have no rational goal or meaning."[30] Historicism therefore led inevitably to cynicism about the value of the great philosophies of the past. This, in turn, led to a general loss of nerve among European intellectuals, a new "doubt about the superiority of the purposes of the West."[31] In the past, the West had striven to construct "a universal society of free and equal nations of free and equal men and women enjoying universal affluence, and therefore universal justice and happiness, through science understood as the conquest of nature in the service of human power."[32] But this had depended on a sure belief in universal principles, among them the "self-evident" values of the American Founding Fathers: liberty, justice, and the pursuit of happiness. Historicism suggested that these principles were culturally-relative and ultimately groundless.

Echoing Nietzsche's *Untimely Meditations*, Strauss writes that a recognition of cultural relativism brings on nihilism by destroying the "protecting atmosphere within which life or culture or action is alone possible."[33] This is a clear disaster for moral theory and practice; but Strauss maintains that "we are able, and hence obliged, to look for a [transcendent] standard with reference to which we can judge of the ideals of our own as well as of any other society."[34] This standard is "natural right," the ostensible subject of Strauss' book. However, the content and consequences of natural right turn out to be remarkably elusive. All we find out for certain is that "all natural right is changeable,"[35] an assertion that seems to undercut its status as transcendent and universal. Strauss' true views about natural right are expressed in his essay on Nietzsche:

> The philosophers' science of morals claimed to have discovered the foundation of morals either in nature or in reason. Apart from all other defects of that pretended science it rests on the gratuitous assumption that morality can or must be natural (according to nature) or rational. Yet every morality is based on some tyranny against nature as well as against reason.[36]

In an essay entitled "On Natural Law," Strauss explicitly states that the belief in *Weltanschauung* (which he shares) has destroyed natural law. "Since every notion of good and right belongs to a specific *Weltanschauung*, there cannot be natural law binding to men as men." Even "Science... is but one historical, contingent form of man's understanding of the world... ."[37]

In works like *Natural Right and History*, Strauss only puts such relativist remarks in the mouths of his purported enemies. His own position is supposed to be antihistoricist. Strauss argues *against* historicism by suggesting that empirical history, "far from legitimizing the historicist inference ..., seems rather to prove that all human thought, and certainly all philosophic thought, is concerned with the same themes or the same fundamental problems, and therefore that there exists an unchanging framework which persists in all changes of human knowledge of both facts and principles"[38] Furthermore, Strauss argues that all of historicism's basic slogans are self-contradictory. For example, whenever the historicist says, "Everything is relative," he thereby claims a universal, timeless truth about human history. Whenever he says, "All ideas are the mere product of their time," he posits a description of all ideas, which—he wants us to believe—is not itself a mere product of its time. Thus Strauss argues that historicism must inevitably slip into nihilism, because the historian, just like his historical subject, is conditioned by his cultural context:

> Historicism thrives on the fact that it inconsistently exempts itself from its own verdict about all human thought. The historicist thesis is self-contradictory or absurd. We cannot see the historical character of 'all' thought—that is, of all thought with the exception of the historicist insight and its implications—without transcending history, without grasping something trans-historical.[39]

But Strauss is one historicist who is willing to be ruthlessly consistent, to apply historicism to itself and thus to undermine the foundations of all rationality by making no reasons appear better than any other. Describing the genesis of his first major work, *Spinoza's Critique of Religion*, Strauss admits that he "therefore began to wonder whether the self-destruction of reason was not the inevitable outcome of modern rationality."[40] Thus for Strauss it is possible to "transcend history"[41] by means of a radicalization of the historical sense—but the Dionysian space one thereby enters is irrational and intoxicating. In his later works, Strauss avoids making this antirational, deconstructive move explicitly, leaving it to readers who recognize his esotericism. Nor does he ever offer any positive account of what a transcendent, "natural" alternative to historicism would be. All he can suggest is that the best societies are those which protect "the highest activity"—that is, philosophy; and that because of its failure to do this, the "contemporary solution" is "*contra naturam.*"[42]

It may seem strange to see societies described as "unnatural" only insofar they are hostile to philosophy. After all, when Strauss describes philosophy as the "highest activity," he seems to imply that it is far removed from nature. And he says explicitly that "every morality is based on some tyranny against nature... ."[43] But Strauss explains his intentions in an essay on Nietzsche's *Beyond Good And Evil*. Here he quotes Nietzsche—"there has never yet been a natural humanity"—to show that all ideas of nature and naturalness are subjective, human creations.[44] But, Nietzsche says, man must be *made* natural [*vernatürlicht*]" by philosophy.[45] Strauss follows Nietzsche in redefining nature as the sphere of Dionysus, and therefore as the province of philosophers who are beyond culture, beyond any contingent good and evil. The role of Nietzsche's Overman is to create values, to set up moral and aesthetic criteria which seem to ordinary people to carry the sanction of nature. So "nature" is a myth, the creation of Dionysian Overmen. Therefore, any society that fails to tolerate the Dionysian philosopher is, by definition, "*contra naturam*." Like Nietzsche, Strauss holds that cultures are only justified by the geniuses that they create; and genius means, above all, being beyond culture.

A closer examination of Strauss' idea of "philosophy" reveals that he means by this precisely the radicalization of historicism, the use of historical relativism to undermine the very structures of rationality which gave it birth. He writes, "the enlightenment critique of the tradition must be radicalized, as it was by Nietzsche, into a critique of the principles of the tradition... . The 'historicization' of philosophy is therefore, and only therefore, justified and necessary."[46] Thus the true Straussian philosopher is a Nietzschean nihilist. But he dares not state his view openly, for he depends upon society—at least for leisure and sustenance—and he knows that philosophy, if openly preached, will destroy society. Therefore, Strauss says:

> Philosophers or scientists who hold this view about the relations of philosophy or science and society are driven to employ a peculiar manner of writing which would enable them to reveal what they regard as the truth to the few, without endangering the unqualified commitment of the many to the opinions on which society rests. They will distinguish between the true teaching as the esoteric teaching and the socially useful teaching as the exoteric teaching; whereas the exoteric teaching is meant to be easily accessible to every reader, the esoteric teaching discloses itself only to the very careful and well-trained readers after long and careful study.[47]

The epitome of such a philosopher is Nietzsche. It might be objected that Nietzsche certainly tried to undermine his readers' "unqualified commitment" to the values on which society rests. But Nietzsche's description of his own project includes several comments like the following:

> Do we immoralists do virtue any *harm?*—As little as anarchists do princes. Only once they have been shot at do they again sit firmly on their thrones. Moral: one must shoot at morals.[48]

True enough, Nietzsche wants his *übermenschlich* readers to recognize the contingency of all values; but he only wants this message to get through to those who are strong and crafty enough to create *new* morals. Nietzsche's worst nightmare is a herd which has seen all its morals dethroned, but is unable to say a new "Yes." The "Last Man" is Nietzsche's caricature of the relativist, nihilist weakling, who, contemplating the dogmas of the past, can say only: "In the past, all the world was mad." "'What is love? What is creation? What is longing? What is a star?' thus asks the Last Man and blinks."[49] Rather than suffer the regime of the Last Man, Nietzsche would rather "drive [people] to extremes, pit them one against each other, people against people, and this for centuries; then perhaps, as from a stray spark from the terrible energy thus ignited, the light of genius will blaze up suddenly."[50] Nietzsche's preference for a culture based on commitment (any commitment)— and his abhorrence for the Last Man's nihilistic tolerance— is shared by Strauss. Hence Strauss' decision to embrace Judaism, despite his esoteric atheism.[51] Hence also Francis Fukuyama's nostalgia for the Cold War, despite his lack of commitment to either communism or democratic capitalism. Allan Bloom follows Strauss and Nietzsche when he writes, "it was not necessarily the best of times in America when Catholics and Protestants were suspicious of and hated one another, but at least they were taking their beliefs seriously."[52] Bloom's target in *The Closing of the American Mind* is the bourgeois nihilist who, open to everything, is in fact closed to any serious commitment.

III. Strauss' Duplicitous Texts

But the opponent of nihilism who is himself "beyond" all values cannot simply announce this position openly, without risking the conversion of all his readers to Last Men. Like Nietzsche, therefore, Strauss developed an intricate method for presenting his two-tiered philosophy, such that it would serve a conservative, antirelativist purpose when read by the many, but reveal the "truth" of nihilism to the sophisticated few. All of his works contain "readings" of political philosophers from the past. These interpretations allegedly reveal that all the great political philosophers possessed esoteric teachings, which they clothed in exoteric garb. These teachings are described in the most elliptical and vague fashion; for example, Bloom merely says that Strauss "enabled [him] to learn strange and wonderful things" from old books.[53] What these strange things are, Bloom does not specify; but they seem to involve at least a secret repudiation of God and a privileging of (Nietzschean) philosophy as the only ennobling activity. Strauss provides a series of clues that he believes can be used to reveal his predecessors' esoteric doctrines. For example, he claims that great philosophers always place their "truths" not at the beginning of books, but in the exact middle, surrounded by great quantities of dry and irrelevant material; they use numerological clues to reveal their true intent; and they attribute their esoteric doctrines to past thinkers whom they pretend to attack.

Strauss claimed to have learned his hermeneutic methods by imitating the medieval Islamic and Jewish interpreters of Plato, who read Plato as an esoteric author. Medieval philosophers outside the Christian tradition had been faced with a problem that Plato also faced: the problem of practicing philosophy in an age when philosophy was not tolerated. Socrates had died because he had openly expressed his views, so his disciple Plato had begun a tradition of concealing esoteric philosophical truths under an exoteric cover. Strauss and his medieval antecedents had recognized the esoteric meaning in Plato because they belonged to a transhistorical class of persecuted philosophers, adept at communicating with each other in subtle and esoteric ways. Thus Strauss adopted Nietzsche's vision of the "republic of geniuses: each [intellectual] giant calls to his brother across the desolate intervals of the ages, and, undisturbed by the wanton noises of the dwarfs who carry on beneath them, they continue their high spirit-talk."[54] Like Nietzsche, Strauss raises "the possibility that all philosophers form a class by themselves, or that what unites all genuine philosophers is more important than what unites a given philosopher with a particular group of non-philosophers [such as the ordinary people of his time]."[55] Along these lines, Strauss concluded that, not only was Plato not a mere child of his time; but he was actually a secret critic or enemy of the world around him—he was Untimely. Strauss further suggested that modern democracies that tolerate philosophy are the exception rather than the rule, so that modern historians, because of their lack of experience with persecution, are unique in not responding to esoteric messages.

He cited Lessing, Bodin, Hobbes, Burke, Condorcet, and others as his predecessors in the art of "reading between the lines."[56]

Plato was, in Strauss' view, the first esoteric philosopher. His philosophy was, moreover, fundamentally a discussion of esoteric philosophy, rather than a statement of any metaphysical view: it was metaphilosophy. "Strictly," he says, "there is then no Platonic teaching... ." Instead of teaching us anything about justice, Plato merely meditated about the process of meditating about justice, i.e., about the role of philosophy. Thus Plato "succeeds in reducing the question of the possibility of the just city to the question of the coincidence of philosophy and political power."[57] Plato answers his own question by concluding that philosophy in its pure form is incompatible with politics, as the fate of Socrates proves; but philosophers can still serve a useful purpose if they disseminate their truths skillfully to a chosen few, and try to bring the mass of people around to their opinions by means of rhetoric and even convenient lies. Strauss is able to elicit all of this out of a text, the *Republic*, which says something quite different on the surface. He makes Plato into an antimetaphysical philosopher without a doctrine—in other words, into Nietzsche. To do this, he relies on a number of clues which (he tells us) Plato placed in the text in order to inform the true philosopher that he was speaking ironically. Thus, for example, Strauss says that Plato cannot have been serious about the doctrine of Forms, which "is utterly incredible, not to say... fantastic."[58] And since the theory of Forms is necessary as a justification for the rule of philosopher-kings, Plato obviously disapproved of the rule of philosophers. Thus the *Republic* was actually a veiled warning against the tyranny of Socratic men; but only those philosophically sophisticated enough to reject the theory of Forms can recognize Plato's ironic intent.[59]

As a tool for interpreting the history of political philosophy, Strauss' method has appeared arbitrary to most critics. Miles Burnyeat, for example, remarks that "Exegesis is Strauss' substitute for argument."[60] But Strauss' methods can also be applied to his own writing, in which case they reveal his total adherence to Nietzsche. For example, we discover that Strauss does not straightforwardly oppose historicism, as he claims at the *beginning* of *Natural Right and History*; rather he endorses the cultural relativism that he puts in the mouths of Nietzsche, Weber, and Heidegger, his apparent enemies.[61] He attacks these thinkers for doing damage to the tradition of natural right, which is the source of the vitality of the West, and therefore for committing a "crime" in the terms of herd morality—but he never claims that they are wrong from a perspective that is beyond good and evil.

What is more, Strauss' hermeneutic tools apply well to Nietzsche, many of whose duplicitous methods he simply borrowed. When Strauss tried to show that Plato was a secret nihilist by arguing that the theory of the Forms was "fantastic," he was offering a deeply improbable interpretation. But Nietzsche's doctrines of the Will to Power and Eternal Return really are fantastic and were deliberately designed to subvert themselves. Strauss' "Note on the Plan of *Beyond Good and Evil*" reveals his understanding of, and indebtedness to, Nietzsche's esotericism. (On his request, this essay was published in the exact center of his *Studies in Platonic Political Philosophy*.) Since Strauss' death, Michael Allen Gillespie has drawn attention to Nietzsche's use of numerological clues—just the kind of signals that Strauss found throughout the canon of great books.[62] Finally, David Allison points out that Nietzsche deliberately undermines the status of his own genealogical method with a comment that appears in the *precise center* of the *Genealogy of Morals*:

> All events in the organic world are a subduing, a becoming master, and all subduing and becoming master involves a fresh interpretation, an adaptation through which any previous "meaning" and "purpose" are necessarily obscured or even obliterated.[63]

This is Nietzsche's most radical statement of his approach to history; it is so radical that it rules out any understanding of the past, and therefore any comprehension of the "meaning" or "purpose" of human life (for Nietzsche constantly reminds us that life *is* history). This is precisely the nihilistic turn of history against itself which Straussians endorse, but which they labor to hide from their average reader. Nietzsche places it in the exact center of a book that purports to reveal the true "meaning" of morals.

In *Natural Right and History*, Strauss remarks that historicism left Nietzsche with a dilemma: "he could insist on the strictly esoteric character of the theoretical analysis of life—that is, restore the Platonic notion of the noble delusion—or else he could deny the possibility of theory proper and so conceive of thought as essentially subservient to, or dependent on, life or fate."[64] Nietzsche's postmodern followers have "adopted the second alternative," and have become unabashed prophets of the end of morality and metaphysics.[65] But Nietzsche and Strauss follow the former path, keeping the full "truth" of nihilism a secret. In practical terms, this decision has led Straussians to champion the most traditional form of humanism imaginable: a canon of great books from the past which—they claim in public—contains a transhistorical set of objectively binding values. Like Nietzsche, they adopt the guise of new "ancients." "One must regard it as possible that we live in an age which is inferior to the past ..., or that we live in an age of decline or decay." "One must be swayed," Strauss writes, "by a sincere longing for the past."[66]   By exposing students to prehistoricist thinkers and interpreting them all as holding precisely the same views, Straussians hope to prevent the spread of relativism and nihilism to the masses.

On the surface, the canon of Western literature appears to be rife with disagreements and the most fundamental diversity of perspectives. But not (say the Straussians) if one reads these texts esoterically. "The works of the great writers of the past are very beautiful even from without. And yet their visible beauty is sheer ugliness, compared with the beauty of those hidden treasures which disclose themselves only after very long, never easy, but always pleasant work."[67]   This work bears little resemblance to what we normally think of as scholarship. One characteristic aspect of Strauss' writing is his

> complete abandonment of the form as well as the content of modern scholarship. Strauss no longer felt bound... to see the texts [of the past] through the screen of scholarly method or categories. He had liberated himself and could understand writers as they understood themselves. He talked with them as one would talk with a wise and subtle contemporary about the nature of things.[68]

Strauss' eagerness to abandon scholarly method is as great as Derrida's, and equally Nietzschean. Strauss' books, like Nietzsche's, avoid the scholarly apparatus of footnotes, bibliographies and references to other scholars. Bloom states that Strauss' "refutation of historicism" consisted in his discovery of "truths" in a subterranean tradition of texts from the past—truths that he could only recognize once he had abandoned the contingent premises of historicist scholarship.[69] Thus Strauss' alleged refutation of historicism was actually a radical version of historicism. He claimed that modern scholars were trapped in a contingent culture, unable to understand the various worldviews of the past on their own terms; but *he* had transcended modernity and understood the ancients as they understood themselves. Thus, for example, he chose to examine Xenophon's view of Socrates, "because Xenophon

seems to us a fool but appeared wise to older thinkers."[70]
The change in attitudes towards Xenophon revealed a gap between
ancient and modern world views; and Strauss, seeking to move
beyond his culture, tried to see things as the ancients had.
His goal was to escape from the *Weltanschauung* of historicism in
order to see attain the perspective of closed societies from the past.
"In short," writes Bloom, "Strauss returned to the cave."[71]
Ostensibly, he found there the universal truths that had been
secretly held by philosophers in a tradition begun by Plato.

But if this is what he found, one wonders why Straussians
refuse to say what the ancient "truths" are, except to call them
"strange and wonderful things." It seems more likely to me that
Strauss thought he had gained a vantage point exterior to *all* culture
by learning to see things through the eyes of many nonhistoricist
epochs. He then embraced the civilization of the "ancients," knowing
that they had not actually possessed universal truths, and knowing
also that his vision of them was by no means objective. This move
was analogous to Nietzsche's praise of the Greeks in *The Birth of
Tragedy* and elsewhere. Both Strauss and Nietzsche claim that
the "ancients" were homogeneous and noble; but neither thinker
believes this. "To be able to reproduce that older thought in full
awareness of the objections to it is to philosophize," writes Bloom.[72]
Similarly, Nietzsche had held that the Overman would endorse
classical cultural values, *despite* his knowledge that they were
merely contingent.

So perhaps Strauss discovered no real "truths" when he learned
to understand the ancients as they understood themselves.
Or perhaps Strauss discovered Nietzscheanism as the esoteric
meaning contained in all canonical texts. In other words, I am not
sure whether Strauss "discovered" that Socrates, Plato, and other
ancients were nihilists (as he sometimes implies), or that a study
of past writers would lead to nihilism by revealing the contingency
of all thought. In either case, the "truth" that Strauss discovered
was the impossibility of truth, and this explains his reticence
about the content of his discoveries. At times, Strauss seems
eager to claim that past philosophers were Nietzscheans, but it is
hard to know whether this is his real belief or his "noble delusion."
Bloom claims that Strauss really believed he was understanding
the ancients as they understood themselves. But Strauss praised
Heidegger for understanding the Greeks creatively, that is, *not* as
they understood themselves. Yet Heidegger wrote as if he *meant*
his interpretations to be accurate. Thus it is extremely difficult to decide
at what level or levels Strauss (like Nietzsche and Heidegger) is
being duplicitous. For example, Strauss claims that Socrates

already knew that reason was groundless and that philosophy would ultimately lead to nihilism. Plato, Maimonides, Spinoza, and the rest of the Straussian canon were all active nihilists, supporters of cultural norms who had seen the abyss that lies beyond culture. If this seems strange, recall that Nietzsche had remarked—admittedly, when he was on the verge of madness—that he was "all the names in history."[73] Strauss' vision of a homogeneous tradition of esoteric Nietzschean philosophers allows him to argue for a humanistic education based on a univocal canon. But Nietzsche too had argued for an education based on imitation of the ancients, knowing that his vision of Greek culture was a myth, and that the ancients he described were really just objectified versions of himself.

Since *The Closing of the American Mind* is the best-known Straussian text—and since it has been widely misread as a conservative polemic—it may be worth trying to demonstrate specifically that Bloom, too, is an esoteric Nietzschean nihilist.[74] Bloom begins with a denunciation of modern America that recalls Nietzsche's attack on the Last Man. Nietzschean allusions are rife throughout *The Closing of the American Mind*. "Practically all that young Americans have today,"[76] Bloom writes, "is an insubstantial awareness that there are many cultures, accompanied by a saccharine moral drawn from that awareness: We should all get along. Why fight?"[75] Our modern sense of "openness has driven out the local deities... ."[76] Bloom holds that "not only to prefer one's own way but to believe it best, superior to all others, is primary and even natural.... . Men must love and be loyal to their families and their peoples in order to preserve them."[77]

According to Bloom, the greatest threat to culture is historicism, which reached its apogee with Nietzsche and Heidegger. These thinkers and their acolytes contributed to the renunciation of liberalism in Germany and the rise of fascism. Bloom denies that historicism is "true" (as would Nietzsche), but he does not argue against it, except by claiming that it produced Hitler. And he suggests that, "while we were fighting [Hitler], the thought that had preceded him in Europe conquered here."[78] Carried to America by refugee scholars, made dogma by the counter-culture of the 1960s, Weimar historicism has become the dominant outlook. So, for example, when Louis Armstrong sang "Mack the Knife," he was not only quoting Brecht and Weill directly, but *Zarathustra* indirectly. Similarly, when a rock star tells people to "stay loose," he is inadvertently translating Heidegger's term *Gelassenheit*. "[B]ehind it all, the master lyricists are Nietzsche and Heidegger."[79]

Bloom attempts no solution to the crisis of nihilism. He certainly does not propose a philosophical solution, e.g., a refutation of cultural relativism. No Straussian text ever mentions such philosophical critics of nihilism as Wittgenstein or Habermas; Rawls merely makes an appearance as a "parody" of the Last Man.[80] For Bloom, no modern philosophy outside the Nietzschean-existentialist tradition has any value at all; analytic philosophers who discuss relativism and rationality are wasting their time, for Nietzsche has already spoken. But, in the absence of a solution to Nietzschean nihilism, Bloom does at least offer a reasonable paraphrase of Nietzsche's own position:

> All ages and places, all races and cultures can play on [the modern] stage. Nietzsche believed that the wild costume ball of the passions was both the disadvantage and the advantage of late modernity... . The advantage hoped for is that the richness and tension present in the modern soul might be the basis for comprehensive new worldviews... . This richness, according to Nietzsche, consisted largely in thousands of years of inherited and now unsatisfied religious longing. But this possible advantage does not exist for young Americans, because their poor education has impoverished their longings, and they are hardly aware of the great pasts [notice the plural: Bloom means cultures] that Nietzsche was thinking of and had within himself.[81]

If Bloom were content to call for better multicultural education in history, art and literature, then he would be a humanist and I would agree with him. But, like Nietzsche, Bloom hopes that the eclectic regime of the Last Man can be replaced by "comprehensive new worldviews." In other words, he looks forward to new authentic cultures, the products, presumably, of charismatic *übermenchlich* individuals like his master, Strauss.

Strauss' educational program represents an interesting version of Nietzschean esotericism, and it is based on a reasonably accurate reading of Nietzsche. But Strauss' *Weltanschauung*-historicism is, if anything, even cruder than Nietzsche's. Strauss imagines all humans, except Overmen like himself, as absolutely committed members of herds (cultures) whose values are incompatible with those of other herds. He sees no possibility of communication among cultures, which he imagines as completely discrete entities. One integrated set of values defines each culture precisely and serves as the foundation of all its members' lives; these values have no validity for members of other cultures. Like Nietzsche, Strauss believes that one either follows herd morality, or else one plunges into an abyss of nihilism. In Chapter IX, I will argue that "cultures" are terms that we use to categorize people according to salient characteristics which they share; but such categories can be conceived in numerous, overlapping ways. We each differ from those around us in fundamental aspects of our character and background, just as we may be similar in some respects to people living far away or long ago. A paradigm that dispenses with reified notions of culture will avoid the nihilist conclusions that Strauss reached because of his crude *Weltanschauung*-historicism. In order to live and act in the world, we do not require an absolute commitment to values that all the people around us share; in fact, it is rare for such a situation to occur. Therefore, nihilism will not overtake a civilization that is aware of cultural difference; and Strauss' program seems an unjustified exercise in deceit.

IV. A "Left" Nietzschean: Jacques Derrida

At the opposite end of the spectrum in the modern quarrel over the humanities are the deconstructionists, who openly endorse Nietzsche's view that "nothing is true." They call for humanistic scholarship to be replaced with a free, creative practice of self-overcoming, just as Nietzsche had argued for philology to be replaced with art and Dionysian philosophy. Their project helps to make clearer what Nietzsche meant by a life "beyond culture." Merely using his own examples—his doctrines of Eternal Return and Will to Power—is not very helpful, because to imitate these doctrines would mean to lack the authenticity and originality of an Overman. So it is instructive to examine the example of a thinker who has tried to move beyond culture in a generally Nietzschean spirit, but without merely appropriating Nietzsche's ideas. One such thinker is Jacques Derrida, whose reading of Nietzsche I have already discussed at some length. In what follows, I will describe his deconstructive method and its relation to Nietzsche's philosophy; I will criticize Derrida for adopting a notion of the *Weltanschauung* much like Nietzsche's; and I will briefly examine Derrida's work on Husserl in order to reply to a potential objection— that Husserl's phenomenology underlies Derrida's position, rather than any form of historicism.

Derrida has tried to "save" Nietzsche from Heidegger's effort to make him the "last metaphysician," a reading that allowed Heidegger to depict himself as the first *non*-metaphysical thinker since the pre-Socratics. According to Derrida, that title belongs to Nietzsche. Derrida argues that, before Heidegger, Nietzsche had already learned to subvert his own metaphysical truth claims, just as Heidegger would later do when he wrote the word "Being" with lines through it to signify its *"Destruktion"*—its purely ad hoc value as an unavoidable term which could, however, claim no objective truth. "Nietzsche," writes Derrida,

> far from remaining *simply* (with Hegel and as Heidegger wished) *within* metaphysics, contributed a great deal to the liberation of the signifier from its dependence or derivation with respect to the logos and the related concept of truth or the primary signified, in whatever sense that is understood.[82]

By the "primary signified," Derrida means the thing-in-itself, Truth or God. Nietzsche's means of avoiding the primary signified was to reveal that the history of thought led to nihilism, and then to embrace nihilism by speaking with many contradictory voices and by teaching self-destructive doctrines, thus freeing himself from "truth." This was a deconstructive move, analogous to the efforts by Heidegger and Derrida to place metaphysical terms "under erasure," crossing them out as they utter them.[83] Derrida imitates Nietzsche's nihilism, but like Heidegger, he invents new ways of conducting a deconstructive practice. And like both Nietzsche and Heidegger, he considers an existence beyond culture to have constructive as well as negative potential: "deconstructive," he writes, "that is to say, affirmative... ."[84]

In *The Genealogy of Morals*, Nietzsche had tried to tell a history of good and evil, in the process showing that any historical understanding was itself the product of a historically contingent morality: thus Nietzsche's *Genealogy* deconstructed. In *Of Grammatology*, Derrida attempts a similar project.[85] Whereas Nietzsche had ascribed all notions of truth to contingent valuations of good and evil, Derrida notes that all truth takes the contingent form of writing. It might be objected that some thoughts are not written down, and that some cultures do not possess writing at all. In response, Derrida examines two authors who attempt to describe and validate cultures *without* writing: Rousseau, whose subject is "barbaric" society before literacy, and Claude Lévi-Strauss, who describes indigenous peoples of South America. Derrida shows that writing actually operates within the cultures that both men describe as illiterate, at least if we take their descriptions of these cultures to be "true." Lévi-Strauss and Rousseau are unable to interpret as "other" a way of life that—they claim—lies beyond the bounds of their own *Weltanschauung*. Writing occurs in these cultures, as they describe them, not in the "literal" sense that pen is put to paper, but in the metaphorical sense that linguistic traces (metaphors) are left to signify things that are not directly present. This practice of metaphor is, as Nietzsche had pointed out, the inescapable structure of language, within which we make any distinctions, even that between "literal" and "metaphorical" varieties of writing. Writing, like thinking, is a metaphor about metaphors; so, too, is the word "metaphor." For Derrida, as for Nietzsche, metaphors have no referent in a transparent world of things-in-themselves: they can be neither truth nor lie. It is impossible to imagine in our metaphorical language a culture without writing— in other words, without metaphors—just as it is impossible to describe in historical terms a culture outside of history. "No reality or concept would therefore correspond to the expression 'society without writing.'"[86]

Thus Derrida describes "logocentrism," or the "metaphysics of phonetic writing" as a contingent but inescapable value, which, when we recognize its contingency, makes all of our ideas appear arbitrary and contingent. (In the same way, Nietzsche had described all of our ideas as dependent upon the arbitrary but universal distinction between good and evil). A simple relativism about writing would suggest that it forces thought into contingent, limited paths that "other cultures" have avoided; but writing is a universal condition for thought as we know it, and any relativist theory could only be expressed within writing. "The privilege of the *phoné* does not depend on a choice which could have been avoided. [Logocentrism] has dominated the history of the world during an entire epoch, and has even produced the idea of the world... ."[87] In logocentrism, Derrida finds a kind of ethnocentrism which "for enigmatic yet essential reasons [is] inaccessible to a simple historical relativism... ."[88] Only in "an original and non-'relativist' sense, logocentrism is an ethnocentric metaphysics. It is related to the history of the West."[89]

The limits of this "epoch" and the domain of the "we" who think in recognizable terms are unclear, although Derrida sometimes speaks of "three millennia" of the "civilization of the book" in "the West,"[90] or the *"epoch* of the full speech,"[91] now "disappearing in its very globalization."[92] But this uncertainty about the limits of our epoch is not due to a failure of Derrida's scholarship. Rather, he adopts the Nietzschean position that we cannot see beyond our own *Weltanschauung*, which Derrida renames the *epistémè*. As far as we look in any direction, we see human life conforming to the rules of our culture, for example, by implicitly assuming the presence of a Primary Signified. We have no means of recognizing any fundamental rules alien to our own; that is why we cannot imagine a culture that does not rely on "writing." Thus ethnocentrism is unavoidable, but the moment of realizing our total dependence upon our *epistémè* is also a moment of recognizing its contingency, of deconstructing it and thereby moving beyond it. If we see writing as a contingent historical fact, then we must be standing at a vantage point outside writing, at least implicitly. This outside is the "beyond" of Nietzsche's *Beyond Good and Evil*, and the "margin of philosophy" from which Derrida conducts his deconstruction.

The realization that writing is a contingent phenomenon with a history comes through the achievements of what in Nietzsche's day was called philology. The "history of writing [among other disciplines] teaches us that phonetic writing, the medium of the great metaphysical, scientific, technical, and economic adventure of the West, is limited in space and time and limits itself even as it is in the process of imposing its laws upon the cultural areas that had escaped it."[93] The study of writing reaches its zenith in structural linguistics, which shows "that the origin assigned to writing [is] always analogous in the most diverse cultures and that it communicate[s] in a complex but regulated manner with the distribution of political power as with familial structure...."[94] But such a discovery applies reflexively; structural linguistics, too, is the mere product of structures of power, and this perhaps explains its tendency to find the same (subjectively imposed) structures everywhere it looks. Discussing the turn of structuralism against itself, Derrida remarks, "A well-known pattern"—well-known indeed, to anyone familiar with Nietzsche's subversion of nineteenth-century philology.[95] Derrida's *post*-structuralist conclusion "refers to a common and radical possibility that no determined science, no abstract discipline, can think as such."[96] The alternative—as Derrida immediately remarks—is to take up a vantage point beyond culture, "beyond the field of the *epistémè*" which is marked by writing. But such a perspective is also beyond any positive philosophical position that could be stated in words: "*thought* is here for me a perfectly neutral name, the blank part of the text, the necessarily indeterminate index of a future epoch of differance [sic]. *In a certain sense, 'thought' means nothing*."[97] Thus Derrida's project is a constant deconstruction of the *epistème*, not the teaching of an alternative doctrine.

To 'deconstruct' philosophy, thus, would be to think—in the most faithful, interior way—the structured genealogy of philosophy's concepts, but at the same time to determine—from a certain exterior that is unqualifiable or unnameable by philosophy—what this history has been able to dissimulate or forbid, making itself into a history by means of this somewhere motivated repression.[98]

This genealogical practice has the "affirmative" effect of freeing us, in the moment of deconstruction, from the straightjacket of our *epistémè*.

Recognizing the inadequacy of relativism, Nietzsche had chosen to write in a deliberately mythical (or "consciously innocent") form about the early Greeks who, he said, lacked a distinction between truth and lie; and Heidegger wrote deconstructively about the pre-Socratic thinkers who, he believed, had thought without metaphysics. In other words, neither philosopher had ascribed "truth" to his own interpretations of an alien culture, but each had recognized that his own texts participated in the historical, metaphysical *Weltanschauung* of modernity, despite any efforts to subvert this *Weltanschauung*. So too, Derrida admits that it is impossible to subvert the structures of writing without participating in them— without writing. We can, he writes in a passage that I have already cited, "pronounce not a single destructive proposition which has not already had to slip into the form, the logic, and the postulations of precisely what it seeks to contest."[99] Like Nietzsche, Derrida holds that the roots of grammar and writing are "metaphysico-theological"—God is just a name for the Being which writing presupposes: a "transcendental signified" for which "logocentrism and the metaphysics of presence [show an] exigent, powerful, and systematic desire... ."[100] But Derrida cautions:

> Of course, it is not a question of 'rejecting' these [metaphysico-theological] notions; they are necessary and, at least at present, nothing is conceivable for us without them. It is a question of first demonstrating the systematic and historical solidarity of the concepts and gestures of thought that one often believes to be innocently separated. The sign and divinity have the same place and time of birth. The age of the sign is essentially theological. Perhaps it will never *end*. Its historical *closure* is, however, outlined.[101]

This is analogous to Nietzsche's view that the Last Man represents the closure of Western civilization (that is why he is "last"); but there is no permanent regime of the Last Man, totally free from the contingencies of history. A truly posthistorical individual would not even be able to think. Thus, writes Derrida, "What is held within the demarcated closure may continue indefinitely."[102] One "does not leave the epoch whose closure one can outline. The movements of belonging or not belonging to the epoch are too subtle, the illusions in that regard are too easy, for us to make a definite judgment."[103] As usual, Nietzsche says the same thing better:

> After Buddha was dead, his shadow was still shown for centuries in a cave—a tremendous, gruesome shadow. God is dead; but given the way of men, there may still be caves for thousands of years in which his shadow will be shown.—And we—we still have to vanquish his shadow, too.[104]

In trying to demonstrate the inescapable, all-encompassing role of writing, Derrida seeks to attain a perspective outside of writing, just as Nietzsche had entered a space beyond truth and lie. Derrida achieves this perspective in the course of writing a book, just as Nietzsche had told "truths" about the identity of truth and falsehood. Thus Derrida's achievement of an *übermenschlich* perspective is, like Nietzsche's achievement before him, fragmentary and unstable. Just as Nietzsche was both beyond culture or Dionysian, and within culture or the Crucified, so Derrida is—and knows himself to be—both beyond writing and the author of books about writing.

Like Zarathustra, Derrida conceives the activity of transcending culture by analogy to a dance or game: "One could call *play* the absence of the transcendental signified as the limitlessness of play, that is to say the destruction of onto-theology and the metaphysics of presence."[105] "To risk meaning nothing is to start to play, [it is a means to prevent] any word, any concept, any major enunciation from coming to summarize and to govern... ."[106] Derrida's "style" of play, insofar as it serves to supersede metaphysics, is reminiscent of Nietzsche. He too uses diverse and eccentric styles, and deliberately contradicts himself. For Derrida, the moment of transcending history arrives when we are able to see the realm of history as a phenomenon, as something that has an outside, albeit an outside in which Being and the self cannot exist. This moment is, as Nietzsche had discovered, a wild, Dionysian one. To "think the history of the system [sc. of logocentrism], its meaning and value must, in an *exorbitant* way, be somewhere exceeded."[107] "Exorbitant" means outside of the "*orbit* of the system" (a phrase that Derrida uses), but it also means excessive, unrestrained, Dionysian. Derrida allows himself the Nietzschean thought of a regime after writing, analogous to

Nietzsche's regime of the Overman; but this remains a purely heuristic fantasy, a kind of chimaera. If we had the means to describe it, it would already exist; but it *cannot* be described in logocentric terms:

> The future can only be anticipated in the form of absolute danger. It is that which breaks absolutely with constituted normality and can only be proclaimed, *presented*, as a sort of monstrosity. For that future world and for that within it which will have put into question the values of sign, word, and writing, for that which guides our future anterior, there is yet no exergue.[108]

When Nietzsche tried to conceive a world seen from a perspective beyond culture—a world therefore without Being—he imagined the Will to Power. This was a vision of mere quanta of energy, mere relations *per se* that were not relations among "things." Derrida provides a similar vision. For him signs have no referent to things; they simply have their "differance" from other signs.[109] "*Différance*," he tells Julia Kristeva, "is the systematic play of differences, of the traces of differences, of the *spacing* by means of which elements are related to each other."[110] Nietzsche did not intend the Will to Power to serve as a cosmological doctrine; it applied above all to itself, and described the process of interpretation and artistic invention by which any vision of the world is conjured up. Our Will to Power creates the world as we know it, so interpreting the world according to its "intelligible character" means seeing it as Will to Power, i.e., seeing it as if "viewed from the inside."[111] Similarly for Derrida, all that we can say we say in metaphors, in texts, the principle of which is "*différance*." However, the word "*différance*" is not a sign that signifies some kind of truth about the nature of language; indeed, "I am not sure if it signifies at all... ."[112] So even in discussing the all-pervading rule of *différance*, we cannot escape its rule. We cannot say anything "true." There is no outside-text, says Derrida, punning: "*Il n'y a pas de hors-texte.*"[113]

I have tried to show that the pattern of deconstruction—whether in Nietzsche's version or in Derrida's—is as follows: the radical contingency of all "our" thought is taken as a premise, and from this it is concluded that all theories and premises are inadequate; the premise leads to its own destruction. The "logic" of deconstruction is compelling enough, once we accept its premise. But the "truth" of the premise can only be shown empirically. This both Nietzsche and Derrida attempt to do; they both turn empirical history against itself. "A history of writing," writes Derrida, "should turn back toward the origin of historicity."[114] As Nietzsche writes:

> the origin of historical culture... *must* itself in turn be historically understood. And the problem of history *must* be solved by history itself; knowledge *must* apply the goad to knowledge.[115]

And along the same lines, Leo Strauss wrote, "we need... an understanding of the genesis of historicism that does not take for granted the soundness of historicism."[116] In other words, the historical sense must be revealed—by means of historical research—to be a merely contingent phenomenon, just as the phenomenon of writing must be shown (in writing) to have contingent origins.

Before Nietzsche or Derrida can begin to write their books, they already "know" the truth of nihilism that comes at the *end* of the evolution of historical thinking, namely the truth that there is no truth. Therefore, they caution us constantly that their empirical arguments and narratives about "good and evil" (Nietzsche) and "writing" (Derrida) are neither truth nor lie. Nevertheless, it seems to me that the force of deconstruction depends upon the empirical truth of its basic premise: the contingency of "our" thought, however "we" is defined. Furthermore, a deconstructionist must define and describe our thought in detail; otherwise, deconstruction will amount to nothing more than the trite claim that human thinking is contingent. The practice of deconstruction involves gaining a vantage point external to culture, in order to describe—and thereby transcend—cultural biases. Therefore, Nietzsche did not simply say that all our thought is conditioned by contingent, hidden valuations of good versus evil; rather, he described the origins, nature and history of such valuations. Similarly, in *Of Grammatology*, Derrida expends considerable effort in treating—in a careful and conventionally scholarly way— the history of linguistics, in order to show its ultimately deconstructive consequences.

Derrida believes that it is important to deal with the history of Western thought "in the most faithful, interior way," just as he thinks it is important to deconstruct the most advanced and sophisticated forms of Western thinking: Husserl's metaphysics and Saussure's linguistics, for example. It would not suffice to show hidden biases in some obviously inferior or superannuated example of Western thought, just as it would not suffice to discuss the history of Western concepts of history, culture and language without reading and citing numerous representative texts. A "mistake" of this kind would doom deconstruction to failure at its earliest stages. Derrida admits as much when he says that, without respect for "all the instruments of traditional criticism ..., critical production would risk developing in any direction at all and authorize itself to say almost anything."[117] In the Preface to *Of Grammatology*, Derrida calls for reading to "free itself, at least on its axis, from the classical categories of history," some of which Derrida then enumerates. But it "goes without saying," he immediately adds, "that around that axis I have had to respect classical norms, or at least I have attempted to respect them."[118] Thus Derrida considers it important not to make certain kinds of mistake in his descriptions of the civilization of the West.

V. A Critique of Deconstruction

The "mistake" that I have identified within Nietzsche's deconstructive premise is his decision to treat historical contexts as reified *Weltanschauungen*. In his early writing, Derrida too speaks of epochs and ages, of the "totality of an era... ." His translator hastens to remark in a footnote, "Later Derrida will come to distrust such terms... ."[119] The same pattern of espousing and then denying *Weltanschauung*-historicism is evident in Nietzsche's intellectual biography, as I tried to show in Chapters II and III. Both thinkers have good reasons to abandon their initial vision of a world composed of many discrete *Weltanschauungen*. Derrida, in particular, adopts Nietzsche's point that it is impossible to understand other cultures, so all that we know, by virtue of our knowing it, belongs to our own world-view. Efforts, like those of Lévi-Strauss, to avoid ethnocentrism are completely ethnocentric. Thus Derrida seeks not to transcend some kind of local culture, but to broach "the de-construction of *the greatest totality*—the concept of the *epistémè* and logocentric metaphysics—within which are produced, without ever posing the radical question of writing, all the Western methods of analysis, explication, reading or interpretation."[120] Thus from the totalities of individual cultures (Greece, Germany, modernity), Derrida moves to the greatest totality of all: the "system" of the West. Derrida recognizes that the West can know no other tradition, so it is not a question of our simply choosing between Western ideas and some nonmetaphysical, non-Western *Weltanschauung*. We are either trapped within the confines of our culture, the *epistémè* of the West, which now appears to us to occupy the whole world, or we are—in a flickering and unstable way—beyond *all* culture. These are the same choices that confronted Nietzsche: for him people were either Men of the Fatherlands, or else, in some respects at least, they were able to become Free Spirits, Last Men or Overmen. Each of these last three terms refers to someone who has recognized "language," "grammar," "culture," and "morality" to be mere phenomena, contingent realities which, by means of this recognition, he manages to overcome. Whether Nietzsche would consider Derrida's books *übermenschlich* or passively nihilistic and decadent is hard to tell; but they do attempt to occupy a space beyond culture in the same way that Nietzsche's texts had moved Beyond Good and Evil, truth and lie. Not surprisingly, then, Derrida's project is open to the same critique, at the level of its *premises*, that I have used against Nietzsche.

Derrida's concept of the *épistémè* is a version of the "culturalist fallacy" so prevalent in nineteenth-century historicism. It is, despite all disclaimers, a deeply idealist notion, a universal, and thus out of place in a philosophy that tries to avoid all such totalizing claims. It is all very well to say that philosophical thought inevitably arises from historically limited perspectives and contains unnoticed prejudices. But Derrida treats these prejudices as if they all belonged to a single homogeneous "system"—logocentrism. He first task is always to demonstrate "the systematic and historical solidarity of concepts and gestures of thought that one often believes to be innocently separated."[121] Once he has recognized the system of logocentrism and its limitations, he has, in principle, moved beyond all contingency. But Derrida can only claim to occupy this position because he treats the perspective of "the West" as a reified, homogeneous entity. It seems more likely that the prejudices that constrain any thinker are a heterogeneous collection, loosely related to each other, the product of specific experiences and influences, so that no two thinkers are identically prejudiced. If this is true, then it is impossible to identify the "fundamental prejudice" of the West, and thereby to overcome *all* contingency at one stroke.

If Derrida thinks he can give an account of what the *Weltanschauung* of the West "essentially" involves, then he must make an enormous inductive generalization about a vast array of cultural phenomena over a 3,000-year period. A generalization of this kind seems to be involved when Derrida argues that all the economic, political, epistemological, and linguistic activity of the West is essentially caught up in writing, or when he describes the West as showing a "logocentric longing par excellence": namely, the wish "to distinguish one from the other."[122] Thus Derrida holds that the creation of dualisms is essential or dominant in the West—surely a contentious empirical generalization. Such inductive claims arise in Derrida's work because he *prima facie* accepts the theories of Freudian psychoanalysis, Husserlian phenomenology, Saussurian linguistics, and structuralist anthropology—but all these movements make empirical claims that reasonable people may reject. Similarly, Nietzsche had derived his nihilist position after first accepting nineteenth-century philology (with all its idealist assumptions) as the highest and final form of Western historical thinking.

Of course, Derrida will immediately turn around and announce that his empirical generalizations deconstruct themselves, since they too arise within writing and metaphysics. I am not, therefore, accusing Derrida of believing the "truth" of his historical generalizations—if so accused, he would immediately, I suspect, reply, "But what is 'truth' if not a logocentric category?" Fair enough; the same move is recognizable already in Nietzsche's earliest published writings. My criticism, however, lies at the level of Derrida's premise. Why should we enter a game which ends in the deconstruction of all "belief," if we don't believe that the West is essentially "logocentric" in the first place? In *Speech and Phenomena*, Derrida writes, "what makes the history of the *phone* [i.e., logocentrism] fully enigmatic is the fact that it is inseparable from the history of idealization, that is, from the 'history of mind,' or history as such."[123] So we cannot know anything objective about the history of the West, because *we know* the "fact" that the West has had a contingent idea of history, which still entraps us. This is the deconstructive turn in a nutshell; but notice that it requires an initial belief in the nature of Western history. In the next sentence, Derrida states in more detail what Western history has essentially involved, e.g., an emphasis on the *"technical* mastery of objective being." Thus, although our history is "fully enigmatic," Derrida nevertheless knows what it means. I will argue in the next chapter that it is a mistake to speak of "the West" at all, if we mean by this some kind of reified philosophical concept. I do not think that it would be possible to *disprove* Derrida's claim that "the West"—whatever that means—is essentially logocentric, because the term "logocentrism" is too vague to admit of empirical contradiction. Besides, "the West" can be defined circularly, as the regime of the logos, in which case calling it logocentric is tautologous. On the other hand, I *do* think that one could perhaps give evidence for the dominance of writing (defined in some specific way) in certain areas of the world during a certain period. Derrida achieves much along these lines as part of his effort to tell the history of philosophy in "the most faithful, interior way." But the evidence he cites is open to refutation and counter-example.

If Derrida's notion of Western logocentrism is intended to be a priori and immune to empirical refutation, then it is vacuous and tautological. It may be true a priori that all thoughts are expressed in the form that thought takes, which Derrida calls "writing"; but nothing is achieved by such an empty statement. Clearly, Derrida hopes to move toward a richer understanding of what "writing" has meant. He claims that it has meant different things "according to the language, the era, the culture,"[124] so he has to say something with an empirical basis. The impossibility of escaping writing, he says, "is historically articulated. It does not limit attempts at deciphering in the same way, to the same degree, and according to the same rules [at different times]."[125] In order to produce "a discourse which borrows from a heritage the resources necessary for the deconstruction of that heritage itself,"[126] Derrida must know something objective about the heritage that he wants to transcend. At one point, having declared that everything is and has been writing, Derrida says, "We know this a priori, but only now and with a knowledge that is not knowledge at all."[127] Given the context in which this strange comment appears, I take it to mean that we understand the premise of deconstruction a priori, but only "now," from a particular historical vantage point. Knowledge a priori means knowledge that is universally held by rational creatures regardless of their experience; but for a historicist like Derrida, people are variable, historical phenomena. Thus, what we find when we introspect without explicit regard for empirical facts is something that has a history; so we may know something a priori "now" that we could not know in another age. In particular, we have by now internalized certain empirical facts about the phenomenon and history of writing, for example, "the multiplicity of the *systems* of script."[128] These facts (which are deeply historicist), when interpreted the right way by Derrida, result in a recognition of the impossibility of knowledge either a priori or a posteriori.

Therefore, deconstruction does seem to have empirical roots, despite Derrida's claim that we know it a priori. "It may be said," Derrida admits, "that [my] style is empiricist and in a certain way that would be correct. The *departure* [from metaphysics] is radically empiricist."[129] Derrida then proceeds to deny any distinction between the a priori and the empirical, having claimed first that deconstruction belongs to one kind of thought, then to the other. This contradiction is no doubt deliberate. Derrida deconstructs the dualism of *a priori* versus *a posteriori* by suggesting that any such distinction is logocentric. The distinction disappears when viewed from a perspective beyond all "classical conceptual oppositions,"[130] from "the point of a certain exteriority in relation to the totality of the age of logocentrism."[131] "Here the very concept of empiricism destroys itself." However, *within* metaphysics, "one can only judge [deconstruction's] style in terms of the accepted oppositions," e.g., as empirical rather than a priori.[132] But a perspective that is beyond metaphysics, Derrida says, can only be attained by empirical means—or more precisely, by means that *seem* empirical to those of us who remain within metaphysics. In order to deconstruct logocentrism, we have to know what it is, and this is an empirical matter. But it seems hard to believe that Derrida can have put his finger accurately and definitively on the essential structure of all "Western thought."

It would be reasonable to object that there *can be* no neutral empirical methodology, no perspective on the data of history that is objective or universal. The methods that scholars use to understand the past are diverse and contentious; each methodological school relies on its own covert philosophical position, and all such positions are open to attack. Consequently, Derrida cannot be held accountable to someone else's "facts," since any such facts would result from a procedure that Derrida could accuse of logocentric bias. For example, a follower of Noam Chomsky might complain that Derrida's description of logocentrism is not consistent with the best modern linguistics; but Derrida could respond that Chomskian linguistics is just a sub-species of logocentrism, which he is trying to explain and transcend.

However, I do not believe that Derrida can make any progress toward explaining world history without at least heeding pragmatic criteria of truth. Pragmatists would not demand that Derrida's theory conform to some preordained idea of Truth; they would merely require that his alleged facts about the history of writing be testable and falsifiable. One must be able to imagine evidence that could contradict his theory. This is a standard by which mainstream humanist scholars frequently judge theories about history and culture. If Derrida's theory met this test, then it would be an interesting contribution to the history of linguistics; but it would not enable a transcendence of logocentrism, because critics could suggest examples of nonlogocentric behavior within our own society, and could thereby undermine Derrida's claim that logocentrism is an inescapable precondition of all our thought. On the other hand, if the theory is so broad and abstract as to be nonfalsifiable, then it cannot convince skeptics to believe in it.

Derrida himself employs pragmatic criteria in a provisional way. He states, for example, that although the "classical norms" of scholarship can ultimately be deconstructed, this does not "prevent [them] from functioning, and even from being indispensable within certain limits—very wide limits."[133] The success of translation between languages serves as Derrida's example of the efficacy of the classical norms. Thus he makes a pragmatic argument for the importance of these norms; they work. Unfortunately, Derrida does not include pragmatism itself among the norms of mainstream scholarship; rather, he stresses such metaphysical doctrines as the "opposition or difference" between signified and signifier. It is this kind of doctrine that is susceptible to being deconstructed when Derrida points out its contingent roots; but it is not a doctrine that most historians and critics assert.

Derrida (like Nietzsche and Heidegger) seems to assume that any practice or method—for example, pragmatic scholarship in the humanities—must depend upon implicit metaphysical claims. For instance, to say that "X happened" is to assume a difference between the signifier and the signified, the historical theory and the actual event. In fact, the view that truth-claims depend upon *any* particular metaphysical doctrine has been cogently criticized by Wittgenstein and the American pragmatists. But even conceding Derrida's belief that scholarship assumes the existence of human subjects, an objective world, and other metaphysical entities, it nevertheless remains true that one cannot transcend these prejudices simply by refusing the accept them. That is a recipe for silence. We always have to take the vast majority of our language for granted, even as we shine a critical spotlight on some parts of it. Quine describes this process as follows:

> we accept provisionally our heritage from the dim past, with intermediate revisions by our more recent forebears; and then we continue to warp and revise. As Neurath has said, we are in the position of a mariner who must rebuild his ship plank by plank while continuing to stay afloat in the open sea.[134]

That is why I conceive of the humanities as an eternal process of description and criticism, an everlasting conversation about both phenomena and procedures from which there is no escape. In discussing Derrida, I have tried to criticize his notion of the *epistémè*, but not, of course, without begging all kinds of questions myself. Derrida, however, seems to think that he can make empirical generalizations about the totality of the West as if these were objectively "true," or as true as any empirical claims will ever be. He then uses these claims to delineate the "closure of the West."

I am aware that he thinks of deconstruction as an "immense and interminable work."[135] It is not a brief chronological moment between the Age of the Logos (now finished) and the Beyond. However, grammatology and deconstruction do seem to adopt a basic orientation towards the whole age of writing which they take to be accurate and in principle final; and they seem to view logocentrism as itself fundamentally closed, at least in the sense that Western thought will undergo no *fundamental* changes in the future. The basic orientation of grammatology will never be surpassed; "there is no *scientific* semiotic work that does not serve grammatology."[136] If all scientific research by definition serves grammatology, then grammatology is in principle irrefutable and therefore vacuous.

According to Derrida, the fundamental presuppositions of logocentrism are truisms in the West, so no one ever states them explicitly; they "never occupied the forefront of the... stage."[137] Thus Derrida has to read between the lines of the "tradition," revealing unnoticed commitments to logical dualism, truth, presence, and Being in texts from the past.[138] This is the business of deconstruction; it is what deconstructionists do. But the "discoveries" that Derrida makes between the lines are not open to refutation. In fact, it seems to me that Derrida's account of logocentrism does have value within the conversation of the humanities, because some of his readings are fruitful. But his work should be taken, like Nietzsche's *Birth of Tragedy*, to be a mere contribution (both methodological and substantive) to a discussion about history and culture which will continue indefinitely as the scholarly "classical norms" evolve, new data arise, and culture itself alters.

VI. Deconstruction as a Kind of Phenomenology

Before closing this chapter, I want to respond to a possible objection. Derrida can be read in a way that explains his position as independent of any generalizations about history or culture. If Derrida's early work on Husserl is taken to be central to his project, rather than his discussions of Nietzsche, the late Heidegger, and structuralism, then a picture emerges of Derrida as a kind of phenomenologist. Phenomenology, in Husserl's version, seeks a universal, ahistorical, "presuppositionless" conception of the things themselves.[139] This is neither an *a priori* nor an empirical project. "I avoid as far as possible," Husserl explains, "the expressions *a priori* and *a posteriori*, partly on account of the confusing obscurities and ambiguities which infect their ordinary use, but also because of the notorious philosophical theories which as an evil heritage from the past are interwoven with them."[140] Pure phenomenology is "established as a science of Essential Being—as an *a priori*... science,"[141] but, on the other hand, it "begins with experience and remains within experience."[142] Husserl treats both individual objects and their Essences as phenomena that can be directly described with a "naive" eye that has been deliberately freed from philosophical distinctions such as that between *a priori* and *a posteriori*, or between subjective and objective. Husserl claims a final and universal status for his phenomenology, which, he says:

> include[s] all sciences and all forms of knowledge in its eidet-
> ic universality... . [It] supplies the definitive criticism of
> every fundamentally distinct science, and in particular [it
> supplies] the final determination of the sense in which their
> objects can be said 'to be.'[143]

Derrida treats Husserl's analysis of signs as the best and purest analysis possible within the terms of logocentrism; it is still metaphysical, but it announces "the closure of metaphysics."[144] Derrida writes, "*within* the metaphysics of presence, within philosophy as knowledge of the presence of the object... we believe, quite simply and literally, in... the *closure* if not the end of history."[145] With Husserl's work, "*such a closure has taken place*." All philosophy is historically contingent, the product of local values and prejudices. Phenomenology, however, is free of every prejudice except the essential one of logocentrism: the belief in Being. Thus phenomenology is the last metaphysical philosophy. History "never meant anything but the presentation of Being,"[146] so within history, Husserl is the last philosopher. (Derrida, like Nietzsche, is *beyond* history, or at least at its margin.) Despite Husserl's best efforts to put metaphysical notions "out of play," Derrida argues that his thought "nevertheless conceal[s] a metaphysical presupposition." This last, unnoticed presupposition is the privileging of presence: the "living present" is "the conceptual foundation of phenomenology as metaphysics."[147] In carrying to still more radical extremes Husserl's method of "putting out of play" all metaphysical notions, Derrida attempts to examine the phenomenon of language *without* assuming the presence of things.[148] The result is a view that "language never escapes analogy"; it is "analogy through and through," without any referent in some thing which is present.[149] There is, then, no way to distinguish between "sign and non-sign"; there is no outside-text; "the thing itself always escapes."[150]

A historicist might criticize Husserl's claim that he had gotten back to the things themselves by suggesting that the vantage point of scientific phenomenology was culturally contingent. In his last years, even Husserl began to see phenomenological investigation as contingent, so that it was impossible merely to reflect on the phenomena in a naive way. We have "become what we are thoroughly and exclusively in a historical-spiritual manner," he wrote. Philosophy, he thought, begins with "a critical understanding of all history—*our* history." "For we are what we are as functionaries of modern philosophical humanity; we are heirs and cobearers of the direction of the will which pervades this humanity... ." But when Husserl admits that his thought is historically contingent, he means that it is the product of a homogeneous system of Western thought. It does not occur to him that phenomenology might contain numerous *individual* prejudices, inherited from past thought. Instead, what limits him is an interrelated set of primal prejudices in Western thought, "which live on in sedimented forms, yet can be reawakened... and, in their new vitality, be criticized... ." For Husserl, as for his student Heidegger, philosophy begins by elucidating the primal goals, "the *unity* running through all the projects... that oppose one another" in Western history; it begins by revealing, "behind the 'historical facts' of documented philosophical theories and their apparent oppositions and parallels, a meaningful, final harmony."[151] These words of Husserl succinctly describe Derrida's project in *Of Grammatology*, where he seeks to uncover the logocentric "essence" of all Western thought, in order to transcend this essence. In his work on Husserl, Derrida describes presence as "historically constituted and demonstrated"; and speaks of "an epoch characterized by the philosophical idea of truth and the opposition between truth and appearance... ."[152] It is this "epoch" that Derrida hopes to transcend by means of his radicalization of Husserl's phenomenology. Thus some kind of understanding of the history of the tradition is assumed by Derrida even in his work on Husserl. Derrida may seek, like Husserl, to get "behind the facts" of history, but he must begin by getting the facts *right*. To do so in a final and irrefutable manner seems impossible; and I have already alluded to some possible errors in Derrida's narrative. But my main point is the following: even if he is interpreted as a disciple of Husserl—as a kind of radical phenomenologist—Derrida's deconstructive conclusions still follow from an empirical account of the nature of culture and history. The basic motif in Derrida's philosophy is a Nietzschean project of turning historicism against itself. But in order for this project to be convincing, the historical account with which Derrida begins must be accurate.

Thus Derrida's claim that, for example, Lévi-Strauss' anthropological "discoveries" lead in the direction of deconstruction proves nothing; we would first have to discuss the validity of Lévi-Strauss' anthropology. When I say that we would "first" have to examine empirical anthropological questions (as well as questions of methodology), I really mean that we would have to study these questions indefinitely, for no ahistorical, aperspectival analysis of human society will ever arise to serve as the foundation of deconstruction or to announce the end of history. To claim that structuralism and phenomenology have in some way brought about the closure of the history of the West seems to me to introduce a faith in these disciplines which runs counter to the perspectivist attitude that Derrida elsewhere professes. Granted, all historical narratives and theories are the product of contentious methodologies and limited perspectives. But structuralism is not, therefore, as good a theory as any other. Structuralism, like phenomenology, may lead to deconstructive conclusions, but the same is not true of other theoretical orientations—such as, for example, the one which I will describe in the following chapter. I think that one can hold a perspectivist view about human knowledge without arriving at skeptical or relativist conclusions. To do so, one has to argue that perspectives can be shared, enlarged and altered as the result of exchanges of ideas and the discovery of new evidence. The result would be a theory that never introduces an idea of "closure," even in the idiosyncratic way that Derrida discusses the "end" of the West. Rather, we would have to imagine an endlessly continuing collaborative enterprise of describing human culture from as many angles as possible.

We might—as I will argue more fully below—do well to abandon the social-scientist's goal of "covering laws" and "structural explanations": these are particularly contentious and always carry the connotation that they represent some kind of universal, ahistorical theory about the nature of all society. But such connotations do not normally attach to the humanities, which aim rather to describe (not to explain) limited pieces of the social world from numerous contingent perspectives. I will try to provide a fuller account of the way the humanities work below. I will not, of course, claim for this account any universal validity or finality. It is, rather, a set of claims about the modern humanities offered as a kind of contribution to an ongoing discussion of these disciplines whose end is nowhere in sight. Such an attitude is characteristic of the humanities, as I describe them. In other words, like deconstruction, my theory is reflexive and even circular; but not, I think, in a self-destructive way.[153]

VII. Strauss or Derrida?

According to Allan Bloom, deconstruction is a "predictable... fad," a "cheapened interpretation of Nietzsche."[154] "Postmodernism," he says, "is an attempt to annihilate the inspiration of Greek philosophy that is more effective than that of the barbarians after the fall of Rome, more effective because it is being accomplished by the force and guile of philosophy itself."[155] Deconstruction is "a dogmatic, academic nihilism of the Left"; it is "platitudinized Nietzsche and Heidegger."[156] Bloom describes deconstruction as:

> a kind of circus performance in which Nietzsche is sawed into many pieces, and then the magician miraculously puts him back together and, lo and behold, Nietzsche is a Marxist, albeit not a 'vulgar' Marxist. The most profound and intense effort of behalf of 'culture'—Nietzsche's effort—is swallowed up by the Last Man.... . The invocation of Nietzsche on the Left is equivalent to Stalin's invocation of God—it makes no sense, but it helps with the simpletons.[157]

It is not surprising that Bloom takes deconstruction seriously, since he secretly agrees with its premises. It is also not surprising that he hates it, for it is in the process of revealing everything that Leo Strauss labored so hard to conceal. His recourse is to call Derrida the "Last Man," and to accuse deconstructionists of being esoterics who try to hoodwink the simpletons. Meanwhile, to postmodernists, Straussians appear to be quintessential reactionaries, craven servants of the existing power structure, and hopelessly naive about "theory."

Since both sides are Nietzschean, to be consistent they must admit that their own values are completely contingent, their styles the mere products of two contrasting cultures. Straussians speak their own dialect, which is replete with phrases like "impoverished souls," "Athens against Jerusalem," "gentlemen and philosophers." Postmodernists speak instead of "phallogocentrism," "the phoné," and "the play of differance." Straussians worry about the connection between nihilism and the holocaust; Derrideans are more interested in the connection between masturbation and writing. Nietzsche was fond of reducing such differences to the basest contingencies; for example, he suggests that the poor cuisine in Leipzig had made him endorse Schopenhauer and a pessimistic worldview.[158] So it is tempting to imagine what Nietzsche would say about the cultures of his purported followers. Straussians wear tweed, smoke cigars, teach seminars on Plato, translate Greek, and celebrate Winston Churchill's birthday; Derrideans wear black, smoke clove cigarettes, conduct seminars on Lacan, deconstruct in French and fondly recollect Paris in 1968. When there is a campus uprising, Straussians fear that the fall of the Weimar Republic is about to repeat itself as farce; Derrideans wish that they were on the barricades. Their heroes and paradigm texts are sometimes different, but Plato, Rousseau, Nietzsche and Heidegger make both groups' short-lists. If Nietzsche was right, then there really is no objective criterion for choosing between these two factions. But if he was wrong, then neither one can make *any* claim on our allegiance. I think Nietzsche was wrong in his definition and analysis of "culture"; and this mistake, inherited by both Strauss and Derrida, means that their critiques of the mainstream humanities are at best irrelevant, at worst deeply misleading.

Chapter 9

The Postmodern Paradigm

I. Two Paradigms for Cultural Diversity

I have already suggested the outline of a critique of the underlying theory of culture that led Nietzsche to abandon humanism and to vilify the pluralist, democratic culture to which the modern humanities are an important contributor. In this chapter, I will try to redescribe the regime of Nietzsche's Last Man in positive terms, suggesting that Nietzsche's distaste for pluralism and democracy stemmed from an implicit commitment to *Weltanschauung*-historicism. This position produced epistemological difficulties that Nietzsche exploited as a way of arguing for the incoherence of rationality in general; but the same difficulties *should* lead us to experiment with an entirely different paradigm for explaining historical differences. Pluralism, democratic institutions, the open society, and humanistic education will all seem more attractive, in the light of this new paradigm, than they seemed to Nietzsche. My purpose here is not to articulate a theory of democracy and education, but simply to point to the general form which such a theory might take, once the Nietzschean critique of humanism is abandoned.

I have described *Weltanschauung*-historicism as the theory that each person belongs to a single delimited culture: Hegel's epoch and nation, Marx's class, Nietzsche's herd.[1] *Weltanschauung*-historicism was Nietzsche's philosophical starting-point; it served as the embarkation point for his extracultural, Dionysian philosophy, which was born out of historicism's contradictions. However, *Weltanschauung*-historicism does not fit the empirical data; it is not, therefore, the best theory that rational investigation can offer. Historicism began as a philosophical reflection on data produced by historians, social observers, explorers, and others, who came to believe that human beings differ in fundamental ways according to their membership in nations, classes, cultures, language groups and so on. The early historicists derived from these data their image of a series of delimited cultures (figure 1). This image was

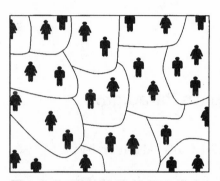

Figure 1. The Modern Paradigm

so prevalent and influential after the late-eighteenth century that it can be called the "modern paradigm" for describing cultural diversity. Nietzsche's "Men of the Fatherlands," shown in figure (1), are each trapped within a narrow horizon which serves to make life and art possible. Nietzsche's "Free Spirits," "Good Europeans," "Last Men," and "Overmen" are all in some way beyond culture, aware of the contingency of all cultural norms and thus living in a parasitical, vicarious "culture of comparison." But the *Übermensch* differs from the Last Man and other decadents insofar as he, recognizing the collapse of reason which results from radical historicism, enters an extracultural, Dionysian state of intoxication and creativity where he can at last be active and authentic. This movement right off the diagram shown in figure (1) represents the revolt against reason that is so pronounced in so-called "postmodern" thought. But it is not a truly *post*-modern development; it is merely a moment of renunciation, a declaration of revolt, a recognition of modernity's contradictions, beyond which nothing comprehensible lies. A more fruitful path beyond the modern paradigm proceeds from a reconsideration of the paradigm itself, and suggests an alternative model that better suits the phenomena of historical diversity.[2]

The *Weltanschaung*-historicists of the nineteenth century quickly ran into inconvenient evidence of diversity within cultures, which belied their modern paradigm. Subcultural groups which failed to fit into a convenient pattern of national or class identity were either ignored or even ruthlessly suppressed, as happened when Nazis murdered Jews, and Stalinists purged the petit bourgeoisie.

Nietzsche too shows disdain for eclecticism and diversity within cultures, especially in his *Untimely Meditations*. However, except in his lectures "On the Future of Our Educational Institutions" (which later served as a basis of the Nazi educational system),[3] he was saved from vicious parochialism by his Dionysian disdain for the Men of the Fatherlands. Diversity *within* cultures is, however, not the only fact that undermines the modern paradigm; the crucial determining factors in our lives also cut *across* cultural lines. "Cultures" represent useful categories into which to place people who share similar characteristics in some salient respect. But these categories can be defined in many ways, and the resulting pattern is not a series of delimited islands, but a tangled crisscross (figure 2). Gender, class, religion, sexual orientation, ethnic identity, and language are all relevant ways to distinguish people, but they do not superimpose neatly on top of each other. Only by privileging one category can the modern paradigm be sustained. But in fact, each of us differs from absolutely everyone else in some respects, although "cultures" remain useful abstractions with which to describe our important similarities. This view reduces the idea of "cultural conditioning"

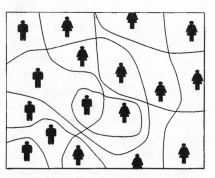

Figure 2. Postmodern Paradigm

from a theory that we are shaped by the defining quality of one crucial group (a nation, say, or a class), to the idea that we are shaped by everything we know, hear, read, and see, to the point at which no two people have identical influences. This nominalist view treats "culture" just as Nietzsche says we should treat causality: "One should not wrongly reify 'cause and effect'... one should use 'cause' and 'effect' only as pure concepts, that is to say, as conventional fictions for the purpose of designation and communication— *not* for explanation."[4] The image of a tangled web of distinguishing lines among people (2) does not invoke the notion of cultures as actually existing entities; and it is much more faithful to the data than the nineteenth-century image of a series of distinct islands, representing reified cultures (1). This more complicated, but truly "postmodern," paradigm leads away from *Weltanschauung*-historicism in the direction of an ethics and aesthetics of pluralism.[5]

The same point can be illustrated with a different analogy. Culture is often compared to a perspective or vantage point.

On this model, the particular point of view from which we observe the world determines how we see everything; thus "culture" is something simple and unitary that determines all of our experiences and judgments. This model fails to account for diversity within cultures, because it suggests that everyone who belongs to a culture occupies the same vantage point. Furthermore, it assumes that we always face every issue and problem from the same starting point, perspective, presupposition, or what have you. Thus the notion of culture as an essential substratum for all experience is built into the metaphor, and this tempts theorists to postulate vast metaphysical interpretations of particular cultures, e.g., the West as the domain of the *logos*. Perhaps this metaphor could be modified to account for differences among members of a single culture; and perhaps it could even take into account the heterogeneity of beliefs—not to mention the downright contradictions—with which we approach issues. Instead of imagining a culture as a group of people who always looked through the same peephole at everything, we could envision them as standing near each other in crowds, so that for periods of time everyone in the culture had nearly the same point of view. Some crowds would be tightly packed and static; they might even punish members who tried to wander away or look in the wrong direction. But even in such highly regimented groups, every member would have a slightly different point of view. Meanwhile, other crowds would be much less disciplined. Members of such groups would drift apart from time to time; they would look in opposite directions from the same vantage point; they would merge with other groups and break apart in different combinations; some of them would imitate members of nearby crowds, and so on. When two loosely ordered and highly mobile crowds stood near to each other, it might be difficult to assign individuals to either group with any certainty. Modified in this way, the metaphor of culture as a perspective would more accurately describe the historical phenomena, for we know that in most cases cultures are loosely defined, evolving, heterogenous entities. But as we begin to view matters in these terms, the very notion of a culture as a perspective begins to fall apart, for each observation by each human being at each point in time can be seen to have its own point of view. Once again, the modern paradigm dissolves under scrutiny, and a nominalist, postmodern paradigm emerges.

II. The Question of Interpretation

A postmodern paradigm has several claims to superiority over *Weltanschauung*-historicism. A central problem for

Weltanschauung-historicists is that they have no means of knowing
that outside the boundaries of their own culture lie several others.
Nietzsche, envisioning a cultural map much like figure (1), often
claimed that understanding across cultural barriers was impossible,
for belonging to a culture meant being closed to all others. But if we
cannot understand alien languages and ways of thought, then we
surely cannot even recognize that cultural barriers exist, or that a
given group of people different from us constitutes a
distinct culture. For Nietzsche, a recognition of cultural plurality
was possible only for someone who had moved beyond culture;
it was therefore an extramoral, nonrational recognition, neither
truth nor lie. On the other hand, some modern thinkers have
claimed that communication *is* possible among cultures. But if we
can understand and communicate with people from an alien culture,
then it is unclear how they are qualitatively more distinct from us
than people in our own culture. There does not seem to be much
reason to invoke boundaries or essential differences among classes,
languages, or national mentalities; they explain nothing.
The postmodern paradigm solves these problems at one stroke.
On this view, I am likely to share certain background characteristics
with many people, and these commonalities provide the grounds
for our mutual understanding. Communication is easier when we
share more, but it is almost never impossible. Even if two people
can identify no similarities in cultural background, they are likely
to be able to find a third party who bridges some of the gap
between them, or a chain of such people. And what is alien in any
person's background (my next-door neighbor's or an ancient
Greek's) can gradually be understood by building on commonalities.
Thus we do not have to be "beyond culture" in order to recognize
the existence of alternative cultures; this recognition is accessible
from within the world of history and rationality.

This account never invokes the notion of a universal "human
nature" as the precondition of communication; it only assumes a
complex web of differences that ultimately includes us all. For an
adherent to the modern paradigm, everything "cultural" is
explained by a diagram like that in figure (1), while everything
that is not included in such a diagram is considered "natural" and
universal. Thus, for example, a Marxist would make important
distinctions between the *Weltanschauung* of the proletariat and
that of the bourgeoisie, but would hold that humans are "naturally"
laboring animals, engaged in self-objectification through work.
But the line between the natural and the cultural is difficult to
draw, to say the least. Nietzsche never discusses the problem in a
sustained way, but I have already shown that there is a tension in

his thought between psychologism, which considers parts of human psychology to be natural, and *Weltanschauung*-historicism, which stresses cultural differences. Nietzsche resists distinctions between ethics and logic, mind and body, language and thought— and so also he resists any artificial barrier between nature and culture. Since he is acutely aware of cultural differences, he tends to place all human experience in the category of the cultural, and even remarks that there "has never yet been a natural humanity."[6] But adherents to the modern paradigm who believe, as Nietzsche does, that humans are not in any sense "natural" can find no common ground to serve as a precondition of communication. On the other hand, *Weltanschauung*-historicists who *do* exempt aspects of human life from the variety of "culture" tend to do so *a priori*, as an assumed requirement for communication. Unfortunately, this position cannot be supported empirically, for any empirical claim about the universality of a given aspect of psychology can always be explained away as the product of a contingent cultural perspective. On the other hand, the claim that *no* human attributes are universal seems equally impossible to prove empirically. The postmodern paradigm does not run into any of these difficulties, however, for it does not require human attributes to be universal as a basis for communication. It may be the case that certain attributes are universal. If this could be discovered, then it would be an interesting, if contingent, fact, and it would lead us to draw a line around *all* of the people in figure (2). But if such a universal human attribute could not be discovered, the paradigm would lose none of its explanatory power.

The postmodern paradigm also sheds light on a problem that has plagued historicist philosophy since the time of Hegel and Schleiermacher: the problem of the hermeneutic circle. On a *Weltanschauung*-historicist picture, every act, person and artifact is a product of its culture and is unintelligible except within the context of the local language, value system, historical tradition, and so on. But the languages and traditions within which each artifact is situated are, in turn, only accessible to us insofar as we have already interpreted the individual artifacts which form the broader cultural context. Thus understanding any culture appears to require a magical ability to leap into the circle from the outside, comprehending at one instant the whole and its parts. Any experience in the interpretation of ideas and events from the past does reveal, I think, that we gain a greater understanding of a work as we comprehend its context better; and we gain a gradually richer sense of an alien epoch or nation by examining its representative works and ideas. But this process requires no magical abilities, if we understand cultural diversity according to the postmodern paradigm. On this view, most alien texts confront us with some intelligible characteristics. Perhaps, for example, we understand the immediate political situation within which a text was written. We therefore find ourselves enclosed within the same horizon as the text in one important respect, for its political context is part of our direct or vicarious experience. In other respects, the text may require mediation if we are to understand it. For example, if we do not understand the language in which the text is written, then we will require the services of a translator: that is, of someone whose linguistic horizon crosses those of both the reader and the author. The text may also confront us with some thoroughly mysterious allusions, vocabulary, logical moves or fundamental values. We will only begin to recognize these as we come to share the cultural background of the text and its author by exposing ourselves to similar experiences and information. But whereas *Weltanschauung*-historicism calls for us to understand the abstract "cultural context" of a work, nominalist historicism requires only that we attempt to uncover its specific influences and its place in an individual narrative.

Thus, for example, we will gain little useful understanding of Nietzsche by seeing him as a part of the "discourse of modernity," but much by recognizing that he read the works of Lange while a student, and approved of them for such and such reasons. Meanwhile, Lange too has to be understood in the light of his personal experiences and influences. Thus—as traditional humanists have always been willing to admit—there is no end to the process of historical interpretation, no single authoritative "reading" that can end the process of inquiry. Nevertheless, we come to share more of an author's experiences through the labor of historical scholarship, as our understanding of the web of causal chains and narratives in which the author stands grows richer. In the process, we gain access to a broader range of experiences and options for living our own lives. Thus the experience of encompassing another person's background, and understanding his or her perspective, is broadening and liberating; it is valuable in itself, regardless of any "universal" themes or doctrines that may be contained in a text.[7]

The question of language still provokes worries of a hermeneutic circle, even within the postmodern paradigm. For it is not clear how we can understand any single word or proposition without first grasping the grammar and vocabulary of the entire language; nor how we can learn a language's vocabulary and grammar without first understanding individual words and propositions. However, it seems clear that translation among languages can occur, that people can occupy several linguistic horizons at different times or even simultaneously, that the boundaries among languages are often far from clear, that we can speak a given language with varying degrees of facility, and that differences in language can be almost as great among several speakers of English (for example) who have radically different occupations or backgrounds, as between speakers of English and French.[8] All of this makes it seem likely that a map of the world's linguistic horizons would resemble the tangled web of figure (2), more than the clearly delineated islands of figure (1). The hermeneutic circle makes learning a second language appear impossible. But we normally learn languages with the aid of people who are to some degree bilingual. The very existence of such people, with their broad, inclusive linguistic horizons, makes *Weltanschauung*-historicism appear unconvincing in the realm of language. In general, the nominalist presuppositions of the postmodern paradigm should lead us to dispense with any cultural categories that seem abstract and simplified. Thus, if the overlapping horizon lines in figure (2) are taken to represent nations, epochs or languages, it should be recognized that these broad horizons can in turn be broken down into overlapping subsets, until all that defines a person's background is a set of individual events, words, values, logical rules, language-games and so on. Sharing more of the items in a person's background makes interpreting him or her easier; gaps in interpretation occur when we fail to recognize items that do not exist within the horizons of our own experience.

All of this assumes that a primary goal of interpretation is to understand the intentional background of a work or event. However, the "meaning" of a work is not exhausted by an understanding of its author's intentions, even supposing that we *could* exhaustively understand any such intentional background. We take a special interest in an author's intentions for (and interpretations of) his or her own work. But there is no reason to suggest that the author's interpretation is the only interesting one. Shakespeare may not have intended his *Tempest* to serve as a commentary on imperialism, but it can be applied interestingly to the case of European colonialism down to the twentieth century; and this is therefore part of its "meaning." The writing of the *Tempest* was a historical event, carried out because of the intentions of an author. But the full meaning of that event for later readers could not have been predicted by Shakespeare. Thus Habermas notes:

> The predicates with which an event is narratively presented
> require the appearance of later events in the light of which

the event in question appears an historical event. Consequently, the historical description of events becomes in the course of time richer than empirical observation at the moment of their happening permits.[9]

A full or complete interpretation of a text would therefore mean perceiving it from every possible perspective; and each such perspective would have to be understood on its own terms, that is, through a comprehension of *its* historical context and intentional background. "We could give a definitive and complete description of a historical event," writes Habermas, "only if we could be certain that new points of view would no longer appear...."[10] And Nietzsche wrote, "A fact, a work is eloquent in a *new* way for every age and every new type of man. History always enunciates *new truths*."[11] Thus the methods of humanistic scholarship do not promise closure; but they do allow for progress toward an ever richer understanding of the past. This is precisely the limitless project at which Nietzsche hinted on several occasions. However, his *Weltanschauung*-historicism made it difficult for him to endorse such a view with confidence or to provide a theoretical understanding of it. Given his commitment to the "modern paradigm," Nietzsche could not make sense of the process by which we come to understand better another person's perspective. Nietzsche believed that any escape from the prison-house of subjectivity was impossible if we relied on rational methods, for he saw each epoch's effort to understand the past as the product of its own distinct, incommensurable "conceptual scheme." But it is possible to argue, by means of a history of humanism, that much *has* been achieved in the effort to fuse our horizons with those of other times, to confront dialectically what is ours with what is foreign. Reflecting on that long series of conflicting interpretations of the past which humanistic scholarship had produced, Nietzsche sometimes concluded—not that all of these perspectives must be wrong—but that true knowledge consists in comprehending *several* perspectives at once. "Problem: to see things as they are! Means: to be able to see them from a hundred eyes, from many persons."[12] This was how Nietzsche spoke in favor of *Wissenschaft*:

But precisely because we seek knowledge, let us not be ungrateful to such resolute reversals of accustomed perspectives and valuations with which the spirit has, with apparent mischievousness and futility, raged against itself

for so long: to see differently in this way for once, to *want* to
see differently, is no small discipline and preparation of the
intellect for its future 'objectivity'—the latter understood not as
'contemplation without interest' (which is a nonsensical absurdity),
but as the ability *to control* one's Pro and Con and to dispose
of them, so that one knows how to employ a variety of
perspectives and affective interpretations in the service of
knowledge.[13]

Thus Nietzsche was sometimes interested in a project that
would fuse the modern "historical sense" with a humanistic interest
in literature as a means of education. The more horizons we were
able to comprehend through the study of others' perspectives, the
broader our own sense of possibilities would become, and the more
sensitive we would become to the values of our fellow human beings.
In the culture of comparison, "the various *Weltanschauungen*,
customs, cultures are compared and experienced next to each other,
which was not possible earlier, when there was always a localized
rule for each culture, just as all artistic styles were bound in place
and time."[14] Thus we open up for ourselves "an immense field of
work. All kinds of individual passions have to be thought through
and pursued through different ages, peoples, and great and small
individuals; all their reason and all their evaluation and perspectives
on things have to be brought to light."[15] At times, Nietzsche conceived
of this as a liberating and ennobling project. Unfortunately, however,
such unqualified humanism was not a particularly prominent
motif in his thought. It was almost always accompanied by the hope
that someday some of us would step completely outside history, into
some kind of posthistorical, extracultural stage. Thus, for example,
the passage quoted above concludes as follows:

we will conceive the task that this [historicist] age sets us to
be as great as *possible*. Then posterity will bless us—
a posterity that knows it has transcended both the completed
original folk cultures, as well as the culture of comparison,
but which looks back on both kinds of culture as on venerable
antiquities, with gratitude.[16]

This, then, is the best that Nietzsche can say about the modern
fusion of historicism and humanism: it is a possible bridge to the
Overman.

III. The Politics of Contingency

On the *Weltanschauung*-historicist view of a "culture," people either belong or they do not. If you belong to a culture, you are utterly committed to its values and recognize alternatives as the province of savages, if at all. Thus Nietzsche writes, "Culture is, above all, a unity of artistic style manifest in all the vital activities of a people."[17] In a master morality, this unity is achieved by means of an unquestioned commitment to the culture's values; in a slave morality, the same commitment is achieved via an unquestioning abhorrence for all other cultures. If, however, you recognize the contingency of your values, then you have no culture at all. You are paralyzed by a lack of belief in received opinion about basic norms and preferences, and, Hamlet-like, you are unable to do anything with conviction: Hamlet is Nietzsche's prototype for the Dionysian Man, the man "beyond culture."[18] Hence the frequent modern decision to affirm the values of *some* culture, even though, deep down, many of Nietzsche's contemporaries already thought that no culture was better or worse than any other. Nietzsche blamed the rise of modern nationalism on a "*need* for a faith, a support, backbone, something to fall back on."[19] Nietzsche's Overman was the figure in his bestiary who had the inner, existential strength to do something affirmative, despite his knowledge that no choice was objectively better than any other. The *Übermensch* was committed to the "modern paradigm," but sophisticated enough about its contradictions and epistemological difficulties that he was ready to abandon reason altogether. The Last Man, on the other hand, was also a creature of the modern paradigm, but one who had neither the strength of character nor the integrity of intellect necessary to transcend it.

Thus Nietzsche's political aesthetics derived from his underlying paradigm for human culture. His rejection of eclecticism and the "culture of comparison" stemmed from his commitment to *Weltanschauung*-historicism, which he shared with many Romantics. Especially in his early work, his ideal remained a vision of Greek culture that—although he knew it was only a fantasy— possessed the Romantic virtues of homogeneity, organic integration and hermetic isolation. In the "archaic Greek world of the great, the natural, and the human," he wrote, no consciousness of historical change or diversity was permitted. There we "find the reality of a basically unhistorical culture, a culture which, despite its lack of history or rather precisely because of it, is unbelievably rich and vital."[20] In Greece before Socrates, "everything had to be fixed for all time."[21] If the world contained cultures like Nietzsche's vision

of classical Greece, it would fit the modern paradigm perfectly; and
Nietzsche, like many of his contemporaries, *wanted* the world to fit
his paradigm. Nietzsche only transcended this Romantic commitment
insofar as he imagined individuals who were propelled by the very
contradictions inherent in the modern paradigm into a space utterly
beyond culture. Describing how these individuals would live
became an increasingly important theme in Nietzsche's mature
work. But their extramoral, untimely, *übermenschlich* posture
could never represent a political alternative for any but the few.
Nietzsche's contempt for the average citizen of the modern world,
the nihilist Last Man, was thorough. His message to the ordinary
modern was therefore an exoteric Romantic doctrine of cultural
renewal, to be achieved by means of a return to the closed societies
of the past.

But Nietzsche's caricature of the Last Man seems a poor
depiction of modern people. Many people today consider their
affiliation to some kind of culture (or sometimes several cultures
at once) to be an important ingredient of who they are. They care
deeply about the values and preferences of their cultures, and they
will resist if these values are threatened. On the other hand, those
of them who are pluralist "Last Men" assign no objective or universal
superiority to their own culture's values. They think that belonging
to a given culture is a matter of contingency, often no more than
an accident of birth. But this in no way lessens their commitment
to their culture, which can even be described as a relation of love.
For when we love another person, we do not claim that everyone
else should too. In many cases, the reason we love one person
instead of another has practically everything to do with accidental
factors: blood relations, for example, or common experiences. But we
build on these accidental ties by investing effort, and thereby create
love. A similar kind of relation ideally exists between modern citizens
and their communities. This can be a relation of serious commitment,
but it implies no claim to universality. Moreover, modern pluralists,
viewing their commitments as important but ultimately contingent
and not necessarily better than anyone else's, will yield in cases of
conflict with other people's values whenever it seems fair to do so.
They may even fight for another person's right to enjoy values
which are different from their own. Thus the modern pluralist has
a kind of second-order commitment to the universal right of people
to live by their own commitments. The contemporary pluralist
hardly lacks values, therefore, and is far from a nihilist.

This is not to say that all moderns are pluralists, nor that all
cultural norms can be viewed in an equally pluralist spirit.
Whereas we can treat our own culture's burial customs, family

structures, and cuisine as contingent—yet dear to us—we cannot treat the belief in an active, omnipotent, universal God in the same way. Certain beliefs are, by definition, incompatible with any alternatives, for they make universal claims. My point is neither to espouse such beliefs nor to attack them; I just want to argue that even people who are thoroughly pluralist are not condemned to the passive nihilism that Nietzsche associated with the Last Man. Although some people believe that all of their customs and beliefs are contingent, nevertheless, these people can still feel profound attachment toward their cultural traditions.

Nietzsche (and many other *Weltanschauung*-historicists) assume that our values and beliefs are always based upon implicit axioms or preconceptions of a general character. Since these axioms are contingent and plural, each is the mere expression of someone's (or some culture's) will to power and there can be no uncoerced consensus among people who begin from different fundamental premises. It is clear that some disputes do arise from differences in basic preconceptions, and these preconceptions are often metaphysical: i.e., since they deal with matters beyond mere experience, they are not susceptible to empirical proof. For example, people who hold one kind of metaphysical theory about human beings may be led to oppose abortion; a different metaphysics can lead to support for abortion rights. Since there is no obvious way to settle this metaphysical dispute, we face a genuine failure of consensus. However, Nietzsche and many other philosophers have found metaphysical presuppositions implicit not only in statements about the nature of human beings, but practically everywhere they look. Nietzsche (followed by Derrida) reveals this tendency when he claims that even our ordinary use of grammar presupposes a metaphysics of Being and a belief in God. It seems much less contentious to suggest that most of our values, beliefs and utterances can stand on their own. They make concrete claims which can be accepted or rejected individually by others. For instance, when we say that X "is" Y, we generally do not *think* that we are affirming a metaphysics of Being; it is only the philosopher who assumes that we must be doing so implicitly. Moreover, since no evidence can be marshalled to show that ordinary statements always rely on implicit metaphysical doctrines, this is usually stipulated by philosophers, rather than argued for. If, however, most of our statements are concrete and susceptible to being tested individually, then the problems created by cultural pluralism are much less pervasive than Nietzsche, Strauss, Derrida, and others have claimed.

Isaiah Berlin is one philosopher who actively affirms a pluralist stance. Although his argument does not have the power to convince people who believe in universal principles to become complete pluralists, he does give a positive formulation of pluralism, showing that a pluralist does not necessarily lack all values and commitments. Berlin's famous essay, "Two Concepts of Liberty," attacks "those who seek for final solutions and single, all-embracing [political] systems, guaranteed to be eternal."[22] Believing that this response is unnecessary and dangerous, Berlin instead advocates pluralism, or the notion "that human goals are many, not all of them commensurable, and in perpetual rivalry with one another."[23] The pluralist's political solution is liberalism, which gives individuals the maximum equal freedom to pursue their own notions of the good. Berlin's position is therefore deontological: it asks—not, what is "the good"?—but how should people live together fairly, regardless of their diverse ethical perspectives? Like Berlin, Nietzsche had no faith in a final political solution: "he has discovered himself who says: This is *my* good and evil: he has silenced thereby the mole and dwarf who says, 'Good for all, evil for all.'"[24] However, Nietzsche thought that no culture could survive unless its members believed in a unifying, if arbitrary, table of values. Thus Zarathustra says:

> No people could live without making values [*schätzen*]; but if it wants to survive, it must not evaluate as its neighbor evaluates.
> Much that one people called good, another called shame and disgrace: this I found. I found much that was called evil here and decked with purple honors there.
> One neighbor never understood another: his soul was always amazed at his neighbor's madness and wickedness.
> A table of values hangs over every people. Look, it is a table of its overcomings; Look, it is the voice of its will to power....[25]

Nietzsche cannot conceive of a creative, life-affirming culture that lacks a coherent, commonly held idea of the good. But this is where Berlin parts company with him. Berlin offers a positive redescription of the life of the pluralist Last Man, whom he portrays as humane and courageous, rather than nihilistic and weak:

> It may be that the ideal of freedom to choose ends without claiming eternal validity for them, and the pluralism of values connected with this, is only the late fruit of our declining capitalist

civilization: an ideal which remote ages and primitive societies have not recognized, and one which posterity will regard with curiosity, even sympathy, but little comprehension. This may be so; but no skeptical conclusions seem to me to follow. Principles are not less sacred because their duration cannot be guaranteed. Indeed, the very desire for guarantees that our values are eternal and secure in some objective heaven is perhaps only a craving for the certainties of childhood or the absolute values of our primitive past. "To realise the relative validity of one's convictions," said an admirable writer of our time, "and yet stand for them unflinchingly, is what distinguishes a civilised man from a barbarian." To demand more than this is perhaps a deep and incurable metaphysical need; but to allow it to determine one's practice is a symptom of an equally deep, and more dangerous, moral and political immaturity.[26]

Another contemporary political theorist who has tried to give a positive formulation of the commitments of the "Last Man" is John Rawls. Rawls' *Theory of Justice* is aimed at the modern citizen who has learned to see the world of cultural diversity from a position of detachment. This citizen may well be committed to an idea of the good, to a "comprehensive religious, philosophical, or moral" view;[27] but he or she recognizes this commitment to be without universal authority. According to Rawls, "we need only suppose in the first stage that the parties assume the fact of pluralism to obtain, that is, that a plurality of comprehensive doctrines exists in society."[28] Rawls believes that this pluralism cannot be resolved through rational debate, for differences of perspective are frequently irreconcilable. But he argues that citizens can distance themselves from their own, contingent ideas of the good sufficiently to ask how a society should be organized in order to allow diverse perspectives to coexist peacefully and fairly. The result, if citizens seek fairness without privileging their own idea of the good, is a theory of justice that is far richer and more substantial than the regime of Nietzsche's Last Man. Jürgen Habermas' notion of a "communications-community" of people who attempt to make common decisions through noncoercive discussion, despite their differences in perspective, leads to remarkably similar results. Habermas believes that— even granting the fact of pluralism—"practical questions admit of truth."[29] But there is no higher authority for the truth or falsehood of moral beliefs than an agreement reached fairly by a community. "It would be meaningless to try to 'justify' practical sentences otherwise than by reference to the fact of an empirically motivated

202 A Vindication of the Last Man

contractual agreement."[30] And the "appropriate model" for such an agreement is the *Kommunikationsgemeinschaft* "of those affected, who as participants in a practical discourse test the validity claims of norms and, to the extent that they accept them with reasons, arrive at the conviction that in the given circumstances the proposed norms are 'right.'"[31] There are, of course, important differences among Rawls, Habermas, Berlin, and other philosophers of the Last Man; but these amount to family squabbles among thinkers who share a basic affirmation of pluralism. They are separated by a great gulf from Nietzsche's antidemocratic, antipluralist position.

For Nietzsche, no values were objectively superior to any others. However, Nietzsche was not a moral relativist, for this position still makes an objective claim about the world and all human values, whereas Nietzsche claimed to have transcended objectivity. Moral relativism also seemed to Nietzsche to contain an implicit egalitarian moral and cultural agenda that he wanted to reject. It represented the last and most pitiable vestige of Christian charity and self-denial. Rawls, Habermas, and other theorists of the regime of the Last Man have shown that it is possible, as Nietzsche thought it was, to draw minimal moral values out of the very presuppositions of relativism. These are, however, precisely the values that comport worst with Nietzsche's political and aesthetic views. Thus, for example, the relativist may be committed to liberal virtues of individual autonomy and noncoercion (à la Rawls and Berlin), solely on the grounds that no religious or moral values have universal validity, and therefore each person should be allowed to live as far as possible according to his or her own idea of the good. These liberal commitments are themselves open to a relativist critique, for one can always demand to know what makes liberty (say) objectively superior to arbitrary bondage. The thoroughgoing relativist can therefore have no commitments at all. But the postmodern paradigm does not entail completely relativist conclusions. Whereas the modern paradigm contained logical contradictions which led Nietzsche to declare it ultimately self-undermining, the postmodern paradigm seems coherent and consistent with the data as we know them. Thus adherents to the postmodern paradigm retain at least one commitment: to the plurality of human perspectives and their essential contingency. They also know that they will be able to recognize the limits of their own horizon and expand their options only if they treat other perspectives with tolerance and attempt to understand them—for they exist within an overlapping web of cultural horizons. Liberation, for adherents to the postmodern paradigm, can proceed only out of a process of mutual understanding. Similarly, postmodern pluralists may well admire those who have broadened their horizons furthest. These kinds of beliefs and preferences retain a *quasi*-objective validity for citizens of a pluralist society.

Many modern political theorists, including Nietzsche and Leo Strauss, have expressed nostalgia for the pre-historicist Closed Society, on the grounds that this is qualitatively different from the nihilist regime of modernity, and allows the creation of "whole," creative individuals. Modern, eclectic society is not a "culture," it is argued, whereas the ancient *polis* or medieval Christendom did deserve this title. But from the perspective of the postmodern paradigm, a closed society is simply a name for a group of people whose array of available ideas and influences is relatively small, and whose background experiences are therefore relatively homogeneous. So, for example, ancient Spartans presumably all thought in a more uniform way than ancient Athenians, as a result of their more uniform upbringing and the very small range of books and ideas that was available to them. But Spartan society was only different in degree from Athenian society. If we judge it as a whole, we might be able to defend it (as many Athenians did) on the grounds of its relative "coherence," "harmoniousness," "stability," and so on. However, the postmodern paradigm does not encourage us to view societies as wholes, because it denies any clear boundaries among them. The postmodern paradigm therefore demands that we examine each Spartan individually, on his own merits. And while we may admire Spartans for their valor and discipline, it seems clear that they did not choose these values from an array of alternatives, but were led to adopt them by an enforced ignorance. This does not mean that someone could not deliberately choose to live like a Spartan; but it becomes more difficult to argue in favor of Spartan life on the grounds that they had a "culture," whereas we do not.

For many philosophers, a society like ancient Sparta— or some imagined "primitive tribe"—is paradigmatic of all culture. In reality, Sparta merely falls near one end of a continuous spectrum, by virtue of the relative homogeneity of its citizenry. Because of draconian laws and customs, Spartans managed to hold together a relatively homogeneous and static society for a fairly long time. However, this just means that the word "Spartan" picks out many common features at once; we can guess that anyone who was a Spartan was also warlike, disciplined, patriotic, white, Greek-speaking, and so on. On the other hand, a phrase such as "Central American" refers to a much more loosely defined culture— but one which is just as paradigmatic of cultures in general. As David A. Crocker writes:

A poor Yucatecan fisherman may be an insider on the piers of Puerto Progresso yet an outsider in the nearby condos of Cancun. A Costa Rican professor of philosophy is an insider in the University of Costa Rica [and perhaps at Harvard] but an outsider among the *vaqueros* of the Costa Rican province of Guanacaste.

Even with respect to the same group we can be both insiders and outsiders. I identify with some of my country's values and practices and not with others.... It follows that the insider/outsider distinction is better understood as a continuum or spectrum rather than a rigid dichotomy whose categories are mutually exclusive.[32]

Hispanics in the United States represent an example of a "culture" that is at least as typical as ancient Sparta. Hispanics do not all speak any one language; they belong to at least four races; there are probably Hispanics of every religion; and they differ by class, profession, national origin, sexual preference, gender, age, and so on. When we speak of "Hispanics," we are using one kind of cultural category, but not the only relevant one, nor the one which may seem most important to some Hispanics. This is not to suggest that ethnic categories are unimportant. In a race-conscious society, it may be wise to make common cause with all people who are categorized as belonging to one's own ethnic group. Besides, there are real and important "family resemblances" linking Hispanics, just as there are resemblances among all lawyers, Americans, Catholics, or women.[33] But abandoning an essentialist notion of culture is valuable for several reasons. First, it allows us to recognize and celebrate diversity within cultures and subcultures. Second, it allows us to acknowledge the claims of many disadvantaged groups simultaneously. For example, no one has to choose feminism *or* antiracism, if it is recognized that categories of race and gender can overlap and be simultaneously important. If, on the other hand, we adopt an essentialist notion of gender or race, then there can only be one struggle of existential importance. Third, avoiding essentialist theories of culture dissolves some apparent epistemological difficulties. There cannot be impenetrable barriers to communication across cultural borders, for we are always crossing such borders, even when we communicate with the people who are most like us. And finally, the recognition that societies are always at least somewhat multicultural helps us to see that uniformity is no prerequisite for becoming a "culture."

Any highly pluralist society would be open to the aesthetically motivated invective that Nietzsche heaped upon the "culture of comparison" of his day; viewed as a whole, it would be merely an "omnium gatherum," a "ragged suit of motley," and so on. But a postmodern, nominalist critic of the idea of a *Weltanschauung* will have no reason to view modern society *as a whole* in aesthetic terms. Nietzsche was thoroughly committed to the modern paradigm and to the Romantic idealization of those civilizations that appeared, in their internal harmony and isolation, to fit the modern paradigm best. If one were to begin instead with the postmodern paradigm, an entirely different political aesthetic would result. According to the postmodern paradigm, understanding who we are means understanding the overlapping horizons in which we live, their limits and their alternatives. Thus it is through interacting with people with whom we share attributes—and also differ in some respects—that we come to understand our own identity and possibilities and the nature of the social world. Adherents to the postmodern paradigm therefore have no reason to favor closed, homogeneous societies, and every reason to prefer pluralism. They have no desire to preserve differences among cultures, and no interest in viewing them separately as aesthetic wholes—for they do not believe that "cultures" exist as objective entities.

To some extent, the Romantic preference for homogeneity may have been strictly aesthetic—a matter of taste, so to speak. But it also had a foundation in the Romantics' erroneous paradigm for cultural life, and their political/cultural program of reform. Nietzsche shared the Romantics' paradigm and (at least exoterically) their political program. By liberating ourselves from these views, we are compelled to reconsider the value of homogeneity, at least in the public sphere. Its only remaining justification will be a purely aesthetic preference that we have inherited from the Romantics; this preference will be difficult to defend rationally and is currently being replaced by an incipient postmodern aesthetic of eclecticism.[34]

As I have said, Nietzsche was sometimes willing to concede the superiority of his own period to all others in its understanding of history and world culture; this was "Our Pre-eminence." But he was equally willing to make a *value-judgment* against this new-found power. I have suggested that Nietzsche's value-judgment against the modern "historical sense" depended on his vision of human cultures as distinct islands, whose narrow perspectives historicist scholarship would undermine. But this vision was inadequate; and his value-judgment is therefore to be viewed with suspicion. Besides, it should be said that the modern "historical sense" at least protects us against the idealization of the past, which has sometimes reached fanatical proportions during our century as the result of admittedly irrationalist political movements. The "historical sense," if pursued with ruthless honesty, will make any idealized description of a closed society from the past appear false. By making closed societies appear to be nothing but relatively parochial versions of the same thing we call "open societies," scholarship makes openness and tolerance appear valuable. From the perspective of the twentieth century, this is one of its greatest merits, for the idealization of past cultures seems a much worse danger than the passive nihilism that Nietzsche attributed (falsely) to pluralists and historicists.

IV. A Vindication of Humanism

In Chapter One, I argued that the traditional humanistic education that Nietzsche encountered at Pforta promoted values of tolerance, openness, pluralism and democracy. In contrast, Nietzsche's exoteric program for cultural reform was explicitly antipluralist and antidemocratic, while his esoteric message was radically apolitical. Today, conservative proponents of traditional humanism attempt to reinforce their position by arguing that a single, transhistorical canon of "great books" contains universal values to which all citizens should be exposed. For example, William Bennett writes:

> our eagerness to assert the virtues of pluralism should not allow us to sacrifice the principle that formerly lent substance and continuity to the curriculum, namely, that each college and university should recognize and accept its vital role as conveyor of the accumulated wisdom of our civilization. We are a part and a product of Western civilization. That our society was founded upon such principles as justice, liberty, government with the consent of the governed, and equality under the law is the result of ideas descended from great epochs of Western civilization—Enlightenment England and France, Renaissance Florence, and Periclean Athens.[35]

This kind of justification fails to take account of the phenomenon of radical diversity *within* Western history, and easily falls prey to a relativist critique. Ironically, Nietzsche himself finds a place on Bennett's very short list of canonical authors, despite Nietzsche's attack on *all* the ideas that Bennett cites as "Western," and Nietzsche's opposition to the very notion of "accumulated wisdom."[36] But the postmodern paradigm provides a new means of conceptualizing and vindicating humanistic education. For on the postmodern paradigm, our only means of gaining self-knowledge and understanding our social context is via exposure to the widest possible array of differing perspectives. But in order to understand these perspectives, we must meet them on their own terms, that is, with the virtues of tolerance and respect included in our very method of interpretation. And in order to understand what an event or idea "means," we must see how it has been interpreted from the widest possible variety of perspectives. Thus the work of describing ourselves and our human environment is necessarily a collaborative and cumulative one, and the apparatus of humanistic scholarship—even the footnotes and appendices that Nietzsche ridiculed—appears indispensable. The labor of humanistic scholarship epitomizes the virtues that are required for life in a pluralist democracy, in the regime of the Last Man.

This explains Nietzsche's contempt for the professional guild of scholars, "herd animal[s] in the realm of knowledge,"[37] who "belong by their very nature and quite involuntarily to the carriers of the democratic idea";[38] but it also explains the evident *value* of a humanistic education in preparing for life in contemporary democracy. It is not that humanism exposes us to universally applicable moral doctrines contained in the works from the past which we read; it is rather that the *methods* of humanistic interpretation inculcate virtues that are required of any citizen in the modern "Culture of Comparison." To say this much is to agree fully with Nietzsche; his only dissent consists in his contempt for the non-culture of modernity, which humanism so powerfully supports.

But if the humanities are to help us learn the virtues required for citizenship in a pluralist regime, they must possess a method that allows us to discover truths about the social world. Many critics of the methods of the humanities assume that humanists claim to "understand" culture. It is relatively easy to attack such a claim from a skeptical position, as both deconstructionists and "new historicists" have shown. Thus, for example, Claude-Lévi Strauss states that structuralism "aims at discovering *general laws*...";[39] and this project proves an easy target for the Nietzschean post-structuralist, Jacques Derrida. But it seems useful to distinguish the relatively modest claims of the humanities from the social-scientific study of culture, which does often aim to provide causal explanations of past events, predictions of future developments, and models or covering laws to explain "systems." The humanist wishes, not to explain, but to describe culture. This is all that is required to broaden our horizons and make us better moral agents. At best, the humanities offer detailed, "thick" descriptions, which place events in a rich context and provide accounts of people's motives. To use Gilbert Ryle's example of a thick description, humanists hope to be able to speak about "conspiratorial winks," rather than mere contractions of eyelids. To interpret the latter as the former does require a labor of understanding and empathy; but it does not entail that the wink has been "explained" in a quasi-scientific fashion. Even the notion of a culture or *Weltanschauung*, used in a reified way, is too abstract and explanatory for the humanities. Thus Clifford Geertz remarks, "culture is not a power, something to which social events, behaviors, institutions, or processes can be causally attributed; it is a context, something within which they can be intelligibly—that is, thickly, described."[40] To explain events by reference to "vast, a priori *Weltanschauungen*, is to pretend a science that does not exist and imagine a reality that cannot be found."[41] Karl Popper too has criticized the predilection for covering laws, quantitative methods, "holism" (i.e., the reification of cultures), predictive theories, and essentialism. He attacks social scientists for misunderstanding the natural sciences, and then importing their misunderstandings into the study of culture.[42] But the nominalist, descriptive method that he advocates for the "social sciences" is not really scientistic at all; it is humanistic. Similarly, Wittgenstein endorsed a humanistic approach when he wrote, "We must do away with all *explanation*, and description alone must take its place."[43] His method epitomized the thick, empathetic descriptions characteristic of the humanities. "In order to see more clearly," he writes, "we must focus on the details of what goes on; must look at them *from close to*."[44]

One kind of context in which humanists often place events is that of a narrative. A narrative does not gain its coherence because of causal connections, nor does it make even an implicit claim to being a definitive explanation of the relationship among events.[45] If I string together the events of my day into a narrative, I am not recounting a chain of causes and effects, nor am I suggesting that my narrative is the only one that could fit the data that I have described. For one thing, my narrative makes me a protagonist, and other people mere bystanders; but in the narrative of *their* lives, the reverse would be true. Moreover, from the perspective of some future time, the same events might take on an entirely different significance. Thus the humanist is something like the director of a film, who portrays events from a perspective that he or she hopes will be particularly interesting and coherent. If we want to know "what actually happened," then the more films we can see, the better, especially if they are shot from a diverse range of perspectives. Of course, the humanist is more like a director of a documentary film than a fictional drama, because the events that he or she describes are not inventions, but discoveries, viewed from an admittedly subjective perspective. Thus the humanities differ from fiction, but also from the social sciences. Perhaps a clear line could not be drawn distinguishing these three kinds of thought; but even an indistinct picture of the humanities allows us to see that any effort to explain a culture or event the way a scientist would explain a reaction or a system is clearly *not* a humanistic endeavor. Thus the humanities do not have to be defended by analogy to the natural sciences.[46]

My description of the humanities is heavily indebted to Geertz. Geertz is an anthropologist; but this only demonstrates that the line between the social sciences and the humanities does not follow institutionalized disciplinary boundaries. The "aim of anthropology," Geertz writes, "is the enlargement of the universe of human discourse."[47] Faced with the peculiarities of an alien way of life, anthropology "renders them accessible: setting them in the frame of their own banalities, it dissolves their opacity." This project is made more difficult if we fall prey to *Weltanschauung*-historicism, which asks us "to imagine that culture is a self-contained 'super-organic' reality with forces and purposes of its own; that is, to reify it."[48] Geertz concludes, "The essential vocation of interpretive anthropology is not to answer our deepest questions, but to make available to us answers that others, guarding their sheep in other valleys, have given, and thus to include them in the consultable record of what man has said."[49]

In recent years, a fierce debate has broken out concerning the value of the humanities as a means of moral education.[50] In this new "battle of the books," conservatives argue for a return to an Arnoldian canon of Western literature, containing the permanent values of civilization. Historicism has become an explicit target for these conservative proponents of a homogeneous, humanistic curriculum that would still allegedly convey "the accumulated wisdom of our civilization"[51] and provide students with "a clear vision of what is worth knowing and what is important in our heritage, [our] great works, ideas, and minds."[52] The conservatives in this new *Querelle* receive apparent support from Straussians, although Strauss' esoteric position was actually far from conservative. Against them are arrayed various critics of the allegedly narrow, exclusive, and ethnocentric curriculum that prevails in modern schools. The "new historicists," for example, attack the idea that texts from the past can ever serve as "compelling embodiments of timeless and universal truths."[53] They oppose the claim "that the traditional literary canon and the canon of traditional critical readings embody an essential and inclusive range of human experience and expression."[54]

The new battle of the books is a legacy of the quarrels of Nietzsche's day; Allan Bloom's *Closing of the American Mind* even alludes deliberately and pervasively to Nietzsche's *Use and Disadvantage of History*. What almost all factions share is a commitment to one form of *Weltanschauung*-historicism, a belief in "the West" as a coherent intellectual entity, a world-view. For Nietzsche, the West constituted the "history of an error [sc. objectivity]"; for Heidegger, the domain of metaphysics; for Derrida, the epoch of logocentrism; and for Popper, the story of liberty and individualism. Similarly, for contemporary conservatives it embodies a tradition culminating in democracy, Christianity, and capitalism, whereas for modern radicals it represents an imperialist and objectifying attitude. *All* such definitions abandon the common-sense idea that "the West" is a vast geographical area, containing a huge diversity of perspectives, spanning millennia of intricate history, and defined—if at all—by extremely vague borders. "The West" is a phrase misleadingly attached to concepts—from democracy to imperialism—that people either want to imbue with legitimacy or condemn, depending upon their attitude toward "Western civilization." But Western civilization is a huge fiction, the amalgam of numerous sub-fictions from "Hellas" to "modernity." It is a category which can lump together Republican Romans and Biblical prophets, cowboys and crusaders, but separate Thomas Aquinas by a great gulf from Avicenna, on the grounds that "Islam" is not Western. Or it can be defined even more contentiously, as for example by Popper, who makes Plato, Hegel and Marx great enemies of "the West." Is an African-American nationalist Western or non-Western? Is democracy a Western imperialist imposition? Was Nazism a betrayal of Western ideals, or their inevitable outcome? These are the kind of sophistical dilemmas which the unself-conscious use of a fiction can create. Of all the *Weltanschauungen* which the nineteenth century invented, "the West" is the most abstract and polemical. It may be useful in some contexts, but its status as an enormous generalization must never be forgotten. And so it seems to me that the contemporary battle of the books deals with a pseudo-problem, which a nominalist view would quickly dissolve.

A humanistic education requires exposure to a wide range of perspectives. But "Western civilization"—however this is defined—

contains an unimaginable variety of ideas, values, preconceptions and vantage points.[55] Thus people who claim to oppose multiculturalism in the name of "Western values" really just oppose someone else's multicultural canon. Multiculturalism is the human condition. Even the limiting case, a curriculum totally devoted to one book, would be "multicultural" insofar as any interesting author would betray influences from diverse sources. And a Western curriculum that included (say) Calvin, Rabelais, Freud, Wilde and Lenin would be enormously diverse.

Therefore, the West would provide adequate material for any curriculum. However, there is no reason to restrict the curriculum to works by people who happen to be European, white, Judeo-Christian, or otherwise "Western." In fact, in a race- and gender-conscious society, it would be harmful to present a curriculum that contained exclusively white male authors; this might give the impression that white males are superior. On the other hand, there is a very good reason to restrict the curriculum in *some* way. For the postmodern paradigm implies that our understanding of a text improves as we begin to grasp its local context as if "from close to"; and no one has the capacity to grasp an unlimited number of local contexts. The primary value of a humanistic education lies in its ability to teach us how to understand another perspective. Thus its primary value is methodological, and it is therefore better to concentrate on gaining a deep understanding of a limited number of interrelated authors and ideas, rather than trying to be "inclusive." Indeed, the kind of humanistic pedagogy which claims to provide a broad education by imparting "information" about a large number of people and their opinions—without attempting to resurrect the rigorous process of thought that produced these opinions—may actually be counter-productive. It obscures the difficult nature of mutual understanding and encourages fatuous generalizations. Thus a good humanistic curriculum might concentrate on a relatively small number of interrelated texts in their specific contexts.[56]

To suggest that the primary value of the humanities is methodological is not to obscure the difference between great and mediocre works. It may well be more profitable to concentrate on painting in Renaissance Florence and drama in Elizabethan England, rather than (for example) the reverse—or Chinese philosophy rather than television sitcoms. The need to *choose* subjects for a curriculum appears to bring into play difficult philosophical problems. But we never make these choices in a vacuum, as if we were simply observing the course of past civilization with a naive eye. Humanistic scholarship is a collective and cumulative enterprise, with a history. Centuries of commentary from a vast diversity of perspectives has already grown up around Renaissance painting, which has thereby proved itself pragmatically to be worthy of discussion, contemplation and analysis. The only way to prove that another work or set of works deserves similar treatment is to offer an interpretation and try to create a dialogue. One can discuss and interpret sitcoms, for example, but I suspect that we would relatively quickly run out of things to say about them.

At first glance, it seems possible to imagine that the "best" works from the past might *never* receive appropriate respect and consideration, or that any canon is arbitrary and even deliberately exclusive. But what court of appeal is higher than the collective enterprise of humanistic scholarship? What imaginable criterion could show that a work is "great," but that it has somehow been ignored by a transhistorical conversation that is, in theory, open to all perspectives? Admittedly, professional humanists frequently fail to live up to their own ideals of openness, candor and fairness; but when this happens, it is their weakness and not a fault implicit in the ideal of humanism. If we are clear, at least, about what humanism ideally entails, then hypocritical efforts at exclusion should be relatively easy to unmask. And at least one criterion emerges for deciding what works are worth studying and teaching: the group of people making this decision must be inclusive with regard to race, gender, class and cultural background, for otherwise the decision made would clearly fail to be just.[57] A procedural definition of quality in the curriculum avoids the chimaera of an aperspectival, ahistorical canon of "the great books," but it nevertheless sets stringent requirements and allows for gradual progress towards consensus.

V. The Good European

Throughout this book I have tried to suggest that the modern humanist with a "historical sense" can be described in positive terms, and not merely caricatured as a Nietzschean Last Man. From time to time, I have admitted that Nietzsche saw value in the Last Man, and not merely as a precondition for the Overman. Moreover, he counted himself among the historicist scholars and educators, speaking consistently of "we philologists," "we scholars," and "we good Europeans." Above all, a "good European" was Nietzsche's term of praise for the modern historicist liberal, who lived up to all the tolerant and cosmopolitan promises of the new, nineteenth-century humanism. I have suggested that Nietzsche's theory of culture and communication made it difficult for him to explain or defend the life of the Good European. His comments about this figure are particularly elliptical and metaphorical, as if he was unable to get an adequate conceptual grip on what it meant to be a humanist in the nihilistic "Culture of Comparison." I hope to have helped in providing some of the necessary conceptual foundations. My goal has been to suggest, against Nietzsche, that historicism need not lead to nihilism, and that historicism and humanism can be fruitfully combined or synthesized. But Nietzsche's own description of the Good European, despite its marginal place in his philosophy, will perhaps never be surpassed in eloquence and promise. It is full of democratic and optimistic spirit, of empathy for every human experience. It is a call to continue a collective labor that will never cease, but that provides its own extraordinary reward:

> *The 'Humaneness' of the Future*—When I contemplate the present age with the eyes of some remote age, I can find nothing more remarkable and distinctive in present-day humanity than its distinctive virtue and disease which goes by the name of the 'historical sense.' This is the beginning of something altogether new and strange in history: If this seed should be given a few centuries and more, it might ultimately become a marvelous growth with an equally marvelous scent that might make our old earth more agreeable to live on. We of the present day are only just beginning to form the chain of a very powerful future feeling, link by link—we hardly know what we are doing.... Anyone who manages to experience the history of humanity as a whole as *his own history* will feel in an enormously generalized way all the grief of an invalid who thinks of health, of an old man who thinks of the dreams of his youth, of a lover deprived of his beloved, of the martyr whose ideal is perishing, of the hero on the evening after a battle that has decided nothing but brought him wounds and the loss of his friend. But if one endured, if one *could* endure this immense sum of grief of all kinds while yet being the hero who, as the second day of battle breaks, welcomes the dawn and his fortune, being the heir of all the nobility of past spirit—an heir with a sense of obligation, the most aristocratic of all old nobles and at the same time the first of a new nobility—the like of which no age has yet seen or dreamt of; if one could burden one's soul with all of this—the oldest, the newest, losses, hopes, conquests, and the victories of humanity;

if one could finally contain this in one soul and crowd it into a single feeling—this would surely have to result in a happiness that humanity has not known so far: the happiness of a god full of power and love, full of tears and laughter, a happiness that, like the sun of the evening, continually bestows its inexhaustible riches, pouring them into the sea, feeling richest, as the sun does, only when even the poorest fisherman is still rowing with golden oars! This godlike feeling would then be called—humaneness.[58]

Notes

Introduction

1. Article of 1941, quoted as an epigraph in William J. Bennett, *To Reclaim a Legacy* (Washington, 1984).

2. Bloom, "Western Civ." (1988) in *Giants and Dwarves: Essays 1960–1990* (New York, 1990), p. 24.

3. See, e.g., Nietzsche, *Homer und die klassische Philologie* (Schlechta, III:165).

4. *Tractatus Logico-Philosophicus*, trans. D. F. Pears and B. F. McGuiness (London, 1922), section 6.54.

5. *Twilight of the Idols*, "'Reason' in Philosophy," 5 (Schlechta II:960).

6. See, e.g., *Genealogy of Morals* I:13.

7. *Über den Humanismus*, 1947 (French/German edition, Paris, 1964), p. 50.

8. See, e.g., William Musgrave Calder III, "The Wilamowitz-Nietzsche Struggle," in *Studies in the Modern History of Classical Scholarship, Antiqua* xvii (Naples, 1984), p. 185.

9. For Wilamowitz' role as a cultural icon, see Luciano Canfora, *Cultura classica e crisi tedeschi: gli scritti politici di Wilamowitz, 1914–1931* (Bari, 1977), p. 8 and passim.

215

10. Bennett, pp. 3 and 29, paraphrasing Matthew Arnold.

11. White, "New Historicism: A Comment," in H. Aram Veeser, ed., *The New Historicism* (New York, 1989), p. 294.

Chapter 1

1. Daniel Halévy, *The Life of Friedrich Nietzsche*, translated by J. M. Hone (London, 1911), pp. 26ff. Halévy's biography is untrustworthy as an interpretation of Nietzsche, being based on his sister's recollections, but it is probably accurate concerning childhood incidents. Ronald Hayman tells the same story with additional details, but does not cite a source: *Nietzsche: A Critical Life* (New York, 1984), p. 28. The best biography, Kurt Paul Janz' *Friedrich Nietzsche* (Munich, 1978), omits the incident. Livy was central to the curriculum at Pforta: see Ulrich von Wilamowitz-Möllendorff, *Recollections, 1848-1914*, translated by G. C. Richards (London, 1930), p. 83.

2. Hayman, p. 25. The first quotation is identified as professor Pitzker writing in the *Tägliche Rundschau* during the summer of 1893, and recalled by Elizabeth Förster-Nietzsche; Hayman does not identify the other two witnesses. Charles Andler describes the young Nietzsche in a similar way, relying for the most part on his autobiographical juvenalia: *Nietzsche: sa vie et sa pensée* (Paris, 1921), II, p. 40, 42.

3. For the dominant influence of humanism at Pforta, see Wilamowitz, *Recollections*, p. 83 and *passim*; Janz, vol. 1, pp. 65-6; and Halévy, p. 26: "In this old monastery German rigour, the spirit of humanism, and the ethic of Protestantism formed a singular and deep-rooted alliance, a fruitful type of life and sentiment." See also: Gerhard Arnhardt, *Schulpforte: Eine Schule im Zeichen der humanistischen Bildungstradition* (Berlin, 1988).
Ranke's slogan, *"wie es eigentlich gewesen,"* is taken from the following passage: "To history has been given the function of judging the past, of instructing men for the profit of future years. The present attempt does not aspire to such a lofty undertaking. It merely wants to show how, essentially, things happened." From the "Preface" to the first edition of the *Histories of the Latin and German Nations*, translated by Iggers and von Moltke, *The Theory and Practice of History* (Indianapolis, 1973), p. 137. Ranke's quest for what essentially happened was still value-laden. Consider, e.g., the following pronouncement from 1820: "God lives and is observable in the whole of history. Every deed bears witness to him, every moment proclaims his name, but especially do we find it in the connecting line that runs through history." Quoted in Pieter Geyl, "Ranke in the Light of the Catastrophe," in *Debates with Historians* (Cleveland, 1958), p. 16. Geyl, p. 21, cites Droysen, von Sybel, and Treitschke as followers of Ranke and members of a "Prussian School" that hoped to legitimize the German nation-state through positivistic history.

4. The Rector's Tercentenary Address, quoted in Janz, vol. 1, p. 65. I have borrowed the use of Voltaire's comment about Prussia from Hayman. Andler

doesn't cite the Rector's address, but calls Pforta "*une petite république sco-laire unique de son espèce en Allemagne.*" The metaphor must have been a commonplace; it is used again by Otto Benndorf in anon., "*Der Primaner Nietzsche*" (1900), trans. in Gilman and Parent, eds., *Conversations with Nietzsche* (Oxford, 1987), p. 16.

5. For descriptions of Pforta, see Janz, Chapter III; Hayman, p. 27; Andler, II, pp. 47ff.; Halévy, pp. 26ff; and Wilamowitz, *Recollections*, p. 68.

6. Dryden, "Life of Plutarch" (1683), in Works, edited by H. T. Swedenberg et al. (Berkeley, 1971), vol. XVII, pp. 270–271, 274. Compare "the like revolutions of former times" with Nietzsche's "eternal return." For a brief account of humanism and its relation to history, see Paul Oskar Kristeller, *Renaissance Thought II: Papers on Humanism and the Arts* (New York, 1965), pp. 3, 26ff. Regarding the humanists' belief in a constant human nature, Kristeller, p. 28, writes of Machiavelli that "he states his underlying assumption more clearly than any [other humanists] had done: human beings are fundamentally the same at all times, and therefore it is possible to study the conduct of the ancients, to learn from their mistakes and from their achievements, and to follow their example where they were success-ful." An explicit statement of the same view comes in Marsilio Ficino's letter to Giocomo Bracciolini (the son of Poggio), quoted in Erwin Panofsky, "The History of Art as a Humanistic Discipline," in *Meaning in the Visual Arts* (New York, 1955), p. 25.

7. See Fritz K. Ringer, *The Decline of the German Mandarins: The German Academic Community 1890–1933* (Cambridge, Massachusetts, 1969), pp. 16–19.

8. Leibniz, *Theodicy*, II:148. See also Leibniz' memoire of July 1, 1692 in Bodemann, *Zeitschift des historischen Vereins für Niedersachsen* (1885), p. 21. Cf. *Nouveaux essais*, IV, XVI:11, in Gerhardt, *Die Philosophischen Schriften von ... Leibniz* (Berlin, 1882), V, pp. 452–453. For Leibniz' belief in the historical basis of religion, see *Leibniziana*, XX, in Feller, *Des seel. Herrn von Leibniz Lebenslauf* (1717), p. 148: "Except by means of history, it is not possible to demonstrate the truth of Christian religion."

Whether Leibniz held that human nature was constant is a matter of dispute: Croce thought so, but Antonio Corsano and Robert Flint hold that Leibniz was only a proto-historicist: see Croce, *La storia come pensiero e come azione*, fourth ed. (Bari, 1943), pp. 62–63; Corsano, "*Leibniz e la storia*," in *Il Giornale critico della filosofia Italiana*, XXXIII, 3, viii; and Flint, *The Philosophy of History in Europe* (London, 1874), I, p. 345. J. H. De Vleeschauwer, in *Perennis quaedem philosophia: exégèse et antécédents d'un texte leibnizien*, (Pretoria, 1968), p. 4, criticizes the view that Leibniz was a historicist at all.

9. Wilamowitz (*Recollections*, p. 92) recalls that when the chaplain "put before us the 22nd Psalm as a prophesy of Christ, we had just read it in Hebrew with Siegfried (he was presently made Professor of Old Testament at Jena and did good work on Philo), and received a scientific explanation."

Nietzsche remained very pious while at Pforta, but he did shock his mother by recommending to his sister *Das Leben Jesu* by the rationalist, Hase: see Hayman, p. 39, and Andler, pp. 53ff. Nietzsche and his friend Paul Deussen had the 45th Psalm explained to them "completely as a secular wedding song" by the Pforta classicist, Steinhart. See Deussen, pp. 3ff. Bendorf (op. cit.) thought that Steinhart influenced Nietzsche deeply.

10. Deussen's *Errinerungen an Friedrich Nietzsche* (Leipzig, 1922), pp. 15ff., in Gilman and Parent, *Conversations with Nietzsche*, p. 19.

11. Nietzsche, autobiographical writings (1856–69) in Schlechta, III:21.

12. *Twilight of the Idols*, "Was ich den Alten verdanke," 1 (Schlechta, II:1027). Cf. *Human, All-Too Human*, 203 (Faber): "Of all the things the Gymnasium did, the most valuable was its training in Latin style ...."

13. G. B. Kerferd, *The Sophistic Movement* (Cambridge, 1981), p. 18.

14. *Birth of Tragedy* (Kaufmann), 13.

15. Ibid., 15.

16. See Werner Jaeger, *Paideia: The Ideals of Greek Culture*, translated by Gilbert Highet (New York, 1943), p. 301, on the parallels between modern humanism and ancient Sophism.

17. Nietzsche, *Twilight of the Idols*, "Das Problem des Sokrates," 5 (Schlechta, II:953). As a matter of fact, Socrates himself specifically warns the young (anyone under 30) to stay away from dialectic: *Republic* 537e1–539a4. But this is probably a middle-period passage (thus more Platonic than Socratic); the Socrates of the early dialogues engages in spirited dialectic with young men, leaving them in a state of *aporia*, or confusion, regarding traditional values. This is the Socrates whom Nietzsche has in mind generally.

18. Ibid., 9 (Schlechta, III:954).

19. *Will to Power*, 427 (Kaufmann).

20. This is the question which Nietzsche says he was the first to raise: see his "Attempt at a Self-Criticism," appended to *The Birth of Tragedy* in 1886, sec. 2: "What I then got hold of, something frightful and dangerous but not necessarily a bull, but in any case a *new* problem—today I should say that it *was the problem of science itself*, science considered for the first time as problematic, as questionable" (Kaufmann). The German word *Wissenschaft*, translated here as "science," includes humanistic scholarship.

21. See, e.g., *Zarathustra*, "Of the Apostates," II.

22. *Birth of Tragedy* (Kaufmann), 13. The dependence of scholarly values upon "naïveté, venerable, childlike, and boundlessly clumsy naïveté" is the theme of *Beyond Good and Evil* (Kaufmann), 58.

23. *Twilight of the Idols*, "Das Problem des Sokrates," 12 (Schlechta, II:956).

24. It is characteristic of Nietzsche's method to discuss not ideas, but people, who serve as incarnations of organic collections of concepts. So rather than speaking separately of humanism, democracy, and rationalism, Nietzsche describes Socrates; instead of attacking historicism, tolerance, openness, and multiculturalism, he criticizes David Strauss (see Chapter IV). "I never attack persons," he says; "I merely avail myself of the person as a strong magnifying glass that allows one to make visible a general but creeping and elusive calamity." (*Ecce Homo*, "Why I Am So Wise," 7 [Kaufmann].) This method has limitations, but I will try to show that there are often legitimate connections among the separate beliefs and concepts which Nietzsche groups together under such rubrics as "Socrates," "Wagner," "Strauss," "Woman," the "Last Man," "We Scholars," and the "Good European."

25. However, Aristophanes depicted Socrates as a Sophist in the *Clouds*, and Socrates seems to have been convicted on charges, essentially, of acting like a Sophist (making the weaker argument appear stronger, etc.).

26. On Protagoras' prosecution for impiety, see Kerferd, p. 21 (citing Diels-Kranz fragments 80A1 and 3). Nietzsche writes: "The ugly man of the people, Socrates, struck dead the authority of the glorious myth in Greece." From *Nachlaß*, summer 1875, in Colli-Montinari, IV:1, p. 178.

27. This work is reconstructed—somewhat speculatively—by Mario Untersteiner in *The Sophists*, translated by Kathleen Freeman (Oxford, 1953), pp. 26ff. Protagoras refused to speculate about gods or the elements: "I do not know whether they exist or not. It is a difficult question, and life is too short." Fragment 4—Diels, quoted in H. I. Marrou, "The Pedagogical Revolution of the Early Sophists," in J. J. Chambliss, ed., *Nobility, Tragedy, and Naturalism: Education in Ancient Greece* (Minneapolis, 1971), p. 48. Cf. Isocrates, *Antidosis* 268ff. In the *Theaetetus* (157a), Socrates ascribes a secret metaphysics to Protagoras. According to Socrates, since Protagoras does not believe in metaphysical truths, he must believe that the cosmos "is" only becoming. But this is to turn Protagoras' skepticism about metaphysics into a metaphysics of becoming. Protagoras would surely protest, but he is not present in the *Theaetetus*.

28. For Leibniz' skepticism about solving moral dilemmas aprioristically, see, e.g., a fragment of 1676 in Couturat, *Opuscules et fragments inédits de Leibniz* (Paris, 1903), p. 524. See also Louis Spitz, "The Significance of Leibniz for Historiography," in *The Journal of the History of Ideas*, XIII (1952), p. 338.

29. *Protagoras*, 325e–326a. My translation from Burnet, ed., *Platonis Opera* (Oxford, 1958), vol. 1.

30. For a Roman echo of Protagoras' claim that literature is valuable because it contains models for moral edification, see Cicero, *Pro Archia poeta oratio*, vi, 14. Cicero's *Pro Archia*, deeply influenced by the Sophists, was

admired by Quintillian, whose works on education were enormously influential in the Latin West, and by Petrarch, a founder of Renaissance humanism.

31. The quarrel between Plato and the Sophists may be more complex than I have made it sound; but Nietzsche's account is like the one I have supplied here. See his *Description of Ancient Rhetoric* (1872–73) in Sander Gilman, Carole Blair, and David J. Parent, *Friedrich Nietzsche on Rhetoric and Language* (New York: Oxford University Press, 1989), pp. 6–9.

32. Kant, *Grundlegung zur Metaphysik der Sitten (Groundwork of the Metaphysics of Morals)*, edited by Wilhelm Weischedel (Baden-Baden, 1991), p. 36.

33. Jaeger, *Paideia*, I, p. v.

34. See Richard Bett, "The Sophists and Relativism," in *Phronesis* XXXIV (2) 1989, pp. 139–169.

35. Habermas, "On the Logic of Legitimation Problems," in *Legitimation Crisis* (Boston, 1973), p. 100.

36. Nietzsche, *Beyond Good and Evil* (Kaufmann), 186.

37. This according to Plato: *Protagoras*, 322C.

38. Plutarch, *Pericles*, 36.

39. See Bernard Knox, *The Oldest Dead White European Males* (New York, 1993), pp. 90–99 for a popular account of the Sophists as democrats, freethinkers, and cosmopolitans.

40. Karl Popper, *The Open Society and Its Enemies*, I, p. 172.

41. Heidegger, *Über den Humanismus*, especially pp. 47ff., where he provides a brief, critical history of humanism since the Sophists.

42. See, e.g., *Will to Power*, 437 (dated 1888).

43. *Birth of Tragedy*, 11 (I have altered the order of phrases).

44. Burckhardt, *Civilization of the Renaissance*, trans. by S. G. C. Middlemore (London, 1955), p. 81.

45. Burckhardt, *History of Greek Culture*, abridged and translated by Palmer Hilty (New York, 1963), p. 326.

46. Max Weber, *The Protestant Ethic and the Spirit of Capitalism* (New York, 1958), p. 26. According to Arnaldo Momigliano, Burckhardt's attitude towards "occidental rationalism" grew gradually more positive after 1860. See "Burckhardt and the *Griechische Kulturgeschichte*," in *Essays in Ancient and Modern Historiography* (Middletown, Connecticut, 1977), pp. 297ff.

47. Jaeger, in *Paideia*, vol. I, p. 304, comments: "It is easy to understand why Nietzsche and Bachofen felt that the summer of Greece was the time before ratio, conscious reason, appeared—the mythical period, the age of

Homer or the great tragedians." But see "We Philogists," III:76 (Arrowsmith, p. 345): "if we fully understand Greek culture, we see that it's gone for good."

48. Mircea Eliade, *The Myth of the Eternal Return, or Cosmos and History*, trans. Willard R. Trask (Princeton, 1974; 1st French ed., 1949), pp. 48; 36. Eliade makes it clear (p. x) that his subject is "pre-Socratic man."

49. Nietzsche, *Birth of Tragedy* (Kaufmann) 23.

50. Eliade, p. 123. Cf. *Will to Power*, 617: "That everything recurs is the closest approximation of a world of becoming to a world of being."

51. Nietzsche, *Die Philosophie im tragischen Zeitalter der Griechen* (Schlechta, III:356).

52. Popper, *The Open Society and its Enemies*, I, p. 172.

53. Habermas, *The Theory of Communicative Action: Volume One, Reason and the Rationalization of Society* (hereafter, *TCA*), translated by Thomas McCarthy (Boston, 1984), I, p. 70.

54. Isocrates, *Panegyricus* 50. Isocrates seems to have inherited his cosmopolitanism from Gorgias' oration at the Olympic Festival of 408 BC, so this attitude was essential of Sophism from the start.

55. Kerferd, pp. 25–26.

56. Knox, op. cit., p. 104.

57. Nietzsche, *Description of Ancient Rhetoric*, p. 3 (cf. his *History of Greek Eloquence* (1872–73) in Gilman et al., p. 214).

58. *Twilight of the Idols*, (Schlechta, II:991). See also: *Will to Power*, 431: "the mob achieved victory with dialectics"; this is used again in *Twilight of the Idols* (1888), "The Problem of Socrates," 5.
Isocrates was led by the logic of his humanism to a qualified support of popular sovereignty: see *Areopagiticus* 20–27. The same principles applied at Pforta. Wilamowitz, *Recollections*, p. 74, recalls: "The wisdom of the order of life which prevailed in the boarding-house was that it gave self-government to the boys, and thus by obedience trained them in leadership and sense of responsibility." And Andler, II, p. 47, remarks that "*Les élèves aussi se governent; on choisit parmi eux les moniteurs surveillants.*"

59. No such experiment was attempted at Nietzsche's Pforta. Ringer (p. 26) writes: "the ideals of the [18th-century neohumanist] reform period were gradually routinized and transformed into defenses of social privilege. Rigid curricular specifications took the place of neohumanist enthusiasm." (Cf. p. 80.) However, it was clear to many in Nietzsche's day that—because of the situation that Ringer describes—German education was no longer humanistic. By appealing to humanistic ideals, liberals were later able to broaden enrollment at gymnasia and universities. Meanwhile, humanistic rhetoric sounded increasingly hollow on the lips of elitists, until many gave up the

pretense. Thus, to say that humanism has been used as a cover for privilege is like saying that Christianity has excused hatred, and socialism, inequality. It does not constitute an attack upon the idea, nor does it prove that the idea completely lacks efficacy.

60. *Twilight of the Idols*, "The Problem of Socrates," 7 (Schlechta, II:953); "Expeditions of an Untimely Person," 38 (Schlechta, II:1015).

61. Aulus Gellius, *The Attic Nights*, trans. J. C. Rolfe, XVIII: xviii, quoting Varro, fragment 1 (Misch).

62. Kristeller, p. 16.

63. Ovid, *Ex ponto*, II, ix, 47–48, my translation from *P. Ovidi Nasonis tristium libri quinque, Ibis, ex ponto libri quatuor ...*, ed. S. G. Owen (Oxford, 1915). The liberal arts (here, *ingenuae artes* or free-born arts) traditionally include the pure sciences, music, and mathematics as well as the humanities, but Ovid only mentions literature in this poem, which was written long before the list of liberal arts became standardized. He also refers to the *mites artes* or "gentle arts."

64. Gadamer, in *Truth and Method* (Sheed & Ward, 1979), p. 16–58, describes "tact," "common sense" (meaning knowledge of the community), and "taste" as essentially ethical attitudes engendered and required by humanistic practices. He cites von Helmholtz, Shaftsbury, and Kant in defense of this view. See in general Chapter One, "The Significance of the Humanist Tradition."

65. The question of Wilamowitz' anti-Semitism has been hotly debated. But consider this passage from the *Recollections* (p. 39), where he is describing his childhood: "I need not say that there was then no Anti-Semitism ... in spite of the physical and moral uncleanliness of many Jews, and it could not manifest itself in our family or in my own case. The task of Germanizing our Jewish compatriots was difficult and took generations to accomplish, but it was in process and was bound to be completed. Not a few had become loyal Germans.... Now [in 1928] everything is upset since the men of November [the founders of the Weimar Republic], just like the Bolsheviks, began to rely on that creedless, stateless, conscienceless Judaism, whose press long ago poisoned our wells, and have called to their aid the Jews of the East, whom we can neither endure nor get rid of [!]. What will come of it, in the world and in our own country only a prophet could declare, and no one would believe him if he did."

66. Nietzsche, *The Gay Science* (Kaufmann) V:348.

67. Canfora, pp. 9–18.

68. Paul Shorey, *What Plato Said* (Chicago, 1934), p. 2; Calder, *Studies in the History of Classical Scholarship, Antiqua xvii*, p. 223.

69. See Ulrich K. Goldsmith, "Wilamowitz and the *Georgekreis*," in *Wilamowitz nach 50 Jahren* (Darmstadt, 1983).

70. Wilamowitz, "German Intellectuals and their Alleged Espousal of Violence" (1918), translated by Canfora, p. 84; Wilamowitz, *Platon* (Berlin, 1920), p. vi.

71. Calder, pp. 222–223.

72. Janz, vol. 1, p. 66 reaches the same conclusion.

73. Halévy, p. 28.

74. *Recollections*, p. 70.

75. Ibid., p. 60.

76. Ibid., p 20: Of the Poles he knew growing up in Posen, Wilamowitz writes, *Recollections*, p. 33: "In fact they *were* like children, and that they are so no longer they owe exclusively to the Germans."

77. Andler, II, p. 48 reports that Koberstein was a fine scholar; and Jaap Mansfield calls him "presumably the most important historian of German literature in his day." See "The Wilamowitz-Nietzsche Struggle: Another New Document and Some Further Comments," *Nietzsche-Studien* XV (1986), p. 43. See also Ivo Frenzel, *Friedrich Nietzsche: An Illustrated Biography*, trans. Joachim Neugroschel (New York, 1967), pp. 16ff.

78. Nietzsche, letter to his mother and sister, Nov. 10, 1863, in Colli-Montinari, *Nietzsche Briefwechsel (Kritische Gesamtausgabe)*, I;1, p. 266.

79. Hayman, p. 40, quoting Nietzsche without a reference.

80. Janz, vol. 1, p. 79

81. Hayman, p. 55, citing a letter of February 12, 1864.

82. Nietzsche's friend Paul Deussen recalled: "Nietzsche treated the literary composition of Theognis' poems, in which the words 'good' and 'bad' are synonymous with 'aristocratic' and 'plebeian,' respectively. Everyone knows how much these impressions, which were the topic of our daily conversations, influenced Nietzsche's later moral views." *Errinerungen*, p. 11, in Gilman and Parent, *Conversations with Nietzsche*. Cf. *Genealogy of Morals*, Preface, 3, and I:5.

83. Hayman, p. 56, quoting autobiographical fragments by Nietzsche (the German text can be found in Schlechta, III:151).

84. Wilamowitz, *Recollections*, pp. 94; 82.

85. Mansfield, p. 44. Koberstein's *Geschichte der deutschen Nationalliteratur* is described by Mansfield as presenting an idealized view of "the Greeks" and their *Weltanschauung* that was deliberately creative and nonobjective. But Koberstein's brand of Romantic historicism was not widely reflected in the curriculum at Pforta.

86. Wilamowitz, *Recollections*, p. 94.

87. Janz, vol. 1, p. 67.

Chapter 2

1. Nietzsche moved to philology from theology. See Janz, vol. 1, p. 142; Hayman, p. 60; Wilamowitz, *Recollections*, p. 92. On Nietzsche's training as a philologist, see, e.g., Marcello Gigante, *"Friedrich Nietzsche nella storia della filologia classica,"* in *Classico e mediazione: contributi alla storia della filologia antica* (Rome, 1989), pp. 21ff; Jonathan Barnes, "Nietzsche and Diogenes Laertius," in *Nietzsche-Studien* XV (1986), pp. 16-40; M. S. Silk and J. P. Stern, *Nietzsche on Tragedy* (Cambridge, 1981).

2. Isaiah Berlin, forward to Friedrich Meinecke, *Historism:* [sic] *The Rise of a New Historical Outlook*, translated by J. E. Anderson (London, 1972), p. x.

3. Nietzsche uses "the historical sense" frequently; I will discuss many of the relevant passages below. He uses the word *"Historizismus"* to describe Hegel's optimistic teleology: *Will to Power* 415 (Schlechta ed., IV:71). I think that this is a deliberately awkward coinage to describe an unattractive view. Nietzsche also speaks of the "theory of the milieu" (*Theorie vom Milieu*): see *Twilight of the Idols*, "Expeditions of an Untimely Man," 44 (Schlechta, II:1020).

4. For theories of history supported by the historicist "picture," see e.g., Erich Auerbach, *Mimesis: The Representation of Reality in Western Literature*, trans. by Willard R. Trask (Princeton, 1974; written 1942), pp. 443ff; George A. Iggers, *The German Conception of History* (Middletown, 1968), pp. 287ff.; Hans Meyerhoff, ed., *The Philosophy of History in Our Time* (New York, 1959); and Meinecke, *Historism*, p. lv. Meinecke writes: "The essence of historism [sic] is the substitution of a process of *individualising* observation for a *generalising* of human forces in history." Iggers writes that Karl Mannheim defined historicism as the theory that ideas are "reflex functions of the sociological conditions under which they arise." Benedetto Croce, in *History as the Story of Liberty* (New York, 1955), uses "historicism" to mean the collapse of logic and metaphysics into history. And Ortega y Gasset, in "History as a System," argues that "historicism" means: "... Man has no nature, what he has is ... history." Quoted in Raymond Klibansky and H. J. Paton, eds., Philosophy and History (Oxford, 1936), p. 313.

5. *Will to Power*, 224 (Schlechta, II:687).

6. I am using the word "picture" much as Wittgenstein uses it. For example, he describes a general, Augustinian picture (*Bild*) of language-as-naming, which has supported diverse theories of language from the ancient world to his own *Tractatus*. He then proposes a new picture, which has different consequences for theory. See *Philosophical Investigations*, trans. G. E. M. Anscombe (Macmillan, 1953), 1.

7. This is the theme of Edmund Wilson's *To the Finland Station* (London, revised ed., 1972). He traces the history of the idea that "the social world is ... the work of men" (p. 5) from Vico, through Michelet and the French socialists, to Marx and Lenin.

8. "Richard Wagner in Bayreuth," 8 (Arrowsmith, p. 281).

9. Ibid., 11 (Arrowsmith, pp. 301–302).

10. Meinecke, *Die Enstehung des Historismus* (Munich, 1936), quoted without page reference in Meyerhoff, p. 9.

11. Wilamowitz, *History of Classical Scholarship*, translated by Alan Harris (London, 1982; written 1922), p. 1.

12. *Zukunftsphilologie!* p. 31, in Karlfried Gründer, *Der Streit um Nietzsche's 'Geburt der Tragödie'*, (Hildesheim, 1969).

13. Nietzsche, *The Gay Science* (Kaufmann) III:152.

14. Balzac, *La vieille Fille*, in Auerbach, p. 478.
On historicism today, see J. Hillis Miller, "Presidential Address 1986: The Triumph of Theory, the Resistance to Reading, and the Question of the Material Base," *Proceedings of the Modern Language Association*, 102 (1987), p. 283. Philology in Nietzsche's day fits many modern definitions of social science, and particularly the sociology of knowledge. A useful survey of the modern social sciences in the light of Nietzsche's historicism is provided by Richard A. Schweder in his "Post-Nietzschean Anthropology," in Michael Krausz, ed., *Relativism: Interpretation and Confrontation* (Notre Dame, 1989), pp. 99–139. See also Martin Hollis, "The Social Destruction of Reality", in Hollis and Lukes, eds., *Rationality and Relativism* (Oxford, 1982), p. 68.

15. Hayman, p. 61. Art history had come into the German university curriculum as a result of J. J. Winckelmann's proto-historicist work, on which see below. According to Friedrich Schlegel (1795), Winckelmann had conceived "the very idea of a history of art." Quoted in Silk and Stern, p. 6.

16. See Meyerhoff, pp. 12–13; and Henri Pirenne, *Methods in Social Science*, ed. Stuart A. Rice (Chicago, 1931), pp. 435–445, reprinted in Meyerhoff, pp. 87ff.

17. Andler (II:73) writes: "For [Ritschl] philological science was the resurrection of the entire civilization of a people." He calls Ritschl (II:67) *"un puritain de la science."* Carlo Antoni discusses Ritschl's historicist interpretation of Christian doctrine in *Lo Storicismo* (Turin, 1968), p. 11. And Francisco Rodriguez Adrados says that Ritschl was skeptical of universalist doctrines of human nature, preferring descriptions of people in their diverse cultural contexts: see *"Nietzsche y el concepto de la filologia classica,"* in *Habis*, I (1970), p. 88.

18. Hayman, p. 63, citing Deussen's recollections. On Strauss, see Karl Löwith, *From Hegel to Nietzsche*, trans. David E. Green (New York, 1967), pp. 330ff.

19. Nietzsche, letter of June 11, 1865 (Schlechta, III: 953). Andler (II:69) writes of Nietzsche in the Bonn period that: "His new cult of scientific truth affected, in the presence of his sister and mother, airs of superiority."

226   Notes

20. Gadamer, *Truth and Method*, p. 204.

21. See Gadamer, p. 207; Dilthey, "The Dream" (1903) in Meyerhoff, p. 41.

22. T. M. Campbell, "Aspects of Nietzsche's Struggle with Philology to 1871," *Germanic Review* XII (1937), p. 251.

23. For discussion of the latter view, see Meinecke, *Historism*, p. 266; and H. R. Trevor-Roper, *The Romantic Movement and the Study of History* (London, 1969), pp. 2ff.

24. On the alleged vicious circle implied by historicism, see Leo Strauss, *Natural Right and History* (Chicago, 1953), p. 25: "Historicism thrives on the fact that it inconsistently exempts itself from its own verdict about [the relativity of] all human thought." For Gadamer's response, see *Truth and Method*, pp. 308ff., and 484. Strauss' charge, fair or not, could be levelled against the first historicist work, Vico's *New Science*, the frontispiece of which depicts the whole variety of human institutions from an implicitly detached viewpoint: that of Vico and his readers. See Thomas Goddard Bergin and Max Harold Fisch, translators, *The New Science of Giambattista Vico* (Ithaca, 1988), pp. 2ff.

25. See J. M. Levine, *The Battle of the Books* (Ithaca, 1991). Helmut Rheder comments, à propos of Nietzsche: "Ever since the '*querelles des anciens et des modernes*' demonstrated the relativity of historical judgment, the question of surpassed standards and outdated models has disquieted literary criticism." See "The Reluctant Disciple: Schiller and Nietzsche," in James O'Flaherty, et. al., *Studies in Nietzsche and the Classical Tradition* (Chapel Hill, 1979), p. 159. And Gadamer notes (*Truth and Method*, p. 482): "That querelle was, as it were, the last form of an unhistorical debate between tradition and the modern age."

26. See John Edwin Sandys, *A History of Classical Scholarship* (Cambridge, 1908), III, pp. 33–35. For Leibniz' view that they were forgeries, which was cited by German scholars of Nietzsche's time as an example of Leibniz's historicism, see: Leibniz, *Dissertatio de principio individuii*, ed. Guhrauer (Berlin, 1837), pp. 68ff. (Corollaria #7); Wilamowitz, *History of Classical Scholarship*, p. 80; Sandys, III, p. 1; and Mauriz Haupt, "*Über Leibnizens Beziehungen zur classischen Philologie*," in his *Opuscula* (Leipzig, 1876), III, i, p. 219.

27. Wilamowitz, *Zukunfstphilologie!*, p. 32. Cf. Meinecke, pp. 240ff.

28. Letter to Erwin Rohde, July 16, 1872, in Colli-Montinari, *Nietzsche Briefwechsel* II:iii, p. 23. In the same letter, Nietzsche describes Homer as emerging from an "enormous, savage struggle," a period of "brutality and cruelty."

29. *The Gay Science* (Kaufmann), II:83.

30. Nietzsche makes this point: *Beyond Good and Evil*, 224.

31. Trevor-Roper, p. 14. Scott's short story, "The Two Drovers," from *Chronicles of Cannongate*, is a classic account of the perennial conflict (only recognizable to historicists) between one person's cultural background and the allegedly absolute standards of an alien culture's law. On Scott as a historicist, see *We Philologists*, 39 (Arrowsmith, p. 335). Cf. *Will to Power*, 831 (Kaufmann): "Winckelmann's and Goethe's Greeks, Victor Hugo's orientals, Wagner's Edda characters, Walter Scott's Englishmen of the thirteenth century—some day the whole comedy will be exposed! it was all historically false beyond measure, but—modern."

32. Racine, *Théâtre complet* (Paris, 1960), pp. 476–477.

33. *Père Goriot*, trans. E. K. Brown et. al. (New York, 1950), p. 3.

34. See, e.g., Ernst Gombrich, *Art and Illusion: A Study in the Psychology of Pictorial Representation* (Princeton, 1969). Cf. Burckhardt, *Civilization of the Renaissance*, p. 100 and passim.

35. Compare also Manet's "Odalisque" and its model, Titian's "Venus of Urbino" (1538). Like Giorgione's "Fête champêtre," the "Venus of Urbino" was a canonical picture, hanging in the Louvre. Titian depicted Venus lying nude in a Venetian bourgeois bedroom; Manet's "Odalisque" reclined in an equally contemporary setting. But Titian was historically naive, whereas Manet possessed a subtle historical sense, and was therefore guilty of deliberately offending bourgeois sensibilities.

36. Gadamer writes (*Truth and Method*, p. 77): "The historical picture ..., the historical novel, but above all the historicizing forms in which the architecture of the nineteenth century indulged in constant stylistic reminiscence, show the close relationship between the aesthetic and the historical elements in the cultural consciousness." Cf. Meyerhoff, p. 10.

On the growing prevalence of perspectivism, see Auerbach's *Mimesis*, the theme of which is the gradual emergence of numerous forms of perspective in Western literature. See also Karsten Harries, review of Hans Blumenberg's *Genesis of the Copernican World* (*Inquiry* XXIII, 1980), p. 264: "As man learned to understand the mechanism of perspectival illusion he also learned to 'see' through what he observed to an underlying reality .... 'More than a form of thought, perspectivity becomes a form of life ....'" From Blumenberg, *Die Genesis der Kopernikanischen Welt* (Frankfurt, 1975), p. 619.

Erwin Panofsky, in *La Perspective comme forme symbolique*, Guy Ballangé, trans. (Paris, 1975; German ed., 1932), argues that Renaissance linear perspective was not an objective discovery about the world, but a contingent product of its age. But Panofsky seems to treat his own historical perspectivism as absolutely valid.

37. Wilamowitz, *History of Classical Scholarship*, p. 92.

38. Iggers, p. 3. Iggers (p. 31) accuses Meinecke of ignoring "the emergence of a historical approach to cultural reality in the eighteenth century." He argues that Meinecke dwells too much on metaphysical theories of culture:

but the same could be said of Iggers. Meinecke, after all, had proposed the definition of historicism as the substitution of an individualising approach to history for a generalising approach—a definition which applies best to the empirical historians of the period.

39. Vico claimed that his New Science originated as a result of philological research: "To discover the way in which this first human thinking arose in the gentile world, we [sc. Vico] encountered exasperating difficulties which have cost us the research of a good twenty years. [We had] to descend from these human and refined natures of ours to those quite wild and savage natures, which we cannot imagine at all and can comprehend only with great effort": *New Science*, p. 100.

40. Meinecke, p. lvii.

41. *Will to Power*, (Kaufmann) 218 (1887–88).

42. *Human, All-Too Human*, 2 (Schlechta, I:448).

43. *Use and Disadvantage of History*, 1 (Schlechta, I:219). Cf. the following comment by Catherine Gallagher: "This is not to claim that the desire for historical knowledge is itself historically unplaced or 'objective'; it is, rather, to insist that the impulses, norms, and standards of a discipline called history, which has achieved a high level of autonomy in the late twentieth century, are a profound part of the subjectivity of some scholars ...." From her "Marxism and the New Historicism," in Veeser, p. 46.

44. For treatments of Nietzsche's perspectivism which demonstrate its consistency but ignore its empirical origins, see Nehamas, *Nietzsche: Life as Literature* (Cambridge, Mass., 1985); Jacques Derrida, *Éperons: Les styles de Nietzsche* (Chicago, 1978); and Arthur Danto, "Perspectivism," in his *Nietzsche as Philosopher* (New York, 1965), pp. 68–99.

I am in general agreement with the position stated by Hendrik Birus: *"je m' attache à démontrer que son* [sc. Nietzsche's] *concept d' interpretation textuelle était profondément enraciné dans la philologie tradionelle ...."* See "Nietzsche's Concept of Interpretation," in *Texte: Revue de Critique et de Théorie Littéraire* III (1984), p. 87 (text in English with French forward by Birus).

45. See, e.g., *Will to Power* 303 (1888); *The Gay Science*, II:57.

46. See below. But for a clear statement, see "Of the Thousand and One Goals" in *Thus Spoke Zarathustra* (Schlechta, II:322). Cf. *The Gay Science*, III:159, entitled "Every virtue has its age"; and *Will to Power*, 354 (in Schlechta, III:724), discussed below.

47. See, e.g., *Gay Science* (Kaufmann), I:7, discussed below.

48. Edmund Husserl, *Logical Investigations*, trans. J. N. Findlay (London, 1970; 1st ed., 1900), para. 35.

49. "On Truth and Lying in an Ultramoral Sense" (1873), in Gilman, Blair,

and Parent, eds., *Friedrich Nietzsche on Rhetoric and Language* (New York: Oxford University Press, 1989), pp. 246, 253.

50. *Will to Power* (Kaufmann), 515.

51. Ibid.

52. Husserl, *Logical Investigations*, paragraph 38.

53. "Truth and Lying" (Gilman et al.) p. 246.

54. These are the thinkers attacked by Husserl. Husserl's arguments depend heavily upon the *reductio ad absurdum*, which Nietzsche might not accept, because Nietzsche would welcome such "absurd" consequences as the loss of any distinction between truth and falsehood. Husserl recognizes "individual" and "special" (i.e., species-based) relativism, and dismisses them both. He does not recognize cultural relativism, which would undermine many of his arguments. For his belated response to cultural relativism, see the aptly entitled *Crisis of the European Sciences*, trans. David Carr (Evanston, 1970; written before 1938), esp. Appendix IX.

On Lange's psychologism, see Claudia Crawford, *The Beginnings of Nietzsche's Theory of Language* (Berlin/New York, 1988), p. 80, citing Lange's *Geschichte des Materialismus* (Iserlohn, 1866), pp. 499ff.; and Husserl, *Log. Invest.*, para. 28, quoting a lengthy passage from Lange's *Logische Studien* (1877 ed.).

55. "On Music and Words" (Mügge), p. 30.

56. "On Truth and Lying" (Gilman et al.), p. 248.

57. For an alternative view, cf. Nehamas, "Immanent and Transcendent Perspectivism in Nietzsche," in *Nietzsche-Studien*, XII (1983), pp. 473–490; and Nehamas, *Nietzsche: Life as Literature*, pp. 42ff.

58. Consider Gadamer's view of Hegel's educational project (*Truth and Method*, pp. 14–15, citing Hegel's *Nurnberger Schriften*, ed. J. Hoffmeister, p. 312). Hegel claims that the world of antiquity is ideal for giving us an objective distance from ourselves, yet also providing "all the exit points and threads of the return to oneself ...." Gadamer writes that Hegel is overly focussed on classical antiquity; "But the basic point is correct. To seek one's own in the alien, to become at home in it, is the basic movement of spirit, whose being is only return to itself from what is other."

59. *The Gay Science* (Kaufmann), IV:337.

60. *Will to Power* (Kaufmann), 254.

61. See, e.g., "We Philologists," V:156 (Arrowsmith, p. 378): "What always *cuts us off* from *ancient culture* is that its *foundations* have become for us completely *invalid*." But cf. V:171, where Nietzsche suggests that if a cultural model, such as Greece, "is very remote," we can still employ it by "devising proximate approaches." And cf. Silk and Stern, p. 13.

62. *Will to Power* (Kaufmann), 561.

63. Nietzsche, *Der letze Philosoph* (1872), MS p. 33, translated in Mark Warren, *Nietzsche and Political Thought* (Cambridge, Mass., 1988), p. 104.

64. "Of the Thousand and One Goals," in *Thus Spoke Zarathustra* (Schlechta, II:322).

65. Nietzsche, "On Truth and Lying," pp. 247–248.

66. *The Gay Science* (Kaufmann), II:76.

67. Ibid., V:354.

68. *Genealogy of Morals*, (Kaufmann), Preface, 2. See also *The Wanderer and His Shadow*, 44.

69. Mark Warren (p. 107) writes that, for Nietzsche, "meaning resides in a correspondence between concepts, ideals, systems of ideas, words, or statements and some metaphysical set of referents." I think that this "set of referents" constitutes the structure of a culture. Warren cites *Human, All-Too Human*, 1; *Will to Power*, 253, 254, 579.

70. *Phenomenology*, Preface, para. 20.

Chapter 3

1. Donald Davidson, "On the Very Idea of a Conceptual Scheme" (1974) in *Inquiries into Truth and Interpretation* (Oxford, 1984), pp. 183–198.

2. Habermas, "Philosophy as Stand-In and Interpreter" in K. Baynes, J. Bohman & T. McCarthy, eds., *After Philosophy: End or Transformation?* (Cambridge, 1987), p. 304. Cf. Foucault's "regimes of truth," described in ibid., p. 12.

3. Iggers, p. 8, citing Ranke's *Das Politische Gespräch*. Nietzsche describes Ranke as "that born classical *advocatus* of every *causa fortior,* that most prudent of all prudent 'realists.'" (*Genealogy of Morals* [Kaufmann] III:19.) Nietzsche's ideal historian was the more diffident Burckhardt: see, e.g., Peter Heller, *Studies on Nietzsche* (Bonn, 1980), pp. 89–117. Burckhardt's "historical philosophizing" epitomized the virtues of "intellectual restraint and moderation"—to quote *Human All Too Human*, sec. 2, where Burckhardt is not explicitly mentioned.

4. Meinecke, *Weltbürgertum und Nationalstaat*, in *Werke* (Munich, 1962), V, p. 83, translated in *Historism*, p. 9.

5 Hollis and Lukes, "Introduction" to *Rationality and Relativism*, pp. 2ff., quoting M. Herkovitz, *Man and His Works* (Knopf, 1947), p. 76.

6. W. Newton-Smith, "Relativism and the Possibility of Interpretation," borrowing a phrase from Ian Hacking, in Hollis and Lukes, p. 115.

To J. G. Droysen, an unquestioning identification with one's state seemed a way out of mere subjectivity: see his *Historik Vorlesungen über Enzyklopädie und Methodologie der Geschichte*, Rudolf Hübner, ed., (Munich, 1960), p. 287. Charles Taylor speaks of the appeal of historicism to "the anti-imperialist conscience, wary of ethnocentrism": see his "Rationality," in Hollis and Lukes, p. 99.

7. "Use and Disadvantage of History," 3 (Arrowsmith, pp. 100–101).

8. "Richard Wagner in Bayreuth," 6 (Arrowsmith, p. 273).

9. "Use and Disadvantage of History," 4 (Arrowsmith, p. 105).

10. *The Gay Science* (Kaufmann), V:377.

11. *Human, All-Too-Human*, I:475 (Schlechta, I:684).

12. See John Hollowell, *The Decline and Fall of Liberalism as an Ideology with Particular Reference to German Politico-Liberal Thought* (Berkeley, 1943); Iggers, p. 14 and passim. Ernst Troeltsch describes the "ideas of 1789" as positing the "isolated individual and his always identical rationality." But because of historicism, writes Troeltsch, today "There is no pure idea of political freedom." See his *"Die Ideen von 1914"* in *Deutscher Geist und Westeuropa*, p. 49, in Iggers, p. 16. Similarly, Leo Strauss criticizes historicism for having led to an unfortunate "doubt about the superiority of the purposes of the West." These purposes are defined in terms of classical liberalism. Quoted from Nathan Tarcov and Thomas Pangle, epilogue to Joseph Cropsey and Leo Strauss, eds., *History of Political Philosophy* (Chicago, 1987), p. 908; cf. Strauss, *Natural Right and History*, p. 33.

13. Antoni, *Lo storicismo*, p. 17.

14. Mansfield, pp. 44ff.

15. Hayman, p. 113. Erwin Rohde pointed out Nietzsche's debt to this school in *Afterphilologie*, pp. 26ff.

16. Gadamer (*Truth and Method*, p. 8) attributes *Weltanschauung*-historicism to the whole tradition of nineteenth-century hermeneutics: "Even Dilthey, on whom the scientific method and the empiricism of Mill's *Logic* had a much stronger effect, retained the romantic, idealist heritage in the concept of *Geist*."

Hayden White describes the "new historicism" of the 1980s as adopting a similarly reified notion of culture: "For the New Historicists, the historical context is the 'cultural system.' Social institutions and practices, including politics, are construed as functions of this system, rather than the reverse. Thus, New Historicism appears to be based on what might be called the 'culturalist fallacy,' which marks it as a brand of historical idealism." See his "New Historicism: A Comment," in Veeser, p. 294.

Charles Taylor suggests that reified notions of culture gained impetus from the "new theory of language that arises at the end of the 18th century, most notably in the work of Herder and Humboldt, [which] places the capacity to speak not simply in the individual but primarily in the speech community." See his "Overcoming Epistemology" in Baynes et al., p. 478.

17. *"Homer und die klassische Philologie,"* in Schlechta, III:164; III:165; III:167; III:174.

18. Nietzsche, "On the Future of Our Educational Institutions," Colli-Montinari, III:2, p. 214.

19. "Homer and Classical Philology" (Schlechta, III:174).

20. *Encyclopädie der klassischen Philologie* (an unpublished book-length MS by Nietzsche, presumably used in his teaching and written in 1871), in Colli-Montinari, *Nietzsche Werke,* II:3, p. 368.

21. In *Beyond Good and Evil* (V:199), Nietzsche lists examples of "herds of men" in which everyone follows a single command; these include "clans, communities, tribes, peoples, states, churches ....'"

22. Gadamer, *Truth and Method,* p. 271.

23. Hegel was not a relativist, at least in the usual sense. He believed that conceptual schemes were commensurable, in that one scheme could be *aufgehoben* by another. He writes: the "World-Spirit itself, has had the patience to pass through these shapes [of consciousness] over the long passage of time [and] embodied in each shape as much of its entire concept as that shape was capable of holding ...." But for the modern philosopher, all of the contingent perspectives of the past are available; their achievements have "been implicitly accomplished; the content is already actuality reduced to a possibility; its immediacy overcome, and the embodied shape reduced to abbreviated, simple determinations of thought." See *Phenomenology,* Preface, para. 29, trans. A. V. Miller (Oxford, 1977), p. 17.

24. Thus Charles Taylor writes: "The Nietzschean position too stands and falls with a certain construal of knowledge: that it is relative to various ulti-mately imposed 'regimes of truth,' to use Foucault's expression." See his "Overcoming Epistemology," p. 484.

25. "On Music and Words," translated by Maximilian A. Mügge in Nietzsche, *Early Greek Philosophy and Other Essays* (New York, 1964), p. 30.

26. Donald Davidson, "On the Very Idea of a Conceptual Scheme," p. 185.

27. *Beyond Good and Evil* (Kaufmann), I:20.

28. *Will to Power* (Kaufmann), 408: "What do philosophers lack? an histor-ical sense ...." Cf. ibid., 382, on Kant as "absolutely unhistorical." Kant is not the only philosopher whom Nietzsche attacks as unhistorical. "You ask me what are the idiosyncrasies of philosophers? ... For example, their lack of historical sense, their hatred of even the idea of becoming, their

Egyptianism. They think they are *honoring* something when they dehistoricize it, *sub species aeterni*—when they make a mummy of it." *Twilight of the Idols*, "'Reason' in Philosophy," 1 (Schlechta, II:957).

29. Hollis and Lukes, "Introduction" to their *Rationality and Relativism* (Oxford, 1982) p. 9. Cf. Habermas, TCA, p. 58: "If a statement is true, it merits universal assent, no matter in which language it is formulated." Habermas therefore describes a "worldview" or "form of life" as something more organic than a collection of statements.

30. Nietzsche, *Will to Power* 568 (1888), in Schlechta, III:769. The term "incommensurable" is used by Kuhn and Paul Feyerabend. See the latter's *Science in a Free Society* (London, 1978), pp. 65–70, 1970–71; and the former's "Reflections on My Critics," pp. 266ff. Cf. Nietzsche's use of the term *"inkongruent."* David Wong has usefully distinguished among incommensurability with respect to translation, evaluation and justification. Nietzsche believes in all three: this is a consistent position, but Wong shows that no form of incommensurabilty *entails* the others. See his "Three Kinds of Incommensurability," in Krausz, ed., pp. 140–158.

31. Barry Barnes and David Bloor, "Relativism, Rationalism, and the Sociology of Knowledge," in Hollis and Lukes, p. 24.

32. Peter Winch, *The Idea of a Social Science and its Relation to Philosophy* (London, 1958), p. 100.

33. Nietzsche, "On Truth and Lying" (Gilman et al.) p. 252.

34. Barry Barnes and David Bloor, "Relativism, Rationalism, and the Sociology of Knowledge," in Hollis and Lukes, p. 27.

35. Davidson, "On the Very Idea of a Conceptual Scheme," pp. 184. Davidson cites the following: B. L. Whorf, "The Punctual and Segmentative Aspects of Verbs in Hopi," in *Language, Thought and Reality*, ed. J. B. Carroll (Cambridge, Mass., 1956); T. S. Kuhn, *The Structure of Scientific Revolutions* (Chicago, 1962); and W. V. Quine, "Speaking of Objects," in *Ontological Relativity and Other Essays* (New York, 1969).

36. Newton-Smith, p. 114.

37. Hacking, p. 60.

38. Hollis, "The Social Destruction of Reality," in Hollis and Lukes, p. 75, citing D. P. F. Strawson, *Individuals* (London, 1959), p. 10.

39. Kluckhohn, *Culture and Behavior* (New York, 1962), p. 280, quoted in Clifford Geertz, "The Impact of the Concept of Culture on the Concept of Man," in *The Interpretation of Cultures* (New York, 1973), pp. 40–41.

40. Barnes and Bloor, "Relativism, Rationalism, and the Sociology of Knowledge," p. 35.

41. Davidson, pp. 197; 196. See also Davidson's "The Myth of the Subjective," in Krausz, pp. 159–172.

42. "We Philologists," 137, (Arrowsmith, p. 372).

43. Peter Winch, "Understanding a Primitive Society," in Bryan Wilson, ed., *Rationality* (Oxford, 1970), pp. 92–93.

44. Robin Horton, "African Traditional Thought" in Wilson, *Rationality*, p. 170.

45. Habermas, *TCA*, p. 65.

46. Section I:1 (Kaufmann).

47. Habermas, *TCA*, p. 55.

48. Habermas, "The Hermeneutic Claim to Universality," in Joseph Bleicher, ed., *Contemporary Hermeneutics* (London, 1980), p. 194.

49. Habermas, "Review of Gadamer's *Truth and Method*," in *Understanding and Social Inquiry* (Notre Dame, 1977), pp. 336, 336, 339, 342, 337, 341. Cf. Krausz, "Introduction," p. 1: "Cultural or historical diversity is logically compatible with either relativism or anti-relativism."

50. *Homer und die klassische Philologie* (Schlechta), III:165.

51. Consider, e.g., *Zarathustra*, "Of the Thousand and One Goals."

52. *Human, All-Too Human*, 23.

53. *Will to Power* (Kaufmann), 354. I have translated *Art* as "kind" instead of Kaufmann's "species."

54. "Use and Disadvantage," 1 (Arrowsmith, p. 90).

55. "Use and Disadvantage," 10 (Schlechta, I:284 ff.).

56. "Truth and Lying," (Gilman et al., p. 250).

57. "Use and Disadvantage," 1 (Arrowsmith, p. 90).

58. "Use and Disadvantage," 6 (Schlechta, I:247).

59. *Über die Zukunft unserer Bildungstalten, Vortrag* II (Schlechta, III:200–201). Nietzsche often attacks the parochialism and authoritarianism that he preaches here. Derrida points out that he never published these essays, and did not want to be associated with them in a straightforward way. (See Derrida, "Otobiographies: the Teaching of Nietzsche and the Politics of the Proper Name," in Avital Ronell, trans., *The Ear of the Other* (Lincoln, Nebraska, 1985, p. 22.) But Nietzsche's attitude towards the authority of arbitrary cultural norms was, and remained, carefully two-sided, as I will argue in Part II. At the end of "Use and Disadvantage," Nietzsche suggests that there are two "remedies" for modern historicism: the "supra-historical" attitude of those who believe in no cultural norms, and

the "unhistorical" attitude of those who remain committed to local norms because they have "forgotten" all alternatives. See Chapter VI for a discussion of Nietzsche's "esotericism," his advocacy of cultural subordination *for some*, and his teaching of nihilism to others.

60. "On Truth and Lying," (Gilman et al., p. 251).

61. *The Gay Science* (Kaufmann), V:354.

62. *Nachlaß*, in Colli-Montinari, 11:142, 25 (491), dated 1884.

63. *Birth of Tragedy* (Kaufmann), 23.

64. On the relation between Wittgenstein and Nietzsche, see Tracy B. Strong, *Friedrich Nietzsche and the Politics of Transfiguration*, expanded ed. (Berkeley, 1988), pp. 78–86 and passim. At p. 279, Strong notes: "What attracts Nietzsche [to the idea of games] is the fact that games and gaming are only made possible by necessities, yet, while playing, one does not experience the necessities as constraint. They are rather the conditions of freedom which make the game possible." The same is true, for Nietzsche, of the underlying premises and perspectives of a culture.

65. Wittgenstein, *Philosophical Investigations*, 50.

66. *On Certainty* (New York, 1969), 559.

67. *Philosphical Investigations*, 18.

68. Ibid., 23.

69. *Genealogy of Morals* (Kaufmann), II:12.

70. *Philosophical Investigations*, 67.

71. *Genealogy of Morals* (Kaufmann), III:13. Cf. *Wagner in Bayreuth*, 5 (Schlechta, I:387 ff.), where Nietzsche describes language as evolving to a point at which the burden of accumulated meanings makes communication impossible.

72. "Use and Disadvantage," 7 (Arrowsmith, p. 119).

73. We Philologists," IV:196 (Arrowsmith, p. 387).

74. *Philosophical Investigations*, 83.

75. Ibid., 82.

76. Ibid., 83.

77. Ibid, 68.

78. Ibid., 66.

79. Wittgenstein remarks (#206) that "The common behavior of mankind is a system of reference by which we interpret an unknown language." It seems to me unnecessary for Wittgenstein to imply that we *all* share certain

specific forms of behavior. All that we need is to be able to play language-games with each other. This seems to require either that we understand some aspects of our interlocutor's behavior, or that a third party is able to mediate between us. But it does not require that *all* humans act the same way in some respects. For I might share "x" behavior with a Frenchman, and "y" with a Hopi; but the Hopi might not understand "x," and the Frenchman might be perplexed by "y." The chain which connects us all does not have to be a universal substratum of commonalities; it can be like Wittgenstein's thread, whose strength lies in its separate fibers.

Chapter 4

1. I have borrowed the title of this chapter from Paul Feyerabend's *Farewell to Reason* (London, 1987), which duplicates some of the arguments that I ascribe to Nietzsche.

2. "Use and Disadvantage," 2 (Arrowsmith, p. 98).

3. See his letter to Carl von Gersdorff, 25 May, 1865; see also Hayman, p. 67; Gigante, p. 23. Calder (*Nietzsche-Studien*, XII, 214ff.) disagrees, but I think Gigante's reply to him is convincing.

4. *The Gay Science* (Kaufmann), V:357.

5. "Use and Disadvantage," 8, (Arrowsmith, p. 127).

6. "Use and Disadvantage," 8, (Arrowsmith, p. 126).

7. Wilamowitz, *History of Classical Scholarship*, p. 92.

8. Silk and Stern, p. 4.

9. Wilamowitz, *Recollections*, p. 120.

10. *History of Classical Scholarship*, p. 1. Cf. E. M. Butler, *The Tyranny of Greece over Germany: A Study of the Influence Exercised by Greek Art and Poetry Over the Great German Writers of the 18th, 19th, and 20th Centuries* (Boston, 1958). The idea that the two 'races' were actually related goes back to K. O. Müller (1797–1840), admired by Wagner, whose introduction of the issue of race into classical scholarship, according to Wilamowitz, "put [early Greek] history on a sound basis once and for all." See his *History of Classical Scholarship*, p. 107. Hugh Lloyd-Jones, in his introduction to this book, writes: "The new developments in ethnology and linguistics had not only helped to make Germans race-conscious, but had reminded them of their supposed racial connection with the Greeks" [ibid., p. xviii].

11. Winckelmann as quoted in Meinecke, p. 245.

12. "We Philologists," IV:156 (Arrowsmith, p. 378). Nevertheless, Nietzsche applauded the *effort* to recover the Greeks, which served as a means of self-overcoming for moderns.

On pessimism about recapturing Greek culture, see Silk and Stern, p. 10: "whereas the Renaissance aspiration to assimilate Rome was realizable, no analogous aspiration was possible for Germany vis-à-vis Greece. Germany could not assimilate Greece—perhaps because Greece was simply too great, certainly because Greece was too alien."

13. Nietzsche later accused himself of entertaining the hope that Greek culture might be resurrected, although "there was no ground for hope, [and] everything pointed all too plainly to an end!" "Attempt at a Self-Criticism" (Kaufmann), 6.

14. *Encylopädie der klassischen Philologie* (1871), in Colli-Montinari II:3, p. 371.

15. See Nietzsche, *"Rückblick auf meine zwei Leipziger Jahre"* in Schlechta, III:135.

16. letter to von Gersdorff, 7 April, 1866, in Schlechta, III:962.

17. See Nietzsche's *"Rückblick auf meine zwei Leipziger Jahre"* in Schlechta, pp. III:144, III:146ff.
Jonathan Barnes provides a modern philologist's appraisal of Nietzsche's scholarly work; see his "Nietzsche and Diogenes Laertius," *Nietzsche-Studien* XV (1986), pp. 16–40. Barnes remarks (p. 39) that Nietzsche's "Laertian studies are remarkable for their virtues .... the studies are brilliant." They were written, he says (p. 40) "by an industrious, erudite, disciplined, and brilliant young mind." And he adds (p. 40, n. 88): "in the history of Laertian studies two scholars stand out—Menagius and Nietzsche." On this basis, Barnes criticizes the often-quoted comment of Karl Rheinhard that "The history of philology has no place for Nietzsche: he did not make enough positive contributions." See Rheinhardt, *"Die klassiche Philologie und die Klassische"* (1941) in his *Vermächtnis der Antike* (Göttingen, 1966), p. 345. Hermann Diels calls Nietzsche's theory that Diogenes borrowed everything from Diocles "palpably false." See his *Doxographi Graeci* (Berlin, 1879). But Barnes finds Nietzsche's theory as plausible as Diels'. Campbell (p. 25) claims that Nietzsche used "a display of information, penetration, and balance remarkable for one so young. His grasp of the discipline seemed sure and firm."

18. Nietzsche, *"Über Demokrit"* (fragment), quoted in Hayman, p. 92.

19. Nietzsche, letter to Deussen, October, 1868, in Schlechta, III:994.

20. Ritschl, letter to Kiessling, cited in Hayman, p. 101.

21. Nietzsche, *"Aphorismen über Geschichte"* in Hayman, p. 86.

22. *The Gay Science* (Kaufmann), V:345. Emphasis on the word "truth" (*die Wahrheit* in the original) is added.

23. *Human, All-Too-Human*, I:2 (Schlechta, I:448).

24. *Nachlaß* from Naumann ed., *Nietzsche Werke* (Leipzig, 1901), vol. XIV, p. 5.

25. Letter to Hermann Mushsake, November 1866, in Colli-Montinari, *Nietzsche Briefwechsel*, I:2, p. 184.
On Nietzsche and Lange, see Halévy, pp. 57ff; Hayman, p. 82; Birus, "Nietzsche's Concept of Interpretation," p. 93; Crawford, pp. 67–94; Jörg Salaquanda, *"Nietzsche und Lange,"* in *Nietzsche-Studien* XII (1978); and George J. Stack, *Lange and Nietzsche* (Berlin and New York, 1983). For Lange on the conventional nature of "truth" see his *Geschichte des Materialismus* (Frankfurt, 1974), II:936 and Stack, p. 313.

26. Harries, review of Hans Blumenberg's *Genesis of the Copernican World*. In *Inquiry* XXIII, 1980, p. 266.

27. Gadamer, *Truth and Method*, p. 479.

28. *"Homer und die klassische Philologie"* (Schlechta III:159). Lange believed that science and materialism would have to be supplemented by art or myth, created deliberately from the "standpoint of the Ideal," if modern culture were to remain healthy. In his *Geschichte des Materialismus*, II:556, he praised David Strauss' New Faith and (II:968) Ueberweg's "new religious force," as efforts "to join together *Dichtung* and *Wissenschaft* in an aesthetically stimulating cosmic vision" [Stack, p. 312]. See also Lange, I:986 on the union of *Dichtung* and *Wissenschaft* [Stack, p. 304]. Cf. Nietzsche's note of 1869 calling for a combination of objective, scientific *Universitätsphilologie* with the frankly creative force of *klassische Bildung*: *Nachlaß*, in Koch and Schlechta, eds., *Historisch-kritische Gesamtausgabe* (Munich, 1940), V:271 (HKG). This recalls Strauss' call for a new Hellenism (Stack, pp. 79ff.).

29. This is a central theme of the *Untimely Meditations*. For example, in "We Philologists, III:39 (Arrowsmith, p. 335), Nietzsche compares the historicist Walter Scott to the naive artist Homer: "And between Homer and Sir Walter Scott—who takes the prize?" (Answer: Homer.)

30. Consider, for example, Nietzsche's use of a speech by Hans Sachs on p. 2 of *The Birth of Tragedy*. Silk and Stern argue (p. 27) that Nietzsche was converted to Wagnerian aesthetics by *Die Meistersinger*; that it was the only opera accurately described by Nietzsche's account of Wagnerianism; and (p. 52) that it was the only Wagner opera he ever saw. Cf. Frederick R. Love, *Young Nietzsche and the Wagnerian Experience* (Chapel Hill, 1963), p. 63.

31. Dieter Wuttke, *Nürnberg als Symbol deutcher Kultur und Geschichte* (Bamberg, 1987), pp. 12ff.

32. Wagner, *Die Meistersinger von Nürnberg*, ed. Eulenberg (Zurich, n.d.).

33. "We Philologists," V:107 (Arrowsmith, p. 367).

34. Wagner, *Art and Revolution*, in Albert Goldman and Evert Sprinchorn, eds., *Wagner on Music and Drama*, trans. H. Aston Ellis (New York, 1964), p. 65.

35. *The Gay Science* (Kaufmann), II:83. Wilamowitz dismisses early-modern philology as naive: see his *History of Classical Scholarship*, pp. 53, 70, 74.

36. Wagner, *German Art and German Policy* (1867) in Goldman and Sprinchorn, p. 427. See also Butler, *The Tyranny of Greece Over Germany.*

37. Wagner, *Judaism in Music* (1850) in Goldman and Sprinchorn, p. 56.

38. *Opera as Drama II* in ibid., pp. 112–113. Wagner praises Weber, but accuses him (p. 107) of Romantic "unnaturalness." Wagner's view of Jewish culture in many ways resembles that of Marx; both had learned from Feuerbach, and both generalized stereotypes about Jews to the whole culture of modernity: see Marx, *On the Jewish Question* (1843) in Robert C. Tucker, *The Marx-Engels Reader* (New York, 1978), p. 48 and passim.

39. *Judaism in Music*, p. 58.

40. Ibid., p. 59.

41. Nietzsche's comments in this period were sometimes anti-Semitic, but he used the term "Jewish" in a symbolic fashion: "Our 'Jews'—and you know how broadly that concept extends ...." (Letter to von Gersdorff, 11 March, 1870, in Colli-Montinari, *Nietzsche Briefwechsel*, II:i, p. 105).

42. *Beyond Good and Evil* (Kaufmann), 223.

43. "Richard Wagner in Bayreuth," 5 (Arrowsmith, p. 269).

44. "Use and Disadvantage of History," 1 (Arrowsmith, p. 92). In this passage, Nietzsche foreshadows his doctrine of Eternal Return (see Chapter VI). The weakness, he says, of modern nihilists is revealed by the fact that they would refuse to *repeat* their lives, which they have recognized to be meaningless.

45. Ibid. (Arrowsmith, p. 91).

46. *Will to Power* (Kaufmann), 1.

47. *Beyond Good and Evil* (Kaufmann), 207.

48. *Will To Power* (Kaufmann), 10.

49. *Genealogy of Morals* (Kaufmann), III:26.

50. *Beyond Good and Evil* (Kaufmann), VII:224.

51. "Use and Disadvantage," 5 (Arrowsmith, p. 111).

52. *Genealogy of Morals*, (Kaufmann), III:26.

53. "Use and Disadvantage," 1 (Arrowsmith, p. 91).

54. Ibid.

55. Letter of April 7, 1866 in Schlechta, III:962 (Halévy translation, pp. 51ff.). Cf. a similar passage in Goethe, *The Sorrows of Young Werther*, trans. B. Q. Morgan (New York, 1957), pp. 40–41 and passim.

56. Wagner, *Judaism in Music*, p. 58 (quoted from a description of Mendelssohn).

57. Wagner, *Art and Revolution*, p. 65.

58. "Wagner in Bayreuth," 1, 2 (Arrowsmith, pp. 254, 256).

59. *Will to Power* (Kaufmann), 70. Cf. "Use and Disadvantage," 5 (Arrowsmith, p. 111): "Only strong personalities can endure history; the weak are completely annihilated by it."

60. Wagner, *Art and Revolution*, p. 65.

61. *Genealogy of Morals* (Kaufmann), III:5. Cf. The following comment by Schopenhauer, who heavily influenced Wagner's *Zunkunftsmusik* (1860): "the composer reveals the innermost nature of the world, and expresses the deepest wisdom in a language that his reasoning faculty does not understand." *The World as Will and Representation*, translated by E. F. J. Payne (New York, 1969), I:260. See also Silk and Stern, pp. 55, for further discussion.

62. "On Music and Words," (Mügge), pp. 30–31.

63. Ibid., p. 31. In *Beyond Good and Evil* (204), Nietzsche describes Schopenhauer's lack of historicism: "with his unintelligent wrath against Hegel he [sc. Schopenhauer] has succeeded in wrenching the whole last generation out of the context of German culture—a culture that was, considering everything, an elevation and divinatory subtlety of the *historical sense*. But precisely at this point Schopenhauer was poor, unreceptive, and un-German to the point of genius."

64. See *"Die Philosophie im tragischen Zeitalter der Griechen,"* Schlechta, III:361ff.

65. "On Music and Words," pp. 31–32.

66. Ibid., p. 36.

67. Ibid., pp. 31–32.

68. "Wagner in Bayreuth," 10 (Arrowsmith, p. 299). Nietzsche wanted Wagner's art to serve the same purpose that humanistic education had served: to provide meaning for the culture. "His writings contain nothing canonical ... but the canon lies in his works." (ibid., p. 298).
S. Morris Engel's article, "An Early Nietzsche Fragment on Language," *Journal of the History of Ideas*, XXIV, no. 2 (1963), pp. 279–286, is devoted to Nietzsche's *"Über Musik und Wort."*

69. But now Nietzsche viewed philology "skeptically and pessimistically": see "We Philologists," III:60 (Arrowsmith, p. 339).

70. "David Strauss," 7 (Arrowsmith, p. 40).

71. *Will to Power*, (Kaufmann), 315. Nietzsche seems to have ignored the neo-pagan, Romantic side of Strauss, and especially his call for a revival of *"die freie, harmonische Menschlichkeit des Griechentums...."* See Strauss' essay *Julian*, as quoted in Lange, II:556 and Stack, p. 79. Strauss belonged to a school of late Romantics who believed in the value of the "deliberately created mythical ideal" [Stack, p. 312]. Nietzsche was highly sympathetic to this attitude, but seems to have read Strauss as a pure rationalist and an enemy of all myths.

72. "David Strauss," 7 (Arrowsmith, p. 40).

73. *Beyond Good and Evil* (Kaufmann), VI:208. "Virile" was by no means an unambiguously positive term in Nietzsche's lexicon. "Supposing truth is a woman—what then?" Nietzsche asks in the Preface to *Beyond Good and Evil*. The answer is that dogmatic, "virile," clumsy philosophers have failed to win her heart.

74. "David Strauss," 1 (Arrowsmith, p. 17). Cf. *Zarathustra*, "The Land of Culture."

75. "David Strauss," 1 (Arrowsmith, p. 17).

76. "Use and Disadvantage," 4 (Arrowsmith, p. 104); repeated in "We Philologists," III:66 (Arrowsmith, p. 341).

77. "David Strauss," 1 (Arrowsmith, p. 17).

78. *Beyond Good and Evil* (Kaufmann), 224.

79. *Genealogy of Morals* (Kaufmann), III:23. Cf. *Beyond Good and Evil*, 6. I have altered Kaufmann's translation by replacing "science" with *"Wissenschaft,"* since the German term includes humanistic scholarship.

80. *Will to Power*, (Kaufmann), 421.

81. *Genealogy of Morals* (Kaufmann), III:21.
Stephen Nimis provides a modern defense of Nietzsche's argument against scholarly methods. Nimis analyses the phenomenon of the "Wilamowitz foot-note" in modern philological writing. According to Nimis, Wilamowitz is cited in articles today solely in order to show philologists' masochistic devotion to authority. Even when Wilamowitz is attacked, this is done in the belief that one proves oneself as a scholar by refuting petty points made by great predecessors, preferably those who wrote enormous tomes in German. References to scholarship in "minor" languages serve a similar purpose. He concludes (p. 117), "the Wilamowitz footnote is an institutional function .... [It] is an inevitable concomitant of a discipline which continues to reproduce, without self-reflection and without any clearly defined goals, its own discourse." See his *"Fußnoten: Das Fundament der Wissenschaft,"* in *Arethusa* XVII, no. 2 (1984), pp. 105–134.

82. "We Philologists," III:18 (Arrowsmith, pp. 329–330).

83. "We Philologists," V:59 (Arrowsmith, pp. 358–359). Yet Nietzsche remained respectful of individual classicists. He called Ritschl "*vir incomparabilis Ritschlius*" and "a truly great man" in a letter to Mushake of July, 1867: quoted in Gigante, p. 33. Gigante claims (p. 23) that Nietzsche always felt for Pforta "a sentiment of loyalty and even of love." In 1869, certainly, Nietzsche was still praising Pforta to the skies: see his "*Autobiographisches aus den Jahren 1856 bis 1869*," in Schlechta III:153 and passim. Here he says that Pforta's faculty were very different from "narrow-minded, cold-blooded pedants, who know nothing of learning but its scholarly dust."

84. "Richard Wagner," 4 (Arrowsmith, p. 263).

85. "We Philologists," V:109 (Arrowsmith, pp. 367-8).

86. Ibid., III:31 (Arrowsmith, p. 333).

87. "Richard Wagner in Bayreuth," 4, (Arrowsmith, p. 263).

88. Notes on literary history, quoted by Campbell (p. 257).

89. *Beyond Good and Evil* (Kaufmann), VII:230.

90. letter of March 28, 1870, in Colli-Montinari, *Nietzsche Briefwechsel* II:1, p. 112.

91. Wilamowitz comments: "Apollonian and Dionysian are aesthetic abstractions like Schiller's naive and sentimental poetry, and the old gods merely supply sonorous names for a conceptual antithesis." *Erinnerungen* (Leipzig, 1928), pp. 128ff.

Cf. Nietzsche's letter to von Gersdorff of April 6, 1867 (Schlechta III:977): "most philologists lack any uplifting total view of antiquity [*erhebende Gesamtanshauung des Altertums*] ...."

92. See Nietzsche, "*Homer und die klassische Philologie*," in Schlechta III:157ff.

93. "We Philologists," IV:17 (Arrowsmith, p. 349); V:149 (p. 376). Cf. Silk and Stern, pp. 13–14; and Lloyd-Jones "Introduction," to Wilamowitz' *History of Classical Scholarship* p. xi.

94. Describing *The Birth of Tragedy* to a potential publisher, Nietzsche wrote, "As you will see, I am trying to explain Greek tragedy in a completely new way, in that I completely ignore all philological treatments of the question and, for the time being, I keep an eye only on the aesthetic problem." Letter in draft of April 20, 1871, in Colli-Montinari, *Nietzsche Briefwechsel*, II:1 p. 194.

95. Stack, p. 310, quoting Czolbe. See also Lange, II:552–560, and Nietzsche's notes from 1867–68 in HKG, 3:393. According to Crawford (p. 94, n. 58), Czolbe introduced a version of *amor fati*.

96. Stack, p. 313.

97. Stack, p. 302.

98. Stack, p. 304; cf. Lange, II:936ff and I:986. Lange was skeptical about science, but he thought that it would create a "necessarily occurring picture of an unknown state of things." I.e., it was unavoidable, but could be *supplemented* by art. See his *Geschichte* in the 1866 ed., p. 500, as quoted in Crawford, p. 79.

99. Stack, pp. 79ff.

100. Stack, p. 311; cf. Lange, II:968.

101. *Philosophy in the Tragic Age of the Greeks* (Schlechta, III:362).

102. *Nachlaß* in Naumann, ed., *Nachgelassene Werke* (Leipzig, 1901), X:119.

103. Cf. Helmut Rehder, "The Reluctant Disciple: Nietzsche and Schiller," in O'Flaherty et al., p. 160.

104. "We Philologists," V:156 (Arrowsmith, p. 378).

105. Ibid.

106. "We Philologists," III:76 (Arrowsmith, p. 344).

107. Ibid.

108. "We Philologists," V:11 (Arrowsmith, p. 348).

109. "Truth and Lying," (Gilman et al., p. 250).

110. Hollis and Lukes, p. 3. They claim that "Nietzsche's imagery is uncommon but his theme has become a commonplace. It is a Romantic version of the thought that reality is socially constructed."

111. *TCA*, p. 24.

112. Derrida, "Interpreting Signatures (Nietzsche\Heidegger): Two Questions" in Laurence A. Rickels, ed., *Looking After Nietzsche* (Albany, 1990), p. 16.

113. This was the book that Nietzsche considered the beginning of his mature phase: see *Ecce Homo*, "*Human All-Too-Human*," 1.

114. *Twilight of the Idols*, "'Reason' in Philosophy," 5 (Schlechta II:960).

115. Ibid.

116. Derrida, "Structure, Sign, and Play in the Discourse of the Human Sciences," in *Writing and Difference*, trans. Allan Bass (Chicago, 1978), pp. 280ff.

117. Derrida, "Otobiographies," p. 15.

118. Nehamas, *Nietzsche*, p. 37.

119. *Beyond Good and Evil*, VII:231 (discussed by Derrida, in *Éperons: Les styles de Nietzsche*).

120. Nehamas, *Nietzsche*, p. 73. For a critique of Nehamas' reading, see Tracy B. Strong, "Comment" in *Nietzsche-Studien*, XII (1983), p. 493. However, for Strong's general agreement with the thesis that Nietzsche uses multiple personas to avoid making truth-claims, see his *Nietzsche*, p. 308.

121. *Ecce Homo*, "Why I Write Such Excellent Books" (Kaufmann), 4.

122. *Will to Power*, (Kaufmann) 25.

123. *Zarathustra*, "Of the Spirit of Gravity," 2 (Schlechta, II:443).

124. Ibid., "Of the Poets," 1 (Schlechta, II:382).

125. Ibid., "The Last Supper," (Schlechta, II:521).

126. *Ecce Homo*, Preface, 4.

127. *"Über Demokrit,"* in Hayman, p. 93.

128. Habermas, *TCA*, p. 24.

129. Ibid., citing B. R. Burleson, "On the Foundations of Rationality," in *Journal of the American Forensic Association*, XVI (1979), p. 113. Habermas argues that "anyone acting communicatively must, in performing any speech action, raise universal validity claims and suppose that they can be redeemed." See "What is Universal Pragmatics?" in *Communication and the Evolution of Society*, trans. Thomas McCarthy (London, 1976), p. 5.

130. Nietzsche, letter to Carl Fuchs of August 26, 1888, in Schlechta, III:1312.
Expressions of skepticism about the one true interpretation are a humanist platitude, as Birus (p. 96) points out. He cites Grotius' aphorism, *"Alia legimus in his pueri, alia viri,"* which was used by Goethe in a poem and thereby became famous. Goethe has: *"Anders lesen Knanben den Torenz\ Anders Grotius."* See also Friedrich Schlegel (*Kritische ausgabe*, Ernst Behler, ed., Munich, 1958, II, p. 189): "Everyone has found in the ancients what he needed, or wished: preferably himself." Quoted in Adrian del Caro, *Nietzsche Contra Nietzsche* (Baton Rouge, 1989), pp. 121–122.

131. Habermas, "Philosophy as Stand-In and Interpreter," in *After Philosophy: End or Transformation?* (Cambridge, 1987), p. 310.

132. *TCA*, p. 18, quoting Toulmin, Rieke, and Janik, *An Introduction to Reasoning* (New York, 1979), p. 13.

133. Wilamowitz, *Zukunfstphilologie!*, p. 6.

134. Walter Kaufmann, in *Nietzsche: Philosopher, Psychologist, Antichrist* (Princeton, 1968), p. 86, claims that Nietzsche "had in mind the 'gay science'

of fearless experiment and the good will to accept new evidence and to abandon previous positions, if necessary." Thus Kaufmann makes Nietzsche
sound like a Habermasian rationalist. But Kaufmann fails to support this
position. When he stumbles across Nietzschean comments against truth and
rationality, he declares them self-defeating and announces (p. 204):
"Nietzsche was not at his best with problems of this kind." Against
Kaufmann's domesticated reading of Nietzsche, consider *Ecce Homo*,
Preface (Kaufmann), 3—"error is cowardice."

Chapter 5

1. letter of July 7, 1872, in Colli-Montinari, *Nietzsche Briefwechsel* (Berlin
and New York, 1978), II:iii, p. 19.

2. *Thus Spake Zarathustra* (Schlechta), II:380.

3. *Birth of Tragedy* (Kaufmann), 4.

4. Ibid., 4.

5. Ibid., 3.

6. Ibid.

7. Ibid., 4.

8. Ibid., 3.

9. Friedrich von Schiller, "Naive and Sentimental Poetry," trans. by Julius
A. Elias (New York, 1966).

10. *Birth of Tragedy* (Kaufmann), 22. I have kept Kaufmann's "Apollinian"
in the citations which follow, but "Apollonian" is more commonly used and
seems more reasonable in English.

11. Ibid., 23.

12. *Beyond Good and Evil* (Kaufmann), IX:260.

13. *Birth of Tragedy* (Kaufmann), 1.

14. Ibid.

15. "Why I am a Destiny," 9.

16. See, e.g., *Gay Science* (Kaufmann), V:358: Luther "surrendered the
holy books to everybody—until they finally got into the hands of the philologists, who are the destroyers of every faith that rests on books."

17. In 1888, Nietzsche signed letters at times as Dionysus, and at times as
The Crucified. Nietzsche's deteriorating mental condition could be invoked
to explain this vacillation; but his ambivalence about history had deep roots.
In *The Birth of Tragedy*, Dionysus is contrasted to Apollo; in Nietzsche's
later writings, to The Crucified. What remains constant is the antithesis

between extra-historical forces and the contingencies of history and culture, the latter represented first by Apollo as the symbol of civilization, and then by The Crucified as the symbol of humanity subsumed by history.

Derrida recognizes Nietzsche's role as the "versus." He was "... Nietzsche, Ecce Homo, Christ but not Christ, nor even Dionysus, but rather the name of the versus, the adverse or countername, the combat called between two names ...." "Otobiographies," p. 11.

18. *The Antichrist*, 32 (Schlechta II:1194).

19. Ibid.

20. *Beyond Good and Evil* (Kaufmann), 164.

21. *Will to Power* (Kaufmann), 158.

22. *Antichrist*, 33 (Schlechta, II:1195).

23. *Will to Power* (Kaufmann), 481.

24. See Gilles Deleuze, *Nietzsche and Philosophy*, trans. Hugh Tomlinson (London, 1983), pp. 14, 18; Thomas J. J. Altizer, "Eternal Recurrence and Kingdom of God," in Allison, ed., *The New Nietzsche*, pp. 232ff; and Paul Valadier, "Dionysus Versus the Crucified," in ibid., pp. 247ff.

25. *Birth of Tragedy* (Kaufmann), 2.

26. Ibid.

27. Nietzsche may be thinking of the rigid, formal spirit revealed in archaic kouroi. Nietzsche's view is that this rigidity sprang from a deliberate effort to ward off Dionysian nature. But a more common modern view holds, conversely, that formalism and severity in art are "natural," whereas it took a "miracle" of Greek genius during the fifth century to produce a more free and expressive style. See Ernst Gombrich, *Art and Illusion*, p. 116 and passim.

28. *Birth of Tragedy* (Kaufmann), 5.

29. Ibid., 4. This is thoroughly Schopenhauerian.

30. Lange, II:998 in Stack, p. 49.

31. *Birth of Tragedy* (Kaufmann), 5.

32. *Beyond Good and Evil* (Kaufmann), VII:230.

33. *Philosophy in the Tragic Age of the Greeks* (Schlechta, III:362).

34. Compare my diagram to that presented by Marcus Hester: "The Structure of Tragedy and the Art of Painting," in O'Flaherty, et al., p. 74. See also Crawford, pp. 161ff., on the *Ur-Eine* and its ability to project *Anschauungen* such as "Homer," "nature," etc.

35. *Birth of Tragedy* (Kaufmann), 6.

36. Ibid., 8.

37. Ibid.

38. Ibid.

39. Ibid., 10.

40. Ibid.

41. Ibid., 8.

42. Ibid., 10.

43. Ibid., 8.

44. Perhaps the following description of the lyric genius (ibid., 5) also describes Nietzsche: he "lives in ... images, and only in them, with joyous satisfaction. He never grows tired of contemplating even their minutest traits."

45. Ibid., 11.

46. Ibid.

47. Ibid.

48. Ibid.

49. Ibid., 12.

50. Ibid., 13.

51. Fragment intended for the section on Socrates in Nietzsche's "Philosophy in the Tragic Age of the Greeks" (cited in Strong, *Nietzsche*, p. 175). Cf. similar comments quoted in Chapter I.

52. *Will to Power* (Kaufmann), 430.

53. *Birth of Tragedy* (Kaufmann), 13.

54. Ibid., 15.

55. Ibid.

56. Ibid., 14.

57. Ibid., 15.

58. Ibid.

59. Ibid., 13. For evidence of Nietzsche's admiration for Socrates, see James C. O'Flaherty, "Socrates in Hamann's Socratic *Memorabilia* and Nietzsche's *Birth of Tragedy*," in O'Flaherty, et al., pp. 134ff.

60. "Attempt at a Self-Criticism," (Kaufmann), 1.

61. *Birth of Tragedy* (Kaufmann), 14.

62. *Human, All-Too-Human*, 94 (Schlechta, I772).

63. *Birth of Tragedy* (Kaufmann), 14.

64. Wagner, *Art and Revolution*, p. 65; *Judaism in Music*, p. 58.

65. *Birth of Tragedy* (Kaufmann), 15: trans. slightly modified.

66. "Use and Disadvantage," 3 (Arrowsmith, p. 102). This critical attitude was, however, inadequate on its own; it had to be supplemented by anti-quarian and monumental approaches.

67. "Attempt at a Self-Criticism" (Kaufmann), 7.

68. *Gay Science* (Kaufmann), V:380.

69. "Attempt at a Self-Criticism" (Kaufmann), 6.

70. Ibid.

71. *Zukunftsphilologie!*, p. 32.
For general literature on the Wilamowitz-Nietzsche quarrel, see William M. Calder III, "The Wilamowitz-Nietzsche Struggle: New Documents and a Reappraisal," *Nietzsche-Studien* XII (1983), pp. 214–254; J.H. Groth, "Wilamowitz-Möllendorf [sic] on Nietzsche's *Birth of Tragedy*," *Journal of the History of Ideas* XI (1950), pp. 179–190; Silk and Stern, *Nietzsche on Tragedy*. Most of the relevant documents are collected in Karlfried Gründer, ed., *Der Streit um Nietzsches "Geburt der Tragödie": Die Schriften von E. Rohde, R. Wagner, U. V. Wilamowitz-Möllendorff* (Hildesheim, 1969). Nietzsche felt universally attacked by his colleagues, but Mansfield remarks (p. 57): "condemnation of Nietzsche in academic circles seems to have been neither wholesale nor universal."

72. Cornford, *From Religion to Philosophy* (1912), quoted in Kaufmann's introduction to *The Birth of Tragedy*, p. 8.

73. For judgments about the relative accuracy of Nietzsche and Wilamowitz, see Lloyd-Jones, "Nietzsche and the Study of the Ancient World"; and Gigante, p. 21.

74. "We Philologists," III:62 (Arrowsmith, p. 340).

75. *Zunkunftsphilologie!*, pp. 7–8.

76. Ibid.

77. Ibid., p. 32.

78. *Recollections*, p. 152.
Erwin Rohde attempted to defend Nietzsche partly by showing that his friend belonged to a tradition of philology as established and respected as that of Lachmann and Hermann: Nietzsche's predecessors, according to Rohde, were F. G. Welcker, August Boeckh, and K. O. Müller: see his *Afterphilologie*, pp. 26, 29, 30 n.1; 31 n.1. But Wilamowitz (*Zukunftsphilologie!*, p. 19) compares Nietzsche to Saint-Croix Creuzer (1771–1858), a Romantic "historian" of myth.

Nietzsche's letter to Rohde of 27 May 1872 reveals that he had been visited by Wilamowitz in Naumberg in October 1871; the two men appear to have been friends until the appearance of the *Birth of Tragedy*, whose *Ton und Tendenz* Wilamowitz found reprehensible.

79. *Zukunftsphilologie!*, p. 12.

80. Ibid., p. 13. Hugh Lloyd-Jones, in "Nietzsche and the Study of the Ancient World," pp. 7–8, describes the pamphlets which flew back and forth between Nietzsche and Wilamowitz and their partisans as "distressing reading; the over-excited tone and utter lack of humour of all parties to the dispute— it is significant that the most moderate of them was Richard Wagner—is the kind of thing that makes foreigners despair of the whole German nation."

81. See *Zukunftsphilologie!, zweites Stück* (1873), p. 24; *Recollections*, p. 152; Gigante, p. 25; and J. H. Groth, "Wilamowitz-Moellendorff on Nietzsche's *Birth of Tragedy*," *Journal of the History of Ideas*, VI, no. 2 (1950), pp. 187-8.

82. *De Laertii Diogenes fontibus* and *Analecta Laertiana*, reprinted in Colli-Montinari, *Nietzsche-Werke* II, pp. 75–167 and 171–190.

83. See, e.g., his article *"Zur Geschichte der Theognideischen Spruchsammlung,"* *Rhein. Museum*, NF xxii (1867), pp. 161–200, in Colli-Montinari, II:1, pp. 1–74.

84. Since Nietzsche does not specifically discuss Diogenes 1.4.ii in his dissertation, we must conclude that he thought this passage was derived from Diocles: for (p. 131) *"Ut igitur brevissime loquar: Laertius est Diocles epitome."* However, since Nietzsche was unsure of Diocles' dates and sources, this insight told him little about the reliability of the rumor about Socrates and Euripides. Nietzsche may have had something more specific in mind, but if so, he played his cards very close to his chest.

85. "We Philologists," V:19 (Arrowsmith, p. 349).

86. "We Philologists," IV:149 (Arrowsmith, p. 376).

87. Wilamowitz, *Platon*, vol. I, quoted in Strong, *Nietzsche*, p. 294.
For Wilamowitz' account of the emergence of historicism in the eighteenth century, see his *History of Classical Scholarship*, p. 92–100. He credits this development to the "new spirit" of the German people. He expresses his belief in *Weltanschauungen* in ibid., p. 100: "Insofar as the Romantic movement entailed a shift of emphasis from the individual to the people, from conscious creation to the impersonal march of evolution, from the highest achievements of culture to its humble beginnings, Vico was its precursor thanks to whom religion and myth came to be understood properly for the first time." See also his *Recollections*, p. 117, and *Platon* vol. II (Berlin, 1920), p. 20, for the view that intellectuals are products of their age. On historicism in the latter work, see E. N. Tigerstedt, *Interpreting Plato*, (Uppsala, 1977), p. 42. Harold Cherniss ("The Biographical Fashion in

Literary Criticism," in *Selected Papers*, ed. Leonard Tarán (Leiden, 1977) p. 282) provides examples of historicism from Wilamowitz' writings. For example, see his *Aristophanes: Lysistrate* (Berlin, 1927), p. 5: "One first becomes aware [of Aristophanes' meaning] when with a historically trained eye one sees how this mad sport [Old Comedy] affected on a single day the thousands who were its audience, a whole people that still constituted a single society .... One must also know the conventions of this people, its deportment, its thought and belief in work and leisure, in sorrow and joy .... " In Wilamowitz' *Sappho und Simonides* (Berlin, 1913), p. 3, he claims a "true historical sense," of which "Lessing and Gibbon had scarcely a notion, for they thought that man in all ages is essentially the same" (Cherniss, p. 291).

88. To name just a few "Whig" histories of scholarship, see Sandys' *History of Classical Scholarship*; Moriz Haupt's *Opuscula* on the history of classical philology (Leipzig, 1876); Franz von Wegele's *Geschichte der deutschen Historiographie seit dem Auftreten des Humanismus* (Munich, 1885); Dilthey's "*Weltanschauung und Analyse des Menschen seit Renaissance und Reformation*," in *Gesammelte Werke* (Leipzig, 1923), vol. II; and Edward Füter's *History of Modern Historiography*, available in a French translation by Emile Jeanmaire (Paris, 1914).

Chapter 6

1. Johan Huizinga, "Historical Ideals of Life" (1915), in *Men and Ideas: History, the Middle Ages, and the Renaissance*, trans. James S. Holmes and Hans van Marle (Princeton, 1959), p. 91. On historicism and the quarrel between the ancients and moderns, see, e.g., Gadamer, *Truth and Method*, p. 482.

2. "We Philologists," V:59 (Arrowsmith, pp. 358ff.).

3. Jonathan Swift, *The Battle of the Books* (London, 1908; 1st ed., 1704), pp. 25–26; 27. Swift (pp. 37ff.) calls Bentley "the most deformed of all the Moderns, tall, but without shape or comeliness, large, but without strength or proportion. His armour was patched up of a thousand incoherent pieces, and the sound of it, as he marched, was loud and dry ...."

4. See Max Oehler, ed., *Nietzsches Bibliothek* (Weimar, 1942). Swift is cited by Nietzsche at (e.g.) *Human, All-Too-Human*, 44 and 54. The first is actually a quotation by Pope, misattributed by Nietzsche to Swift.

5. *The Gay Science* (Kaufmann), II:83.

6. *Wanderer and His Shadow*, 216 (Schlechta, I:964).

7. Heller, p. 54.

8. See *Ecce Homo*, "Why I Write Such Excellent Books," 4, for Nietzsche's self-description as an imitator of Sallust's "austerity and terseness." In *Ecce Homo*, "The Case of Wagner," Nietzsche attacks German modernity and praises the Renaissance. See also *Will to Power* (Kaufmann), 94, entitled

"Comparison of Greek culture and that of the French in the age of Louis XIV."

9. On Suidas and Zarathustra, see Karl H. Dannenfeldt, "The Pseudo-Zoroastrian Oracles in the Renaissance," *Studies in the Renaissance* IV (1957), p. 7.

10. Diogenes Laertius I.2.8ff. (citing Aristotle, Hermadorus Platonics, and Xanthus as sources).

11. See Frances Yates, *Giordano Bruno and the Hermetic Tradition* (Chicago, 1964), pp. 15, 416, and passim.

12. Dannenfeldt, p. 14.

13. Charles Schmitt, "Perennial Philosophy from Agostino Steuco to Leibniz," *Journal of the History of Ideas* XXVII:4 (1966), p. 510. The Chaldaic Oracles are translated in Dannenfeldt, pp. 27ff. Dannenfeldt notes (pp. 28ff.) that they were reprinted more than 75 times in Europe between 1538 and 1743.

14. Werner Jaeger, *Aristotle* (Oxford, 1934), pp. 133–134. Cf. *Alcibiades* I 122A, attributed to Plato.

15. Schmitt, p. 509.

16. D. P. Walker, *The Ancient Theology: Studies in Christian Platonism from the Fifteenth to the Eighteenth Century* (Ithaca, 1972), p. 263; p. 144, quoting Robert Parsons, *The First Boke of the Christian Exercise* (London, 1582). p. 96.

17. Letter of Bouvet to Leibniz, dated Beijing, 4 November 1701, discussed by Walker (p. 224). See also Vleeschauwer, p. 40 and passim.

18. Walker, p. 263. Cf. J. E. McGuire and P. M. Rattansi, "Newton and the Pipes of Pan," in *Notes and Records of the Royal Society of London* XXI (1967), pp. 108–143.

19. Walker, p. 49, quoting Pietro Critino, *De honesta disciplina libri xxv* (Basel, 1532), pp. 80ff.

20. *Philosophy in the Tragic Age of the Greeks* (Schlechta, III:356).

21. On the "real" Zoroaster (ca. 660–583 B.C.), see, e.g., *The New Larousse Encyclopedia of Mythology* (London, 1969), p. 312. On the *Zend-Avesta*, see Dannenfeldt, p. 7. Carl G. Jung believes that Nietzsche knew the *Zend-Avesta*: see his *Nietzsche's Zarathustra* (Princeton, 1988), I, pp. 4-9. Elizabeth Förster-Nietzsche provides an outline by Nietzsche of *Also sprach Zarathustra*, written in 1881, which shows that its structure was to follow the *Zend-Avesta*. See her "Introduction" to *Also sprach Zarathustra in Die Unschuld des Werdens*, ed. by A. Baümler (Stuttgart, 1956), VII:xviii. Zoroaster, like Nietzsche's Zarathustra, had pets, lived for many years in a solitary cave on top of a mountain, was tempted by false prophets, and

laughed and rejoiced constantly. On the other hand, he was also a dogmatic theologian who waged a holy war. For studies of the psuedo-Zoroaster's works in Nietzsche's time, see papers by W. Kroll and A. Jahn, both cited in Dannenfeldt, pp. 8ff. Werner Dannhauser remarks that "Nietzsche's Zarathustra shows only the most superficial resemblance to the historical Zarathustra, and Nietzsche seems to have had only the most superficial knowledge of either Zarathustra or Zoroastrianism." This is unsubstantiated and seems to me untrue, but see his *Nietzsche's View of Socrates* (Ithaca, 1974), p. 242.

22. It might seem that Mozart, a Mason, was absolutely serious about using Zarathustra as his mouthpiece; after all, Zarathustra was still considered a prophet by many in Mozart's day. But Mozart casts Sarastro as a bass, and bass rôles were always *buffo* in rococo Italian opera. On the other hand, Sarastro says many things that Mozart actually believed, and he sings them in E-Flat major, the Masonic key. On Mozart's desire that his opera be taken both seriously and ironically, see his letter to Constanze, October 8–9, 1791, in Emily Anderson, ed., *The Letters of Mozart and His Family* (London, 1938).

23. *Ecce Homo*, "Why I am a Destiny" (Kaufmann), 3.

24. *Zarathustra*, "Of the Thousand and One Goals" (Schlechta, II:322). See Thomas J. J. Altizer, "Eternal Recurrence and Kingdom of God," in Allison, ed., *The New Nietzsche*, p. 232.

25. See Auerbach, pp. 443ff.

26. *Ecce Homo*, "Thus Spake Zarathustra" (Kaufmann), 1.

27. *Genealogy of Morals* (Kaufmann), I:13 (cf. Will to Power, 531, 548- 9).

28. *Ecce Homo*, "Thus Spake Zarathustra" (Kaufmann), 1.

29. *Will to Power* (Kaufmann), 417.

30. *Zarathustra*, "Redemption," (Schlechta, II:394).

31. *Will to Power* (Kaufmann), 1062.

32. *Zarathustra*, "Redemption," (Schlechta, II:394).

33. Ibid.

34. Ibid., II:395.

35. Much of this paragraph is derived from Nehamas, *Nietzsche*, Chapter V.

36. *Will to Power* (Kaufmann), 617.

37. Ibid., 462.

38. Ibid., 55.

39. Ibid., 522.

40. Ibid., 1063.

41. *Beyond Good and Evil* (Kaufmann), I:14.

42. *Nachlaß*, from C. G. Naumann, *Nietzsche's Werke* (Leipzig, 1898), XII, p. 118, cited and translated in Strong, *Nietzsche*, p. 265.

43. See *Schopenhauer as Educator*, I (Arrowsmith, p. 163): "Basically every man knows quite well that he is on earth only once, a unicum, and that no accident, however unusual, could ever again combine this wonderful diversity into the unity he is." Nietzsche writes that a belief in eternal return will not be possible unless "astronomers become astrologers once more": "Use and Disadvantage," 2 (Arrowsmith, p. 97.).
Nehamas, *Nietzsche*, p. 145, writes: "the eternal return is 'scientific' in that it is strictly nonteleological ...." This reading seems to me, at best, insufficient. Arthur Danto, *Nietzsche as Philosopher* (pp. 200–213), takes Nietzsche at his word, and tries to come up with the best scientific arguments he can for the Eternal Return; but he finds these ultimately unsatisfactory. See also: Stambaugh, pp. 45–51 (the Eternal Return as "A Fact Belonging to Physics").

44. *Ecce Homo*, "Birth of Tragedy," 3 (Kaufmann): "The doctrine of the 'eternal recurrence,' that is, of the unconditioned and infinitely repeated circular course of all things—this doctrine of Zarathustra *might* in the end have been taught already by Heraclitus." See also his "Lectures on the Pre-Platonic Philosophers," as described in Kaufmann, *Nietzsche*, p. 279.

45. *Ecce Homo*, "Zarathustra," 1 (Kaufmann).

46. Nietzsche, *Nachgelassene Werke*, C. G. Naumann, ed. (Leipzig, 1904), xii:371.

47. *Ecce Homo*, Preface, 4 (Kaufmann).

48. Zarathustra, "The Convalescent," 2 (Schlechta, II:463).

49. Eliade, p. 120, citing Joseph Bidez, *Éos, ou Platon et l'Orient* (Brussels, 1945). Cf. D. O'Brien, *Empedocles' Cosmic Circle* (Cambridge, 1969); and Jonathan Barnes, *The Presocratic Philosophers* (London, 1979), vol. 2, pp. 200–205.

50. Eliade, p. ix.

51. Ibid., p. 153.

52. Cf. Gary Shapiro, "Nietzsche's Graffito: A Reading of the *Antichrist*," in *Boundary* II, pp. 9–10 (1981), p. 136: "The eternal return is an anti-narrative because it knows no isolated agents in the sequence of events; ... it knows no beginning, middle, or end of the narrative but simply the continuous circle of becoming; and it tends to dissolve the mainstay of all narrative, the individual agent into the ring of becoming."

53. "Use and Disadvantage," 1.

54. *Genealogy of Morals* (Kaufmann), III:26.

55. Karl Löwith reads the Eternal Return as strictly Romantic: see *Nietzsches Philosophie der ewigen Wiederkunft des Gleichens* (Berlin, 1935), Chapter IV. Kaufmann, *Nietzsche*, p. 283, provides a brief history of previous Romantic attempts to exchange the modern view of history for an ancient, cyclical one. He cites Lovejoy, *Essays in the History of Ideas* (Baltimore, 1948), on Friedrich Schlegel, who contrasted the classical *System des Kreislaufes*—in which history is a "movement which returns upon itself in repeated cycles"—to the modern theory of infinite progress: the *"System der unendlichen Fortschreitung."* Similar views were held by A. W. Schlegel and Novalis.

56. *Zarathustra*, "The Convalescent," 2 (Schlechta, II:466).

57. Nehamas, *Nietzsche*, p. 147.

58. E.g., *The Gay Science*, 341; *Beyond Good and Evil*, 56.

59. *Will to Power* (Kaufmann), 1057.

60. Zarathustra chooses not to inform a solitary hermit of the death of God, because being solitary, the hermit is not caught up in the historical process of nihilism, and will never find out that God is dead. Zarathustra would rather leave him in peace (see "Zarathustra's Prologue," 2).
Nietzsche told Peter Gast that until he published his actual, explicit "philosophy," *Zarathustra* would "have only a completely personal meaning, as my 'Book of Edification and Consolation'—remaining dark and hidden and ridiculous for Everyman." (Letter of Sept. 2, 1884 in Schlechta III:1222).

61. *Will to Power* (Kaufmann), 595.

62. Ibid., 596.

63. Ibid., 602; used in several places.

64. *Ecce Homo.*, "Why I Write Such Good Books," 5 (Kaufmann).

65. Ibid., 3, quoting *Zarathustra*, "On the Vision and the Riddle," 1.

66. Letter of December, 1888, in Strong, *Nietzsche*, p. 111. This letter does not appear in the Colli-Montinari *Briefwechsel*, and Strong notes that it was never sent.

67. *Beyond Good and Evil*, VII:228

68. "Preface" to *The Dawn*, 5 (Schlechta, I:1016).

69. *Der Wanderer und sein Schatten*, 71 (Schlechta, 909). Cf. *The Gay Science*, V:381 (Kaufmann): "It is not by any means necessarily on objection to a book when anyone finds it impossible to understand: perhaps that was part of the author's intention—he did not want to be understood by just 'anybody.' All the nobler spirits and tastes select their audience when they

wish to communicate; and choosing that, one at the same time erects barriers against 'the others.'"

In *The Birth of Tragedy*, Nietzsche suggests that Socrates was aware of the groundlessness of reason, although he preached a supremely rational exoteric doctrine. Perhaps this explains Nietzsche's comment at ibid., V:340: "I admire the courage and wisdom of Socrates in everything he did, said— and did not say."

70. *Will to Power* (Kaufmann), 132.

71. *Nachlass* in the Colli-Montinari ed., VIII, 1, 5(9).

72. In a lecture, Robert Rethy pointed out this note and described its relation to *Beyond Good and Evil*. See also Stanley Rosen, "Nietzsche's Revolution" in *The Ancients and the Moderns* (New Haven, 1989), p. 223.

73. *Beyond Good and Evil* (Kaufmann), II:36.

74. Ibid., II:27. The translations from Sanskrit are provided by Kaufmann, but were not included in Nietzsche's edition.

75. Ibid., II:30

Chapter 7

1. Rosen, *The Ancients and the Moderns*, p. 225.

2. *Will to Power* (Kaufmann), 171, cf. *Antichrist*, 53.

3. See Birus, p. 96.

4. Preface, 1 (Kaufmann).

5. I am thinking of Deleuze, DeMan, Derrida, Blondel et al., all cited below except Paul DeMan, whose *Blindness and Insight* (New York, 1971), pp. 138–165 and *Allegories of Reading* (New Haven, 1979) both draw heavily on Derrida. For a fuller account of Derrida, see Chapter VIII.

6. *Ecce Homo*, "Why I Write Such Good Books," 1 (Kaufmann). But Nietzsche says that often he is read as the *opposite* of his real nature (e.g., as an "idealist")—and this seems to imply that there can be true and false interpretations of his texts.

7. Robert Pippin, "Irony and Affirmation in Nietzsche's *Thus Spake Zarathustra*," in Gillespie and Strong, eds., *Nietzsche's New Seas*, p. 56.

8. *Genealogy of Morals* (Kaufmann), I:13. Nietzsche refuses to distinguish between an event and an intention: see *Will to Power*, 550. For his view that "the 'subject' is not something that creates effects, but only a fiction," see ibid., 552.

9. Derrida, *Éperons*, p. 106.

10. Derrida, "Interpreting Signatures (Nietzsche\Heidegger): Two Questions" in Laurence A. Rickels, ed., *Looking After Nietzsche* (Albany, 1990), p. 12. See also Derrida's *Of Grammatology*, p. 99: "The names of authors or of doctrines have here no substantial value. They indicate neither identities nor causes. It would be frivolous to think that 'Descartes,' 'Leibniz,' 'Rousseau,' 'Hegel,' etc., are names of authors, of the authors of movements or displacements that we thus designate" (translated by Gayatri Chakravorty Spivak [Baltimore: Johns Hopkins University Press, 1974], and printed by permission).

11. Derrida, "Otobiographies," p. 14.

12. Ibid., p. 4.

13. Ibid., pp. 3–4.

14. *Zarathustra*, "Of the Bestowing Virtue," 2 (Schlechta II:339).

15. Derrida, *Éperons*, p. 136.

16. Ibid., p. 94.

17. Ibid., p. 104.

18. *Human, All-Too-Human*, 377 (Faber).

19. Beyond Good and Evil (Kaufmann), VII:232. Derrida thinks that Nietzsche was praising women when he described them as not believing in truth but enjoying the act of dissembling. "*Mais en tant qu'elle* [sc. "*la Femme*"] *ne croit pas, elle, à la vérité, trouvant néanmoins son intérêt à cette vérité qui ne l'intéresse pas, elle est encore le modèle: cette fois le bon modèle:... elle joue la dissimulation, la parure, le mensonge, l'art, la philosophie artiste, elle est une puissance d'affirmation*" (from *Éperons*, p. 66). On this definition, Nietzsche is a "woman," because this is precisely what he does. Derrida (p. 84) quotes *Twilight of the Idols* ("Maxims and Arrows," #27): "Women are considered deep—why? because one can never discover any bottom to them. Women are not even shallow." But these are words of praise, coming from Nietzsche, who does not believe in the difference between profound meaning and surface appearance. "We no longer believe that truth remains truth when the veils are withdrawn; we have lived too much to believe this." *Gay Science*, Preface (Kaufmann), 4.

20. *Beyond Good and Evil* (Kaufmann), II:40.

21. *Human, All-Too-Human* (Faber), 405.

22. Ibid., 417.

23. See Derrida, Spurs, p. 70: "*Mais la simple formation de cette problématique commune suspend la question «qu'est-ce que la femme?». On ne peut plus chercher la femme ou la féminité de la femme ou la sexualité féminine.*" See also Jonathan Culler, *On Deconstruction* (London, 1983), p. 174. He quotes Julia Kristeva: "The belief that 'one is a woman' is almost as absurd

and obscurantist as the belief that 'one is a man' .... On a deeper level ...,
a woman is not something one can 'be'; it does not even belong to the order
of being."

24. *Will to Power* (Kaufmann), 807.

25. Ibid., 806.

26. *Nietzsche Contra Wagner*, Epilogue, 2 (Schlechta, II:1061), and elsewhere; here the aphorism appears in the context of a discussion of women.

27. *Human, All-Too-Human*, 1:107 (Schlechta, I:515).

28. *Zarathustra*, "Of the Three Metamorphoses," (Schlechta, II:293–294).

29. *Gay Science* (Kaufmann), IV:339. See Paul Valadier, "Dionysus Versus
the Crucified," in Allison, ed., *The New Nietzsche*, pp. 247ff.

30. Eric Blondel, "Nietzsche: Life as Metaphor" (1971), trans. Mairi
Macrae, in Allison, *The New Nietzsche*, p. 157.

31. *Beyond Good and Evil* (Kaufmann), Preface.

32. Nietzsche, *Nachgelassene Werke*, edited by C. G. Naumann (Leipzig,
1904), xiv, p. 369. Heidegger discusses this fragment: *Nietzsche: Vol. I, The
Will to Power as Art*, translated by D. F. Krell (London, 1981), p. 74.

33. It may be that Nietzsche shifts from using the Greeks as his model of
deliberate naïveté to using women because he wants to avoid the charge of
Romantic cultural nostalgia, and he prefers a model which is universal and
transhistorical.

34. *Will to Power* (Kaufmann), 22.

35. Ibid., 55.

36. *Zarathustra*, "Prologue," 5 (Schlechta, II:284).

37. *Beyond Good and Evil* (Kaufmann), V:201. For Nietzsche's ambivalence towards nihilism, see Michel Haar, "Nietzsche and Metaphysical
Language" in Allison, ed., *The New Nietzsche*, p. 6. Nietzsche's caricature of
the Last Man recalls the current conservative polemics against "political
correctness."

38. *Human, All-Too Human*, 23 (Faber).

39. Ibid.

40. *Will to Power* (Kaufmann), 79.

41. *Beyond Good and Evil* (Kaufmann), I:9.

42. "Use and Disadvantage," 1 (Arrowsmith, p. 91).

43. Walter Gropius, *The New Architecture and the Bauhaus*, trans.
P. Morton Shand (Cambridge, Massachusetts, 1965), p. 44.

44. Ibid., p. 82.

45. Ibid., p. 19.

46. Ibid., p. 112.

47. Ibid., p. 92.

48. Ibid.

49. *Will to Power* (Kaufmann), 797.

50. *Zarathustra*, "The Convalescent," 2 (Schlechta, II:465).

51. *Will to Power* (Kaufmann), 887.

52. *Schopenhauer as Educator*, 6 (Arrowsmith, p. 197).
In *Human, All-Too-Human* (Faber), 23, Nietzsche prophesies a "posterity that knows it has transcended both the completed original folk cultures, as well as the culture of comparison, but that looks back on both kinds of culture as on venerable antiquities, with gratitude." But this kind of optimistic prophecy has disappeared by the time of *Zarathustra*, when Nietzsche recognizes that the Last Man, too, eternally recurs.

53. *Gay Science* (Kaufmann), V:343.

54. *Will to Power* (Kaufmann), 5.

55. *Gay Science* (Kaufmann), V:358.

56. Ibid., 343.

57. *Genealogy of Morals*, III:27.

58. *Will to Power* (Kaufmann), 13.

59. See *The Gay Science*, V:377 (discussed above). In *Will to Power*, 829 (Kaufmann), Nietzsche makes fun of Wagner's nationalism. Wagnerians, he says, are attracted by "the charm of exoticism (strange times, customs, passions), exercised on sentimental stay-at-homes .... For nationalism, let us not deceive ourselves, is merely another form of exoticism—"

60. *Will to Power* (Kaufmann), 54.

61. *Twilight of the Idols*, "The Problem of Socrates," 2 (Schlechta, II:951).

62. See Deleuze, *Nietzsche*, pp. 9, 106, 170, 194.

63. *Gay Science* (Kaufmann), V:380.

64. Ibid.

65. Schlechta, II:404.

66. Ibid.

67. *Zarathustra*, "Of the Higher Men," 17 (Schlechta, II:530).

68. *Zarathustra*, Prologue, 3 and *passim*.

69. The same goal is called for by Derrida in *Of Grammatology,* p. 87.

70. *Birth of Tragedy* (Kaufmann), 1.

71. *Ecce Homo,* "Zarathustra" (Kaufmann), 6. For Deleuze, this is the essence of Nietzsche's philosophy. See, e.g., his *Nietzsche,* pp. 25–27.

72. *Philosophy in the Tragic Age of the Greeks,* 5 (Schlechta III:372).

73. Ibid.

74. *Will to Power* (Kaufmann), 1067.

75. Ibid.

76. *Nachlaß,* from A. Baümler, *Die Unschuld des Werdens* (Stuttgart, 1956), II(18), p. 8., cited and translated in Strong, *Nietzsche,* p. 42.

77. *Beyond Good and Evil,* (Kaufmann), II:39.
Cf. "Use and Disadvantage," I (Schlechta, I, 214): "The extreme case [of a being freed from all arbitrary horizons] would be a man who is condemned to see becoming everywhere. Such a man no longer believes in his own existence; he sees everything fly past in an eternal succession and looses himself in the stream of becoming. At last, the logical disciple of Heraclitus, he will hardly dare raise a finger." Unless, of course, he is an Overman. See also *Zarathustra,* "Of Old and New Law-Tables," 8. The "bumpkins" say: "What? ... everything in flux? But there are planks and railings over the stream! Over the stream everything is firmly fixed ... all 'Good' and 'Evil' ...." "O my brothers," replies Zarathustra, "is everything not *now in flux?* Have not all the railings and gangways fallen into the water? Who can still *cling to* 'good' and 'evil'?" (Schlechta III:448).
Heidegger's reading of Nietzsche rests on the thesis that "All Being is for Nietzsche a Becoming" (*Will to Power as Art,* p. 7). Heidegger thus reads Nietzsche's Heraclitean vision as a piece of metaphysics, ignoring Nietzsche's epistemological position and his careful avoidance of metaphysical claims.

78. *Ecce Homo,* "Zarathustra" (Kaufmann), 6

79. See Strong, *Nietzsche,* pp. 108-134.

80. *Genealogy of Morals* (Kaufmann), I:10.

81. Nietzsche, *Nachlaß* in C. G. Naumann, ed., *Nachgelassene Werke von Friedrich Nietzsche* (Leipzig, 1904), XII:13.

82. *Will to Power* (Schlechta), 259.

83. See Friedrich Ohly, "*Vom geistigen Sinn des Wortes im Mittelalter*" (1958), in *Schriften zur mittelalterlichen Bedeutungsforschung* (Darmstadt, 1977), pp. 1–32.

84. *Nachlaß*, in Colli- Montinari, VIII (2), pp. 431ff.

85. *Twilight of the Idols*, "How the 'Real World' at Last Became a Myth" (Schlechta II:963ff.).
Cf. Derrida, *Of Grammatology*, p. 131: "What is going to be called *enslavement* can equally legitimately be called *liberation*." Derrida makes this claim in discussing the turn of structuralist anthropology against itself, which results in the nihilist (but also liberated) position of post-structuralism. For the ambiguous meaning of nihilism in Western civilization, see Heidegger, *Will to Power as Art*, pp. 26ff.

Chapter 8

1. Whether deconstruction really belongs on the Left is a matter of controversy. See, e.g., Terry Eagleton, *Literary Theory* (Oxford, 1981), pp. 140-150.

2. *Ecce Homo*, "Why I Write Such Good Books" (Kaufmann), 1–2.

3. *Gay Science* (Kaufmann), V:365.

4. Lewis A. Coser comments that Strauss attracted a "brilliant galaxy of disciples who created an academic cult around his teaching." See his *Refugee Scholars in America* (New Haven, 1984), p. 4. Strauss' friends included Gadamer, Kojève (who wrote an afterword to Strauss' *On Tyranny*), and Löwith. He studied at Marburg under Husserl and Cassirer, and there "furtively read Schopenhauer and Nietzsche." (See his 1970 lecture, "the Problem of Socrates, quoted in John Gunnell, "Strauss Before Straussianism," unpublished MS.) He wrote that he always remained a "doubting and dubious adherent of the Marburg school," whose great fixation, in his day, was historicism. (See his *Studies in Platonic Political Philosophy* [Chicago, 1983], p. 31; and Gadamer, *Philosophical Apprenticeships*, trans. Robert R. Sullivan [Cambridge, Mass., 1985], pp. 7 ff.) For his relation to Gadamer, see his letter of February 26, 1961 in the *Independent Journal of Philosophy*, vol. I, no. 2, 1978; Gadamer's *Philosophical Apprenticeships*, p. 74 and passim; and *Truth and Method*, pp. 484ff.

5. *The End of History and the Last Man* (New York, 1992). Fukuyama first developed his theme in an article that appeared in *The National Interest*, XVI (1989), pp. 3–18. His target in that article is the Last Man, and his rhetoric is full of Nietzschean allusions. He treats the Cold War as a situation in which two naive cultures gain coherence through their mutual opposition. They are like Nietzsche's slave societies, defined by their abhorrence of outsiders. Nihilism inevitably ensues with the end of ideological conflict, for, without communism to oppose, the West has no raison d'être. Cf. Bloom, "Alexandre Kojève," in *Giants and Dwarves*, p. 273: "After reading [Kojève], one wonders whether the citizen of the universal homogeneous state is not identical to Nietzsche's Last Man, and whether Hegel's historicism does not by an inevitable dialectic force us to a more somber and radical

historicism which rejects reason." Bloom and Fukuyama (p. 3) worry that the demise of communism has brought about a "universal homogeneous state." However, in Fukuyama's book, he seems to be more sanguine about the possibility of a stable universal consensus that is rational (in a Hegelian sense) rather than nihilistic, *pace* Nietzsche.

6. Shadia Drury, *The Political Ideas of Leo Strauss* (Basingstoke, 1988), pp. 15ff.

7. See, e.g., *On Tyranny* (New York, 1968), p. 27.

8. *Natural Right and History*, p. 157 (in a passage that lies at the exact center of the book).

9. For the view that Strauss is an esoteric nihilist, see Drury; Gunnell, op. cit.; "The Myth of the Tradition," *American Political Science Review*, LXXII (1978), pp. 122–134; and "Political Theory and Politics: The Case of Leo Strauss" *Political Theory*, XIII (1985), pp. 339–361. This view has also been confirmed by several Straussians with whom I have spoken. See also Werner Dannhauser, "Remarks on Nietzsche and Allan Bloom's Nietzsche," in *Nietzscheana*, I (May, 1989). Dannhauser, a Straussian (see p. 3), admits that Bloom only differs from Nietzsche in his specific strategy for overcoming nihilism. But Bloom's strategy is Straussian and thus basically Nietzschean: see below.

10. Strauss, "Note on the Plan of Nietzsche's *Beyond Good and Evil*," in *Studies in Platonic Political Philosophy* (Chicago, op. posth., 1983), p. 186.

11. Leo Strauss, "Relativism," in Helmut Schoek and James W. Wiggins (eds.), *Relativism and the Study of Man* (Princeton, 1961), p. 151.

12. Ibid.

13. Ibid., p. 150.

14. "The Problem of Socrates," in Gunnell, "Strauss Before Straussianism," p. 10.

15. *Studies in Platonic Political Philosophy*, p. 107.

16. "Relativism," p. 152.

17. Ibid. Allan Bloom writes: "Leo Strauss believed that the Platonic image of a cave described the essential human condition. All men begin, and most men end, as prisoners of the authoritative opinions of their time and place .... Socrates' assertion that he only knows that he is ignorant reveals that he has attained ... a standpoint [outside the cave], from which he can see that what others take to be knowledge is only opinion, opinion determined by the necessities of life in the cave." (See "Leo Strauss," in *Giants and Dwarves*, pp. 240–241.)

18. "Relativism," p. 152.

19. Ibid.

20. Ibid., p. 153.

21. "Relativism," p. 154.

22. Strauss, *What is Political Philosophy?* (New York, 1959), p. 241.

23. Ibid., p. 246. Cf. Laurence Berns, "Aristotle and the Moderns on Freedom and Equality," in Kenneth Deutsch and Walter Soffer, *The Crisis of Liberal Democracy: A Straussian Perspective* (New York, 1987), p. 152.

24. Strauss, *The Rebirth of Classical Political Rationalism* (Chicago, 1989), p. 43 (cf. his *Spinoza's Critique of Religion* (New York, 1965), p. 29).

25. "Relativism," pp. 155–156.

26. "The Problem of Socrates," quoted in Gunnell, "Strauss Before Straussianism," p. 6.

27. "Unspoken Prelude to a Lecture at St. John's", in *Interpretation*, VII:iii, p. 2.

28. Strauss, *Natural Right and History*, pp. 1–3.

29. Schacht, "Nietzsche and Allan Bloom's Nietzsche," *Nietzscheana*, I (May, 1989), p. 18.

30. Nathan Tarcov and Thomas Pangle, "Epilogue: Leo Strauss and the History of Political Philosophy" in Leo Strauss and Joseph Cropsey, eds., *History of Political Philosophy*, (Chicago, 1987), p. 908.

31. Ibid.

32. Ibid., p. 907.

33. *What is Political Philosophy?* p. 221. See also Strauss, *Liberalism Ancient and Modern* (New York, 1968), p. 4. Cf. Allan Bloom, *The Closing of the American Mind* (New York, 1987), pp. 38–39: "Cultural relativism succeeds in destroying the West's universal or intellectually imperialistic claims, leaving it to be just another culture .... Unfortunately the West is defined by its need for justification of its ways or values .... This is its cultural imperative. Deprived of that, it will collapse."

34. *Natural Right and History*, p. 3.

35. Ibid., p. 157.

36. "Note on the Plan of Nietzsche's *Beyond Good and Evil*," p. 182.

37. "On Natural Law," in *Studies in Platonic Political Philosophy*, p. 137.

38. *Natural Right and History*, pp. 23ff..

39. Strauss, *Natural Right and History*, p. 25.

40. *Spinoza's Critique*, p. 31.

41. *Natural Right and History*, p. 25.

42. *What is Political Philosophy?*, p. 10; *Studies in Platonic Political Philosophy*, p. 107ff.

43. "Note on the Plan of Nietzsche's *Beyond Good and Evil*", p. 182.

44. *Will to Power*, 120. See Strauss, "Note on the Plan of Nietzsche's *Beyond Good and Evil*," p. 189.

45. *Gay Science*, III:109.

46. Strauss, *Philosophy and Law* (New York, 1987; written 1935), p. 112.

47. Strauss, *What is Political Philosophy?*, pp. 221–222.

48. Nietzsche, *Twilight of the Idols*, Sayings and Arrows, #36 (Schlechta, II:948).

49. *Zarathustra*, Prologue, 5 (Schlechta, II:284).

50. *Human, All-Too-Human* (Faber), 233.

51. See Bloom, "Leo Strauss," p. 242.

52. *Closing of the American Mind*, p. 35 (usefully discussed by Richard Rorty in "On Bloom's Nietzsche," *Nietzscheana*, I [May, 1989], p. 35.) On Bloom's enmity towards the Last Man, see, e.g., *Closing of the American Mind*, p. 194.

53. Bloom, "Leo Strauss," p. 244.

54. "Philosophy in the Tragic Age of the Greeks" (Schlechta, III:356).

55. Strauss, *Persecution and the Art of Writing*, pp. 7–8.

56. Ibid., p. 28.

57. Strauss, "Plato" in Cropsey, ed., *History of Political Philosophy*, p. 33.

58. Ibid., p. 53.

59. Cf. Strauss, *Persecution and the Art of Writing*, pp. 16–17.

60. M. F. Burnyeat, "Sphinx Without a Secret: A Review of Leo Strauss' *Studies in Platonic Political Philosophy*," *New York Review of Books*, May 30, 1985, p. 32; cf. J. G. A. Pocock, "Prophet and Inquisitor," *Political Theory*, vol. 3, no. 4 (1975), pp. 385–401; and Richard Rorty, "Thugs and Theorists," *Political Theory*, vol 15, no. 4 (1987), p. 569.

61. John Finnis, in "Aristotle, Aquinas, and Moral Absolutes (*Catholica*, no. 12, 1990), pp. 7–15, shows that—at the precise center of *Natural Right and History*—lies an alleged paraphrase of Aristotle that (p. 7) "manifestly goes beyond Aristotle into Strauss' own argumentation." At p. 160 of *Natural Right and History* (a 323-page book), Strauss says: "the normally valid rules of natural right are justly changed ...; the exceptions are as just as the rules." He claims that this is Aristotle's position. I assume that he is

referring to *Nicomachean Ethics*, 1134b29–30ff.: "although in our world there is such a thing as natural law, yet everything is subject to change." This passage appears very close to the middle of the *Nicomachean Ethics*; and Aristotle is not speaking in his own voice, but reporting what "appears to some" to be the case. Thus the text is grist for Strauss's mill. Nevertheless, his reading seems implausible. As Finnis states (p. 8): "Whatever Strauss' success in articulating the spirit of 'the classics', he certainly conveyed some characteristic elements of the spirit of the mid- and late twentieth century." The Aristotle whom Strauss presents on pp. 160–162 resembles Nietzsche.

62. See: Michael Allen Gillespie, "Nietzsche's Musical Politics," in *Nietzsche's New Seas*, p. 124; and Christopher Middleton, "Nietzsche on Music and Meter," *Arion*, VI (1967), pp. 58-65.

63. *Genealogy of Morals* (Kaufmann), II:12 (middle of the section), discussed in David B. Allison, Introduction to *The New Nietzsche*, p. xxiii. Strauss' note on *Beyond Good and Evil* is discussed in Drury, pp. 171ff. Dannhauser (*Nietzsche's View of Socrates*, p. 270) points out Nietzsche's esotericism.

64. Strauss, *Natural Right and History*, p. 26.

65. Ibid. Strauss is thinking of Heidegger's *Lebensphilosophie*, not of contemporary postmodernists such as Derrida; but the same point applies to them, and has been made by Bloom (see, e.g., "Western Civ.," p. 28).

66. Strauss, "On Collingwood's Philosophy of History," *Review of Metaphysics*, V, 4, 1952, p. 576.
Bloom, in the final section of *The Closing of the American Mind* (p. 373), brings up the eighteenth-century querelle in order to defend the "ancient" position against Bentley. And in the Preface to his *Giants and Dwarves* (p. 11), he claims that Swift "climbed from the shifting sands of his culture to a firm footing in timeless greatness." Thus Bloom adopts the rhetoric of the "ancients" to praise an "ancient."

67. Strauss, "Plato," p. 37.

68. Bloom, "Leo Strauss," p. 247.

69. Ibid., p. 247.

70. Ibid., p. 246.

71. Ibid., p. 242.

72. Ibid., p. 249.

73. Letter to Jacob Burckhardt, January 6, 1889 (Schlechta III:1351).

74. Bloom seems to deny Walker Percy's charge that he is a nihilist ("Western Civ.," pp. 18–19). But: (1) an esoteric nihilist *would* deny his secret position when giving a public speech at Harvard; and (2) Bloom

avoids saying point-blank that he is not a nihilist, producing instead a convoluted piece of rhetoric whose meaning is very difficult to pin down.

75. *Closing of the American Mind*, p. 35. Cf. Zarathustra's Prologue, 5: "Who still wants to rule? Who obey? Both are too much of a burden" (Schlechta II:284).

76. *Closing*, p. 56. Cf. *Will to Power*, 427: "one thereby loses faith in the sole prerogative of the *deus autochthonous*" (Kaufmann).

77. *Closing*, pp. 36–37. Cf. *Will to Power*, 354: "it seems to be all over for a species of man (people, races) when it becomes tolerant, allows equal rights and no longer thinks of wanting to be master" (Kaufmann).

78. *Closing*, p. 214.

79. Ibid., p. 152.

80. Ibid., p. 30. See also "Justice: John Rawls Versus the Tradition of Political Philosophy," in *Giants and Dwarves*, pp. 315–345.

81. Ibid., p. 156, alluding to *The Gay Science*, IV:337, which I quote on the last page of this book.

82. Derrida, *Grammatology*, p. 19 (see also p. 143).

83. Spivak notes in her Preface to Derrida's *Of Grammatology* (p. xlix), that in the first edition of this work, Derrida used "destruction" (a direct translation of Heidegger's "*Destruktion*"), rather than "deconstruction."

84. *Spurs*, p. 36. See also ibid., pp. 78, 80, 114. Derrida views the loss of all truth as having both affirmative and negative consequences. "Turned toward the presence, lost or impossible, of the absent origin, [the] structuralist thematic of broken immediateness is thus the sad, *negative*, nostalgic, guilty, Rousseauist aspect of the thought of play of which the Nietzschean *affirmation*—the affirmation of a world of signs without fault, without truth, without origin, offered to an active interpretation—would be the other side." (*L'Écriture et la différance*, p. 427, in Spivak, p. xiii). Derrida gains his own affirmative attitude through a kind of *amor fati*, a joyous embrace of meaninglessness (see Spivak, p. xxx).

85. Derrida believes that his project is compatible with Nietzsche's effort to discover the valuations ("good and evil") that lie behind cultural institutions. He recognizes this project in psychoanalysis as well: see *Grammatology*, p. 88.

86. *Grammatology*, p. 109.

87. Ibid., pp. 7-8.

88. Ibid., p. 3.

89. Ibid., p. 79.

90. Ibid., p. 8.

91. Ibid., p. 43.

92. Ibid., p. 52. Not only "the West," but also the period from Descartes to Hegel is an "epoch," according to Derrida. See *Grammatology*, p. 98. Cf. Nietzsche's use of variously defined *Weltanschauungen*: Christianity, Germany, philology, modernity, etc.

93. Ibid., p. 10.

94. Ibid., p. 92.

95. Ibid., p. 129.

96. Ibid., p. 93.

97. Ibid.

98. Derrida, interview with Henri Ronse, 1967, in *Positions*, trans. Alan Bass (London, 1981; first French ed., 1972), p. 6. Cf. p. 24: "Operating necessarily from the inside, borrowing all the strategic and economic resources of subversion from the old structure, borrowing them structurally, that is to say without being able to isolate their elements and atoms, deconstruction always in a certain way falls prey to its own work."

99. Derrida, "Structure, Sign, and Play in the Discourse of the Human Sciences," p. 15.

100. *Grammatology*, p. 49.

101. Ibid, pp. 13–14.

102. *Positions*, p. 13.

103. *Grammatology*, p. 12.

104. Nietzsche, *Gay Science* (Kaufmann), III:108.

105. *Grammatology*, p. 50.

106. *Positions*, p. 14.

107. *Grammatology*, p. 85.

108. *Grammatology*, p. 5. Derrida calls a short first section of *Of Grammatology* an "exergue," which *Webster's Dictionary* defines as "a space on a coin, token, or medal usu[ally] on the reverse below the central part of the design."

109. Deleuze reads Nietzsche's Will to Power as the play of differences: Nietzsche, pp. 44, 62-3.

110. Derrida, *Positions* (interview of 1968), p. 27.

111. *Beyond Good and Evil* (Kaufmann), II:36.

112. *Positions*, p. 8.

113. Derrida, *Grammatology*, p. 158.

114. *Grammatology*, p. 27.

115. "Use and Disadvantage," 8 (Arrowsmith, p. 126).

116. *Natural Right and History*, p. 33:

117. *Grammatology*, p. 158.

118. Ibid., p. lxxxix.

119. Derrida, *L'Écriture et la différance* (Paris, 1967), p. 411ff., cited by Spivak, p. lxvii (see her note number 78).

120. *Grammatology*, p. 46.

121. *Grammatology*, pp. 13–14.

122. Ibid., p. 167.

123. *Speech and Phenomena*, (1967), trans. David B. Allison (Evanston, 1973), p. 75.

124. *Positions*, p. 33.

125. *Grammatology*, p. 159.

126. *L'Écriture et la Différance*, p. 416, in Spivak, p. xviii.

127. *Grammatology*, p. 164.

128. Ibid., p. 76.

129. Ibid., p. 162.

130. Ibid., p. 162.

131. Ibid., p. 161.

132. Ibid., p. 162.

133. Positions, p. 20.

134. W. V. O. Quine, "On Mental Entities," in *Ways of Paradox* (New York, 1966), p. 210. Cf. p. 213: "I have talked up to now as if there were such entities [sc. experiences]; I had to talk some language and I uncritically talked this one." Quine then *attacks* the notion of experience.

135. *Positions*, p. 35.

136. Ibid., p. 36.

137. *Speech and Phenomena*, p. 16. For Derrida's confidence in his empirical data, see, e.g., *Grammatology*, p. 124: "It is now known, thanks to unquestionable [sic] and abundant evidence, that the birth of writing (in the colloquial sense) was nearly everywhere and most often linked to genealogical anxiety." Derrida "knows" this because of his reading of structuralist anthropology.

138. Cf. Leo Strauss' hermeneutic method, which is also a question of reading between the lines.

139. Husserl, "Philosophy as a Rigorous Science," in *Phenomenology and the Crisis of Philosophy*, Quentin Lauer, trans., pp. 145–147.

140. Husserl, *Ideas* (1913), trans. W.R. Boyce Gibson (New York, 1962), pp. 41-2.

141. Ibid., p. 41.

142. Ibid., p. 45.

143. Ibid., p. 166.

144. *Speech and Phenomena*, p. 52.

145. Ibid., p. 102.

146. Ibid., p. 102.

147. Ibid., p. 99.

148. Derrida's experimental radicalization of Husserl's method resembles Nietzsche's derivation of the Will to Power, which he achieved by means of an experimental radicalization of Schopenhauer's methodology: see *Beyond Good and Evil*, 36, described above.

149. *Speech and Phenomena*, p. 13.

150. Ibid., p. 104.

151. Husserl, *The Crisis of the European Sciences*, 15.

152. Derrida, *Speech and Phenomena*, p. 77.

153. For an excellent general account of Derrida, see Henry Staten, *Wittgenstein and Derrida* (Oxford, 1985).

154. *Closing of the American Mind*, p. 379.

155. "Western Civ.," p. 28.

156. Bloom, "Commerce and Culture," in *Giants and Dwarves*, p. 293.

157. Ibid.

158. *Ecce Homo*, "Why I am So Clever," 1.

Chapter 9

1. On Marx's *Weltanschauung*-historicism, see, e.g., *The Holy Family* (1845): "It is not a matter of what this or that proletarian or even the proletariat as a whole *pictures* at present as its goal. It is a matter of *what the proletariat is in actuality* and what, in accordance with this *being*, it will historically be compelled to do." (Robert C. Tucker, *The Marx-Engels Reader*,

New York: second ed., 1978, pp. 134–135.) Cf. *The Poverty of Philosophy* (1847), in Tucker, pp. 218–219. On "class culture," see the *Communist Manifesto*, in Tucker, p. 487. Not all modern Marxists hold that classes are *Weltanschauungen* or cultures. For a recent article with a useful bibliography, see Jack Amariglio and Bruce Norton, "Marxist Historians and the Question of Class in the French Revolution," *History and Theory*, XXX:1 (1991), pp. 37–55.

2. For an ambitious history of the term "culture," which amply demonstrates its prevalence in modern thought, see A. L. Kroeber and Clyde Kluckholm, *Culture: A Critical Review of Concepts and Definitions* (New York, 1963).

3. See Derrida, "Otobiographies," especially pp. 22ff.

4. *Beyond Good and Evil* (Kaufmann), I:21.

5. In suggesting a paradigm based on the individual person, I am making no claim about the metaphysical status of the human self, any more than one would have to believe in the ontological reality of human beings in order to propose a historical narrative that attributed importance to individual human agents. Whether the human self "really exists" is a question that can be safely passed over in this context.

6. *Will to Power* (Kaufmann), 120.

7. A nominalist method of interpretation is employed and defended by Michael Baxandall, *Patterns of Intention: On the Historical Explanation of Pictures* (New Haven, 1985). Baxandall's "texts" happen to be visual.

8. See E. D. Hirsch, Jr., *Validity in Interpretation* (New Haven, 1967), p. 28: the "argument that a Muttersprache imposes an inescapable Weltanschauung on its speakers seems to overlook the remarkable variety in assumptions and attitudes of speakers who have the same Muttersprache." Cf. *Human, All-Too-Human*, aphorism 267, entitled "Learning many languages."

9. Habermas, "A Review of Gadamer's *Truth and Method*" from *Understanding and Social Inquiry* (Notre Dame, 1977), p. 346.

10. Ibid., p. 349.

11. *Will to Power* (Kaufmann), 511.

12. Nietzsche, *Nachlaß*, in C. G. Naumann, ed., *Nachgelassene Werke von Friedrich Nietzsche* (Leipzig, 1904), xii:13.

13. *Genealogy of Morals* (Kaufmann), III:12 (cf. *Beyond Good and Evil*, 221). Cf. *Will to Power* (Kaufmann), 556: "A thing would be defined once all creatures had asked 'what is that?' and had answered their question. Supposing one single creature, with its own relationships and perspectives for all things, were missing, then the thing would not yet be defined."

14. *Human, All-Too-Human* (Faber), 23.

15. *The Gay Science* (Kaufmann), I:7.

16. *Human, All-Too Human* (Faber), 23.

17. "David Strauss," 1 (Arrowsmith, p. 17).

18. *Birth of Tragedy* (Kaufmann), 7: "In this sense the Dionysian man resembles Hamlet: both have once looked truly into the essence of things, they have gained *knowledge,* and nausea inhibits action .... [A]ction requires the veils of illusion: that is the doctrine of Hamlet."

19. *The Gay Science* (Kaufmann), V:347.

20. "Use and Disadvantage of History," 7 (Arrowsmith, p. 126).

21. "We Philologists," V:197 (Arrowsmith, p. 387).

22. Berlin, "Two Concepts of Liberty," in *Four Essays on Liberty* (Oxford, 1969), p. 170.

23. Ibid., p. 171.

24. Nietzsche, *Zarathustra,* "Of the Spirit of Gravity," 2 (Schlechta, II:441).

25. Ibid., "Of the Thousand and One Goals" (Schlechta, II:322).

26. Berlin, p. 172. Richard Rorty identifies Berlin's "admirable writer" as Joseph Schumpeter. See Rorty's *Contingency, Irony, and Solidarity* (Cambridge, 1989), p. 46.
Leo Strauss chooses Berlin's essay as a target, because he recognizes Berlin as a voice of the Last Man. See Strauss, "Relativism," op. cit.

27. Rawls, "The Domain of the Political and Overlapping Consensus," *New York University Law Review,* LXIV, 2 (1989), p. 243.

28. Ibid., p. 258. In Rawls' recent work, he has provided a historicist, rather than Kantian, interpretation of his *Theory of Justice.* See especially: "Justice as Fairness: Political not Metaphysical," *Philosophy and Public Affairs,* XIV (1985), pp. 223–251; and "Justice as Fairness: A Guided Tour" (unpublished MS, 1989).

29. Habermas, *Legitimation Crisis* (Boston, 1973), Part III: "On the Logic of Legitimation Problems," p. 111.

30. Ibid., p. 104.

31. Ibid., p. 105.

32. Crocker, "Insiders and Outsiders in International Development Ethics," *Ethics and International Affairs,* volume 5, 1991, pp. 156–157.

33. Cf. Wittgenstein, *Philosophical Investigations,* 67–68: "I can think of no better expression to characterize these similarities [sc. among games] than

'family resemblances'; for the various resemblances between members of a family: build, features, colour of eyes, gait, temperament, etc. etc. overlap and criss-cross in the same way .... And for instance the kinds of number form a family in the same way. Why do we call something a 'number'? Well, perhaps because it has a—direct—relationship with several things that have hitherto been called number; and this can give it an indirect relationship to other things we call the same name. And we extend our concept of number as in spinning a thread we twist fibre on fibre. And the strength of the thread does not reside in the fact that some one fibre runs through its whole length, but in the overlapping of many fibres ....

"I *can* give the concept 'number' rigid limits ..., that is, use the word 'number' for a rigidly limited concept, but I can also use it so that the extension of the concept is not closed by a frontier. And this is how we use the word 'game'. For how is the concept of a game bounded? What still counts as a game and what no longer does? Can you give the boundary? No." (I think that this is also how we use the term "Hispanic.")

34. Consider Umberto Eco's diagnosis of a certain strand of American culture: "It is like making love in a confessional with a prostitute dressed in a prelate's liturgical robes reciting Baudelaire while ten electronic organs reproduce the *Well-Tempered Clavier* played by Scriabin." See his *Travels in Hyperreality*, trans. William Weaver (London, 1987), pp. 23ff. Postmodern aesthetics, having overcome the desire for a consistent, ideal, reified culture, celebrates the *omnium gatherum*, rather than denouncing it. Thus Eco (p. 26) writes with evident relish of "eclectic frenzy, and compulsive imitation," of (p. 24) "Chopin's Sonata in B flat minor sung by Perry Como in an arrangement by Liberace and accompanied by the Marine Band." In the same spirit, Jean-Francois Lyotard declares a "war on totality; let us be witness to the unpresentable; let us activate differences and save the honor of the name." See the conclusion of his "What is Postmodernism?" appendix to *The Postmodern Condition* (Minneapolis, 1984).

35. Bennett, *To Reclaim a Legacy*, pp. 29-30.

36. Ibid., p. 11.

37. *Will to Power* (Kaufmann), 421.

38. *Gay Science* (Kaufmann), V:348.

39. Lévi-Strauss, *L'Anthropologie structurale*, pp. 39ff., in Gayatri Chakravorty Spivak's Introduction to Derrida, *Of Grammatology*, p. lvi.

40. Clifford Geertz, "Thick Description: Toward an Interpretive Theory of Culture," in *The Interpretation of Cultures*, p. 14.

41. Ibid., p. 20.

42. *The Poverty of Historicism* (London, 1957). Popper defines "historicism"—somewhat confusingly—as "theoretical history," (p. vi) or the use of induction in the social sciences as a source of predictions and covering laws.

His definition of "historicism" is therefore diametrically opposed to the "individualizing" approach to history that Meinecke labelled "historicist." In the terms which I have been using, Popper seems to be something like a "nominalist historicist," rather then a critic of historicism.

43. Wittgenstein, *Philosophical Investigations*, 109.

44. Ibid., 51.

45. See William Dray, "Explanatory Narrative in History," *Philosophical Quarterly*, iv, no. 14 (1954), pp. 15–27.

46. For a compelling account of narrative in history, see Alasdair MacIntyre, After Virtue (Notre Dame, 1981).

47. Geertz, p. 14.

48. p. 11.

49. p. 30.

50. For a view very close to mine, see George Levine, Peter Brooks, Jonathan Culler, Marjorie Garber, E. Ann Kaplan, and Catharine R. Stimpson, *Speaking for the Humanities*, ACLS occasional paper #7 (1989).
For other views, see: Bennett, *To Reclaim a Legacy*; Otto A. Bird, *Cultures in Conflict: An Essay in the Philosophy of the Humanities* (Notre Dame, 1976); Allan Bloom, *Giants and Dwarves* and *The Closing of the American Mind*; Wayne C. Booth, *The Vocation of a Teacher* (Chicago, 1988); Lynne V. Cheney, *American Memory: A Report on the Humanities in the Nation's Public Schools* (Washington, 1988); Commission on the Humanities, *The Humanities in American Life* (Berkeley, 1980); W. R. Connor et al., *The Humanities in the University: Strategies for the 1990's*, ACLS occasional paper #6 (1988); Chester E. Finn, Jr., Diane Ravitch, and P. Holley Roberts, eds., *Challenges to the Humanities* (New York, 1985); A. Bartlett Giamatti, *A Free and Ordered Space* (New York, 1988); Darryl Gless and Barbara Hernstein Smith, *The Politics of Liberal Education* (South Atlantic Quarterly, winter 1990; vol. 89, no. 1); Stephen R. Graubard, *The Agenda for the Humanities and Higher Education for the 21st Century*, ACLS occasional paper #8 (1989); E. D. Hirsch, Jr., *Cultural Literacy: What Every American Needs to Know* (Boston, 1987); Roger Kimball, *Tenured Radicals: How Politics has Corrupted Our Higher Education* (New York, 1990); Robert E. Proctor, *Education's Great Amnesia: Reconsidering the Humanities from Petrarch to Freud, With a Curriculum for Today's Students* (Bloomington, 1988); John Searle, "The Storm Over the University," *New York Review of Books*, xxxvii:19 (December 6, 1990), pp. 34–42—and letters in the February 14th, 1991 edition.

51. Bennett, p. 29.

52. Ibid., p. 6.

53. Louis A. Montrose, "The Poetics and Politics of Culture," in H. Aram Veeser, ed., *The New Historicism* (New York, 1989), p. 24.

54. Ibid., p. 26.

55. See Michael Stanford, "The Stanford Library: 'Great Books,' Broadly Defined," *New Republic*, October 2, 1989, pp. 18–20.

56. See George Levine et al., pp. 16ff.

57. I do not mean that every curriculum committee must contain people of both genders and all races; only that no system for arriving at a curriculum should be either de jure or de facto discriminatory. A system discriminates de facto if there are structural impediments—deliberate or not—to any group's participation.

58. *Gay Science* (Kaufmann), IV:337.

Index

perspectivism: in art 32–33, 147, 227
n; Heraclitean, 144; and history,
147–148; Nietzsche's adoption of,
73–74, varieties of, 36–39, 228 n
philology, 27–32, 69–74, 85–89,
112–116. *See also* Nietzsche on
scholarship
Pippin, Robert, 132
Pforr, Franz, 33
Pforta, 3, 5–7, 21–24, 67
Pico della Mirandola, Giovanni,
120–121
Plato, 148, 160–162
Pope, Alexander, xviii, 31, 118
Popper, Karl Raimund, 14, 17, 208,
210
postmodernism, 132–133, 140, 185,
189, 271 n
pragmatism, xvi, 93–95, 179–180
Protagoras, 10–11, 219 n
Pseudo–Dionysius, the Areopagite,
144

quarrel of the ancients and moderns,
xviii, 7; and Bloom, 226 n, 264 n;
and historicism, 30, 226 n;
Nietzsche in, 117–119;
Leo Strauss in, 163–164, 209
Quine, Willard van Orman, 180

Racine, Jean Baptiste, 31–32
Ranke, Leopold von, 4, 45, 216 n,
230 n
Rawls, John, 166, 201–202
relativism, 50–57; and historicism,
35–38; Nietzsche on, xiv, 73, 202;
politics of, 45–46; and the
Sophists, 12; Leo Strauss on,
153–156. *See also* historicism,
perspectivism, nihilism
Ritschl, Albrecht Benjamin, 28,
47–48, 68, 71–72, 225 n, 242 n
Rohde, Erwin, 86, 99, 248 n
Romantic movement: historicism of,
31; and the Greeks, 69–71, 76–77,
86–87; and Nietzsche, 22,
110–111, 139; politics of, 197, 205;

Leo Strauss on, 154
Rosen, Stanley, 131
Rousseau, Jean-Jacques, 168–169
Ryle, Gilbert, 208

Sallust, 7, 119
Schacht, Richard, 155
Shakespeare, William, 194
Schiller, Johann Christoph Friedrich
von, 100–101, 107
Schinkel, Karl Friedrich, 77, 139
Schleiermacher, Friedrich Ernst
Daniel, 192
Schopenhauer, Arthur: and historicism, 68, 240 n; homogeneity
principle of, 129–130; and the
Greeks, 49; Nietzsche and, 71,
80–81, 100, 105; psychologism
of, 38
Schulpforte. *See* Pforta
slave morality, 146, 197, 260 n
Socrates: as esoteric, 109, 164–165,
255 n; and humanism, 108; negative stance of, 146; as rationalist,
4–5, 108, 218 n; and the Sophists,
8–13, 107–108; and tragedy,
107–110, 114
Sophists: and humanism, 8–13, 219 n;
and liberalism, 17–18;
and Plato, 220 n; and tragedy,
107–108.
Stack, George, 87
Strauss, David: historicism of,
28–29; rationalism of, 28–29,
67–68; Nietzsche's attack on,
82–84; romanticism of, 241 n
Strauss, Leo: and Derrida, 185–186;
esotericism of, xviii–xix, 153–165;
on historicism, 153–159, 226 n,
231 n; as Nietzschean, xi, 117,
152–167
Strawson, Peter Frederick, 53
Strong, Tracy B., 146
Suidas, 71, 119
Swift, Jonathan, xviii, 118, 264 n

Theognis, 22, 71, 222 n